Real-World ML Projects: Hands-on Learning

Gilbert Gutiérrez

A Practical Guide to Building, Deploying, and Scaling Machine Learning Models

Machine Learning (ML) is no longer just a buzzword—it is transforming industries, powering intelligent applications, and reshaping how businesses operate. However, most ML learners and aspiring data scientists struggle to bridge the gap between theoretical concepts and practical applications. While many books and courses focus on algorithms and mathematical foundations, few provide hands-on, project-based guidance that aligns with real-world challenges.

Real-World ML Projects: Hands-on Learning is the ultimate guide to mastering machine learning through practical, end-to-end projects. As the sixth installment in the *AI from Scratch: Step-by-Step Guide to Mastering Artificial Intelligence* series, this book is designed to equip you with the skills needed to tackle industry-grade ML problems, deploy models, and navigate the complexities of MLOps.

Why This Book?

This book goes beyond traditional ML textbooks and online courses by focusing on practical, hands-on projects that mirror real-world business scenarios. Each chapter covers a complete ML project—from defining the problem and preparing data to model development, evaluation, and deployment. By the end of this book, you will have built a diverse ML portfolio that showcases your ability to solve real-world problems.

Whether you're a beginner eager to gain hands-on experience or an experienced professional looking to refine your ML deployment skills, this book will guide you through a structured approach to working on ML projects that are industry-relevant, scalable, and impactful.

What You Will Learn

This book is divided into four sections: Foundations of Real-World ML, Hands-On ML Projects, Deployment & Scaling, and Advanced Topics & Future Trends.

1. Foundations of Real-World ML

Before diving into projects, this section provides a solid foundation on how real-world ML projects are structured and executed. You will learn:

- The complete ML project lifecycle from problem identification to deployment.
- Best practices for data collection, cleaning, and feature engineering.

- The role of MLOps in managing ML workflows efficiently.
- How to define success metrics and ensure reproducibility in ML experiments.

2. Hands-On ML Projects

This section is the heart of the book, covering 10 real-world ML projects across different domains, each designed to strengthen your practical knowledge.

Project 1: Predicting House Prices with Regression

- Learn how real estate pricing models work.
- Implement linear regression, decision trees, and ensemble models.
- Deploy a Flask-based API for serving predictions.

Project 2: Customer Churn Prediction

- Understand why churn prediction is vital for businesses.
- Train classification models to predict customer retention.
- Use SHAP analysis for interpretability.

Project 3: Sentiment Analysis on Social Media

- Work with text data and NLP techniques.
- Implement word embeddings (Word2Vec, BERT) for classification.
- Deploy a real-time Twitter sentiment analysis dashboard.

Project 4: Fraud Detection in Financial Transactions

- Learn how to detect anomalies in financial data.
- Implement unsupervised ML methods like Isolation Forest.
- Handle imbalanced datasets effectively.

Project 5: Demand Forecasting for Retail

- Learn time series analysis with ARIMA and LSTMs.
- Predict sales trends for retail businesses.
- Deploy a forecasting model with an interactive dashboard.

Project 6: Image Classification with CNNs

- Work with deep learning and convolutional neural networks.
- Train models using TensorFlow and PyTorch.
- Implement transfer learning for improved accuracy.

Project 7: Recommender System for E-Commerce

- Build a hybrid recommendation system.
- Use collaborative filtering and content-based filtering.
- Deploy the recommender system on a web app.

Project 8: Chatbot with NLP

- Understand how chatbots and conversational AI work.
- Implement transformer-based NLP models (BERT, GPT-3).
- Deploy the chatbot on WhatsApp or Telegram.

Project 9: Autonomous Vehicle Simulation

- Work with reinforcement learning for self-driving cars.
- Train Deep Q-Networks (DQN) and PPO models in simulators.
- Understand real-world applications and challenges of autonomous vehicles.

Project 10: Edge AI with TinyML

- Deploy ML models on microcontrollers like Raspberry Pi and Arduino.
- Optimize ML models for low-power embedded systems.
- Learn about real-world applications of Edge AI.

3. Deployment & Scaling

Building ML models is just one part of the puzzle—deploying and maintaining them in production is where real-world challenges arise. This section covers:

- MLOps & CI/CD pipelines for deploying ML models.
- Model monitoring to detect performance drift.
- Handling bias, fairness, and explainability in AI.
- Ensuring data privacy and security in ML applications.

4. Advanced Topics & Future Trends

The final section explores cutting-edge trends in ML, including:

- Scaling ML for Big Data using Apache Spark and Dask.
- LLMs & Generative AI, including GPT-based applications.
- AutoML & No-Code ML, making AI accessible to non-experts.
- Ethical considerations and regulatory frameworks in AI.

Who This Book is For

This book is ideal for:

✓ Aspiring data scientists and ML engineers looking for real-world projects to add to their portfolio.

✓ Software engineers wanting to integrate ML into their applications.

✓ Business professionals and analysts interested in data-driven decision-making.

✓ Students and researchers looking for hands-on ML experience.

Prior knowledge of Python and basic ML concepts is recommended but not mandatory.

Why This Book Stands Out

✓ **Hands-On Learning** – Instead of just reading about ML, you'll build and deploy real projects.

✓ **Industry-Relevant Projects** – Covering use cases in finance, retail, NLP, healthcare, and more.

✓ **Deployment Focus** – Learn to deploy models, not just train them.

✓ **Cutting-Edge Topics** – Covers LLMs, AutoML, and Edge AI.

✓ **Practical Code Examples** – Step-by-step implementation with real-world datasets.

By the end of this book, you won't just understand machine learning—you'll be able to apply it to real-world problems, build scalable AI systems, and deploy them into production.

Take the Next Step in Your ML Journey!

If you're ready to move beyond theory and start building and deploying real-world ML projects, this book is for you. With practical, hands-on guidance and real industry use cases, you'll gain the confidence to tackle complex ML challenges and advance your AI career.

🔥 *Start your hands-on ML journey today with Real-World ML Projects: Hands-on Learning!* 🚀

1. Introduction to Real-World ML Projects

Machine learning is transforming industries, but applying it in real-world scenarios requires more than just theoretical knowledge—it demands hands-on experience with real data, scalable workflows, and deployment strategies. In this chapter, we set the stage for your journey into practical machine learning by exploring the end-to-end ML project lifecycle, from problem formulation and data collection to model development, evaluation, and deployment. You'll gain insight into the common challenges faced in real-world ML applications, best practices for building robust and scalable models, and how to think like an industry professional when tackling ML problems. By the end of this chapter, you'll have a clear roadmap for approaching ML projects with confidence and efficiency. 🚀

1.1 Understanding the gap between theory and practice

In the world of machine learning (ML), there's often a significant gap between theoretical concepts and their practical application. This gap can be daunting, especially for newcomers who have learned the mathematical principles and algorithms behind ML but may struggle when it comes to implementing them in real-world scenarios. Understanding this gap is critical for anyone aiming to work with machine learning in an industry setting, as the complexities of real data, diverse use cases, and ever-evolving technologies can challenge even the most well-versed theoretical practitioners.

Theoretical Foundations of Machine Learning

The foundation of machine learning theory is based on algorithms and statistical models that work under controlled, ideal conditions. Concepts like supervised learning, unsupervised learning, and reinforcement learning are explored in detail, often focusing on mathematical models such as linear regression, decision trees, support vector machines, and neural networks. These models are usually studied in terms of accuracy, precision, recall, and other well-defined metrics. The theoretical curriculum is structured to ensure you grasp the underlying mechanics of these models, such as how a decision tree splits data, or how neural networks adjust weights during training.

In theory, the process is straightforward: the data is well-organized, models are well-defined, and performance metrics are easy to calculate and interpret. You typically deal with structured datasets with no missing values, minimal noise, and well-labeled information. Moreover, the goal of these models is usually confined to solving small-scale problems where inputs and outputs are easily comprehensible.

The Complexity of Real-World Data

When moving from theory to practice, one of the most significant challenges you face is the quality and nature of real-world data. Unlike the controlled, clean datasets used in theoretical machine learning exercises, real-world data is often messy, incomplete, and inconsistent. In practice, data comes in various forms: structured (like tables or spreadsheets), semi-structured (such as JSON files), and unstructured (like images, audio, and text). Handling these different types of data requires distinct approaches, which is a skill that's rarely deeply emphasized in theoretical ML education.

Data preprocessing is one of the first tasks where theory meets practice. In theory, you might be given a pristine dataset, with all the features neatly aligned and no missing values. However, in the real world, you often encounter data with missing values, outliers, inconsistent formats, and noisy signals. This means you have to spend a significant portion of time just cleaning and transforming data before you can even think about training a model. Common techniques such as imputation, data normalization, and feature engineering are crucial for ensuring the model can perform well with the available data.

Furthermore, data might not always be labeled, which creates additional challenges in tasks like supervised learning. In practice, labeling large datasets can be time-consuming and expensive. When labels are unavailable or unreliable, you might have to turn to unsupervised learning or semi-supervised learning techniques, adding another layer of complexity.

Model Selection and Tuning

Another gap between theory and practice lies in the process of model selection and hyperparameter tuning. In theory, we often focus on a small set of algorithms that are mathematically elegant and easy to implement, such as linear regression or decision trees. In real-world scenarios, the choice of model is rarely clear-cut, and often, there are many competing algorithms, each with its strengths and weaknesses.

For example, in practice, you may have to decide whether a random forest, gradient boosting, or deep learning model is more suitable for a given dataset, considering factors like the size of the dataset, the computational resources available, and the interpretability of the model. Theoretical frameworks often do not go into the nitty-gritty details of these trade-offs. In a classroom setting, students might experiment with a couple of models on a small dataset, but in practice, the selection process requires intensive experimentation.

Furthermore, real-world machine learning often involves hyperparameter tuning, a process of adjusting parameters like learning rate, regularization strength, or the number of layers in a neural network. While theory provides us with a general understanding of the role of these hyperparameters, in practice, selecting the optimal combination is an art form that often requires trial and error, intuition, and domain knowledge. The use of techniques like grid search, random search, and Bayesian optimization can help automate this process, but tuning models for optimal performance remains a complex task in practice.

Overfitting, Underfitting, and Model Validation

Another key area where theory and practice diverge is in understanding and handling overfitting and underfitting. In theory, we know that overfitting occurs when a model becomes too complex, capturing the noise and random fluctuations in the training data, thus failing to generalize to unseen data. Similarly, underfitting occurs when a model is too simple to capture the underlying patterns of the data. In practice, detecting and preventing these issues is not always straightforward.

In real-world settings, the datasets are often more heterogeneous, and cross-validation techniques may need to be tailored based on the specific dataset and the business problem at hand. For example, time-series data requires temporal cross-validation, while in the case of large datasets, shuffling may lead to poor results, necessitating more sophisticated validation schemes. Furthermore, the distribution of the data and the presence of biases can often make model evaluation trickier, requiring careful selection of performance metrics that align with real-world objectives.

Scalability and Model Deployment

While theoretical machine learning often operates in a static environment—where models are trained on a single machine and evaluated on small-scale datasets—scalability becomes a critical issue when moving to production environments. Real-world ML models often need to handle massive datasets, perform real-time predictions, and integrate seamlessly into operational pipelines. This is where concepts like distributed computing, parallel processing, and cloud computing come into play, tools that are typically not discussed in depth in the theoretical framework.

Deploying machine learning models involves creating end-to-end pipelines that are robust, maintainable, and scalable, which is a far cry from the simple model training scripts often used in classrooms. You will need to consider how to manage model versioning, monitor performance, and automate model updates in production environments, which are concepts that extend well beyond theoretical learning.

Closing the Gap Between Theory and Practice

To bridge the gap between theory and practice, it's essential to embrace hands-on learning. Practical experience—through working on real-world projects, participating in competitions like those on Kaggle, or contributing to open-source ML projects—can help solidify your theoretical knowledge and expose you to the challenges that arise when applying machine learning in real environments.

Additionally, focusing on problem-solving skills rather than memorizing algorithms is key. While knowing the theory behind algorithms is important, the ability to adapt and customize models to meet the unique demands of different datasets and business problems is what will make you a successful machine learning practitioner. This means continuously experimenting, learning from failures, and iterating on models until they are production-ready.

The gap between theory and practice in machine learning is substantial, but not insurmountable. Understanding the theoretical concepts is essential, but it is the ability to apply them to real-world data that defines a true ML practitioner. By engaging with messy data, tackling model selection, and navigating the complexities of deployment and monitoring, you will develop the practical skills required to work in real-world machine learning environments. Embracing this challenge and taking a hands-on approach will ultimately transform you from a theoretical learner to a competent and capable machine learning practitioner.

1.2 What makes an ML project "real-world"?

Machine learning (ML) projects can vary greatly in terms of complexity, data sources, and the specific challenges they aim to solve. However, a key distinction exists between theoretical exercises and what is considered a "real-world" ML project. While theoretical models often focus on idealized data and simplified problems, real-world ML projects involve tackling messy, dynamic, and multifaceted challenges in business, healthcare, finance, and other domains. But what truly makes an ML project "real-world"?

In this section, we'll break down the characteristics that define a real-world machine learning project. From working with raw, noisy data to managing business objectives and scaling models in production, we'll explore the complexities that elevate an ML project from an academic exercise to something applicable in the real world.

1.1 Complex, Unstructured, and Noisy Data

One of the defining features of a real-world machine learning project is the nature of the data. While theoretical projects often use curated, clean, and well-labeled datasets, real-world ML projects rarely enjoy such luxuries. Real-world data comes in various forms—structured, semi-structured, and unstructured—and is often messy and noisy.

In a real-world scenario, data may be incomplete, unbalanced, or plagued with missing values. Data preprocessing steps such as data cleaning, imputation, and feature engineering are essential before you can even begin model building. For instance, in a real-world sales forecasting project, you may need to handle customer data that includes missing purchase history, inconsistent formatting across multiple sources, or irrelevant noise due to inconsistent labeling practices.

Unstructured data such as text, images, and audio is increasingly prevalent in real-world projects. Dealing with natural language, image classification, or speech recognition requires different preprocessing techniques and model architectures than structured data. Tackling these challenges involves not only selecting the right models but also engineering features that can adequately represent this complex data.

1.2 Problem Framing and Domain Expertise

Real-world ML projects often require an understanding of the problem domain. It's not enough to simply apply machine learning algorithms—domain knowledge is necessary to ensure that the right problems are being framed and that the outcomes are interpretable and valuable. For instance, in healthcare, understanding clinical pathways, patient behaviors, or medical conditions is critical to framing problems in ways that make the most sense for the business or research objectives.

In practice, defining a clear problem is often a collaborative process between data scientists, business stakeholders, and domain experts. This requires the ability to translate business goals into machine learning objectives and to continuously adjust the scope as new insights are uncovered. A clear, well-defined problem makes it easier to choose the right algorithms, data sources, and performance metrics.

For example, if you're building a fraud detection system for a financial institution, knowing how fraud manifests in financial transactions and the typical behaviors of fraudsters can guide your feature engineering and model selection. Real-world problems often evolve over time, which means the definition and scope of the project may change as new challenges arise.

1.3 Model Complexity and Algorithm Selection

Real-world machine learning projects typically involve selecting and adapting multiple algorithms to suit the nature of the data, the business objectives, and available computational resources. Unlike in theoretical settings, where models are often chosen based on simple criteria (e.g., linear regression for continuous outcomes, decision trees for classification), real-world projects require a more nuanced approach to model selection.

For example, when dealing with a large-scale recommendation system, an ML practitioner may have to choose between collaborative filtering, content-based filtering, or hybrid models, depending on the available data and the desired outcome. In addition to model choice, you must also consider the interpretability of the model, especially in industries like finance or healthcare, where stakeholders need to understand how predictions are made.

Tuning these models is another challenge. Hyperparameter tuning, while theoretically discussed, takes on a real meaning when you have to tweak learning rates, number of layers, or regularization terms for models that handle petabytes of data. Tools like grid search or random search help in systematically finding optimal configurations, but the decision-making process is far more iterative in practice.

1.4 Handling Imbalanced and Skewed Data

In real-world machine learning projects, one of the most significant challenges is dealing with imbalanced datasets—where some classes are significantly underrepresented compared to others. This is common in tasks such as fraud detection, disease diagnosis, or spam filtering, where the positive class (e.g., fraud, disease, spam) is much rarer than the negative class.

Addressing data imbalance requires using specialized techniques, such as resampling, synthetic data generation (SMOTE), or cost-sensitive learning, to ensure that models don't become biased toward predicting the majority class. In real-world projects, evaluation metrics like precision, recall, and F1-score take precedence over accuracy, as they better capture model performance in the face of class imbalance.

Skewed data distribution can also affect model training. For example, in a time-series forecasting project for sales data, data may follow a seasonal or cyclical pattern that needs to be accounted for. In real-world ML projects, ensuring your model can adapt to these complexities is a key part of the process.

1.5 Scalability and Model Deployment

In academic exercises, models are often tested on small datasets or simplified environments. Real-world ML projects, however, require models to scale effectively. Scaling ML means managing vast amounts of data and ensuring that models can make predictions in real-time or on massive batches of data. Whether you're predicting customer churn in an e-commerce platform or detecting fraudulent transactions in a banking system, the ability to deploy and scale a model is critical.

In practice, model deployment involves creating an end-to-end pipeline, where data is ingested, processed, and used to generate predictions in a streamlined manner. This means understanding how to integrate your model with production environments, maintain it over time, and ensure its performance does not degrade. MLOps (machine learning operations) plays a vital role in this aspect, helping data scientists manage continuous integration, testing, monitoring, and updating of deployed models.

For example, a fraud detection system might need to handle millions of transactions per second while maintaining low-latency predictions. This requires not only optimizing the machine learning model itself but also ensuring it works seamlessly within a distributed computing environment, using tools such as Docker, Kubernetes, or cloud platforms like AWS or Google Cloud.

1.6 Monitoring, Maintenance, and Adaptability

A real-world ML project is not a one-time endeavor but an ongoing process that involves monitoring the model's performance and making updates as needed. In production, models may face concept drift, where the data distribution changes over time, or data drift, where new types of input data appear that were not present during training. For example, in a customer churn prediction system, changes in customer behavior or external factors (e.g., market conditions, product changes) can cause the model to lose its predictive accuracy.

Real-world ML systems require the ability to monitor performance metrics continually and adapt models when necessary. Automated retraining, continuous monitoring, and alerting mechanisms need to be in place to ensure that the system remains reliable and useful.

1.7 Business Impact and Feedback Loops

Finally, real-world ML projects are driven by business objectives. The true value of a machine learning model comes from its ability to address a specific business problem and provide actionable insights. A "real-world" project involves working with stakeholders to assess the impact of the model, whether it's improving customer retention, reducing costs, or increasing revenue.

Moreover, real-world ML projects often involve feedback loops, where the model's predictions influence future data collection and decision-making. For instance, a recommendation system might influence what products customers are shown, and customer behavior in turn provides feedback that can be used to improve future recommendations. These feedback loops make continuous model improvement and retraining crucial.

A machine learning project becomes "real-world" when it addresses complex, messy data, integrates domain expertise, involves algorithmic selection and tuning, and requires real-time scalability. It's about solving practical business problems, ensuring models deliver tangible value, and adapting to changing environments over time. By understanding what makes an ML project real-world, you can approach machine learning with a broader, more comprehensive perspective that prepares you for the challenges ahead.

1.3 Common challenges in real-world ML implementation

Machine learning (ML) offers immense potential to revolutionize industries, solve complex problems, and drive business success. However, the transition from theory to practical application presents a range of challenges that data scientists, machine learning engineers, and business professionals must navigate. In real-world ML implementation, problems are rarely straightforward, and solutions often require creative thinking, iteration, and a combination of tools and techniques. In this section, we'll explore the most common challenges faced when implementing ML in the real world.

1.1 Data Quality and Preprocessing

One of the most significant challenges in any ML project is dealing with the quality and format of the data. In theory, machine learning models often work with ideal, clean datasets that contain no missing values, outliers, or inconsistencies. However, in practice, data is often incomplete, noisy, and may come in different formats (structured, unstructured, semi-structured). Poor-quality data can lead to inaccurate predictions, biases in model training, and increased time spent in data cleaning.

Challenges include:

- **Missing or incomplete data**: Real-world datasets often have missing values, which can affect model accuracy. Handling missing data requires strategies like imputation, data augmentation, or even removing entire rows or columns.
- **Inconsistent data**: Inconsistent formatting, such as varying date formats, different units of measurement, or conflicting data from different sources, can introduce errors and confusion.
- **Outliers and noise**: Extreme outliers and noise in data can significantly affect model performance. Identifying and handling these correctly through techniques like outlier detection or robust models is essential.

Data preprocessing becomes time-consuming and often requires iterative approaches to get the dataset into a format that is clean, structured, and ready for machine learning. This is a critical, but often underappreciated, part of a real-world ML project.

1.2 Model Complexity and Overfitting

Choosing the right model for a given problem and dataset is a tricky endeavor. While theoretical ML education provides a strong foundation in the math behind algorithms, real-world data is rarely clean or well-behaved enough to guarantee success with a specific model. Real-world machine learning tasks often require a model with more complexity or adaptability to capture the intricacies of the data, but this also raises the risk of overfitting.

Challenges include:

- **Overfitting**: In practical settings, it's easy for a model to memorize the training data rather than learning generalizable patterns, especially when the dataset is small or not representative of the population. Overfitting leads to poor model performance when evaluated on unseen or future data.
- **Underfitting**: On the flip side, using overly simple models (e.g., linear regression for complex non-linear data) can result in underfitting, where the model fails to capture important patterns in the data.

- **Feature selection**: Real-world datasets often contain a vast number of features, some of which may not contribute meaningfully to the model. Selecting relevant features and reducing dimensionality through techniques like Principal Component Analysis (PCA) or feature engineering is crucial for optimizing model performance.

Finding the right balance between underfitting and overfitting requires careful model selection, tuning, and evaluation using techniques like cross-validation, which may not be as straightforward as the theoretical models you're accustomed to.

1.3 Model Interpretability and Explainability

While machine learning models, particularly deep learning models like neural networks, have shown impressive performance, they often operate as "black boxes." In many real-world applications, model interpretability and explainability are vital, particularly in sectors like finance, healthcare, and law, where stakeholders need to understand how a model arrived at its decision.

Challenges include:

- **Lack of transparency**: In complex models, especially neural networks, it's often difficult to explain why certain decisions were made, which can result in a lack of trust from stakeholders and end-users.
- **Regulatory requirements**: In industries like finance and healthcare, regulatory bodies may require that models be interpretable to ensure fairness, transparency, and accountability. Complying with such standards while still maintaining high performance can be a significant hurdle.
- **Complexity of explainability techniques**: While techniques like LIME (Local Interpretable Model-Agnostic Explanations) and SHAP (Shapley Additive Explanations) can help shed light on how a model makes decisions, they often add another layer of complexity to the project and may not always provide satisfactory explanations.

For many real-world ML applications, providing stakeholders with clear, actionable insights from the model is just as important as achieving high accuracy. Balancing performance with interpretability remains a major challenge for practitioners.

1.4 Lack of Sufficient Labeled Data

Many ML algorithms, especially supervised learning models, require a substantial amount of labeled data to train effectively. In real-world scenarios, obtaining high-quality labeled data is often a bottleneck. Labeling data can be time-consuming, expensive, and subject to human biases, especially in specialized domains like medical imaging, legal documents, or sentiment analysis.

Challenges include:

- **High cost of labeling**: Manual labeling of data is labor-intensive and expensive, particularly for large datasets. For example, labeling medical images or transcribing audio data requires domain expertise, which adds to the cost.
- **Data scarcity**: In some domains, the amount of labeled data available may be insufficient for training robust models, leading to poor model generalization.
- **Label bias and inconsistency**: Even when labeled data is available, it may be subject to inconsistencies or bias introduced by human annotators, which can affect the model's fairness and performance.

To mitigate these challenges, practitioners often turn to unsupervised learning, semi-supervised learning, or active learning, where models can be trained on unlabeled or partially labeled data. Another approach is transfer learning, where pre-trained models on large datasets are fine-tuned for specific tasks with less labeled data.

1.5 Model Deployment and Scalability

While building and training a model might be a complex task, deploying it into a real-world environment comes with its own set of challenges. In production, ML models need to handle large volumes of data, make real-time predictions, and integrate smoothly with other systems. Ensuring that models run efficiently and scale as the data grows is not always straightforward.

Challenges include:

- **Real-time prediction**: Many real-world applications, such as fraud detection, demand real-time predictions. Ensuring that a trained model can handle high throughput and low-latency requirements while maintaining accuracy can be challenging.
- **Scalability**: As businesses scale, their data grows exponentially. This requires models to handle larger datasets, often necessitating distributed computing or specialized architectures like cloud-based solutions (e.g., AWS, Google Cloud).
- **Model versioning and updates**: In production, models must be regularly updated to reflect new data or changes in underlying patterns (e.g., concept drift). Keeping

track of different model versions and ensuring seamless updates in a production environment adds complexity.

- **Integration with existing systems**: Deploying models involves integrating them with business systems, databases, and other software tools. Compatibility issues, system architecture constraints, and testing requirements can slow down the deployment process.

Ensuring that models are both efficient and reliable when deployed in real-world settings requires careful planning, collaboration with engineering teams, and robust MLOps practices.

1.6 Model Monitoring and Maintenance

Once deployed, machine learning models must be continuously monitored and maintained to ensure they perform as expected over time. In dynamic environments, such as financial markets or customer behavior analysis, data distributions can shift, causing model performance to degrade.

Challenges include:

- **Concept and data drift**: Over time, the data distribution may change (known as concept drift) or new, unseen data types may appear (data drift). This can lead to reduced model accuracy or even failure.
- **Model monitoring**: It's crucial to monitor a model's performance in real-time to detect issues like model drift, incorrect predictions, or system failures. However, designing a monitoring system that can handle large-scale deployments and flag performance drops can be technically challenging.
- **Retraining models**: As models experience drift or degrade over time, they need to be retrained with new data. Implementing automated retraining pipelines can help, but it's important to balance the tradeoff between retraining frequency and the computational cost involved.

Keeping a model reliable and effective requires a feedback loop, where insights are gathered from its performance and used to refine or update the system. Regular maintenance is a core part of ensuring that the model remains valuable and aligned with business goals.

Real-world machine learning implementation involves overcoming a range of challenges that go far beyond what is covered in theoretical studies. From working with messy, incomplete data to deploying models in scalable, production-ready environments, these challenges require data scientists to think critically, adapt to changing conditions, and collaborate with cross-functional teams. By understanding and anticipating these challenges, ML practitioners can more effectively navigate the complexities of real-world ML applications and create models that deliver lasting value.

1.4 Tools and frameworks for practical ML

When it comes to implementing machine learning (ML) in real-world applications, choosing the right tools and frameworks is a crucial step that can significantly impact the success of your project. While there are numerous ML tools available, selecting the most suitable ones depends on the specific task at hand, the size and nature of the data, and the level of expertise available. From data preprocessing to model building, evaluation, deployment, and monitoring, a variety of tools can help you streamline the ML pipeline.

In this section, we'll explore the essential tools and frameworks that are commonly used in real-world ML projects. These tools are designed to make machine learning tasks more efficient, scalable, and manageable, whether you're working on a small-scale project or a large, complex system.

1.1 Data Collection and Preprocessing Tools

Data collection and preprocessing form the foundation of any machine learning project. Handling data from multiple sources, cleaning it, and transforming it into a usable format requires specialized tools. In practice, you'll often work with structured data from databases, unstructured data from web scraping, or streaming data from real-time sources. Here are some popular tools for these tasks:

Pandas: A powerful Python library for data manipulation and analysis. It provides data structures like DataFrames to handle structured data, making it easy to clean, filter, and preprocess data. Pandas is often used for tasks like data wrangling, feature engineering, and handling missing values.

NumPy: A core package for scientific computing in Python. It provides support for large multi-dimensional arrays and matrices and a collection of mathematical functions to operate on them. It's essential for numerical computations, especially when dealing with numerical data transformations.

OpenCV: For image data processing, OpenCV is a widely used library that allows image preprocessing, transformations, resizing, and even more complex tasks like object detection.

BeautifulSoup & Scrapy: For web scraping and data collection, these Python libraries are indispensable. They allow you to extract data from HTML and XML documents, making them useful for collecting unstructured data from websites.

Apache Kafka: For real-time data streams, Kafka is a distributed event streaming platform that handles high throughput data ingestion. It's ideal when working with real-time data or in environments requiring continuous data collection.

1.2 Model Building and Training Frameworks

Once the data is preprocessed and ready for training, the next step is to build and train the machine learning model. Depending on the problem you're solving—whether it's classification, regression, clustering, or another type of ML task—you'll need to choose the right algorithms and tools to train the model effectively.

Scikit-learn: One of the most popular ML libraries for beginners and intermediate practitioners. Scikit-learn provides simple, efficient tools for data mining and data analysis, including well-implemented algorithms for classification, regression, clustering, and dimensionality reduction. It's excellent for building traditional machine learning models (like decision trees, SVMs, and linear regression) and for easy experimentation.

TensorFlow: A deep learning framework that offers an open-source platform for building and training machine learning models. TensorFlow supports neural networks and large-scale ML workflows and is particularly useful for deep learning applications, including natural language processing (NLP), computer vision, and reinforcement learning. TensorFlow also includes tools for model deployment through TensorFlow Serving and TensorFlow Lite for mobile.

Keras: A high-level deep learning API built on top of TensorFlow. Keras simplifies the process of building neural networks by providing an intuitive interface for designing and training models. It is particularly useful when working with complex deep learning architectures.

PyTorch: Another widely adopted deep learning framework, PyTorch has grown in popularity for research and production. Known for its dynamic computation graph, PyTorch is well-suited for rapid experimentation and developing custom models, especially in research settings. It supports deep learning applications in NLP, computer vision, and more.

XGBoost: A highly efficient, scalable machine learning library designed for gradient boosting. XGBoost is widely used in Kaggle competitions and real-world applications due to its ability to handle large datasets and deliver high-performance models.

LightGBM: A gradient boosting framework that uses tree-based learning algorithms. It's optimized for speed and scalability, especially when dealing with large datasets. It is particularly useful for handling categorical features directly, making it a good choice for problems involving tabular data.

1.3 Model Evaluation and Hyperparameter Tuning

Once your models are trained, the next crucial step is evaluating their performance and optimizing them through hyperparameter tuning. Real-world machine learning projects often require careful evaluation to ensure that models generalize well and are not overfitting to the training data.

Cross-Validation: Cross-validation is a method of evaluating a model's performance by dividing the data into multiple subsets (folds) and training the model on each fold. This technique helps mitigate overfitting and provides a more reliable estimate of model performance. Scikit-learn provides built-in support for cross-validation.

Hyperopt: A library for hyperparameter optimization using algorithms like random search and Bayesian optimization. Hyperopt allows you to find the best set of hyperparameters for your model by searching the hyperparameter space more intelligently.

Optuna: An open-source hyperparameter optimization framework that automates the search for the best hyperparameters using efficient algorithms. Optuna is particularly useful when you need to tune multiple hyperparameters at once in a complex search space.

TensorBoard: A visualization toolkit for TensorFlow that provides powerful ways to monitor model training, visualize performance metrics, and track hyperparameters. TensorBoard helps to assess how well a model is training and adjust parameters accordingly.

1.4 Model Deployment and Scalability Tools

Deploying machine learning models into a production environment introduces new complexities. The model needs to be integrated with business processes and handle live data inputs while maintaining real-time performance. Moreover, models must be easily retrained, monitored, and scaled as data grows.

Docker: Docker allows you to containerize machine learning models along with their dependencies. Containerization ensures that the model can be deployed consistently across different environments, whether it's on a local server, in the cloud, or within an organization's IT infrastructure.

Kubernetes: Kubernetes is an open-source container orchestration system that helps you manage and scale machine learning applications. It automates deployment, scaling, and operations of machine learning models in distributed computing environments, ensuring efficient resource allocation and high availability.

Flask/FastAPI: Both Flask and FastAPI are lightweight web frameworks that allow you to serve machine learning models as REST APIs. Flask is popular for simple applications, while FastAPI offers faster performance and automatic generation of OpenAPI documentation, making it ideal for scalable, production-grade applications.

TensorFlow Serving: This is a flexible, high-performance system for serving TensorFlow models in production environments. It allows for easy deployment, serving multiple versions of models, and is designed for low-latency predictions in production systems.

MLflow: An open-source platform for managing the end-to-end machine learning lifecycle. MLflow helps track experiments, package models, and manage deployments. It includes tools for model versioning, tracking hyperparameters, and monitoring model performance.

Apache Spark: A unified analytics engine for big data processing, Apache Spark is particularly useful for large-scale machine learning workflows. With MLlib, Spark provides distributed machine learning algorithms that can handle large datasets and scale horizontally across clusters of machines.

1.5 Monitoring and Maintenance Tools

Once a machine learning model is deployed in production, ongoing monitoring and maintenance become crucial to ensure that the model continues to deliver accurate results over time. The following tools help track model performance, detect concept drift, and automate model retraining:

Prometheus: An open-source monitoring and alerting toolkit that can be used to monitor machine learning models and infrastructure. Prometheus is particularly useful for monitoring model performance metrics (e.g., accuracy, latency) in real time.

Grafana: Often used alongside Prometheus, Grafana allows you to visualize the data collected by Prometheus, providing interactive dashboards that can display model performance metrics, system health, and more.

Evidently AI: A framework designed for monitoring the performance of machine learning models in production. It helps identify data drift, model decay, and other issues that could negatively affect model accuracy, providing visualizations and alerts for ongoing model monitoring.

Kubeflow: A comprehensive machine learning platform that runs on Kubernetes and simplifies the deployment, monitoring, and retraining of models. Kubeflow supports end-to-end ML pipelines, from data ingestion to model serving, and automates model maintenance processes.

1.6 Collaboration and Version Control Tools

As machine learning projects often involve collaboration among teams of data scientists, engineers, and business stakeholders, managing code, experiments, and models becomes a challenge. Version control and collaboration tools ensure that the project progresses smoothly and everyone is on the same page.

Git & GitHub: Version control tools like Git allow teams to track changes in their code and collaborate effectively. GitHub or GitLab further enhances collaboration by providing repositories, issue tracking, and CI/CD (continuous integration/continuous deployment) pipelines.

DVC (Data Version Control): A version control system specifically designed for machine learning projects. DVC tracks changes in datasets, models, and hyperparameters, making it easier to collaborate and manage large-scale machine learning workflows.

Jupyter Notebooks: Jupyter notebooks are widely used for documenting experiments, exploring data, and building models interactively. They facilitate collaboration, as you can share and reproduce the analysis while combining code, visualizations, and narrative.

The world of real-world machine learning is vast and filled with powerful tools and frameworks that make implementing, deploying, and maintaining ML models more efficient and scalable. Understanding which tools to use for each stage of the ML workflow—data collection, model building, deployment, and monitoring—is essential for ensuring the success of an ML project. By leveraging the right tools, you can overcome many of the challenges that arise in practical machine learning and create models that deliver meaningful and reliable results in production environments.

1.5 Setting up your development environment

Setting up a robust development environment is one of the most important steps in ensuring a smooth and efficient machine learning (ML) project. The right environment not only helps streamline the workflow but also ensures consistency, reproducibility, and scalability throughout the development lifecycle. A well-configured environment can help you avoid compatibility issues, speed up experimentation, and enable easy deployment. In this section, we'll walk through the essential steps to set up your development environment for machine learning, including hardware, software, tools, and best practices to get you started.

1.1 Hardware Requirements

Before diving into software, it's crucial to assess the hardware requirements of your machine learning projects. While some simple ML tasks can run efficiently on a basic laptop, larger datasets and more complex models (such as deep learning tasks) may require specialized hardware. Here's what to consider:

CPU: For smaller machine learning tasks, a multi-core CPU (e.g., Intel i5/i7 or AMD Ryzen) is typically sufficient. However, for computationally intensive tasks like deep learning, using more powerful CPUs will expedite training times.

GPU: Graphics Processing Units (GPUs) are essential for tasks involving large datasets, deep learning, and neural networks. GPUs speed up matrix operations, which are common in deep learning. Popular models include NVIDIA's Tesla and GeForce RTX series, which support frameworks like CUDA (Compute Unified Device Architecture) and cuDNN (CUDA Deep Neural Network library).

RAM: ML tasks can consume a significant amount of memory, especially when processing large datasets. A minimum of 8 GB of RAM is recommended for entry-level projects, but for large-scale machine learning, 16 GB or more may be necessary.

Storage: High-speed storage is also crucial, especially when dealing with large datasets. Consider using an SSD (Solid-State Drive) for faster read/write speeds compared to traditional HDDs, particularly when loading datasets into memory for training.

1.2 Choosing the Right Operating System

The operating system (OS) you choose plays an important role in setting up the development environment. Both Windows and macOS are popular among developers, but Linux is often the preferred choice for many ML practitioners due to its flexibility, performance, and compatibility with open-source tools. Here's a breakdown of each option:

Linux: Most machine learning libraries and frameworks are developed with Linux in mind, making it the most compatible and efficient OS for machine learning. Distributions like Ubuntu, Debian, and CentOS provide an open-source, highly customizable environment, and support for tools like Docker, Kubernetes, and TensorFlow.

Windows: While Windows is widely used in development, it's not always the best option for ML, as some tools and libraries have limited or delayed support. However, Windows Subsystem for Linux (WSL) has made it easier to use Linux-based tools on Windows systems, bridging the gap for ML developers.

macOS: macOS is suitable for smaller-scale ML projects and is preferred by some data scientists for its smooth integration with Apple's ecosystem. However, it's worth noting that macOS doesn't support GPUs from NVIDIA, limiting its potential for large-scale deep learning tasks.

1.3 Installing Python and Conda

Python is the de facto language for machine learning, with a vast ecosystem of libraries and frameworks that make it easy to build and train models. The first step in setting up your ML environment is to install Python and manage dependencies efficiently.

Python: Most ML frameworks and tools are built around Python, so it is essential to install it on your system. The latest version of Python 3.x should be installed, as Python 2.x is no longer supported.

Anaconda: Anaconda is a popular distribution that simplifies Python package management and environment setup. It comes with a large number of pre-installed libraries, such as NumPy, SciPy, Pandas, and Matplotlib, which are commonly used in machine learning. Anaconda also includes Conda, a package manager for easily installing and managing different versions of Python packages, making it easier to set up isolated environments for different projects.

Installation: Once Anaconda is installed, you can create new virtual environments tailored to your ML project requirements by running conda create -n <env-name> python=3.x.

Managing environments: You can manage dependencies and libraries for each project in isolated environments, avoiding conflicts. For example, you can install TensorFlow in one environment and PyTorch in another.

1.4 Installing Machine Learning Libraries and Frameworks

Once Python and Conda are set up, it's time to install the core machine learning libraries. Depending on the type of machine learning you plan to do, the following libraries and frameworks are essential:

NumPy and Pandas: These libraries are foundational for working with arrays, data manipulation, and preprocessing.

Matplotlib and Seaborn: These libraries are used for data visualization and generating plots to gain insights into the data.

Scikit-learn: A versatile library for traditional machine learning tasks such as regression, classification, clustering, and model evaluation.

TensorFlow and Keras: TensorFlow is the go-to library for deep learning. Keras, which is now integrated into TensorFlow, offers a user-friendly API for building neural networks.

PyTorch: Another deep learning framework, popular for its dynamic computational graph, useful for research and complex model development.

XGBoost and LightGBM: These libraries are used for gradient boosting and are commonly employed in structured/tabular data tasks for superior performance in competitions and real-world applications.

OpenCV: For computer vision tasks like image classification, object detection, and image segmentation.

You can install these libraries directly using Conda or pip (Python's package manager). For example, to install TensorFlow in a specific environment, you can run:

conda install tensorflow

Alternatively, for pip-based installations:

pip install tensorflow

1.5 Setting Up Jupyter Notebooks and IDEs

Jupyter Notebooks is a popular tool in the ML community, especially for interactive experimentation, visualization, and documentation. It enables you to combine code, markdown, and visual outputs in one document, making it easier to analyze and share results.

Jupyter Notebooks: You can install Jupyter via Anaconda with the following command:

conda install jupyter

JupyterLab: JupyterLab is an extension of Jupyter Notebooks and offers a more flexible and feature-rich environment for managing notebooks, text editors, terminals, and other tools within one interface.

conda install jupyterlab

IDE Options: While Jupyter is great for experimentation and exploration, integrated development environments (IDEs) like VSCode, PyCharm, or Spyder can help improve your productivity during larger projects. These IDEs offer code suggestions, debugging tools, and a better environment for working with more complex scripts.

VSCode: A lightweight and powerful code editor that supports Python, Jupyter Notebooks, and many ML extensions. You can install the Python extension and other relevant tools to enhance your experience.

1.6 Version Control with Git

For collaborative machine learning projects, version control is crucial. Git allows you to track changes in your code and collaborate with others in a seamless way.

Git: Git is a distributed version control system that tracks changes in your codebase. Install Git from Git's official website.

GitHub/GitLab/Bitbucket: These platforms host Git repositories and offer a collaborative environment for teams. You can push your local changes to these platforms, keep track of code versions, and share your code with others.

DVC (Data Version Control): For ML projects, DVC provides version control for datasets and machine learning models, enabling you to track and share large datasets and model files. DVC integrates seamlessly with Git, helping you manage not just code, but data and models as well.

1.7 Setting Up Docker for Containerization

Containerization has become an essential practice for deploying machine learning models in production. Docker allows you to package your machine learning environment (including all dependencies, libraries, and models) into a container, ensuring that it can run consistently across different environments.

Docker: Install Docker on your system and create a Dockerfile to define your project's environment. This file contains instructions for setting up your machine learning environment, installing necessary libraries, and ensuring compatibility across systems.

Docker Compose: For more complex ML applications involving multiple services (e.g., databases, APIs), Docker Compose is a tool that helps define and run multi-container Docker applications.

Setting up a machine learning development environment requires careful consideration of the hardware, software, libraries, and tools that will be used throughout the project lifecycle. By selecting the right tools for data processing, model building, evaluation, deployment, and monitoring, you can set up a streamlined and efficient environment that maximizes your productivity. Whether you're working on small-scale tasks or large, complex machine learning systems, a properly configured environment will ensure that your projects are reproducible, scalable, and maintainable in the long run.

2. Project Workflow & Best Practices

Successfully executing a machine learning project requires a structured workflow that ensures efficiency, reproducibility, and scalability. In this chapter, we break down the end-to-end ML workflow, covering key stages such as problem definition, data collection, preprocessing, model selection, training, evaluation, and deployment. You'll learn industry best practices for handling data, avoiding common pitfalls, tracking experiments, and optimizing models for production. We also introduce essential tools like version control, MLOps frameworks, and automated pipelines to streamline your workflow. By following a systematic approach, you'll be able to develop ML solutions that are not only accurate but also scalable and maintainable in real-world applications. 🔥

2.1 Problem formulation & defining success metrics

In any machine learning (ML) project, the first and arguably most important step is to properly define the problem you're trying to solve and how you'll measure its success. This phase lays the foundation for your entire project, as the clarity of your problem statement and success metrics directly influences your model selection, data collection, algorithm choice, and evaluation techniques.

Problem formulation and defining success metrics might seem straightforward, but they require a deep understanding of the business or research objectives you're addressing. It's crucial to define both in a way that's measurable, achievable, and aligned with the broader goals of the project. Without this clarity, even the most sophisticated machine learning models may fall short of delivering tangible value.

In this section, we'll break down the essential components of problem formulation and defining success metrics. By the end, you'll have a clear roadmap to guide your machine learning efforts and ensure that your models solve real-world problems effectively.

1. Understanding the Problem

Before jumping into data collection or model development, you need to thoroughly understand the problem you're tackling. This involves discussions with stakeholders, reviewing project requirements, and exploring the business or technical goals you aim to achieve. Here's how to approach the problem formulation process:

Clarify the Objective: What is the goal of the project? Are you trying to predict a future outcome, classify data into categories, or perhaps find patterns in existing data? For instance, if you're working on a customer churn prediction project, your goal may be to predict whether a customer will leave a service based on historical data. If you're building a house price prediction model, you are trying to predict the price of a house based on various features (e.g., location, size, number of rooms, etc.).

Identify the Type of Problem: Machine learning problems can generally be categorized into one of the following types:

- **Classification**: Predicting discrete labels or categories (e.g., email spam classification, customer segmentation).
- **Regression**: Predicting continuous values (e.g., predicting house prices, stock prices).
- **Clustering**: Grouping similar data points together (e.g., customer segmentation based on purchasing behavior).
- **Anomaly Detection**: Identifying unusual patterns or outliers (e.g., fraud detection in transactions).
- **Recommendation**: Suggesting items to users based on preferences (e.g., movie recommendations, product recommendations).

Defining whether your problem is classification, regression, or another type helps determine the appropriate machine learning approach and evaluation strategies.

Specify the Scope: Clearly define the boundaries of the project. What exactly are you trying to predict or uncover? What is outside the scope of this project? For example, in a demand forecasting project, your scope might be limited to forecasting product demand for the next three months, but not the next year.

Gather Domain Knowledge: Understanding the business domain or context of the problem is critical. Collaborate with domain experts (e.g., business analysts, product managers) to gain insights that will help shape your approach. This domain knowledge will be crucial in choosing the right features and interpreting the results.

2. Defining Success Metrics

Once you've formulated the problem, the next step is to define success metrics. These are the quantitative measures that will guide how well your machine learning model performs. Success metrics are essential for model evaluation and determining whether the project has met its objectives.

Here are the key components to consider when defining success metrics:

Align Metrics with Business Objectives: Your success metrics should be directly tied to the goals of the project. For example:

- If your goal is to increase customer retention, a customer churn prediction model might use metrics like precision, recall, or F1-score to evaluate how accurately it predicts which customers are likely to churn.
- In a house price prediction project, metrics like Mean Absolute Error (MAE) or Root Mean Squared Error (RMSE) would measure how close your predicted house prices are to the actual values.

Select the Right Evaluation Metrics: The evaluation metric you choose depends on the type of problem you're solving:

For Classification:

- **Accuracy**: Measures the proportion of correct predictions. It's useful when the classes are balanced, but it may be misleading in imbalanced datasets.
- **Precision**: The proportion of true positive predictions among all predicted positives. Precision is essential when false positives are costly (e.g., predicting fraud).
- **Recall**: The proportion of true positive predictions among all actual positives. Recall is important when false negatives are risky (e.g., predicting cancer).
- **F1-score**: The harmonic mean of precision and recall. It's a good balance between precision and recall when you need to balance both.
- **AUC-ROC (Area Under the Receiver Operating Characteristic curve):** Measures the model's ability to distinguish between positive and negative classes, independent of the classification threshold.

For Regression:

- **Mean Absolute Error (MAE):** The average absolute difference between the predicted and actual values. It's easy to interpret and works well when you want to avoid the effect of outliers.
- **Root Mean Squared Error (RMSE):** Similar to MAE, but it gives more weight to larger errors. It is sensitive to outliers and is often preferred when large errors are undesirable.

- **R-squared (R²):** Measures how well the model's predictions match the actual data, representing the proportion of variance in the dependent variable explained by the independent variables.
- **Mean Squared Error (MSE):** Similar to RMSE but without taking the square root. It penalizes larger errors more than MAE.

For Clustering:

- **Silhouette Score**: Measures the quality of clusters based on how close the points in a cluster are to each other compared to points in other clusters.
- **Davies-Bouldin Index**: Measures the average similarity ratio of each cluster with the cluster that is most similar to it. Lower values indicate better clustering.

For Anomaly Detection:

- **True Positive Rate (TPR):** The rate of correctly identified anomalies compared to the total number of anomalies.
- **False Positive Rate (FPR):** The rate of incorrectly classified normal points as anomalies.

Business Metrics vs. Technical Metrics:

Business Metrics: These metrics focus on the practical outcomes of the ML model in the real world. For example, in a recommendation system, the ultimate business metric could be click-through rate (CTR), which measures how often users click on recommended items. Alternatively, in a customer churn problem, a business metric could be the reduction in churn rate after deploying the model.

Technical Metrics: These metrics assess the model's technical performance, such as training time, inference speed, or memory usage. For a real-time application, latency (inference speed) may be crucial, while for batch processing, model accuracy might take precedence.

Benchmarking Success: Compare your model's performance against a baseline model. A baseline model is a simple, straightforward approach that often involves predicting the mean or median value for regression tasks or the majority class for classification tasks. If your model performs worse than the baseline, it's a sign that something might be wrong with the model or the data.

Defining Acceptable Thresholds: It's essential to define what constitutes an acceptable level of success. For example, you may decide that your model should achieve at least 80% accuracy for a classification task, or an R-squared value greater than 0.9 for a regression task. These thresholds can be refined over time based on testing and further analysis.

Consider Trade-offs: Often, improving one metric may come at the expense of another. For example, increasing precision may reduce recall, or focusing on minimizing RMSE may lead to a longer training time. It's important to consider the trade-offs based on your business needs. Sometimes, balancing multiple metrics (e.g., precision and recall, accuracy and training time) may lead to the best outcome.

3. Defining Success Beyond Metrics

Although numerical metrics are invaluable for model evaluation, defining success in machine learning projects should also account for non-quantitative aspects:

Model Interpretability: In some domains (e.g., healthcare, finance), model interpretability is crucial for stakeholders to trust and act upon the model's predictions. If the model is a "black-box" with no clear explanation of how it arrived at its predictions, it might be difficult to gain acceptance in these fields.

Scalability: The model's ability to handle increasing data volumes or work efficiently in production environments is a key consideration. Scalability often becomes more important in real-world deployment, where the model needs to operate at scale with minimal downtime.

Real-World Impact: Ultimately, the goal of machine learning is not just to perform well on a dataset, but to provide value in real-world applications. Whether it's reducing costs, increasing revenue, improving customer satisfaction, or automating a tedious task, the model's success can be measured by the positive impact it has on the business.

Effective problem formulation and defining success metrics are pivotal to the success of a machine learning project. A well-defined problem statement ensures that you're addressing the right challenge, while success metrics give you a clear path to measuring the value your model provides. By aligning your metrics with business objectives, selecting the right evaluation methods, and understanding the trade-offs involved, you can ensure that your machine learning project delivers measurable value and meets real-world expectations.

2.2 Choosing the right ML approach

Selecting the appropriate machine learning (ML) approach is a crucial step in building a successful ML project. The choice of algorithm depends on several factors, including the nature of the problem, the type and quantity of data available, and the computational constraints of your system. A well-chosen approach can lead to accurate and efficient models, while a poorly chosen one may result in suboptimal performance, wasted resources, and impractical deployment.

In this section, we will explore how to choose the right ML approach by examining different categories of machine learning, understanding the characteristics of each method, and considering key factors that impact decision-making.

1. Understanding the Different Types of ML Approaches

Machine learning approaches can generally be categorized into three main types:

1.1 Supervised Learning

Supervised learning is used when the dataset contains labeled examples, meaning that each training instance includes both input features and a corresponding output (target variable). The model learns from these labeled examples to make predictions on new, unseen data.

Best suited for:

- **Predicting continuous numerical values (Regression):** E.g., house price prediction, stock market forecasting.
- **Classifying data into categories (Classification):** E.g., spam detection, sentiment analysis, fraud detection.

Common algorithms:

- Linear Regression, Decision Trees, Random Forest, XGBoost, Neural Networks (for regression).
- Logistic Regression, Support Vector Machines (SVM), K-Nearest Neighbors (KNN), Random Forest, Deep Learning (for classification).

1.2 Unsupervised Learning

Unsupervised learning is used when the dataset lacks explicit labels. The goal is to identify patterns, structures, or relationships within the data without predefined categories.

Best suited for:

- **Grouping similar data points (Clustering):** E.g., customer segmentation, anomaly detection.
- **Identifying hidden patterns (Dimensionality Reduction):** E.g., feature selection, data compression.

Common algorithms:

- K-Means, DBSCAN, Hierarchical Clustering (for clustering).
- Principal Component Analysis (PCA), t-SNE, Autoencoders (for dimensionality reduction).

1.3 Reinforcement Learning (RL)

Reinforcement learning is a goal-driven approach where an agent learns by interacting with an environment. The agent takes actions to maximize cumulative rewards over time.

Best suited for:

- Decision-making tasks requiring sequential learning: E.g., robotics, game playing, autonomous systems.
- Optimization problems where exploration and exploitation are important: E.g., supply chain optimization, dynamic pricing.

Common algorithms:

Q-Learning, Deep Q-Networks (DQN), Proximal Policy Optimization (PPO), Actor-Critic methods.

2. Key Factors to Consider When Choosing an ML Approach

Selecting the best ML approach requires careful consideration of the problem, dataset, and available resources. Here are some key factors to keep in mind:

2.1 Nature of the Problem

- **If the goal is to make predictions based on historical data** → Choose Supervised Learning (Regression or Classification).
- **If the goal is to discover patterns or structure in the data** → Choose Unsupervised Learning (Clustering, Dimensionality Reduction).
- **If the goal is to develop an agent that learns through trial and error** → Choose Reinforcement Learning.

2.2 Type & Volume of Data Available

- **Labeled data available?** → Supervised learning is the best choice.
- **Unlabeled data?** → Consider unsupervised learning methods.
- **Sequential decision-making or real-time interactions required?** → Reinforcement learning is suitable.
- **Big data requiring scalability?** → Use distributed computing techniques like Spark ML, Hadoop, or cloud-based ML platforms.

2.3 Model Interpretability vs. Accuracy Trade-off

- If explainability is important (e.g., healthcare, finance), consider simpler models like Decision Trees, Logistic Regression, or Rule-Based Systems.
- If high accuracy is the priority and interpretability is less important, consider Deep Learning or Ensemble Models.

2.4 Computational Complexity & Deployment Feasibility

- Simple models like Linear Regression or Decision Trees are easier to deploy in resource-constrained environments.
- Neural Networks and Deep Learning models require more computational power and specialized hardware (e.g., GPUs, TPUs).

2.5 Handling of Noisy or Imbalanced Data

- If data is highly imbalanced (e.g., fraud detection, rare disease classification), consider techniques like SMOTE (Synthetic Minority Over-sampling Technique) or ensemble methods such as XGBoost or Random Forest.
- If data contains noise, consider robust models like Gradient Boosting Machines (GBM) or Neural Networks with dropout techniques.

3. Choosing the Right Algorithm for Different Scenarios

Below is a high-level guide to selecting the right ML approach based on common real-world scenarios:

Problem Type	Recommended ML Approach	Example Use Case
Binary Classification	Logistic Regression, Random Forest, SVM, XGBoost	Spam detection, fraud detection
Multiclass Classification	Decision Trees, Neural Networks, KNN, Naïve Bayes	Sentiment analysis, handwriting recognition
Regression	Linear Regression, Random Forest, XGBoost, LSTM	House price prediction, demand forecasting
Clustering	K-Means, DBSCAN, Hierarchical Clustering	Customer segmentation, anomaly detection
Anomaly Detection	Isolation Forest, One-Class SVM, Autoencoders	Fraud detection, network intrusion detection
Recommendation Systems	Collaborative Filtering, Matrix Factorization	E-commerce recommendations, movie suggestions
Time-Series Forecasting	ARIMA, LSTMs, Facebook Prophet, XGBoost	Stock price forecasting, energy consumption prediction
Reinforcement Learning	Q-Learning, PPO, DDPG, Deep Q-Networks (DQN)	Autonomous driving, game playing, robotics

Choosing the right ML approach is a critical decision that can significantly impact the performance and success of your project. By considering the type of problem, available data, model complexity, computational resources, and business requirements, you can make an informed decision that aligns with your project goals.

In the next section, we will discuss how to structure your ML project workflow effectively, covering best practices in data collection, preprocessing, model selection, and evaluation.

2.3 The iterative nature of ML development

Machine learning (ML) development is not a one-time process—it is highly iterative. Unlike traditional software development, where a program is written, tested, and deployed with minimal need for ongoing changes, ML models require continuous refinement. The process involves multiple cycles of experimentation, evaluation, and tuning to achieve optimal performance.

An iterative approach is necessary because ML models rely on data, which can be noisy, incomplete, or biased. Additionally, real-world conditions change over time, requiring models to be updated or retrained. In this section, we'll explore the iterative nature of ML development, its key stages, and how to efficiently manage multiple iterations to build robust and reliable models.

1. Understanding the ML Development Cycle

A typical ML workflow follows a structured but iterative path:

- **Problem Definition & Data Understanding** – Identify the problem, understand the domain, and gather relevant data.
- **Data Preprocessing & Feature Engineering** – Clean, transform, and select meaningful features from the raw data.
- **Model Selection & Training** – Choose an appropriate ML algorithm and train an initial model.
- **Evaluation & Performance Metrics** – Measure the model's effectiveness using relevant evaluation metrics.
- **Hyperparameter Tuning & Optimization** – Adjust model parameters to improve performance.
- **Deployment & Monitoring** – Deploy the model into a production environment and continuously monitor its performance.
- **Retraining & Updating** – Retrain the model periodically to ensure it adapts to new data trends.

Each of these steps often requires multiple iterations before achieving a satisfactory outcome.

2. Why ML Development is Iterative

Unlike traditional software development, where a predefined set of rules governs program behavior, ML models learn from data. The learning process is unpredictable and requires constant refinement due to the following reasons:

2.1 Data Quality Issues

- **Noisy or incomplete data**: Missing values, inconsistent formatting, or outliers can affect model performance.
- **Changing data distributions**: Real-world data evolves (e.g., consumer behavior shifts over time), requiring retraining.
- **Bias in data**: If the dataset is unbalanced or skewed, the model might not generalize well.

Each time an issue is discovered, the data preprocessing and feature engineering steps need to be revisited, making ML development an ongoing process.

2.2 Model Performance Optimization

- Initial models rarely perform optimally. Developers must experiment with different algorithms, hyperparameters, and feature sets.
- Performance improvements often require multiple rounds of fine-tuning, adjusting learning rates, regularization techniques, and testing various architectures.

2.3 Overfitting & Generalization Issues

- A model might perform well on training data but fail on unseen data.
- Regularization techniques, cross-validation, and feature selection must be adjusted iteratively to balance bias and variance.

2.4 Evolving Business Needs

- Business objectives may change, requiring different success metrics or adjustments in model design.
- New constraints (e.g., regulatory requirements, ethical considerations) might demand modifications in data collection or model behavior.

3. Managing Iterative ML Development Efficiently

To ensure that the iterative process is productive rather than chaotic, structured approaches and best practices should be followed:

3.1 Version Control for Data & Models

- Unlike software development, where version control systems like Git track code changes, ML projects also require versioning for datasets and models.
- Tools like DVC (Data Version Control), MLflow, and Weights & Biases help manage different iterations of models and datasets.

3.2 Experiment Tracking

- Keeping track of different model versions, hyperparameter settings, and evaluation results is essential for efficient iteration.
- Tools like TensorBoard, Comet.ml, Neptune.ai, and MLflow allow developers to log and compare experiment results.

3.3 Automating Model Training & Hyperparameter Tuning

- Instead of manually adjusting hyperparameters, tools like Optuna, Hyperopt, or GridSearchCV can automate hyperparameter search.
- Continuous integration and automated pipelines help streamline model retraining.

3.4 Continuous Monitoring & Feedback Loops

- Deployed models must be monitored for drift in data distributions, concept drift, and performance degradation.
- MLOps frameworks like Kubeflow, MLflow, and AWS SageMaker provide automated monitoring and alert systems.

3.5 Human-in-the-Loop (HITL) Systems

- Incorporating domain experts and users to provide feedback on model predictions helps refine models iteratively.
- Active learning strategies can be used to select the most valuable data points for human review.

4. Case Study: Iterative Development in a Fraud Detection Model

Consider a financial institution developing an ML model to detect fraudulent transactions. The first version of the model achieves 85% accuracy, but further evaluation reveals that:

- Many fraudulent transactions are misclassified as legitimate.
- The model struggles with detecting new fraud patterns that were not present in the training data.

Iteration 1: Improving Data Quality

- Additional fraud-related features (e.g., transaction frequency, geolocation) are engineered.
- More recent transaction data is collected to reflect current fraud trends.

Iteration 2: Model Optimization

- The original model used Logistic Regression, but an ensemble approach (Random Forest + XGBoost) improves recall.
- Hyperparameter tuning is performed using Bayesian Optimization to fine-tune thresholds.

Iteration 3: Deployment & Monitoring

- The model is deployed, but monitoring reveals data drift in customer transaction behavior.
- A mechanism is introduced to retrain the model every three months with updated data.

This case study highlights how ML models require continuous improvement rather than a single development cycle.

Machine learning development is inherently iterative, requiring multiple cycles of experimentation, evaluation, and optimization. Data quality, model performance, and evolving real-world conditions demand continuous refinement. By adopting best practices such as version control, experiment tracking, hyperparameter tuning, and continuous monitoring, ML teams can effectively manage the iterative nature of model development.

In the next section, we'll explore best practices for data collection, cleaning, and preprocessing, which are essential for ensuring high-quality ML models.

2.4 Version control & experiment tracking

Machine learning (ML) projects involve constant iterations—data updates, model tuning, hyperparameter adjustments, and architecture modifications. Unlike traditional software development, where version control systems like Git efficiently track changes in code, ML projects require versioning not just for code but also for datasets, models, and experiments. Keeping track of different versions ensures reproducibility, prevents unnecessary rework, and enables better collaboration in teams.

In this section, we will explore why version control is crucial in ML workflows, how to implement dataset and model versioning, and how to efficiently track experiments to ensure optimal model performance over time.

1. Why Version Control & Experiment Tracking Matter in ML

ML projects involve multiple moving parts—each with frequent updates:

- **Data Changes**: New data is added, cleaned, or modified regularly.
- **Feature Engineering**: Different features are tested for their impact on model performance.
- **Model Architectures**: Experimenting with various ML algorithms or deep learning architectures is common.
- **Hyperparameters**: Tuning parameters like learning rates, regularization factors, and batch sizes significantly impact model performance.

Evaluation Metrics: Different success metrics (e.g., accuracy, precision, recall, F1-score) are tested to determine the best-performing model.

Without proper versioning and tracking, teams may:

✓ **Lose track of what worked best** – Reproducing a high-performing model without knowing its exact parameters is difficult.

✓ **Accidentally overwrite good models** – Older, better models may be lost in an uncontrolled development process.

✓ **Face collaboration issues** – Team members working on different parts of a project need clear tracking to avoid conflicts.

✓ **Struggle with debugging** – Understanding why a model fails in production is hard without knowing its training history.

To address these challenges, version control for datasets and models, along with proper experiment tracking, is essential.

2. Version Control for ML Projects

Traditional version control tools like Git work well for tracking code, but ML projects involve additional components:

2.1 Dataset Versioning

Unlike software code, datasets are often large, making traditional Git impractical for versioning. Instead, specialized tools help track dataset changes:

- **DVC (Data Version Control):** A Git-like tool that versions large datasets efficiently.
- **Pachyderm**: A data lineage and versioning tool for reproducible ML.
- **Delta Lake**: A structured storage layer that tracks changes in datasets.

✦ **Best Practice**: Store raw data separately from processed data and track transformations using pipeline tools like DVC.

2.2 Model Versioning

Each time a model is trained, it generates artifacts such as model weights, configurations, and performance metrics. Versioning these artifacts ensures better reproducibility.

- **MLflow**: A widely used tool that tracks different model versions and logs metrics.
- **Weights & Biases (W&B):** A popular framework for experiment tracking and model versioning.
- **Amazon SageMaker Model Registry**: A cloud-based solution for storing and managing different model versions.

✦ **Best Practice**: Store trained models in a structured format (e.g., .pkl, .h5, or .onnx) with metadata on training conditions.

3. Experiment Tracking in ML

An ML project may involve testing multiple models, tuning hyperparameters, and evaluating different datasets. Manually tracking these experiments using spreadsheets or notes can quickly become unmanageable. Experiment tracking tools automate this process by logging all model training runs, configurations, and results.

3.1 Key Components of Experiment Tracking

A well-structured experiment tracking system should log:

- **Dataset versions** – Ensuring each experiment uses a specific dataset version.
- **Model parameters & hyperparameters** – Capturing details like learning rates, batch sizes, dropout rates, etc.
- **Model architecture details** – Defining layers, activation functions, and training epochs.
- **Performance metrics** – Logging accuracy, precision, recall, loss curves, etc.
- **Hardware specifications** – Tracking GPU/CPU usage and execution time for optimization.

3.2 Popular Experiment Tracking Tools

Several tools make it easy to track experiments efficiently:

Tool	Key Features
MLflow	Model tracking, versioning, and deployment tools.
Weights & Biases	Experiment logging, visualizations, and team collaboration.
Neptune.ai	Cloud-based experiment tracking for ML workflows.
Comet.ml	Real-time experiment tracking with API integrations.
TensorBoard	Visualization tool for TensorFlow-based models.

◆ **Best Practice**: Use a dedicated tool like MLflow or Weights & Biases to automatically log experiments instead of manual tracking.

4. Implementing Version Control & Tracking in an ML Workflow

Here's how to integrate version control and experiment tracking in a real ML project:

Step 1: Initialize a Git Repository for Code Versioning

git init
git add .
git commit -m "Initial ML project setup"

Step 2: Set Up DVC for Dataset Versioning

```
pip install dvc
dvc init
dvc add data/raw_data.csv
git add data/.gitignore data/raw_data.csv.dvc
git commit -m "Track dataset with DVC"
```

Step 3: Use MLflow for Experiment Tracking

```
import mlflow

mlflow.start_run()
mlflow.log_param("learning_rate", 0.001)
mlflow.log_metric("accuracy", 0.92)
mlflow.log_artifact("model.pkl")
mlflow.end_run()
```

Step 4: Automate Experiment Tracking in a Jupyter Notebook

```
import wandb

wandb.init(project="fraud-detection")
wandb.config.learning_rate = 0.001
wandb.log({"accuracy": 0.92, "loss": 0.08})
```

5. Case Study: Version Control in a Fraud Detection Model

A financial services company builds a fraud detection model using ML. Their ML team encounters challenges:

🕮 **Problem 1**: Different team members train models on different datasets, causing inconsistencies.
🕮 **Problem 2**: It's unclear which hyperparameters led to the best-performing model.
🕮 **Problem 3**: The deployed model performs poorly, but no one knows which dataset version was used for training.

Solution: Implementing Version Control & Experiment Tracking

✅ DVC is used to version datasets, ensuring everyone works with the same data.

✓ MLflow logs model hyperparameters, architectures, and metrics for comparison.

✓ Weights & Biases provides visualizations for performance tracking.

After implementing these solutions, the team improves collaboration, eliminates confusion, and can confidently reproduce the best-performing model.

Version control and experiment tracking are essential for ML development, ensuring reproducibility, collaboration, and efficient model optimization. By using tools like DVC for datasets, MLflow for model tracking, and Weights & Biases for logging experiments, teams can streamline ML workflows, avoid costly mistakes, and build robust models that can be confidently deployed in real-world applications.

In the next section, we will explore best practices for data collection, cleaning, and preprocessing—a foundational step for building high-quality ML models.

2.5 Collaboration in ML projects

Machine learning (ML) projects are rarely solo endeavors. They require cross-functional collaboration among data scientists, engineers, domain experts, product managers, and stakeholders. Unlike traditional software development, where code is the primary deliverable, ML projects involve datasets, models, experiments, and deployment pipelines—all of which demand efficient coordination.

In this section, we explore the key challenges of collaboration in ML projects, best practices for effective teamwork, and the tools that facilitate seamless collaboration in modern ML workflows.

1. Why Collaboration is Critical in ML Projects

Unlike typical software projects, where well-defined requirements lead to a predictable development cycle, ML projects are inherently iterative and exploratory. This makes collaboration essential for:

✓ **Aligning objectives** – Ensuring data scientists, engineers, and business stakeholders have a shared understanding of goals.
✓ **Efficient data management** – Handling large datasets while ensuring consistency across team members.

✓ **Experiment tracking & model reproducibility** – Keeping track of different versions of models, hyperparameters, and datasets.

✓ **Smooth deployment & monitoring** – Coordinating between data scientists, ML engineers, and DevOps teams.

✓ **Ethical and responsible AI development** – Ensuring models are fair, unbiased, and aligned with business and societal goals.

Without proper collaboration, teams risk misaligned expectations, inefficient workflows, redundant efforts, and poor model deployment outcomes.

2. Challenges in ML Collaboration

Despite its necessity, collaboration in ML projects presents several challenges:

2.1 Communication Gaps Between Teams

- Business teams focus on KPIs, success metrics, and customer impact, while data scientists are concerned with model accuracy and performance.
- ML engineers prioritize efficient deployment, scalability, and monitoring, but may not fully understand the nuances of model training.

◆ **Solution**: Establish clear documentation and regular meetings to align priorities and expectations.

2.2 Reproducibility Issues

- Different team members may train models using different dataset versions or hyperparameters, leading to inconsistent results.
- Code, data preprocessing scripts, and experiment settings are often not properly tracked.

◆ **Solution**: Use version control (Git, DVC), experiment tracking (MLflow, Weights & Biases), and containerization (Docker, Kubernetes) to ensure consistency.

2.3 Managing Large Datasets & Shared Resources

- ML teams often work with massive datasets, making it difficult to share and store efficiently.
- Computational resources (GPUs, cloud instances) need to be allocated efficiently across multiple team members.

✦ Solution: Utilize cloud storage (Google Cloud Storage, AWS S3), data versioning (DVC, Delta Lake), and resource orchestration (Kubernetes, Ray, Airflow) for efficient collaboration.

2.4 Integration Between Research & Production Teams

- Many ML models work well in Jupyter Notebooks but are difficult to deploy in real-world applications.
- Research teams may build models in TensorFlow or PyTorch, while engineering teams require optimized versions for production (e.g., TensorFlow Serving, ONNX, or FastAPI).

✦ Solution: Implement MLOps practices to bridge the gap between research and production.

3. Best Practices for Collaboration in ML Projects

To ensure smooth collaboration, teams should adopt structured workflows, use the right tools, and follow best practices.

3.1 Define Roles & Responsibilities

Clearly outline each team member's role to avoid confusion:

Role	Responsibilities
Data Scientist	Data preprocessing, feature engineering, model training, and evaluation.
ML Engineer	Optimizing models for deployment, creating APIs, and managing inference pipelines.
Data Engineer	Managing data pipelines, ETL processes, and database systems.
DevOps Engineer	Infrastructure automation, CI/CD pipelines, and cloud deployments.
Domain Expert	Providing business insights, evaluating model relevance, and defining success metrics.

✦ Tip: Use project management tools like JIRA, Trello, or Asana to track tasks and progress.

3.2 Establish a Shared Development Environment

To prevent "it works on my machine" problems, teams should work in a consistent environment:

- Use Docker to create portable and reproducible environments.
- Leverage JupyterHub or Google Colab for collaborative model development.
- Utilize cloud-based platforms (Google Vertex AI, AWS SageMaker, Databricks) for shared computing resources.

3.3 Implement Version Control for Code, Data & Models

Use a structured versioning approach to maintain reproducibility:

- **GitHub/GitLab** → Track source code, scripts, and configurations.
- **DVC (Data Version Control)** → Version datasets and preprocessing steps.
- **MLflow/Weights & Biases** → Track and compare model experiments.

3.4 Use CI/CD for Model Deployment

- Set up continuous integration & deployment (CI/CD) pipelines to automate model testing and deployment.
- Use Kubeflow, TFX, or SageMaker Pipelines to streamline ML production workflows.

3.5 Encourage Documentation & Knowledge Sharing

- Maintain clear README files, Wiki pages, and internal documentation.
- Use Notion, Confluence, or Google Docs for shared knowledge bases.
- Hold weekly knowledge-sharing sessions to discuss experiments, findings, and challenges.

4. Collaboration Tools for ML Projects

Category	Recommended Tools
Code Versioning	GitHub, GitLab, Bitbucket
Data Versioning	DVC, Delta Lake, Pachyderm
Experiment Tracking	MLflow, Weights & Biases, Comet.ml
Collaboration & Docs	Notion, Confluence, Google Docs
Cloud-based ML	Google Vertex AI, AWS SageMaker, Azure ML
MLOps & Deployment	Kubeflow, TFX, Airflow, Docker, Kubernetes

5. Case Study: Collaborative ML in a Healthcare AI Project

A hospital research team is developing an ML model to predict patient readmission rates. The project involves data scientists, ML engineers, doctors, and software developers.

Challenges Faced:

🔬 Doctors and data scientists struggle to communicate technical details.

🔬 Data preprocessing is inconsistent across team members.

🔬 ML engineers face difficulties in deploying the trained models.

Solution: Implementing a Collaborative Workflow

✔ Weekly sync meetings are introduced to align medical experts and ML teams.

✔ DVC & MLflow are used to track data and model versions, ensuring reproducibility.

✔ Google Cloud AI & Vertex AI provide a shared development environment.

✔ MLOps pipelines automate model retraining and deployment.

Outcome: The project achieves faster iteration cycles, better model performance, and seamless deployment into the hospital's IT system.

Collaboration in ML projects is essential but challenging due to interdisciplinary team structures and the iterative nature of ML workflows. By defining clear roles, using version control, automating workflows, and adopting MLOps best practices, teams can build reliable, scalable, and impactful machine learning solutions.

In the next section, we will explore data collection, cleaning, and preprocessing—a fundamental step for building high-quality ML models.

3. Data Collection, Cleaning & Preprocessing

Data is the backbone of any successful machine learning project, and the quality of your model is directly tied to the quality of the data you use. In this chapter, we dive into the critical steps of data collection, cleaning, and preprocessing. You'll learn how to gather relevant data from diverse sources, handle missing values, remove duplicates, and deal with noisy or inconsistent data. We also cover techniques for feature engineering, transforming raw data into meaningful inputs for your models. By mastering data preprocessing, you'll be able to turn messy datasets into high-quality input, ensuring your machine learning models are accurate and reliable from the start. ✸

3.1 Sourcing and scraping real-world datasets

Data is the foundation of any machine learning (ML) project. Without high-quality, diverse, and representative data, even the most sophisticated models will struggle to deliver meaningful results. In real-world ML applications, data often comes from multiple sources—structured and unstructured, static and dynamic. This chapter explores effective strategies for sourcing real-world datasets, scraping data from the web, and handling ethical and legal considerations when acquiring data.

1. Understanding Data Sources

Before diving into data collection, it's important to understand the different types of datasets:

- **Open Datasets**: Publicly available datasets curated by governments, research institutions, and organizations.
- **Proprietary Datasets**: Private or purchased data from companies or third-party providers.
- **Scraped Data**: Extracted data from websites, APIs, or online repositories.
- **User-Generated Data**: Data from social media, reviews, or user interactions.
- **Sensor & IoT Data**: Data collected from smart devices, cameras, or industrial sensors.

Each source has its advantages and challenges, and selecting the right one depends on the ML project's objectives.

2. Finding Open Datasets

If your ML project can leverage publicly available data, there are numerous high-quality sources to explore:

2.1 Popular Open Data Repositories

Source	Description
Kaggle Datasets	A vast collection of datasets across domains, often used for competitions.
Google Dataset Search	A search engine for publicly available datasets across the web.
UCI Machine Learning Repository	Classic datasets used for ML benchmarking.
AWS Open Data Registry	Datasets stored in AWS for easy access and analysis.
Data.gov	Open government datasets from the U.S.
World Bank Open Data	Economic and financial datasets from global organizations.
FiveThirtyEight	Data journalism site with structured datasets on various topics.

◆ **Best Practice**: Always check dataset licenses before use, as some require attribution or restrict commercial applications.

3. Scraping Data from the Web

When specific datasets are not publicly available, web scraping can help extract valuable information from websites, news sources, social media, and e-commerce platforms.

3.1 Web Scraping Techniques

There are two main ways to collect data from websites:

- **Static Scraping**: Extracting data from HTML pages using libraries like BeautifulSoup (Python).
- **Dynamic Scraping**: Interacting with JavaScript-rendered content using Selenium or Playwright.

3.2 Scraping Data Using Python

Example: Extracting Product Prices from an E-commerce Website

```
import requests
from bs4 import BeautifulSoup

url = "https://example.com/products"
response = requests.get(url)
soup = BeautifulSoup(response.text, "html.parser")

for product in soup.find_all("div", class_="product-item"):
    name = product.find("h2").text
    price = product.find("span", class_="price").text
    print(f"Product: {name}, Price: {price}")
```

◆ **Best Practice**: Always check the website's robots.txt file to ensure compliance with scraping policies.

Example: Scraping Dynamic Content Using Selenium

```
from selenium import webdriver

driver = webdriver.Chrome()
driver.get("https://example.com/dynamic-content")

content = driver.page_source
print(content)
driver.quit()
```

◆ **Best Practice**: Use headless browsers for efficiency and avoid overloading servers with frequent requests.

4. Using APIs for Data Collection

Many organizations provide APIs to access their data in a structured and legal manner. APIs are often the most reliable way to collect real-time data.

4.1 Popular APIs for ML Projects

API Provider	Data Type
Twitter API	Social media posts, sentiment analysis.
Google Maps API	Geolocation, business data.
OpenWeatherMap API	Weather data for forecasting models.
Alpha Vantage API	Stock market and financial data.
NewsAPI	Aggregated news data from multiple sources.

Example: Collecting Tweets Using Twitter API

```
import tweepy

api_key = "your_api_key"
api_secret = "your_api_secret"

auth = tweepy.OAuthHandler(api_key, api_secret)
api = tweepy.API(auth)

tweets = api.search_tweets(q="machine learning", count=10)
for tweet in tweets:
    print(tweet.text)
```

♦ **Best Practice**: Use API rate limits responsibly to avoid getting blocked.

5. Handling Data Ethics and Legal Considerations

When sourcing and scraping data, it's critical to follow ethical and legal guidelines:

✓ **Respect Privacy Laws** – Follow regulations like GDPR (Europe) and CCPA (California) when handling personal data.

✓ **Check Licensing Agreements** – Some datasets have restrictions on commercial use or require attribution.

✓ **Avoid Overloading Websites** – Excessive scraping can violate Terms of Service (ToS) agreements and result in IP bans.

✓ **Ensure Data Anonymization** – If handling sensitive user data, anonymize personally identifiable information (PII).

6. Case Study: Collecting Data for a Customer Sentiment Analysis Project

A company wants to analyze customer sentiment about its brand on social media.

Approach:

- **Step 1:** Use the Twitter API to collect recent tweets mentioning the brand.
- **Step 2**: Scrape reviews from e-commerce platforms (if permitted).
- **Step 3:** Apply NLP techniques to analyze sentiment trends.

Challenges & Solutions:

🔊 **API rate limits** → Implement caching and scheduled data collection.

🔊 **Handling noisy data** → Use text preprocessing to remove spam and irrelevant content.

🔊 **Ethical concerns** → Obtain proper permissions and anonymize user data.

Sourcing real-world datasets is a crucial step in any ML project. Whether leveraging open datasets, scraping web content, or using APIs, selecting the right data source depends on the project's objectives and constraints. While web scraping can provide valuable insights, it must be done ethically and within legal guidelines.

In the next section, we will explore data cleaning and preprocessing—essential steps for transforming raw data into high-quality inputs for ML models.

3.2 Handling missing values, outliers, and noise

Raw data is rarely perfect. Real-world datasets often contain missing values, outliers, and noise, which can significantly impact the performance of machine learning models. If these issues are not handled properly, they can lead to biased models, incorrect predictions, and reduced accuracy. In this chapter, we will explore techniques to detect and manage missing data, outliers, and noisy data to ensure a high-quality dataset for ML training.

1. Handling Missing Values

Missing data occurs when some observations lack values for certain features. This can happen due to sensor failures, human errors in data entry, or system issues. There are three main types of missing data:

- **Missing Completely at Random (MCAR)** – Data is missing independently of any factors (e.g., a random network issue).
- **Missing at Random (MAR)** – The missingness depends on another observed variable (e.g., older customers not providing their phone numbers).
- **Missing Not at Random (MNAR)** – The missingness is related to the missing value itself (e.g., people with high incomes not disclosing their salaries).

1.1 Identifying Missing Values

In Python, we can check for missing values using pandas:

```
import pandas as pd

df = pd.read_csv("data.csv")
print(df.isnull().sum())  # Count missing values in each column
```

1.2 Strategies to Handle Missing Data

1.2.1 Removing Missing Values (When to Use It)

If missing values are few and random, we can drop rows or columns:

```
df_cleaned = df.dropna()  # Remove rows with missing values
df_cleaned = df.dropna(axis=1)  # Remove columns with missing values
```

✓ **Best for**: Large datasets with few missing values where removal won't cause data loss.

✗ **Avoid if**: The missing data is significant or removal reduces dataset quality.

1.2.2 Imputation (Filling Missing Values)

A more common approach is to fill in missing values using imputation techniques:

Mean/Median/Mode Imputation (for numerical data)

```
df["Age"].fillna(df["Age"].mean(), inplace=True)  # Fill with mean
df["Salary"].fillna(df["Salary"].median(), inplace=True)  # Fill with median
```

✓ **Best for**: Normally distributed numerical data.

✗ **Avoid if**: The data is skewed or contains outliers (use median instead of mean).

Forward/Backward Fill (for time-series data)

```
df["Temperature"].fillna(method="ffill", inplace=True)  # Forward fill
df["Temperature"].fillna(method="bfill", inplace=True)  # Backward fill
```

✓ **Best for**: Time-series data where missing values are related to previous/future observations.

K-Nearest Neighbors (KNN) Imputation (for complex relationships)

```
from sklearn.impute import KNNImputer

imputer = KNNImputer(n_neighbors=5)
df_filled = imputer.fit_transform(df)
```

✓ **Best for**: Data where missing values can be inferred based on similar observations.

2. Handling Outliers

Outliers are data points that significantly deviate from the normal pattern. They can distort statistical summaries and negatively impact ML model performance.

2.1 Identifying Outliers

2.1.1 Using Box Plots (Visual Inspection)

A box plot helps identify outliers by visualizing the distribution of values:

```
import seaborn as sns
sns.boxplot(x=df["Price"])
```

Any value outside the whiskers (1.5 times the interquartile range) is considered an outlier.

2.1.2 Using Z-Score (Statistical Approach)

The Z-score measures how far a value is from the mean in terms of standard deviations:

from scipy import stats

z_scores = stats.zscore(df["Price"])

df_no_outliers = df[(z_scores < 3) & (z_scores > -3)] # Keep values within 3 standard deviations

✅ **Best for**: Normally distributed data.

❌ **Avoid if:** The dataset has skewed distributions.

2.1.3 Using IQR (Interquartile Range) Method

The IQR method is useful for detecting extreme values in non-normally distributed data:

Q1 = df["Price"].quantile(0.25)
Q3 = df["Price"].quantile(0.75)
IQR = Q3 - Q1

*df_no_outliers = df[(df["Price"] >= (Q1 - 1.5 * IQR)) & (df["Price"] <= (Q3 + 1.5 * IQR))]*

✅ **Best for**: Skewed datasets and distributions with long tails.

2.2 Handling Outliers

Once outliers are detected, we can handle them in different ways:

Remove Outliers (if they are errors or anomalies)

df_cleaned = df[df["Price"] < df["Price"].quantile(0.99)]

✅ **Best for**: Clearly erroneous data points.
❌ **Avoid if**: Outliers contain useful information (e.g., fraud detection).

Transform Data (for skewed distributions)

Log transformation: df["Price"] = np.log(df["Price"] + 1)

Winsorization (limiting extreme values):

```
from scipy.stats.mstats import winsorize
df["Price"] = winsorize(df["Price"], limits=[0.05, 0.05])  # Cap extreme values
```

Use Robust Models (if removing is not an option)

- Decision Trees and Random Forests handle outliers better than linear regression.
- Use Huber loss in regression instead of mean squared error (MSE).

3. Handling Noise in Data

Noise refers to random variations and irrelevant information in data. It can come from sensor inaccuracies, human errors, or inconsistent recording practices.

3.1 Identifying Noisy Data

- **Visual Inspection** – Scatter plots and histograms can reveal noisy patterns.
- **Statistical Methods** – High variance in numerical features or frequent spelling errors in categorical data suggest noise.

3.2 Techniques for Reducing Noise

3.2.1 Data Smoothing

Smoothing helps reduce variability in noisy datasets:

Moving Average for Time-Series Data

```
df["Smoothed"] = df["Price"].rolling(window=3).mean()
```

Gaussian Smoothing for Images

```
import cv2
blurred = cv2.GaussianBlur(image, (5,5), 0)
```

3.2.2 Removing Inconsistent Data

- Use Levenshtein Distance to correct typos in categorical data.
- Apply Natural Language Processing (NLP) techniques to clean textual noise.

Handling missing values, outliers, and noise is a critical step in preparing high-quality data for machine learning models. By imputing missing values, detecting and managing outliers, and filtering noise, we can significantly improve model performance and ensure reliability in real-world applications.

In the next section, we will explore feature engineering—a key process in transforming raw data into meaningful input features for ML models.

3.3 Feature engineering & selection strategies

Feature engineering is the art of transforming raw data into meaningful inputs that improve machine learning (ML) model performance. The right features can make a simple model highly effective, while poor feature selection can cause even the most complex models to fail. This chapter explores feature engineering techniques, feature selection strategies, and best practices to enhance model accuracy and efficiency.

1. Understanding Feature Engineering

Feature engineering involves creating, modifying, or selecting features that improve an ML model's predictive power. It includes:

- **Feature Transformation** – Scaling, encoding, or modifying features for better representation.
- **Feature Extraction** – Deriving new features from existing data (e.g., PCA, text embeddings).
- **Feature Selection** – Choosing the most relevant features to reduce dimensionality and enhance model performance.

2. Feature Transformation Techniques

Raw features often need preprocessing before being used in ML models.

2.1 Scaling Numerical Features

Many ML algorithms (e.g., linear regression, SVMs, neural networks) perform better when numerical data is scaled.

2.1.1 Standardization (Z-score Scaling)

Standardization ensures that all features have a mean of 0 and a standard deviation of 1.

from sklearn.preprocessing import StandardScaler

scaler = StandardScaler()
df_scaled = scaler.fit_transform(df[["Age", "Salary", "Experience"]])

✓ **Best for**: Normally distributed numerical data.

2.1.2 Min-Max Scaling (Normalization)

Scales data to a fixed range $[0, 1]$ or $[-1, 1]$.

from sklearn.preprocessing import MinMaxScaler

scaler = MinMaxScaler()
df_scaled = scaler.fit_transform(df[["Age", "Salary"]])

✓ **Best for**: Neural networks and distance-based algorithms (e.g., k-NN, K-means).

2.2 Encoding Categorical Features

Machine learning models cannot work directly with categorical data, so we convert it into numerical form.

2.2.1 One-Hot Encoding (OHE)

Converts categorical values into binary columns.

import pandas as pd

df = pd.get_dummies(df, columns=["City"], drop_first=True)

✓ **Best for**: Low-cardinality categorical features.

2.2.2 Label Encoding

Assigns unique numerical values to each category.

```
from sklearn.preprocessing import LabelEncoder

encoder = LabelEncoder()
df["Gender"] = encoder.fit_transform(df["Gender"])
```

✓ **Best for**: Ordinal data (e.g., education level: "High School" → 0, "Bachelor" → 1).

2.2.3 Target Encoding

Encodes categorical variables based on the mean of the target variable.

```
df["City_Encoded"] = df.groupby("City")["Price"].transform("mean")
```

✓ **Best for**: High-cardinality categorical features in regression problems.

2.3 Creating New Features (Feature Extraction)

Generating additional features can often improve model performance.

2.3.1 Date & Time Features

Extract useful information from timestamps:

```
df["Year"] = df["Date"].dt.year
df["Month"] = df["Date"].dt.month
df["DayOfWeek"] = df["Date"].dt.dayofweek
```

✓ **Best for**: Time-series forecasting and trend analysis.

2.3.2 Text Feature Engineering

Convert text data into numerical features using TF-IDF (Term Frequency - Inverse Document Frequency):

```
from sklearn.feature_extraction.text import TfidfVectorizer

vectorizer = TfidfVectorizer(max_features=500)
X = vectorizer.fit_transform(df["Review"])
```

✓ **Best for**: Sentiment analysis and NLP applications.

2.3.3 Feature Interaction (Polynomial Features)

Create new features by combining existing ones:

from sklearn.preprocessing import PolynomialFeatures

poly = PolynomialFeatures(degree=2, interaction_only=True)
df_poly = poly.fit_transform(df[["Age", "Salary"]])

✅ **Best for**: Non-linear relationships in regression models.

3. Feature Selection Strategies

Too many features can lead to overfitting, slower training, and increased complexity. Feature selection helps identify the most relevant features while removing irrelevant or redundant ones.

3.1 Filter Methods (Univariate Selection)

Filter methods select features based on statistical tests and intrinsic properties.

3.1.1 Using Pearson Correlation

Drop highly correlated features to avoid redundancy:

import seaborn as sns
import matplotlib.pyplot as plt

corr_matrix = df.corr()
sns.heatmap(corr_matrix, annot=True, cmap="coolwarm")

✅ **Best for**: Removing multicollinearity in regression models.

3.1.2 SelectKBest (Chi-Square Test for Classification)

from sklearn.feature_selection import SelectKBest, chi2

selector = SelectKBest(score_func=chi2, k=5)
X_new = selector.fit_transform(X, y)

✅ **Best for**: Classification tasks with categorical target variables.

3.2 Wrapper Methods (Model-Based Selection)

Wrapper methods evaluate subsets of features based on model performance.

3.2.1 Recursive Feature Elimination (RFE)

```
from sklearn.feature_selection import RFE
from sklearn.ensemble import RandomForestClassifier

model = RandomForestClassifier()
selector = RFE(model, n_features_to_select=5)
X_new = selector.fit_transform(X, y)
```

✅ **Best for**: Finding the most important features for a specific ML model.

3.3 Embedded Methods (Regularization Techniques)

Embedded methods select features during model training using techniques like Lasso Regression and Tree-Based Models.

3.3.1 Lasso Regression (L1 Regularization)

```
from sklearn.linear_model import Lasso

lasso = Lasso(alpha=0.01)
lasso.fit(X, y)
selected_features = X.columns[lasso.coef_ != 0]
```

✅ **Best for**: Sparse datasets and feature elimination in regression tasks.

3.3.2 Feature Importance from Random Forest

```
from sklearn.ensemble import RandomForestClassifier

model = RandomForestClassifier()
model.fit(X, y)
```

```
importances = model.feature_importances_
feature_names = X.columns
sorted_features = sorted(zip(importances, feature_names), reverse=True)

for importance, feature in sorted_features:
    print(f"{feature}: {importance}")
```

✓ **Best for**: Understanding feature importance in tree-based models.

4. Case Study: Feature Engineering for House Price Prediction

Dataset Overview

A real estate company wants to predict house prices based on various attributes like location, size, and amenities.

Feature Engineering Steps:

- **Transform Numerical Data**: Scale features like square footage and price using MinMaxScaler.
- **Encode Categorical Data**: Convert location into numerical values using one-hot encoding.
- **Create New Features**: Extract Year Built and Renovation Year from timestamps.
- **Select the Best Features**: Use RandomForestClassifier to rank important features.

Outcome:

After applying feature engineering and selection, the final model achieved 15% lower error compared to using raw features.

Feature engineering and selection are critical steps in machine learning projects. By applying scaling, encoding, and extraction techniques, we can improve model accuracy. Additionally, using filter, wrapper, and embedded methods helps remove irrelevant features and optimize performance.

In the next section, we will explore data splitting, feature selection validation, and model performance optimization techniques to build more reliable ML models.

3.4 Data augmentation for low-resource scenarios

Machine learning models thrive on large, diverse datasets, but in many real-world applications, data collection is limited by cost, privacy concerns, or domain-specific constraints. Data augmentation provides a powerful way to artificially expand datasets, improve model generalization, and reduce overfitting—especially in scenarios where acquiring labeled data is challenging. This chapter explores various data augmentation techniques for structured data, text, images, and time-series data, along with best practices for applying them in real-world ML projects.

1. Why Data Augmentation is Important

1.1 Challenges in Low-Resource Scenarios

- **Limited Labeled Data** – Collecting and annotating data can be expensive and time-consuming (e.g., medical images, financial fraud detection).
- **Class Imbalance** – Some classes may have significantly fewer samples, leading to biased models.
- **Domain-Specific Constraints** – Certain fields, like cybersecurity or rare disease diagnosis, have very little historical data.
- **Privacy and Compliance Issues** – Industries like healthcare and finance have strict data-sharing restrictions.

Data augmentation helps mitigate these challenges by creating synthetic variations of existing data to enhance model performance.

2. Data Augmentation for Structured (Tabular) Data

While data augmentation is more common in computer vision and NLP, structured datasets (e.g., financial records, customer data) can also benefit from augmentation techniques.

2.1 Synthetic Data Generation

2.1.1 Random Perturbation

Introduce small variations in numerical features to simulate real-world variability.

import numpy as np

```
df["Price"] = df["Price"] * np.random.uniform(0.95, 1.05, size=len(df))
```

✅ **Best for**: Financial data, sensor readings.

❌ **Avoid if:** Data needs to remain highly precise.

2.1.2 Synthetic Minority Over-sampling Technique (SMOTE)

Generates synthetic samples for underrepresented classes.

```
from imblearn.over_sampling import SMOTE
```

```
smote = SMOTE()
X_resampled, y_resampled = smote.fit_resample(X, y)
```

✅ **Best for**: Handling class imbalance in classification problems.

2.1.3 Generative Models (GANs & VAEs)

Use Generative Adversarial Networks (GANs) or Variational Autoencoders (VAEs) to generate realistic tabular data.

```
from ctgan import CTGANSynthesizer
```

```
ctgan = CTGANSynthesizer()
ctgan.fit(df, epochs=300)
synthetic_data = ctgan.sample(1000)
```

✅ **Best for**: Privacy-preserving synthetic data generation.

3. Data Augmentation for Text Data (NLP)

Text data augmentation helps create diverse training samples for tasks like sentiment analysis, text classification, and chatbot training.

3.1 Synonym Replacement (Word-Level Augmentation)

Replace words with synonyms using NLP libraries.

```
from nltk.corpus import wordnet
```

```
def synonym_replacement(text):
    words = text.split()
    new_words = [wordnet.synsets(word)[0].lemmas()[0].name() if wordnet.synsets(word)
else word for word in words]
    return " ".join(new_words)


text = "The product is excellent and highly recommended."
augmented_text = synonym_replacement(text)
```

✅ **Best for**: Sentiment analysis, text classification.

3.2 Back Translation

Translate text to another language and back to introduce variations.

```
from deep_translator import GoogleTranslator


text = "The customer service is outstanding."
translated = GoogleTranslator(source="en", target="fr").translate(text)
back_translated = GoogleTranslator(source="fr", target="en").translate(translated)
```

✅ **Best for**: Creating diverse text variations.

3.3 Text Noise Injection

Randomly swap or remove words to simulate noisy user input.

```
import random


def add_noise(text, p=0.1):
    words = text.split()
    noisy_text = [word if random.random() > p else "" for word in words]
    return " ".join(noisy_text)


augmented_text = add_noise("The service was fast and reliable.")
```

✅ **Best for**: Improving chatbot robustness to typos and incomplete inputs.

3.4 Large Language Models (LLMs) for Text Augmentation

Use LLMs (e.g., GPT, BERT) to generate paraphrases or synthetic training data.

```
from transformers import pipeline

paraphraser = pipeline("text2text-generation", model="t5-small")
augmented_text = paraphraser("The delivery was quick and efficient.", max_length=30)
```

✓ **Best for**: Data augmentation in low-data NLP scenarios.

4. Data Augmentation for Image Data

Computer vision models require diverse training images to generalize well. Image augmentation applies transformations like rotation, flipping, and color adjustment to artificially expand the dataset.

4.1 Using Albumentations for Image Augmentation

```
import albumentations as A
import cv2

augment = A.Compose([
    A.HorizontalFlip(p=0.5),
    A.RandomBrightnessContrast(p=0.2),
    A.Rotate(limit=30, p=0.5),
])

image = cv2.imread("image.jpg")
augmented_image = augment(image=image)["image"]
```

✓ **Best for**: Enhancing generalization in deep learning models.

4.2 Generating Synthetic Images with GANs

Use Generative Adversarial Networks (GANs) to create realistic synthetic images.

```
from tensorflow.keras.models import load_model
generator = load_model("gan_generator.h5")

latent_points = np.random.randn(100, 100)
```

```
synthetic_images = generator.predict(latent_points)
```

✅ **Best for**: Medical imaging, rare object detection.

5. Data Augmentation for Time-Series Data

Time-series data, such as stock prices and sensor readings, can be augmented using techniques like jittering and time-warping.

5.1 Jittering (Adding Noise to Time-Series Data)

```
def jitter(series, noise_level=0.05):
    return series + np.random.normal(loc=0.0, scale=noise_level, size=series.shape)

df["Temperature_Augmented"] = jitter(df["Temperature"])
```

✅ **Best for**: Financial data, IoT sensor readings.

5.2 Time-Warping (Elastic Distortion)

```
import tsaug

augmenter = tsaug.TimeWarp(n_speed_change=5, max_speed_ratio=2)
augmented_series = augmenter.augment(df["Signal"].values)
```

✅ **Best for**: Speech recognition, ECG signal analysis.

6. Best Practices for Data Augmentation

- **Maintain Label Integrity** – Ensure augmented data does not alter class labels incorrectly.
- **Avoid Over-Augmentation** – Too much synthetic data can introduce noise and reduce model accuracy.
- **Test on Real Data** – Always validate model performance on real-world data, not just augmented samples.
- **Use Task-Specific Augmentations** – Choose augmentation techniques based on the data type and ML task.
- **Combine Multiple Techniques** – Using a mix of augmentation methods can enhance diversity and robustness.

Data augmentation is a powerful strategy for improving model performance in low-resource ML scenarios. By applying augmentation techniques across structured, text, image, and time-series data, we can create diverse, high-quality training datasets without requiring extensive manual labeling.

In the next section, we will explore data splitting and validation strategies to ensure that models generalize well across unseen data.

3.5 Scaling and normalizing features

Scaling and normalizing data are critical preprocessing steps in machine learning (ML) that help improve the performance of many algorithms. These techniques ensure that the input features are on a comparable scale, which is particularly important for distance-based models, optimization algorithms, and models that assume certain distributions. This section will explore the key methods for scaling and normalizing features, the differences between them, and how to apply them in real-world machine learning projects.

1. Why Scaling and Normalization Matter

Before diving into the techniques themselves, it's important to understand why scaling and normalizing features are necessary:

1.1 The Problem of Different Feature Scales

In datasets, features often vary in their magnitude or units. For example, one feature might represent "income" in thousands of dollars, while another might represent "age" in years. If these features are not scaled or normalized, models that rely on distance calculations (such as K-nearest neighbors, support vector machines, and neural networks) may give undue importance to higher-magnitude features. For instance, the model might focus too much on "income" while ignoring the "age" feature, which can degrade performance.

1.2 Impacts on Optimization Algorithms

Many ML algorithms, such as gradient descent, rely on the optimization of model parameters to minimize a loss function. If the input features are on different scales, the optimization process can be inefficient or converge slowly because features with larger ranges will dominate the gradient updates. In the worst case, it can lead to poor convergence and suboptimal results.

1.3 Improving Model Convergence and Accuracy

Proper scaling and normalization make it easier for the algorithm to converge and improve the overall accuracy by treating all features equally. This is particularly true for models like linear regression, logistic regression, and neural networks, which depend on gradient-based optimization.

2. Scaling Techniques

Scaling refers to changing the range of your data, usually by transforming the data into a standard scale. Below are the most common scaling techniques:

2.1 Standardization (Z-Score Normalization)

Standardization transforms data such that each feature has a mean of 0 and a standard deviation of 1. This ensures that the features are centered around 0, with a consistent unit variance. Standardization is especially useful when data is not uniformly distributed or when you have outliers.

Formula:

$$z = \frac{x - \mu}{\sigma}$$

Where:

- x is the original data point.

- μ is the mean of the data.

- σ is the standard deviation of the data.

from sklearn.preprocessing import StandardScaler

scaler = StandardScaler()
X_scaled = scaler.fit_transform(X)

✅ **Best for**: Models that assume data is centered around 0 (e.g., linear regression, neural networks).

❌ **Avoid if**: The data has many outliers, as they could impact the mean and standard deviation.

2.2 Min-Max Scaling (Normalization)

Min-Max scaling, also known as **Normalization**, transforms the data into a specific range—typically $[0, 1]$ or $[-1, 1]$. It is useful when you want all features to have the same scale, but unlike standardization, it does not change the distribution of the data.

Formula:

$$x_{normalized} = \frac{x - x_{\min}}{x_{\max} - x_{\min}}$$

Where:

- x is the original data point.

- $x_{\min}$ and $x_{\max}$ are the minimum and maximum values of the feature.

from sklearn.preprocessing import MinMaxScaler

scaler = MinMaxScaler()
X_scaled = scaler.fit_transform(X)

✅ **Best for**: Models that rely on distances between data points (e.g., KNN, neural networks).

❌ **Avoid if**: The data contains outliers, as they will squash the rest of the data into a narrow range.

2.3 Robust Scaling

Robust scaling uses medians and interquartile ranges to scale features, making it more resilient to outliers. Unlike Min-Max scaling, robust scaling doesn't use the extreme values, making it a good choice for datasets with significant outliers.

Formula:

$$x_{\text{scaled}} = \frac{x - \text{Median}(x)}{\text{IQR}(x)}$$

Where:

- Median(x) is the median value of the feature.
- IQR(x) is the interquartile range (the difference between the 75th percentile and 25th percentile).

from sklearn.preprocessing import RobustScaler

scaler = RobustScaler()
X_scaled = scaler.fit_transform(X)

✔ **Best for**: Datasets with many outliers, especially in tree-based models.

✗ **Avoid if:** The data is normally distributed and you don't have outliers, as it may distort relationships.

3. Normalization Techniques

Normalization is typically used for transforming data into a certain range. The most common normalization techniques are Min-Max Scaling and L2 Normalization, but we'll also cover some other approaches to normalization.

3.1 L2 Normalization (Vector Normalization)

L2 normalization scales each feature such that the sum of the squares of the feature values equals 1. This technique is often used when the data is represented as vectors (e.g., word embeddings in NLP) or when working with cosine similarity.

Formula:

$$\text{Norm}_2 = \frac{x}{\|x\|_2}$$

Where:

- $\|x\|_2$ is the L2 norm (Euclidean length) of the vector.

from sklearn.preprocessing import Normalizer

scaler = Normalizer(norm='l2')
X_normalized = scaler.fit_transform(X)

✅ **Best for**: Text data (e.g., in NLP models), recommendation systems, and when working with distance-based algorithms.

❌ **Avoid if**: The data has a lot of sparsity, as normalization might distort the feature relationships.

3.2 MaxAbs Scaling

MaxAbs scaling scales each feature by its maximum absolute value, which ensures that all feature values fall within the range [−1,1] but retains the sign of the data. MaxAbs scaling is typically used for sparse data and is less sensitive to outliers than Min-Max scaling.

from sklearn.preprocessing import MaxAbsScaler

scaler = MaxAbsScaler()
X_scaled = scaler.fit_transform(X)

✅ **Best for**: Sparse data (e.g., text data in bag-of-words format).

❌ **Avoid if**: Your data has large outliers, as they could dominate the scaling.

4. When to Use Scaling and Normalization

4.1 Choose Scaling for Algorithms Sensitive to Feature Scale:

Use scaling techniques for models like:

- Linear regression
- Logistic regression
- SVM (Support Vector Machines)
- K-nearest neighbors (KNN)
- Neural networks (Deep learning)

4.2 Choose Normalization for Distance-Based Models:

Normalization techniques like Min-Max scaling and L2 normalization are ideal for:

- KNN
- Clustering (K-means)
- Distance-based anomaly detection
- Image data pre-processing

4.3 Avoid Scaling for Decision Trees:

Decision trees, including random forests and gradient boosting, are insensitive to feature scaling and normalization.

5. Best Practices for Scaling and Normalizing

Fit Scaling on Training Data Only:

Always compute the scaling parameters (e.g., mean, std, min, max) based only on the training data. This ensures that no data leakage occurs during training.

Apply Same Transformation to Test Data:

Once you've fit the scaler on the training data, use the same transformation for the test dataset to maintain consistency.

Consider the Distribution of Your Data:

Choose a method based on the distribution and characteristics of your dataset. For example, use Standardization if the data is normally distributed, and use Min-Max Scaling if data has bounded limits.

Monitor the Impact of Scaling on Model Performance:

Sometimes scaling may not improve model performance. Always validate your results using cross-validation to ensure that scaling techniques are beneficial for your specific use case.

Scaling and normalization are essential steps in machine learning that prepare your features for modeling by making them more comparable and improving convergence in optimization algorithms. Choosing the appropriate technique—whether it's standardization, Min-Max scaling, or others—depends on the specific characteristics of your data and the ML algorithm you are using. By applying these preprocessing steps effectively, you can improve model accuracy and reduce the risk of overfitting.

4. Predicting House Prices with Regression

In this chapter, we tackle a classic problem in machine learning: predicting house prices. Using regression techniques, you'll learn how to develop a model that predicts property prices based on various features like location, size, and amenities. We'll walk you through the entire process, from data exploration and feature selection to model building using algorithms like linear regression and decision trees. You'll also learn how to evaluate your model's performance and make improvements. By the end of this project, you'll be equipped with the skills to tackle real-world regression problems and create models that can predict continuous values with accuracy. 🏠

4.1 Understanding real estate data and features

Predicting house prices using machine learning is a classic application of regression models, where the goal is to predict the sale price of a property based on various features or attributes. Understanding real estate data is the first step in building an effective predictive model. Real estate datasets typically include a mix of numerical, categorical, and sometimes text-based features that provide insights into a property's characteristics. In this section, we will explore the key types of data and features commonly found in real estate datasets and how each one contributes to predicting house prices.

1. Key Features in Real Estate Data

1.1 Numeric Features

Numerical features are the backbone of any regression model, as they provide quantitative information that can be directly used for prediction. These features typically describe the physical characteristics of a property, its location, and its historical context.

1.1.1 Sale Price (Target Variable)

The most important numerical feature in real estate datasets is the sale price of the house. This is the target variable we aim to predict. Understanding how the sale price varies with respect to other features is key to building an effective model. The distribution of sale prices can vary greatly depending on the market (urban vs rural, luxury vs affordable homes), so it's essential to understand this feature's behavior before starting the modeling process.

1.1.2 Square Footage (Size of the Property)

The size of the house, typically measured in square feet or square meters, is a significant predictor of the price. Larger homes usually command higher prices. However, the relationship is not always linear, and a larger home in a less desirable location may not necessarily be worth much more than a smaller home in a prime area.

1.1.3 Number of Bedrooms and Bathrooms

The number of bedrooms and bathrooms is often an indicator of how comfortable the house is. Typically, more bedrooms and bathrooms lead to a higher price, but it's important to consider this in conjunction with other features like the size and location of the house. For example, a five-bedroom house in a low-demand area may not be as expensive as a three-bedroom house in a prestigious neighborhood.

1.1.4 Lot Size

Lot size refers to the area of the land the house sits on. Larger lots can be more expensive, but this depends on factors like zoning laws, location, and demand for land in that area. In suburban and rural areas, larger lot sizes often lead to higher prices, whereas in dense urban areas, lot size might not have as much of an impact.

1.1.5 Year Built and Age of the House

The year built and age of the house provide important context for understanding the property's condition and marketability. Newer homes often command higher prices due to their modern amenities, but older homes in prime locations or with historical value can be equally or more expensive. This feature can be combined with others like renovation to assess how a house has been maintained.

1.1.6 Home Condition and Quality

While condition and quality are often categorical, certain ratings or indices can be quantified. Houses in better condition generally fetch higher prices. The age of the home can be a proxy for condition if detailed condition data is missing, though it is better to have explicit feature values like renovated, newly painted, or modernized interiors.

1.2 Categorical Features

Categorical features represent non-numerical data that describe qualitative attributes of a property. These features must be converted into a numerical format (using encoding methods) before they can be used in a machine learning model. Categorical data can offer valuable insights into the desirability and price range of a home.

1.2.1 Location (Neighborhood, Zip Code, City)

The location of the property plays a crucial role in pricing. Features like neighborhood, zip code, and city can provide context for determining the value of a property. Homes in affluent areas with good schools, low crime rates, and easy access to amenities tend to fetch higher prices. This is often referred to as the location premium.

Geographical features can also influence price predictions by identifying spatial patterns or clusters of high-value properties, such as proximity to parks, commercial centers, or the ocean. In machine learning models, encoding location data into meaningful categories can help improve predictions.

1.2.2 Property Type

The type of property (single-family home, townhouse, condominium, apartment, etc.) is another important categorical feature. Different property types come with different price ranges, with single-family homes generally commanding higher prices than condominiums or apartments. Even within a particular property type, the market trends may differ, so segmenting property types helps in accurate price predictions.

1.2.3 Condition of the House

This can include categorical features like whether the house is renovated, new, or needs repair. A home in excellent condition will generally be priced higher than one that requires significant repairs. Sometimes, this data can be provided as ratings (e.g., a scale from 1 to 5). The level of detail in these features can vary, so it's essential to ensure proper encoding.

1.3 Time-Related Features

The time of sale is another important feature, especially when dealing with real estate data. The housing market fluctuates based on seasons, economic conditions, and various external factors.

1.3.1 Time on the Market (Days Listed)

A property's time on the market can be indicative of demand and pricing. Homes that sell quickly may be priced below market value or are in high-demand areas. Conversely, homes that have been listed for a long time might be overpriced or located in less desirable areas. This feature helps to understand market trends and pricing strategy.

1.3.2 Month/Season of Sale

The month or season in which a house is sold can also influence its price. For example, homes sold in spring or summer might command higher prices due to better weather and a more active market. In contrast, homes sold in the winter months often experience lower demand, potentially leading to lower prices.

2. Handling Real Estate Data for ML Models

Understanding the data and the relationships between various features is crucial when preparing for machine learning. There are several considerations and preprocessing steps to take before using real estate data in predictive models:

2.1 Missing Data

Real estate datasets often have missing values. For example, the lot size might be missing for some properties, or the condition might not be recorded for others. Depending on the amount of missing data, various imputation methods can be used, including the mean, median, or mode for numerical data, or the most frequent category for categorical data.

2.2 Feature Engineering

Creating new features from existing data can greatly improve the performance of your model. For example:

- Combining the year built and age of the property to create a "renovation year" feature.
- Creating a binary indicator for has a garage (yes/no).
- Encoding property type into numeric categories (single-family = 1, townhouse = 2, etc.).

Feature engineering is particularly important in real estate data because the market dynamics and the impact of various factors on price can be nuanced.

2.3 Encoding Categorical Data

For categorical features like neighborhood or property type, encoding methods like one-hot encoding or label encoding can be used. One-hot encoding creates a separate binary feature for each category, while label encoding assigns a unique numeric value to each category. The choice of encoding method depends on the nature of the categorical data and the modeling technique.

3. Common Pitfalls to Watch Out For

When working with real estate data, certain challenges can skew results if not properly addressed. Here are some common pitfalls:

3.1 Data Leakage

Data leakage occurs when the model has access to information during training that would not be available at prediction time. For example, if the model uses the sale price of a home as a feature during training, it is likely to learn to predict that value trivially and overfit. Always ensure that your features don't inadvertently include future or target variables.

3.2 Outliers

In real estate, outliers can often skew predictions, especially when there are rare, extremely expensive properties. Removing or treating outliers is essential to ensure the model remains robust.

3.3 Multicollinearity

Some features, like square footage and number of rooms, may be highly correlated with one another. This multicollinearity can cause issues for some regression models. One way to handle this is by using Principal Component Analysis (PCA) to reduce dimensionality or simply removing highly correlated features.

Understanding the various features in real estate datasets is a critical step in predicting house prices. By carefully analyzing and preprocessing features such as sale price, square footage, location, and property type, you can build robust predictive models that account for the many variables that influence property values. From feature engineering to handling categorical data, mastering these preprocessing steps will lay a solid foundation for building accurate and interpretable regression models. With a solid grasp of the data, you'll be able to tackle house price prediction with confidence and precision.

4.2 Data preprocessing and feature selection

Data preprocessing and feature selection are two critical steps in the machine learning pipeline that can significantly influence the performance of your predictive model, especially when predicting house prices using regression techniques. Proper preprocessing ensures that the data is cleaned, transformed, and ready for modeling, while feature selection helps focus on the most relevant attributes that contribute to the target variable—house prices in this case. In this section, we will dive into the steps involved in preprocessing real estate data and selecting the best features for building a robust model.

1. Importance of Data Preprocessing

Before building any machine learning model, data preprocessing is essential to prepare raw data for modeling. In real estate datasets, this step typically involves cleaning the data, handling missing values, transforming categorical variables, normalizing numerical data, and scaling the features. Without proper preprocessing, machine learning models may suffer from poor performance due to noisy or irrelevant data, making preprocessing an essential task.

1.1 Cleaning the Data

Data cleaning involves identifying and handling issues such as missing, incorrect, or inconsistent values within the dataset. In real estate datasets, common issues include:

1.1.1 Missing Data

Real estate data may have missing values in various columns such as square footage, number of bedrooms, or year built. Depending on the nature of the data and how much is missing, there are several ways to handle missing values:

Imputation: For numerical features like square footage or lot size, you can impute missing values with the mean, median, or mode of the respective feature. Imputation can also be done using advanced techniques such as K-Nearest Neighbors (KNN) or regression imputation, where missing values are predicted based on other features.

Removal: If a significant proportion of a feature is missing, or if the data is very sparse, it might be best to drop the column or rows containing missing values.

Flagging: Another technique is to create a new binary feature (e.g., "is_missing") that flags whether data for a particular feature is missing or not. This can sometimes reveal useful patterns during model training.

1.1.2 Handling Duplicates

Real estate datasets may contain duplicate entries where the same property appears multiple times with the same features. Duplicates can affect the accuracy of the model and lead to bias. It's important to identify and remove duplicates to ensure that each property is represented only once in the dataset.

1.1.3 Correcting Data Errors

Mistakes in data entry, such as erroneous values or outliers that are not reflective of the real-world scenario (e.g., a house listed as 100,000 square feet instead of 1,000), need to be addressed. These errors can distort predictions and lead to overfitting. Automated checks or manual review may be required to fix such issues.

1.2 Transforming Categorical Variables

Real estate datasets usually contain both numerical and categorical variables. However, machine learning algorithms, especially regression models, work with numerical values. Therefore, categorical variables like property type, neighborhood, or condition must be converted into a numerical format. There are a few methods for transforming categorical data:

1.2.1 One-Hot Encoding

One-hot encoding is a popular technique for transforming categorical variables into binary features (0 or 1) for each category. For example, if you have a property type feature with categories like 'Single Family', 'Townhouse', and 'Condo', one-hot encoding would create three binary features:

- Is_Single_Family
- Is_Townhouse
- Is_Condo

If a property is a single-family home, the Is_Single_Family feature would be 1, while the other two features would be 0. This method is particularly useful for nominal categories where there is no inherent order or hierarchy.

1.2.2 Label Encoding

Label encoding converts categorical variables into numerical labels. For example, 'Single Family' could be encoded as 0, 'Townhouse' as 1, and 'Condo' as 2. Label encoding is more suited for ordinal categories where there is an inherent order (e.g., 'Excellent', 'Good', 'Fair' condition of the house). However, be cautious when applying label encoding to nominal data, as it could introduce unintended ordinal relationships.

1.2.3 Frequency or Target Encoding

In cases where a categorical variable has many levels, and one-hot encoding may lead to high-dimensional data (also known as the curse of dimensionality), frequency encoding or target encoding might be useful. Frequency encoding assigns a numeric value based on the frequency of each category, while target encoding uses the mean target value (house price) for each category.

1.3 Normalizing and Scaling Numerical Features

Numerical features, such as square footage, lot size, and year built, may have vastly different scales. For example, square footage might range from 1,000 to 5,000, while lot size might vary from 1 to 50 acres. Machine learning algorithms that rely on distance metrics or gradient-based optimization (like linear regression, support vector machines, or neural networks) may struggle to converge or give more importance to features with larger ranges. Therefore, normalizing or scaling numerical features ensures all features are treated equally.

1.3.1 Standardization

Standardization (Z-score normalization) transforms features to have a mean of 0 and a standard deviation of 1. This is particularly useful when the data is normally distributed. Standardization helps to ensure that each feature contributes equally to the model.

from sklearn.preprocessing import StandardScaler

scaler = StandardScaler()
X_scaled = scaler.fit_transform(X)

1.3.2 Min-Max Scaling

Min-max scaling rescales the data to a fixed range, typically [0, 1]. This is useful when you want to preserve the relative relationships between the data points but put them on the same scale. However, it's sensitive to outliers, which can distort the scaling.

from sklearn.preprocessing import MinMaxScaler

scaler = MinMaxScaler()
X_scaled = scaler.fit_transform(X)

1.3.3 Robust Scaling

Robust scaling uses the median and interquartile range (IQR) instead of the mean and standard deviation, making it more robust to outliers. This method is particularly useful when dealing with real estate datasets that may contain extreme values (e.g., very large houses or commercial properties).

from sklearn.preprocessing import RobustScaler

scaler = RobustScaler()
X_scaled = scaler.fit_transform(X)

2. Feature Selection

Feature selection is the process of selecting the most relevant features from the dataset that contribute significantly to predicting the target variable—in this case, house prices. Selecting the right features is important for building an efficient model that generalizes well and avoids overfitting.

2.1 Methods of Feature Selection

2.1.1 Correlation Analysis

In real estate data, certain features are likely to be highly correlated with house prices, such as square footage, number of bedrooms, or lot size. Correlation analysis helps identify relationships between features and the target variable (house price). Features that have a high correlation with the target variable should be kept in the model, while features that show little or no correlation can be discarded.

Additionally, it's important to check for multicollinearity—a situation where two or more features are highly correlated with each other. Multicollinearity can reduce model interpretability and inflate variance. One way to handle this is by removing one of the correlated features or combining them into a single feature.

2.1.2 Recursive Feature Elimination (RFE)

Recursive Feature Elimination is a feature selection technique that fits a model and removes the least important features iteratively. RFE ranks features based on their importance and removes the least useful ones until the optimal subset is achieved.

```
from sklearn.feature_selection import RFE
from sklearn.linear_model import LinearRegression

model = LinearRegression()
selector = RFE(model, n_features_to_select=5)
X_selected = selector.fit_transform(X, y)
```

2.1.3 Feature Importance from Tree-Based Models

Tree-based models, such as Random Forest or Gradient Boosting, can be used to calculate the feature importance—the contribution of each feature to the model's predictions. By analyzing these importances, you can identify which features have the most significant impact on predicting house prices.

```
from sklearn.ensemble import RandomForestRegressor

model = RandomForestRegressor()
model.fit(X, y)
importances = model.feature_importances_
```

2.1.4 L1 Regularization (Lasso Regression)

L1 regularization, also known as Lasso Regression, adds a penalty to the model for using too many features. It forces some of the less important features' coefficients to zero, effectively performing feature selection.

```
from sklearn.linear_model import Lasso
```

```
model = Lasso(alpha=0.1)
model.fit(X, y)
```

Data preprocessing and feature selection are essential for building robust machine learning models, especially in predicting house prices. By cleaning the data, handling missing values, transforming categorical features, and scaling numerical data, you ensure the dataset is ready for model training. Feature selection further enhances the model by focusing on the most important features, reducing noise, and improving model performance. Whether using correlation analysis, RFE, or tree-based models, choosing the right features will allow you to develop a predictive model that accurately estimates house prices in real-world scenarios.

4.3 Implementing linear regression models

Linear regression is one of the most widely used algorithms for predicting continuous values, and it's particularly well-suited for predicting house prices based on various features like square footage, number of bedrooms, and location. In this section, we will explore how to implement a linear regression model for predicting house prices. We will cover the steps involved in building the model, evaluating its performance, and interpreting the results. Let's break this down into manageable steps: from data preparation to model evaluation.

1. What is Linear Regression?

Linear regression is a simple yet powerful supervised learning algorithm used to model the relationship between a dependent variable (target) and one or more independent variables (features). In the context of predicting house prices, the dependent variable would be the price of the house, while the independent variables could include factors such as square footage, number of bedrooms, location, and year built.

1.1 Simple vs. Multiple Linear Regression

Simple Linear Regression: Involves a single independent variable. The model assumes that there is a linear relationship between the independent variable and the dependent variable. For example, predicting house price based solely on square footage.

Multiple Linear Regression: Involves multiple independent variables. This is the more typical scenario for house price prediction, where multiple features (e.g., square footage, number of bedrooms, neighborhood) are used to predict the target variable.

Equation for Linear Regression

The general form of the linear regression model is:

$$y = b_0 + b_1 x_1 + b_2 x_2 + \cdots + b_n x_n$$

Where:

- y is the target variable (house price),

- b_0 is the intercept (the price when all the features are zero),

- $b_1, b_2, \ldots, b_n$ are the coefficients for the features,

- $x_1, x_2, \ldots, x_n$ are the input features (e.g., square footage, number of bedrooms).

The goal of linear regression is to find the optimal values for the coefficients $b_0, b_1, \ldots, b_n$ that minimize the difference between the predicted and actual house prices.

2. Preparing the Data for Linear Regression

Before implementing the linear regression model, the dataset needs to be properly prepared. We have already discussed data preprocessing steps, such as handling missing values, encoding categorical variables, and scaling the features, so let's briefly outline the necessary preparations:

2.1 Feature Selection

To build an effective model, it's crucial to select relevant features. In a house price prediction model, features like square footage, number of bedrooms, location, condition of the house, and age of the house might be important predictors. Using techniques like correlation analysis, feature importance from tree-based models, or recursive feature elimination (RFE) can help identify the most significant features to include.

2.2 Train-Test Split

It's essential to split the data into training and testing datasets to evaluate the performance of the model. Typically, the training set consists of about 70–80% of the data, while the testing set consists of the remaining 20–30%.

from sklearn.model_selection import train_test_split

```
# Split the data into features (X) and target (y)
X = data.drop('Price', axis=1)  # All features except 'Price'
y = data['Price']  # Target variable: house prices

# Split into train and test sets
X_train, X_test, y_train, y_test = train_test_split(X, y, test_size=0.2, random_state=42)
```

3. Building and Implementing the Model

Now that the data is prepared, we can proceed to build and implement the linear regression model. In Python, scikit-learn provides an easy-to-use API for implementing linear regression.

3.1 Fitting the Model

Once the data is ready, we can initialize the linear regression model and fit it to the training data. This step involves estimating the coefficients $b_0, b_1, \ldots, b_n$ that minimize the loss function (typically the Mean Squared Error) and fit the best line to the data.

```
from sklearn.linear_model import LinearRegression

# Initialize the model
model = LinearRegression()

# Fit the model to the training data
model.fit(X_train, y_train)
```

3.2 Making Predictions

After the model has been trained, we can use it to predict house prices on the test set. This step is crucial for evaluating the performance of the model.

```
# Predict house prices on the test data
y_pred = model.predict(X_test)
```

3.3 Model Coefficients

The linear regression model will output a set of coefficients for each feature, which represent the impact of each feature on the predicted house price. For example, if the coefficient for square footage is 100,000, it means that for every additional square foot, the house price is expected to increase by 100,000 units (e.g., dollars).

```
# Get the model's coefficients
coefficients = model.coef_

# Get the intercept
intercept = model.intercept_

# Display the coefficients for each feature
for feature, coef in zip(X.columns, coefficients):
    print(f"{feature}: {coef}")
```

4. Model Evaluation

Once the model is trained and predictions are made, we need to evaluate the model's performance to ensure it's accurately predicting house prices. Common evaluation metrics for regression models include:

4.1 Mean Absolute Error (MAE)

The Mean Absolute Error measures the average magnitude of the errors between predicted and actual values, without considering their direction (positive or negative).

$$MAE = \frac{1}{n} \sum_{i=1}^{n} |y_i - \hat{y}_i|$$

Where y_i is the true value and $\hat{y}_i$ is the predicted value.

```
from sklearn.metrics import mean_absolute_error

mae = mean_absolute_error(y_test, y_pred)
print(f"Mean Absolute Error: {mae}")
```

4.2 Mean Squared Error (MSE)

The Mean Squared Error penalizes large errors more than small ones and is calculated as the average of the squared differences between predicted and actual values.

$$MSE = \frac{1}{n} \sum_{i=1}^{n} (y_i - \hat{y}_i)^2$$

from sklearn.metrics import mean_squared_error

mse = mean_squared_error(y_test, y_pred)
print(f"Mean Squared Error: {mse}")

4.3 R-squared (R²)

R-squared is a measure of how well the regression model fits the data. It indicates the proportion of the variance in the dependent variable (house prices) that is explained by the independent variables (features). An R-squared value close to 1 means the model explains most of the variance, while a value close to 0 means the model performs poorly.

$$R^2 = 1 - \frac{\sum (y_i - \hat{y}_i)^2}{\sum (y_i - \bar{y})^2}$$

Where $\bar{y}$ is the mean of the actual values.

from sklearn.metrics import r2_score

r2 = r2_score(y_test, y_pred)
print(f"R-squared: {r2}")

5. Model Interpretation and Insights

Once the linear regression model is trained and evaluated, the next step is to interpret the model's results. The coefficients of the features will indicate the significance of each feature in predicting the house price.

For instance:

- A positive coefficient for square footage means that as the size of the house increases, the price also increases.
- A negative coefficient for distance from city center might indicate that properties further away from the city center tend to have lower prices.

Interpreting the coefficients can provide valuable insights into how different features impact house prices and guide further improvements in the model, such as adding or removing features based on their significance.

Implementing a linear regression model for predicting house prices is a straightforward process, but it requires careful attention to data preprocessing, feature selection, and model evaluation. By following the steps outlined in this section, you can build a robust linear regression model that effectively predicts house prices based on relevant features. While linear regression is a simple algorithm, it offers a solid foundation for understanding relationships between features and target variables, and can serve as a baseline for more advanced modeling techniques.

4.4 Evaluating model performance (MAE, RMSE, R²)

Once the linear regression model for predicting house prices is built and trained, the next critical step is to evaluate its performance. The purpose of model evaluation is to assess how well the model is able to predict house prices based on the given features. In this section, we will discuss three important evaluation metrics used in regression tasks: Mean Absolute Error (MAE), Root Mean Squared Error (RMSE), and R-squared (R^2). Each of these metrics provides a unique insight into the accuracy and effectiveness of the model. Let's dive into each metric in detail, understand what it measures, and how to calculate it.

1. Mean Absolute Error (MAE)

1.1 What is MAE?

The Mean Absolute Error (MAE) is a metric that measures the average magnitude of the errors in a set of predictions, without considering their direction (whether the predicted values are higher or lower than the actual values). It represents the absolute difference between the predicted house prices and the actual house prices, averaged over all data points.

The formula for MAE is:

$$MAE = \frac{1}{n} \sum_{i=1}^{n} |y_i - \hat{y}_i|$$

Where:

- y_i is the actual house price (ground truth),

- $\hat{y}_i$ is the predicted house price,

- n is the total number of predictions (test samples).

1.2 Why Use MAE?

Interpretability: MAE is simple and intuitive. It directly tells you the average absolute error in the model's predictions. For example, if MAE is 10,000, this means that, on average, the model's predictions are off by $10,000 from the actual house prices.

Robustness: MAE is not sensitive to large outliers. If the dataset has extreme values (e.g., extremely expensive houses), MAE will not be disproportionately affected by them. This makes it a useful metric when you want to get a general sense of model performance across all predictions.

1.3 How to Calculate MAE in Python?

Here's how to calculate the MAE in Python using scikit-learn:

```
from sklearn.metrics import mean_absolute_error

# Assuming y_test are the true house prices and y_pred are the predicted house prices
mae = mean_absolute_error(y_test, y_pred)
print(f"Mean Absolute Error (MAE): {mae}")
```

2. Root Mean Squared Error (RMSE)

2.1 What is RMSE?

The Root Mean Squared Error (RMSE) is another common metric for regression tasks that measures the average magnitude of the error, but unlike MAE, it penalizes larger errors more heavily. RMSE is the square root of the average of the squared differences between predicted and actual values.

The formula for RMSE is:

$$RMSE = \sqrt{\frac{1}{n}\sum_{i=1}^{n}(y_i - \hat{y}_i)^2}$$

Where:

- y_i is the actual house price (ground truth),

- $\hat{y}_i$ is the predicted house price,

- n is the total number of predictions (test samples).

2.2 Why Use RMSE?

Penalty for Larger Errors: RMSE gives more weight to larger errors because it squares the differences before averaging. This means that if your model makes large prediction errors, RMSE will reflect them more strongly. For example, an RMSE of 15,000 means that the model is making errors that, on average, are larger than those reflected by MAE.

Sensitivity to Outliers: RMSE is sensitive to outliers in the data. If there are extreme values or large errors, RMSE will tend to inflate, indicating the presence of larger-than-expected prediction errors.

Units: The units of RMSE are the same as the units of the target variable (house price), making it easy to interpret in terms of the actual problem.

2.3 How to Calculate RMSE in Python?

Here's how to calculate RMSE in Python using scikit-learn:

```
from sklearn.metrics import mean_squared_error
import numpy as np

# Calculate Mean Squared Error (MSE)
mse = mean_squared_error(y_test, y_pred)
```

```
# Calculate RMSE by taking the square root of MSE
rmse = np.sqrt(mse)
print(f"Root Mean Squared Error (RMSE): {rmse}")
```

3. R-squared (R²)

3.1 What is R-squared?

The R-squared (R^2) metric is one of the most widely used metrics to assess the goodness of fit for a regression model. It measures the proportion of the variance in the dependent variable (house price) that is explained by the independent variables (features).

The formula for R-squared is:

$$R^2 = 1 - \frac{\sum(y_i - \hat{y}_i)^2}{\sum(y_i - \bar{y})^2}$$

Where:

- y_i is the actual house price (ground truth),

- $\hat{y}_i$ is the predicted house price,

- $\bar{y}$ is the mean of the actual house prices,

- The numerator represents the residual sum of squares (RSS), and the denominator represents the total sum of squares (TSS).

3.2 Why Use R²?

Explained Variance: R^2 tells you how well the independent variables explain the variation in the dependent variable. An R^2 value of 0.8 means that 80% of the variance in house prices can be explained by the selected features, while the remaining 20% is unexplained or due to random noise.

Interpretation: R^2 ranges from 0 to 1. A value of 1 indicates a perfect fit, where the model perfectly predicts the house prices. A value of 0 means that the model does not explain any of the variance in the target variable.

Comparative Metric: R^2 is often used to compare different models. A higher R^2 value typically indicates better model performance, although it's important to note that R^2 can be artificially inflated by overfitting.

3.3 How to Calculate R² in Python?

Here's how to calculate R² in Python using scikit-learn:

```
from sklearn.metrics import r2_score

# Calculate R-squared value
r2 = r2_score(y_test, y_pred)
print(f"R-squared (R²): {r2}")
```

4. Comparison of MAE, RMSE, and R²

Each of the metrics discussed—MAE, RMSE, and R²—provides different insights into model performance, and each has its own strengths and limitations.

4.1 MAE vs. RMSE

MAE is easier to interpret because it tells you the average error in the same units as the target variable, and it's less sensitive to large errors. However, it does not penalize large errors, so it might be less informative if the model makes significant mistakes on some predictions.

RMSE, on the other hand, penalizes large errors more heavily, making it more sensitive to outliers. This can be useful when you want to focus on reducing larger errors, but it might not always be ideal if the dataset contains extreme values that do not represent typical cases.

4.2 R²

R² provides a high-level understanding of how well the model fits the data. It is especially useful for comparing models, as it gives a proportion of variance explained by the model. However, R² can sometimes be misleading in cases of overfitting or when the relationship between the target and features is not linear.

In this section, we explored how to evaluate the performance of a linear regression model using three essential metrics: Mean Absolute Error (MAE), Root Mean Squared Error (RMSE), and R-squared (R²). Each metric offers unique insights into model performance, helping you understand the accuracy of the predictions, the impact of larger errors, and how well the model fits the data. By calculating these metrics, you can assess how effectively your model is predicting house prices and whether it needs improvement or adjustments.

4.5 Deploying a simple Flask API for predictions

Once you have developed and trained a machine learning model to predict house prices, the next step is to deploy it in a way that allows users to make predictions easily. One of the most popular approaches for deploying machine learning models is through a web API. This allows clients (such as web browsers, mobile apps, or other systems) to send input data to your model and receive predictions as responses.

In this section, we will learn how to deploy a simple Flask API to serve predictions from your machine learning model. Flask is a lightweight web framework for Python that makes it easy to set up APIs quickly.

1. Why Flask for Deployment?

- **Simplicity**: Flask is lightweight, which makes it a great choice for simple projects and quick deployments.
- **Flexibility**: Flask doesn't enforce a specific project structure, so it's highly flexible and easy to modify as your project grows.
- **Integration**: Flask can easily integrate with machine learning models and allows you to expose them via RESTful APIs, making it suitable for building services that interact with your model.

2. Preparing the Model for Deployment

Before deploying the model, ensure that it is trained, evaluated, and saved properly. Once the model is ready, you can use libraries like Pickle or Joblib to save it for later use. In this example, we'll use Pickle to save and load the model.

import pickle

 # Save the trained model to a file
with open('house_price_model.pkl', 'wb') as file:
    pickle.dump(model, file)

This will save the model to a file called house_price_model.pkl in the current directory. You can later load this model to make predictions via the Flask API.

3. Setting Up Flask

Now that the model is saved, it's time to set up a simple Flask API. Below are the steps to follow:

3.1 Installing Flask and Required Libraries

To begin with, you need to install Flask, Pickle (for loading the model), and any other necessary libraries. You can install them via pip:

pip install flask scikit-learn pandas

3.2 Creating the Flask Application

Now, let's create the Flask app. The main components of the Flask app will include:

- Loading the trained model when the app starts.
- Accepting input data from users.
- Making predictions using the loaded model.
- Returning the prediction as a response.

Here's the code to create a basic Flask app:

```
from flask import Flask, request, jsonify
import pickle
import numpy as np

# Initialize the Flask app
app = Flask(__name__)

# Load the pre-trained machine learning model
with open('house_price_model.pkl', 'rb') as file:
    model = pickle.load(file)

@app.route('/')
def home():
    return "Welcome to the House Price Prediction API!"

@app.route('/predict', methods=['POST'])
```

```python
def predict():
    # Get data from the request (assuming it's in JSON format)
    data = request.get_json()

    # Extract features from the input data (adjust the keys to match your features)
    try:
        sqft = data['sqft']
        bedrooms = data['bedrooms']
        bathrooms = data['bathrooms']
        year_built = data['year_built']

        # Put the data into a format suitable for prediction (e.g., a numpy array)
        input_features = np.array([[sqft, bedrooms, bathrooms, year_built]])

        # Make a prediction using the loaded model
        prediction = model.predict(input_features)

        # Return the prediction as a JSON response
        return jsonify({'predicted_price': prediction[0]})

    except KeyError:
        return jsonify({'error': 'Invalid input format. Please provide valid feature values.'}), 400

if __name__ == '__main__':
    # Run the Flask app
    app.run(debug=True)
```

3.3 Explanation of the Flask Code

- **Importing Libraries**: We import Flask for the web framework, request to get the input data from the user, and pickle to load the saved model.
- **Model Loading**: The trained model is loaded from the house_price_model.pkl file when the Flask app starts, so it can be used for making predictions.

Route Definitions:

- **Home Route (/):** A simple welcome page when you visit the root of the API.
- **Prediction Route (/predict):** This route handles POST requests containing data for house price prediction. The data is expected to be in JSON format. It extracts

the features from the request, uses the model to make a prediction, and returns the predicted price as a JSON response.

- **Error Handling**: If the input data is in an incorrect format or missing expected values, the API will return an error with a 400 status code and an error message.

4. Running the Flask API

To run the Flask application, open a terminal and navigate to the directory where the Flask app file is located. Then, run the following command:

python app.py

This will start the Flask development server. You will see output similar to this:

 * Running on http://127.0.0.1:5000/ (Press CTRL+C to quit)

Now, your Flask API is running locally on http://127.0.0.1:5000/. You can send requests to this API to get predictions.

5. Testing the API

To test the API, you can use Postman or any HTTP client, such as requests in Python, to send a POST request to the /predict route. The request body should contain the necessary features in JSON format.

Example Request Using Postman

URL: http://127.0.0.1:5000/predict
Method: POST
Request Body (JSON):

```
{
    "sqft": 2000,
    "bedrooms": 3,
    "bathrooms": 2,
    "year_built": 1995
}
```

Example Request Using Python (requests)

You can also send a POST request using Python's requests library:

```python
import requests

# Define the API endpoint
url = 'http://127.0.0.1:5000/predict'

# Define the data to send in the request
data = {
    'sqft': 2000,
    'bedrooms': 3,
    'bathrooms': 2,
    'year_built': 1995
}

# Send the POST request and get the response
response = requests.post(url, json=data)

# Print the response (predicted house price)
print(response.json())
```

The response from the API will look something like this:

```json
{
    "predicted_price": 350000
}
```

In this section, we have successfully deployed a simple Flask API that takes input features for house price prediction and returns the predicted price. Deploying machine learning models using Flask makes it easy to integrate your model into a web-based application and serve predictions in real-time. This is a crucial step in making your machine learning model accessible to others and putting it into practical use.

Once the basic Flask app is running, you can further enhance it by adding additional features like authentication, logging, error handling, and more advanced deployment options, such as using Docker or deploying the app to cloud platforms like Heroku or AWS.

5. Customer Churn Prediction

In this chapter, we explore how machine learning can help businesses retain customers by predicting customer churn—the likelihood of a customer leaving a service. You will learn how to apply classification algorithms such as logistic regression, decision trees, and random forests to identify at-risk customers based on factors like usage patterns, customer service interactions, and demographics. We'll guide you through the process of data preprocessing, feature selection, and model evaluation using metrics like precision, recall, and F1-score. By the end of this project, you'll be able to create predictive models that not only help businesses understand customer behavior but also take proactive steps to reduce churn and improve customer retention. ⊞

5.1 What is churn, and why does it matter?

Customer churn, often referred to as customer attrition, is a critical metric that businesses across industries must track in order to understand and manage customer retention. The term refers to the phenomenon where customers stop using a service or product over a given period of time. Churn is commonly measured as the percentage of customers who leave or discontinue their relationship with a business during a specified time frame, such as monthly or annually. For businesses that rely heavily on repeat customers or subscriptions, churn can have significant financial implications, making it an essential concept in customer retention strategies.

This sub-chapter will explore the concept of churn in detail, discussing what churn is, why it matters to businesses, and how predicting it can provide valuable insights for companies to take proactive measures to improve customer retention.

1. Defining Churn

Customer churn refers to the loss of customers who were once using a product or service but have stopped engaging with it. In subscription-based businesses, churn specifically refers to customers who cancel their subscriptions or fail to renew them. This loss can occur for a variety of reasons, from dissatisfaction with the product or service to simply finding a better or cheaper alternative.

Churn can be categorized into two main types:

Voluntary Churn: This happens when customers consciously decide to leave the service. For instance, they may cancel their subscription or stop purchasing due to dissatisfaction with the product, pricing, or customer support.

Involuntary Churn: This occurs when customers are forced to leave, often due to external factors like payment failures, account freezes, or service interruptions. While this type of churn is not usually a result of customer dissatisfaction, it still impacts the business.

The definition and type of churn may vary depending on the industry and business model. For example, in the telecommunications industry, churn could involve customers leaving due to high prices or poor network coverage, while in e-commerce, churn could mean customers abandoning shopping carts or ceasing to make repeat purchases.

2. Why Does Churn Matter?

Churn is a major concern for businesses for several reasons, as it directly affects profitability, growth, and long-term success. Below are some of the key reasons why churn matters:

2.1 Loss of Revenue

For businesses that rely on recurring revenue, such as subscription-based models, customer churn directly impacts their revenue stream. When customers leave, they stop paying for the service, leading to a loss in predictable income. This can be especially damaging for startups and businesses in their growth stages, where a steady customer base is essential for survival. Even for established companies, churn can slow down growth and reduce revenue.

2.2 Higher Acquisition Costs

Acquiring new customers is often more expensive than retaining existing ones. Marketing, sales, and customer acquisition efforts can require a significant investment in terms of advertising, promotions, and time. When customers churn frequently, a company must continuously replace lost customers with new ones to maintain its customer base. This cycle of high acquisition costs can be financially draining and unsustainable in the long run.

2.3 Impact on Customer Lifetime Value (CLV)

Customer Lifetime Value (CLV) is a key metric that represents the total revenue a company can expect from a single customer during their entire relationship with the company. High churn rates significantly reduce CLV, as customers leave before they can make enough purchases to offset the cost of acquiring them. A high CLV indicates that a business is able to retain customers over time, while low CLV signals that churn is undermining the potential profitability of each customer.

2.4 Brand Reputation and Word-of-Mouth

Churn is not only about financial loss, but also about customer experience and perception. When customers leave, they often share their negative experiences through reviews, social media, or word-of-mouth. This can harm the company's reputation and dissuade potential customers from signing up or purchasing. Negative churn signals a gap in the company's ability to meet customer expectations, which can lead to a negative feedback loop where high churn feeds into poor brand perception, which in turn leads to more churn.

2.5 Retention is More Cost-Effective than Acquisition

From a financial standpoint, it's much more cost-effective to retain existing customers than to acquire new ones. Research consistently shows that acquiring a new customer can cost five to seven times more than retaining an existing one. By focusing on reducing churn, businesses can maximize the value they get from their current customers and reduce the need to invest heavily in acquiring new ones. This is especially important for businesses with high customer acquisition costs, as retaining customers has a direct impact on profitability.

3. The Costs of High Churn

The effects of churn extend beyond just the loss of revenue. High churn rates can result in several operational and strategic challenges for businesses:

3.1 Decreased Market Share

When customers leave, the company loses not just revenue but also market share. In highly competitive industries, this can have a long-term impact, as competitors may capitalize on the customer's dissatisfaction or offer better alternatives. If a company doesn't take action to reduce churn, it risks losing ground to competitors, which can be difficult to recover from.

3.2 Decreased Morale and Company Culture

When churn is high, it can also affect employee morale. Staff members in customer-facing roles may become disheartened by the constant need to deal with dissatisfied customers or find solutions to retention problems. This can lead to a reduction in engagement and productivity, which ultimately impacts the overall performance of the business.

3.3 Lower Customer Satisfaction

Churn is often a result of unmet customer needs or dissatisfaction. High churn indicates that a company's product or service is not aligning with customer expectations, whether in terms of quality, functionality, support, or price. If customers are not satisfied, they are more likely to leave for a competitor that can better meet their needs.

4. Predicting and Reducing Churn

Understanding why churn occurs is vital for taking preventive measures. Predicting churn with machine learning models allows companies to identify customers at risk of leaving and intervene with targeted retention strategies. Common predictive techniques include:

Customer Segmentation: Grouping customers based on their behaviors, demographics, and engagement levels can help identify segments with higher churn rates. Companies can then tailor retention strategies to these specific segments.

Predictive Analytics: By analyzing historical data, businesses can develop models to predict which customers are most likely to churn. These models can factor in usage patterns, engagement, customer feedback, and other variables to generate risk scores for individual customers.

Retention Strategies: Once customers at risk of churn are identified, companies can act to retain them. This might involve personalized offers, discounts, loyalty programs, improving customer support, or addressing specific pain points that lead to dissatisfaction.

4.1 Retaining Customers

To reduce churn, businesses should focus on improving customer satisfaction, adding value, and addressing pain points. Offering personalized experiences, improving product quality, and providing excellent customer support are key strategies to increase retention. Additionally, regular engagement with customers—through email newsletters, satisfaction surveys, or loyalty programs—can foster long-term relationships and reduce the likelihood of churn.

Churn is an unavoidable reality for businesses, but understanding it and managing it effectively can make a significant difference in a company's long-term success. Churn directly impacts revenue, customer lifetime value, and brand reputation. By predicting churn using machine learning and taking proactive steps to retain customers, businesses can reduce the financial and operational costs of customer attrition. Understanding churn, why it matters, and how to address it is essential for any business that values sustainable growth and long-term customer loyalty.

5.2 Exploratory Data Analysis (EDA) on customer data

Exploratory Data Analysis (EDA) is a crucial step in the data science workflow, particularly in the context of customer churn prediction. It involves analyzing and visualizing data to gain insights, identify patterns, and understand the relationships between variables before diving into the modeling process. For churn prediction, EDA helps uncover key features that could drive customer churn and guides the choice of modeling techniques. In this sub-chapter, we will explore the importance of EDA in churn prediction, the key steps involved, and the types of analyses that should be performed on customer data.

1. The Importance of EDA in Churn Prediction

Before building any machine learning model, it is essential to understand the data you are working with. For churn prediction, understanding the underlying patterns and distributions in the customer data can significantly improve the model's performance. By performing EDA, we can uncover relationships between customer behaviors, demographics, and the likelihood of churn. Additionally, EDA helps in:

- **Identifying Data Quality Issues**: Missing values, duplicates, and incorrect data entries can interfere with the accuracy of the model. EDA allows us to clean the data effectively.
- **Feature Engineering**: Insights from EDA help in creating new features that could have a higher predictive power.
- **Determining Outliers**: Identifying extreme values or anomalies in the data can help ensure the integrity of the model and guide decisions on how to treat outliers.
- **Choosing the Right Model**: By understanding the structure of the data and the relationships between variables, EDA helps to choose the appropriate modeling techniques, whether linear models, decision trees, or more advanced methods.

2. Steps in Performing EDA for Churn Prediction

When performing EDA on customer churn data, the process typically involves several key steps:

2.1 Loading and Preprocessing the Data

The first step in EDA is to load the dataset and prepare it for analysis. This includes loading the data from CSV, databases, or other formats, cleaning it, and transforming it into a suitable format for analysis.

For example, in Python, we might use libraries such as Pandas and NumPy to handle data manipulation, and Matplotlib or Seaborn for data visualization. The following are common preprocessing tasks:

- **Handling missing data**: Identifying and filling missing values using mean, median, mode, or other imputation techniques.
- **Removing duplicates**: Ensuring that there are no duplicate entries in the dataset.
- **Converting categorical variables**: Encoding categorical features into numerical format using techniques such as one-hot encoding or label encoding.

2.2 Descriptive Statistics

Before diving deeper into visualizations, it's important to perform some basic statistical analysis to get an overview of the dataset. This includes:

- **Summary Statistics**: Use functions like .describe() in Pandas to get the mean, median, standard deviation, minimum, and maximum values of numeric features. This helps identify the central tendency and spread of the data.
- **Distribution Analysis**: Understanding how data is distributed is crucial, especially for numerical features like age, account balance, or tenure. Histograms and box plots can reveal skewed distributions or the presence of outliers.

Example:

```
import pandas as pd

# Load data
df = pd.read_csv('customer_data.csv')
```

```
# Display basic statistics
print(df.describe())
```

2.3 Visualizing Data

Visualization is an essential part of EDA. It helps to identify patterns, trends, and anomalies in the data more easily. Here are some common visualizations used in churn prediction analysis:

2.3.1 Univariate Analysis

Univariate analysis focuses on understanding the distribution of individual features. It includes:

Histograms: Used to visualize the distribution of continuous features like Age, Tenure, or AccountBalance.

Example: Plotting the distribution of account balances.

```
import seaborn as sns
import matplotlib.pyplot as plt

sns.histplot(df['AccountBalance'], kde=True)
plt.title('Account Balance Distribution')
plt.show()
```

Box Plots: Useful for identifying outliers and understanding the spread of the data.

2.3.2 Bivariate Analysis

Bivariate analysis involves exploring relationships between two features. For churn prediction, it's essential to explore the relationship between customer attributes and churn status. Examples include:

Bar Plots: Show the relationship between categorical variables (e.g., customer Gender, PaymentMethod) and the target variable Churn (Yes/No).

Example: Visualizing churn distribution by gender.

```
sns.countplot(x='Gender', hue='Churn', data=df)
plt.title('Churn by Gender')
plt.show()
```

Correlation Heatmap: A correlation matrix shows how numeric variables relate to one another. In churn prediction, understanding correlations between features like Tenure, AccountBalance, and Churn can help identify key drivers of customer behavior.

Example:

```
correlation_matrix = df.corr()
sns.heatmap(correlation_matrix, annot=True, cmap='coolwarm')
plt.title('Correlation Matrix')
plt.show()
```

2.3.3 Pair Plots

Pair plots visualize pairwise relationships between multiple features at once, allowing us to see how different features interact with one another. This can help reveal underlying patterns that might suggest factors that influence churn.

```
sns.pairplot(df[['Age', 'AccountBalance', 'Tenure', 'Churn']])
plt.show()
```

3. Identifying Key Features That Influence Churn

One of the primary goals of EDA in churn prediction is to identify which features have the most impact on whether a customer will churn or stay. This can be done by examining:

Customer Demographics: Features like Age, Gender, Income, Region, and SubscriptionType may have an impact on churn. For example, younger customers or those in specific regions may have higher churn rates.

Customer Behavior: Features like Tenure, AccountBalance, UsageFrequency, and SupportCalls can indicate whether customers are engaged with the service or not. High churn rates in customers with low usage may point to product dissatisfaction.

Customer Feedback: If available, customer feedback data such as SurveyScore, NPS (Net Promoter Score), or SatisfactionRating can be key indicators of churn risk.

Using feature importance techniques (e.g., decision trees, random forests) after performing EDA can help in quantifying which features matter the most for predicting churn.

4. Identifying Patterns and Trends in Churn

EDA also helps in identifying key patterns and trends that may indicate why customers are churning. For example, churn may vary by:

- **Subscription Type**: Customers on a monthly plan may be more likely to churn than those on an annual plan.
- **Usage Patterns**: Customers who rarely use the service or make fewer transactions may be more likely to churn.
- **Support Interactions**: A high number of support calls or negative interactions with customer support could correlate with higher churn rates.

By identifying these patterns, businesses can better target retention strategies to prevent churn before it happens.

Exploratory Data Analysis is a vital step in churn prediction, as it helps uncover key insights from customer data, identify potential features that influence churn, and guide the modeling process. Through the use of descriptive statistics, visualizations, and correlation analysis, businesses can understand the underlying drivers of churn and take proactive steps to improve retention. By using EDA to its full potential, companies can make data-driven decisions to reduce churn, optimize customer experience, and ultimately drive long-term profitability.

5.3 Training decision tree & random forest classifiers

In customer churn prediction, machine learning models play a critical role in identifying customers who are most likely to churn. Among the various algorithms available, Decision Trees and Random Forests are some of the most commonly used techniques. These models provide interpretable insights and are well-suited for classification tasks like churn prediction, where the goal is to predict whether a customer will leave or stay based on their features.

This sub-chapter will focus on training Decision Tree and Random Forest classifiers, explaining how they work, when to use them, and how to implement them for churn prediction.

1. Understanding Decision Tree Classifiers

A Decision Tree is a supervised machine learning algorithm that splits the dataset into subsets based on the most significant features. It creates a tree-like structure where each internal node represents a decision based on a feature, each branch represents an outcome of that decision, and each leaf node represents a class label (in this case, "Churn" or "No Churn").

The key feature of decision trees is their interpretability. By visually following the path from the root to a leaf, you can easily understand the reasoning behind a model's prediction. For churn prediction, a decision tree can help identify which customer characteristics are most strongly associated with churn.

1.1 Key Components of a Decision Tree

- **Root Node**: Represents the entire dataset and the first decision point.
- **Splitting**: The process of dividing the dataset into subsets based on a feature's value.
- **Leaf Nodes**: Represent the final output or prediction (i.e., "Churn" or "No Churn").
- **Branches**: Represent the decision rules that connect the nodes based on feature values.

The goal of a decision tree is to split the data in such a way that the resultant subsets are as homogeneous as possible with respect to the target variable (churn or no churn).

1.2 Training a Decision Tree

To train a decision tree, we need to choose an algorithm that splits the data based on the best feature at each decision point. Popular splitting criteria include:

- **Gini Impurity**: Measures the "impurity" or uncertainty in a set of data. A lower Gini impurity indicates that a node is more pure and homogenous with respect to the target class.
- **Entropy**: Measures the amount of disorder or randomness in the data. The goal is to reduce entropy, making the nodes more predictable.

In practice, we will use a decision tree classifier from Python's scikit-learn library to train the model. Below is a basic implementation for training a decision tree classifier on a churn dataset.

```
from sklearn.model_selection import train_test_split
from sklearn.tree import DecisionTreeClassifier
from sklearn.metrics import accuracy_score, confusion_matrix

# Load the churn data (assumed to be preprocessed)
X = df.drop(columns='Churn')
y = df['Churn']

# Split the data into training and testing sets
X_train, X_test, y_train, y_test = train_test_split(X, y, test_size=0.3, random_state=42)

# Create the Decision Tree model
dt_model = DecisionTreeClassifier(criterion='gini', max_depth=5)

# Train the model
dt_model.fit(X_train, y_train)

# Make predictions on the test set
y_pred = dt_model.predict(X_test)

# Evaluate the model
accuracy = accuracy_score(y_test, y_pred)
conf_matrix = confusion_matrix(y_test, y_pred)

print(f"Accuracy: {accuracy}")
print(f"Confusion Matrix:\n{conf_matrix}")
```

In this code, we:

- Split the data into training and test sets.
- Create a DecisionTreeClassifier model with a maximum depth of 5 to prevent overfitting.
- Train the model on the training data using .fit().
- Evaluate the model's accuracy and confusion matrix on the test set.

2. Understanding Random Forest Classifiers

A Random Forest is an ensemble method that combines multiple decision trees to improve performance. Unlike a single decision tree, which can easily overfit the data, a random forest reduces overfitting by averaging the results of multiple trees, each trained on different subsets of the data and features. This aggregation process makes the random forest more robust and accurate.

2.1 How Does a Random Forest Work?

Random Forests create multiple decision trees using the following steps:

- **Bootstrap Sampling**: Randomly sample subsets of the original data (with replacement) to create multiple training datasets.
- **Feature Randomness**: At each split in the tree, consider a random subset of features instead of all features. This decorrelates the trees and leads to a more diverse set of models.
- **Ensemble Prediction**: Each tree makes a prediction, and the random forest aggregates these predictions (usually by voting for classification) to produce the final output.

The advantage of a random forest over a single decision tree is that it balances bias and variance. While individual decision trees may have high variance (overfitting), the random forest's ensemble nature reduces this risk, leading to a more generalizable model.

2.2 Training a Random Forest

Training a random forest is very similar to training a decision tree, but instead of creating a single tree, we create a forest of many trees. The scikit-learn library provides an implementation of the Random Forest Classifier, which is simple to use.

```
from sklearn.ensemble import RandomForestClassifier
from sklearn.metrics import accuracy_score, confusion_matrix

# Create the Random Forest model
rf_model = RandomForestClassifier(n_estimators=100, random_state=42)

# Train the model
rf_model.fit(X_train, y_train)

# Make predictions on the test set
y_pred_rf = rf_model.predict(X_test)

# Evaluate the model
```

accuracy_rf = accuracy_score(y_test, y_pred_rf)
conf_matrix_rf = confusion_matrix(y_test, y_pred_rf)

print(f"Random Forest Accuracy: {accuracy_rf}")
print(f"Random Forest Confusion Matrix:\n{conf_matrix_rf}")

In this code, we:

- Use the RandomForestClassifier to create a random forest with 100 trees (specified by n_estimators).
- Train the model using .fit() on the training data.
- Evaluate the model's performance using accuracy and confusion matrix.

3. Comparison Between Decision Trees and Random Forests

When it comes to churn prediction, both decision trees and random forests have their strengths and weaknesses. Here's a comparison of the two:

Metric	Decision Tree	Random Forest
Overfitting	Prone to overfitting, especially with deep trees.	Less prone to overfitting due to ensemble learning.
Interpretability	Very interpretable, easy to visualize.	Less interpretable due to the complexity of multiple trees.
Accuracy	Often less accurate due to overfitting.	More accurate due to averaging over many trees.
Training Time	Faster to train than Random Forests.	Slower to train because of multiple trees.
Model Complexity	Simpler, easier to understand and debug.	More complex, harder to debug.

4. Tuning Decision Trees and Random Forests

Both decision trees and random forests have several hyperparameters that can be tuned to improve model performance. For example:

- **Maximum Depth (max_depth):** Controls how deep the tree can grow. Limiting depth can prevent overfitting.

- **Minimum Samples Split (min_samples_split):** The minimum number of samples required to split an internal node. Increasing this number can prevent the tree from growing too deep.
- **Number of Trees (n_estimators):** For random forests, this controls how many trees are in the forest. More trees generally lead to better performance, but also increase computation time.

By using grid search or random search, we can find the optimal combination of hyperparameters.

Training Decision Trees and Random Forests is a powerful approach for churn prediction. Decision trees offer interpretability and are easy to understand, while random forests mitigate overfitting and provide better generalization. Random forests are often the preferred choice for churn prediction due to their robustness and accuracy. Both models, when trained and tuned correctly, can help businesses identify at-risk customers and take proactive measures to improve customer retention.

5.4 Feature importance and SHAP analysis

In machine learning, particularly in models used for customer churn prediction, understanding which features influence the model's predictions the most is critical for interpreting model behavior and gaining actionable insights. One of the key methods for understanding feature influence is feature importance. Additionally, SHAP (SHapley Additive exPlanations) values have become a powerful tool for interpreting complex models like decision trees and random forests.

In this sub-chapter, we will discuss feature importance, explain its significance, and explore SHAP analysis to provide detailed insights into the predictive power of different features in churn prediction.

1. Feature Importance in Machine Learning

1.1 What is Feature Importance?

Feature importance refers to a technique used to determine which input features are the most influential in making predictions for a model. In the context of churn prediction, feature importance helps identify which customer characteristics (such as age, account balance, or subscription type) are most strongly associated with a customer's likelihood to churn.

Many machine learning models, including decision trees, random forests, and gradient boosting machines, are capable of calculating feature importance automatically. These models can rank the features based on how useful they are in reducing uncertainty or improving the accuracy of the model. Features with higher importance are considered more relevant to the prediction task.

1.2 How is Feature Importance Calculated?

Feature importance can be computed in various ways depending on the model. For decision trees and random forests, it is typically calculated by evaluating how much each feature reduces a model's overall error (e.g., Gini impurity or entropy) when used to split the data at each node.

Decision Trees: For decision trees, the importance of a feature is typically computed by measuring the reduction in the Gini impurity or entropy when the feature is used to split the data. The more a feature reduces uncertainty, the higher its importance.

Random Forests: Random forests aggregate the feature importance scores of individual trees in the forest. The overall importance of a feature is the average of its importance across all trees.

For example, if a feature like "Age" significantly improves the accuracy of the churn prediction model by helping to split data into homogenous subsets, its importance will be higher than less impactful features.

1.3 Feature Importance in scikit-learn

In Python's scikit-learn library, feature importance can be easily extracted from decision trees and random forests. Here's an example of how to retrieve and visualize feature importance using a random forest model for churn prediction:

```
import matplotlib.pyplot as plt
import numpy as np
from sklearn.ensemble import RandomForestClassifier

# Train a random forest model (assuming 'X_train' and 'y_train' are prepared)
rf_model = RandomForestClassifier(n_estimators=100, random_state=42)
rf_model.fit(X_train, y_train)
```

```
# Get feature importance
importances = rf_model.feature_importances_

# Sort the features based on importance
indices = np.argsort(importances)[::-1]

# Plot feature importance
plt.figure(figsize=(10, 6))
plt.title("Feature Importance (Random Forest)")
plt.barh(range(len(importances)), importances[indices], align="center")
plt.yticks(range(len(importances)), [X_train.columns[i] for i in indices])
plt.xlabel("Importance")
plt.show()
```

In this code:

- rf_model.feature_importances_ retrieves the importance scores of the features.
- We use np.argsort() to sort the feature importance values in descending order.
- A bar plot is created to visualize the importance of each feature.

This provides a quick visual interpretation of which features are driving churn predictions, allowing you to focus on the most relevant variables.

2. SHAP Analysis: An Advanced Technique for Model Interpretability

2.1 What is SHAP?

SHAP (SHapley Additive exPlanations) is a powerful technique derived from cooperative game theory, specifically the concept of Shapley values. SHAP values provide a way to explain the output of any machine learning model by assigning each feature an importance score that represents its contribution to a given prediction.

SHAP values decompose a model's prediction into the sum of the contributions from each feature, providing a detailed explanation of the model's output. The key benefit of SHAP is that it offers a unified framework for explaining both global model behavior (which features matter the most) and local model behavior (how features affect individual predictions).

2.2 How Does SHAP Work?

SHAP values are based on Shapley values, which were originally introduced in game theory. The Shapley value of a feature is computed by considering all possible combinations of features and how the feature contributes to the prediction when added to each combination. Essentially, it measures the average contribution of a feature across all possible subsets of features.

In churn prediction, SHAP values can provide insights into how specific features, such as "Tenure" or "Support Calls", influence a particular customer's churn prediction. For example, if the SHAP value for "Tenure" is negative, it means that a longer tenure is associated with a lower likelihood of churn for that specific customer.

2.3 Visualizing SHAP Values

One of the most powerful aspects of SHAP is its ability to produce clear visualizations that help explain both global and local patterns. Two commonly used visualizations are:

SHAP Summary Plot: A summary plot shows the impact of each feature on the model's predictions across all instances in the dataset. It displays both the magnitude and direction (positive or negative) of each feature's contribution.

SHAP Force Plot: The force plot is used to show how a specific feature's value contributes to an individual prediction. It provides an intuitive, visual breakdown of why a model made a specific decision.

2.4 Implementing SHAP for Churn Prediction

To use SHAP for churn prediction, you need to install the SHAP library and apply it to a trained model. Below is an example of how to use SHAP to explain a random forest model's predictions:

```
import shap

# Initialize the SHAP explainer
explainer = shap.TreeExplainer(rf_model)

# Compute SHAP values
shap_values = explainer.shap_values(X_test)

# SHAP summary plot
shap.summary_plot(shap_values[1], X_test)
```

```
# SHAP force plot for a specific prediction (e.g., first instance)
shap.force_plot(shap_values[1][0], X_test.iloc[0])
```

In this example:

- We use shap.TreeExplainer to create an explainer for the random forest model.
- explainer.shap_values(X_test) computes the SHAP values for the test set.
- The summary plot is generated using shap.summary_plot(), and the force plot shows the contribution of features to the first instance's prediction.

The summary plot will display the importance of each feature across the test set, while the force plot will explain the prediction for a specific customer, showing how each feature contributed to the churn or non-churn prediction.

2.5 Interpreting SHAP Results

By analyzing SHAP values, you can gain deeper insights into the factors driving customer churn:

Global Insights: The summary plot can tell you which features are the most important across the entire dataset. For example, if Tenure has the highest SHAP value, it indicates that customers who have been with the company for a longer time are less likely to churn, on average.

Local Insights: The force plot provides a detailed breakdown for a specific customer. If the model predicts that a customer will churn, SHAP can show which features (such as a high number of support calls) contributed to that prediction.

Feature importance and SHAP analysis are critical tools for understanding and interpreting machine learning models in churn prediction. While feature importance provides a global view of which features are most important for the model's predictions, SHAP values offer more granular, individual explanations for each prediction. Together, these techniques allow businesses to not only improve the accuracy of their models but also build trust and transparency by explaining why certain customers are more likely to churn.

By leveraging these methods, businesses can make data-driven decisions to optimize customer retention strategies and gain a deeper understanding of the factors influencing customer behavior.

5.5 Building a dashboard for churn prediction insights

In customer churn prediction, presenting the insights gained from machine learning models in an easily interpretable and actionable format is crucial for business stakeholders. A well-designed dashboard can help visualize key metrics, model predictions, and feature importance, allowing teams to make informed decisions based on data. A dashboard offers the ability to monitor churn predictions in real-time, track trends over time, and dive into detailed customer insights.

In this sub-chapter, we will walk through the process of building a churn prediction insights dashboard using Python libraries like Dash and Plotly. The dashboard will allow users to interact with the churn model's results, visualize key data points, and explore customer behavior patterns.

1. Introduction to Dashboards for Churn Prediction

Dashboards are interactive tools that allow users to visualize and explore data in a dynamic way. In the context of churn prediction, a dashboard can:

- Show the overall churn rate and trends over time.
- Visualize feature importance for the churn model.
- Display customer-level insights based on the churn prediction.
- Allow stakeholders to filter and segment data based on various parameters such as customer demographics, subscription type, or service usage patterns.

Building a dashboard for churn prediction insights provides business users with the necessary information to take action, such as identifying at-risk customers, designing targeted retention campaigns, and measuring the effectiveness of retention strategies.

2. Tools for Building Dashboards

For this dashboard, we will use the following libraries:

- **Dash**: An open-source Python framework for building analytical web applications. It is built on top of Flask, Plotly, and React.js, which makes it easy to build interactive and dynamic dashboards.

- **Plotly**: A graphing library used to create interactive visualizations. Plotly works seamlessly with Dash to generate various types of charts, such as bar plots, line graphs, and scatter plots.
- **Pandas**: For data manipulation and preprocessing.
- **Scikit-learn:** For the churn prediction model and metrics.

Dash provides a simple structure where you can define HTML components (such as graphs, tables, and input fields) and link them to Python code for interactivity.

3. Step-by-Step Guide to Building the Dashboard

3.1 Set Up the Environment

First, you need to install the necessary libraries. If you haven't already installed Dash and Plotly, you can do so by running the following command:

pip install dash plotly pandas scikit-learn

3.2 Prepare the Data and Model

For the dashboard, we'll assume you have already built a churn prediction model (such as a random forest) and have preprocessed the churn dataset.

Here's an example of how to prepare the data and the trained model for deployment:

```
import pandas as pd
import joblib
from sklearn.model_selection import train_test_split
from sklearn.ensemble import RandomForestClassifier

# Load the churn data (assuming it's already preprocessed)
df = pd.read_csv('customer_churn_data.csv')

# Prepare the features (X) and target (y)
X = df.drop(columns='Churn')
y = df['Churn']

# Train a Random Forest Classifier
X_train, X_test, y_train, y_test = train_test_split(X, y, test_size=0.3, random_state=42)
rf_model = RandomForestClassifier(n_estimators=100, random_state=42)
```

```
rf_model.fit(X_train, y_train)

# Save the trained model
joblib.dump(rf_model, 'churn_model.pkl')
```

In this example:

- We load and preprocess the churn data.
- We split the data into training and testing sets.
- We train a random forest model for churn prediction.

We save the trained model using joblib.dump() so that it can be loaded into the dashboard application.

3.3 Define the Dashboard Layout

Now that we have the model ready, we can start building the Dash app. Dash apps are composed of two main parts:

- **Layout**: Defines the structure of the dashboard, including graphs, tables, and input elements.
- **Callbacks**: Define the interactivity between the components, such as filtering data or updating charts.

Here's an example layout that includes key components for the churn prediction dashboard:

```
import dash
from dash import dcc, html
import plotly.express as px
import joblib
import pandas as pd

# Load the trained model
rf_model = joblib.load('churn_model.pkl')

# Load the churn data (or any other relevant dataset)
df = pd.read_csv('customer_churn_data.csv')

# Initialize the Dash app
```

```python
app = dash.Dash(__name__)

# Layout of the dashboard
app.layout = html.Div([
    html.H1("Customer Churn Prediction Dashboard"),

    # Dropdown for selecting customer segment
    html.Div([
        html.Label("Select Customer Segment:"),
        dcc.Dropdown(
            id="segment-dropdown",
            options=[
                {'label': 'All', 'value': 'all'},
                {'label': 'Churned Customers', 'value': 'churned'},
                {'label': 'Non-Churned Customers', 'value': 'non-churned'}
            ],
            value='all'
        ),
    ], style={'width': '30%', 'margin-bottom': '20px'}),

    # Churn Prediction Probability Graph
    dcc.Graph(id="churn-probability-graph"),

    # Feature Importance Bar Chart
    dcc.Graph(id="feature-importance-graph"),

    # Customer Insights Table
    html.Div(id="customer-table"),
])

# Callback to update churn probability graph based on customer segment selection
@app.callback(
    [dash.dependencies.Output('churn-probability-graph', 'figure'),
     dash.dependencies.Output('feature-importance-graph', 'figure')],
    [dash.dependencies.Input('segment-dropdown', 'value')]
)
def update_graphs(selected_segment):
    # Filter data based on segment
    if selected_segment == 'churned':
        segment_data = df[df['Churn'] == 1]
```

```
elif selected_segment == 'non-churned':
    segment_data = df[df['Churn'] == 0]
else:
    segment_data = df

# Predict churn probabilities for the filtered data
X_segment = segment_data.drop(columns='Churn')
y_pred_prob = rf_model.predict_proba(X_segment)[:, 1]

# Plot churn probabilities
churn_prob_fig = px.histogram(x=y_pred_prob, nbins=30, title="Churn Prediction
Probability Distribution")

# Plot feature importance
feature_importance = rf_model.feature_importances_
feature_names = X_segment.columns
feature_importance_fig = px.bar(
    x=feature_names,
    y=feature_importance,
    labels={'x': 'Feature', 'y': 'Importance'},
    title="Feature Importance"
)

return churn_prob_fig, feature_importance_fig

# Run the app
if __name__ == '__main__':
    app.run_server(debug=True)
```

3.4 Key Features of the Dashboard

- **Customer Segment Dropdown**: Users can filter the data by selecting different customer segments (e.g., churned or non-churned customers). This allows the user to focus on specific customer groups.
- **Churn Probability Graph**: This graph shows the distribution of churn probabilities for the selected customer segment. It helps visualize how likely customers are to churn based on the model's predictions.
- **Feature Importance Bar Chart**: This chart displays the importance of various features in predicting churn, based on the trained random forest model. It provides valuable insights into the factors that contribute most to churn.

- **Customer Insights Table**: A table can be added to display individual customer details, such as churn probability, feature values, and model prediction.

3.5 Running the Dashboard

Once the dashboard is complete, run it by executing the script. The app will start a web server, and you can access the dashboard by navigating to the provided URL (usually http://127.0.0.1:8050/).

Building a churn prediction dashboard offers several benefits for businesses, providing a visual and interactive interface to explore churn data and insights. With tools like Dash and Plotly, it is easy to design a user-friendly dashboard that allows stakeholders to explore model predictions, understand feature importance, and make data-driven decisions.

By deploying such a dashboard, you can help teams proactively manage customer retention efforts, identify at-risk customers, and develop targeted interventions based on real-time data and predictions. This approach empowers businesses to stay ahead in competitive markets by leveraging churn prediction models effectively.

6. Sentiment Analysis on Social Media

Social media is a goldmine for understanding public opinion, and in this chapter, we dive into the power of sentiment analysis to extract insights from text data. You'll learn how to build a model that can classify social media posts, tweets, or reviews as positive, negative, or neutral using natural language processing (NLP) techniques. We'll cover the fundamentals of text preprocessing, including tokenization, stopword removal, and vectorization using methods like TF-IDF and word embeddings. You'll also explore more advanced models like LSTM and BERT for better accuracy. By the end of this project, you'll be able to analyze social media sentiment at scale, enabling businesses to gauge customer feedback and trends in real-time. 💬

6.1 Introduction to NLP and sentiment analysis

Sentiment analysis is one of the most widely used applications of Natural Language Processing (NLP), and its importance has only grown with the rise of social media, where millions of people share their opinions, thoughts, and emotions every day. Sentiment analysis refers to the use of computational methods to identify and extract subjective information from text, often to determine whether the expressed opinion in a document, sentence, or even a word is positive, negative, or neutral.

This sub-chapter introduces the basics of NLP, the field that enables machines to understand, interpret, and generate human language. We will specifically focus on sentiment analysis in the context of social media, where the vast amount of unstructured text data presents both challenges and opportunities for machine learning and AI.

1. What is Natural Language Processing (NLP)?

1.1 Defining NLP

Natural Language Processing (NLP) is a subfield of Artificial Intelligence (AI) and Computational Linguistics that focuses on enabling machines to understand, interpret, and respond to human language in a way that is both meaningful and useful. The goal of NLP is to bridge the gap between human communication and machine understanding, allowing machines to process large amounts of natural language data (text or speech) in ways that are meaningful.

NLP encompasses a wide range of tasks, including:

- **Text classification**: Categorizing text into predefined categories.
- **Named entity recognition (NER):** Identifying proper names, organizations, locations, and other important entities within a text.
- **Part-of-speech tagging (POS):** Identifying the grammatical structure of a sentence by tagging each word with its corresponding part of speech (noun, verb, adjective, etc.).
- **Machine translation**: Translating text from one language to another.
- **Text generation**: Creating new text that resembles the style and content of an existing corpus.

1.2 How NLP Works

NLP tasks typically require several steps to process raw text data, and various techniques are employed depending on the complexity of the task. The process often includes:

- **Tokenization**: Breaking the text into smaller units (tokens), such as words or phrases.
- **Stop word removal**: Removing common words (like "the", "and", "is") that do not contribute significant meaning.
- **Stemming and Lemmatization**: Reducing words to their root forms (e.g., "running" becomes "run").
- **Vectorization**: Converting text data into numerical format so that machine learning algorithms can process it.

NLP is continuously evolving, and with advances in machine learning (particularly deep learning) and access to larger datasets, modern NLP techniques are achieving impressive results across a variety of tasks.

2. Sentiment Analysis

2.1 Defining Sentiment Analysis

Sentiment analysis is a form of text classification in which the goal is to determine the emotional tone or attitude of the text. The primary task in sentiment analysis is to categorize text as expressing positive, negative, or neutral sentiment. In a more advanced form, sentiment analysis can also detect emotions like anger, joy, sadness, fear, or disgust.

In the context of social media sentiment analysis, sentiment analysis algorithms are designed to process large volumes of unstructured text data—such as tweets, Facebook posts, product reviews, or blog comments—and determine how users feel about a given topic. Sentiment analysis can be applied to a variety of applications:

- **Brand Monitoring**: Understanding customer opinions about products, services, or brands.
- **Customer Support**: Analyzing customer feedback to identify satisfaction levels or complaints.
- **Political Analysis**: Gauging public opinion about political candidates, policies, or issues.
- **Market Research**: Analyzing consumer sentiment for product development and marketing strategies.

2.2 Types of Sentiment Analysis

Sentiment analysis can be classified into different types depending on the granularity of analysis and the scope of the model. There are three primary levels of sentiment analysis:

Document-level sentiment analysis: At this level, the algorithm assesses the overall sentiment of the entire document (or piece of text). The goal is to classify the document as expressing positive, negative, or neutral sentiment.

Sentence-level sentiment analysis: Here, the focus is on individual sentences. The algorithm determines the sentiment of each sentence, which can then be aggregated to evaluate the overall sentiment of the document.

Aspect-based sentiment analysis: This is a more advanced form of sentiment analysis, where the goal is to identify specific aspects (or features) of a product or service that are being discussed. For example, in a product review, sentiment analysis might determine whether the customer is positive about the price, quality, or customer service of the product.

Each type of sentiment analysis has its own challenges and use cases, with document-level analysis being the most common and aspect-based analysis often requiring more sophisticated models.

3. Sentiment Analysis on Social Media

3.1 Social Media as a Source of Data

Social media platforms such as Twitter, Facebook, Instagram, and Reddit generate massive amounts of text data every second. Users frequently post their opinions on various topics, making social media an incredibly valuable source of data for sentiment analysis. Understanding the sentiments expressed on these platforms can help businesses and organizations to:

- Track public sentiment toward products, services, or brands.
- Understand customer feedback in real-time.
- Measure the success of marketing campaigns.
- Detect emerging trends or issues in society.

Unlike structured datasets (like product ratings), social media posts are often informal and unstructured, containing slang, emojis, hashtags, misspellings, and abbreviations, making them more challenging to analyze.

3.2 Challenges of Social Media Sentiment Analysis

Sentiment analysis on social media is fraught with unique challenges due to the informal and dynamic nature of social media content. Some of the challenges include:

- **Ambiguity**: Words or phrases can have different meanings depending on context. For example, the word "sick" can be used to mean either "ill" or "awesome" in different contexts.
- **Sarcasm and Irony**: Social media users often express sarcasm or irony, which can be difficult for sentiment analysis algorithms to interpret. A sentence like "This product is the worst thing I've ever bought" may be meant sarcastically, but a simple sentiment analysis model may classify it as negative.
- **Emojis and Hashtags**: Emojis are widely used on social media to express emotions, and hashtags often represent topics or trends. Properly interpreting emojis and hashtags is crucial for accurate sentiment analysis.
- **Short Texts**: Social media posts are often short, which makes it challenging to accurately capture the full context and sentiment of the text.

To address these challenges, more advanced NLP models, such as those built using deep learning techniques (e.g., LSTM, BERT), are often employed to capture subtle nuances in text.

3.3 Sentiment Analysis Models for Social Media

There are several approaches to sentiment analysis, ranging from traditional machine learning models to more sophisticated deep learning techniques:

Traditional Machine Learning: Traditional sentiment analysis techniques typically rely on methods like Naive Bayes, Support Vector Machines (SVM), and Logistic Regression. These models often use bag-of-words or TF-IDF (Term Frequency-Inverse Document Frequency) representations of text data and rely on manually engineered features.

Deep Learning Models: Deep learning models, particularly Recurrent Neural Networks (RNNs), Long Short-Term Memory (LSTM) networks, and Transformers (like BERT), are capable of capturing more complex patterns in the text. These models can better understand context, word order, and semantic meaning, making them more suited for analyzing social media data.

Pre-trained Models: Pre-trained models such as BERT and RoBERTa (and their variants) have revolutionized sentiment analysis. These models are trained on vast amounts of text data and can be fine-tuned for specific tasks, making them powerful tools for sentiment analysis, even in challenging domains like social media.

Sentiment analysis is a powerful application of Natural Language Processing that has become essential in understanding public opinion, particularly on social media platforms. By analyzing sentiment, businesses can gain valuable insights into how customers feel about their products, services, or brands. However, the informal and noisy nature of social media data poses unique challenges for sentiment analysis, requiring advanced NLP techniques to achieve accurate results.

As machine learning and NLP technologies continue to evolve, sentiment analysis will play an even more critical role in understanding and responding to the opinions of customers and the public. By mastering sentiment analysis techniques, businesses can stay ahead of trends, respond to customer needs, and make data-driven decisions in an increasingly opinionated and connected world.

6.2 Text preprocessing (tokenization, stopwords, stemming)

Text preprocessing is a crucial step in any Natural Language Processing (NLP) project. Before diving into building and training sentiment analysis models, the raw text data needs to be processed in a way that makes it suitable for machine learning algorithms to understand. This process involves several key steps, each with a specific purpose, including tokenization, stopwords removal, and stemming.

In this sub-chapter, we will explore these text preprocessing steps in detail and explain their importance in the context of sentiment analysis on social media.

1. Tokenization

1.1 What is Tokenization?

Tokenization is the first step in text preprocessing and involves breaking down text into smaller, manageable pieces called tokens. These tokens could be words, sentences, or even characters, depending on the level of tokenization. In most cases, we perform word-level tokenization, where a sentence is split into its constituent words.

For example:

Sentence: "I love this product!"
Tokens: ['I', 'love', 'this', 'product']

Tokenization is crucial because machine learning algorithms do not understand raw text. By breaking the text into tokens, we can convert the input into a structured format that can be processed further.

1.2 Types of Tokenization

Word Tokenization: The most common type of tokenization is word-level tokenization, where the text is split into words based on spaces and punctuation. In Python, you can use libraries like NLTK or spaCy to tokenize text into words.

Sentence Tokenization: In some NLP tasks, we may want to tokenize text at the sentence level. This is useful for tasks like summarization or when analyzing the sentiment of individual sentences. Sentence tokenization splits text into discrete sentences using punctuation marks like periods or exclamation points.

Tokenization often involves dealing with punctuation, contractions (e.g., "don't" to "do" and "not"), and special characters, which should either be removed or handled appropriately to maintain clean data.

2. Stopwords Removal

2.1 What are Stopwords?

Stopwords are words that are considered insignificant in NLP tasks because they occur frequently in the language but do not carry meaningful information. Examples of stopwords include words like "the," "is," "in," "and," "to," "a," "of," etc.

For example:

Sentence: "I am learning Natural Language Processing."
Stopwords: ['I', 'am', 'learning', 'to']
Remaining words: ['Natural', 'Language', 'Processing']

The removal of stopwords helps reduce noise in the data and allows the algorithm to focus on more meaningful words, thereby improving model performance.

2.2 Why Remove Stopwords?

The removal of stopwords is particularly useful in sentiment analysis, where we aim to capture the sentiment conveyed by content-specific words (e.g., "happy," "angry," "love," "hate"). Words like "the," "of," and "is" are too common and unlikely to contribute any meaningful insight into the sentiment of the text. Therefore, removing stopwords helps in reducing the dimensionality of the data and streamlining the analysis process.

However, in some cases, stopwords may carry specific importance, depending on the context (e.g., in legal documents, "is" or "are" may be significant). In such cases, stopwords might not be removed.

2.3 Stopwords Removal Tools

NLTK: The Natural Language Toolkit (NLTK) in Python provides a built-in list of stopwords for several languages. It allows easy filtering of stopwords from a text corpus.

Example using NLTK to remove stopwords:

```
from nltk.corpus import stopwords
from nltk.tokenize import word_tokenize

stop_words = set(stopwords.words('english'))
text = "I love coding with Python!"
words = word_tokenize(text)
filtered_text = [word for word in words if word.lower() not in stop_words]
```

print(filtered_text)

Output: ['love', 'coding', 'Python']

spaCy: spaCy is another popular NLP library in Python that also comes with a pre-built list of stopwords and tools to filter them from text data.

3. Stemming

3.1 What is Stemming?

Stemming is the process of reducing words to their root form or stem. The goal of stemming is to remove suffixes and prefixes from words, leaving behind the base form. This is particularly important in sentiment analysis, where different forms of a word (e.g., "run," "running," "runner") might express the same underlying concept.

For example:

Word: "running"
Stemmed form: "run"

Stemming helps to standardize words that are linguistically related, reducing the complexity of the dataset and improving the performance of machine learning models.

3.2 Why is Stemming Important?

In sentiment analysis, it is important to capture the underlying meaning of words without worrying about their different forms. For instance, the words "happy," "happiness," and "happily" all express the same sentiment. Stemming consolidates these words into a single root form, which reduces the number of unique tokens in the dataset and helps the model focus on the actual sentiment, rather than variations of the same word.

Stemming is a relatively simple technique, and it works well in many NLP tasks, but it can sometimes lead to the creation of non-dictionary words, which can affect readability and accuracy. For example, "better" may be reduced to "bet," which can alter its meaning.

3.3 Common Stemming Algorithms

Porter Stemmer: The Porter Stemmer is one of the most widely used stemming algorithms. It applies a series of rules to remove suffixes from words. For example, it reduces "happily" to "happi" and "running" to "run."

Lancaster Stemmer: The Lancaster Stemmer is another popular algorithm. It is more aggressive than the Porter Stemmer and can reduce words like "better" to "bet."

Snowball Stemmer: The Snowball Stemmer is a more advanced version of the Porter Stemmer, designed to be more efficient and produce better results for multiple languages.

3.4 Stemming in Python with NLTK

You can easily perform stemming using NLTK's built-in stemmers. Here's an example of how to use the Porter Stemmer:

```
from nltk.stem import PorterStemmer

stemmer = PorterStemmer()
word = "running"
stemmed_word = stemmer.stem(word)
print(stemmed_word)  # Output: run
```

4. Lemmatization vs. Stemming

While both stemming and lemmatization aim to reduce words to their base form, lemmatization is a more advanced technique. Unlike stemming, which often results in non-dictionary words, lemmatization reduces a word to its lemma, which is the word's dictionary form. For example, "better" becomes "good," and "running" becomes "run" in lemmatization.

Lemmatization requires knowledge of the word's part of speech, making it more computationally expensive than stemming but generally more accurate in preserving meaning.

In this sub-chapter, we've explored essential text preprocessing techniques for sentiment analysis on social media: tokenization, stopwords removal, and stemming. These steps are critical for transforming raw, unstructured text into a format that can be processed by machine learning algorithms.

By breaking text into tokens, removing unimportant words, and reducing words to their root forms, we streamline the analysis and improve the accuracy of sentiment analysis models. These preprocessing steps are foundational for building robust models that can analyze social media content and extract meaningful insights regarding public sentiment.

In the next steps, these preprocessed texts can be vectorized, passed through machine learning models, and used to predict sentiment effectively. With the increasing volume of social media data, these techniques are essential in making sense of textual data and driving actionable insights for businesses and organizations.

6.3 Implementing TF-IDF and word embeddings

In the realm of Natural Language Processing (NLP), transforming text data into numerical representations that machine learning models can understand is a critical step. Among the most effective techniques for achieving this transformation are Term Frequency-Inverse Document Frequency (TF-IDF) and Word Embeddings. Both methods aim to capture the meaning of words in a form suitable for use in various NLP tasks, including sentiment analysis on social media.

In this sub-chapter, we will dive into these two powerful text vectorization methods, explaining how they work, when to use them, and how to implement them in your NLP pipeline.

1. TF-IDF (Term Frequency-Inverse Document Frequency)

1.1 What is TF-IDF?

TF-IDF is a statistical measure used to evaluate the importance of a word in a document relative to a corpus (a collection of documents). It helps transform text into a meaningful numerical representation that emphasizes more relevant words while de-emphasizing less important ones.

TF-IDF is composed of two components:

Term Frequency (TF): This measures how frequently a word appears in a document. The more often a word appears in a document, the higher its term frequency.

$$TF(t, d) = \frac{\text{Number of times term t appears in document d}}{\text{Total number of terms in document d}}$$

Inverse Document Frequency (IDF): This measures how important a term is across all documents in the corpus. Words that appear frequently across all documents are less important, while words that appear in only a few documents are considered more significant.

$$IDF(t, D) = \log \left(\frac{\text{Total number of documents}}{\text{Number of documents containing term t}} \right)$$

TF-IDF: Finally, the TF-IDF score is the product of the TF and IDF values, providing a measure of how important a word is within a specific document in the context of the entire corpus.

$$\text{TF-IDF}(t, d, D) = TF(t, d) \times IDF(t, D)$$

1.2 Why TF-IDF?

TF-IDF is particularly useful for text classification tasks such as sentiment analysis, as it allows us to focus on words that provide the most information about a document, discarding words that are too common (like "the," "is," "in," etc.). It effectively captures word importance, considering both their frequency within individual documents and their rarity across the corpus.

For example, in sentiment analysis, words like "excellent" or "terrible" will likely have higher TF-IDF scores in product reviews, since they provide strong signals of positive or negative sentiment. On the other hand, words like "the," "and," or "of" will have low scores and can be safely ignored.

1.3 Implementing TF-IDF in Python

In Python, scikit-learn provides a straightforward implementation of TF-IDF. Here's how you can use it to convert a set of documents into TF-IDF vectors:

from sklearn.feature_extraction.text import TfidfVectorizer

```
# Sample corpus
documents = [
    "I love programming in Python.",
    "Python programming is great for data science.",
    "I enjoy learning new programming languages."
]

# Initialize the TF-IDF vectorizer
tfidf_vectorizer = TfidfVectorizer()

# Fit and transform the corpus
tfidf_matrix = tfidf_vectorizer.fit_transform(documents)

# View the resulting TF-IDF matrix
print(tfidf_matrix.toarray())

# View feature names (words)
print(tfidf_vectorizer.get_feature_names_out())
```

Output Example:

The matrix will contain the TF-IDF values for each word in the documents, with rows representing documents and columns representing words. For example, the word "Python" will have a higher score in the second document because it appears more frequently there.

2. Word Embeddings

2.1 What are Word Embeddings?

Word embeddings are a type of representation that captures the meaning of words in a dense vector space, where words with similar meanings are represented by similar vectors. Unlike TF-IDF, which is a sparse representation based on frequency counts, word embeddings are continuous and capture semantic relationships between words.

For example, in a well-trained word embedding space, the words "king" and "queen" would have vectors that are closer to each other than to the vector for "dog" or "car," reflecting their similar meanings and relationships in the English language.

2.2 Popular Word Embedding Models

Several models have been developed to learn word embeddings from large text corpora:

Word2Vec: Developed by Google, Word2Vec uses shallow neural networks to learn word representations based on context. There are two primary approaches in Word2Vec:

CBOW (Continuous Bag of Words): Predicts the target word given a context (surrounding words).

Skip-gram: Predicts the context given a target word.

GloVe (Global Vectors for Word Representation): Developed by Stanford, GloVe creates word vectors based on the frequency of word co-occurrence across a large corpus. Unlike Word2Vec, which is predictive, GloVe is based on matrix factorization techniques.

FastText: An extension of Word2Vec, developed by Facebook, that represents words as bags of character n-grams. This makes FastText more effective at handling out-of-vocabulary (OOV) words or rare words.

BERT (Bidirectional Encoder Representations from Transformers): A transformer-based model developed by Google that generates contextualized word embeddings, meaning it can generate different embeddings for the same word based on its context in the sentence. This is particularly useful for tasks like sentiment analysis, where context matters.

2.3 Why Word Embeddings?

Word embeddings are superior to TF-IDF in many situations because they capture the semantic meaning of words, allowing algorithms to understand nuances in language. For sentiment analysis, word embeddings can recognize that "awesome" and "fantastic" have similar meanings, while also understanding that "awful" and "terrible" are negative words. This ability to model relationships between words is essential for effective sentiment analysis, where subtle distinctions between words can have a significant impact on the overall sentiment.

Unlike TF-IDF, word embeddings are more compact and dense. TF-IDF vectors are often sparse and high-dimensional (especially for large vocabularies), while word embeddings offer a much lower-dimensional, dense representation.

2.4 Implementing Word Embeddings in Python

Using pre-trained word embeddings like Word2Vec or GloVe is a common approach to incorporate word vectors into sentiment analysis. Here's an example of how you can use Gensim's Word2Vec model to load pre-trained word embeddings:

```python
from gensim.models import KeyedVectors

# Load pre-trained Word2Vec model (you can use GloVe or FastText similarly)
model = KeyedVectors.load_word2vec_format('GoogleNews-vectors-negative300.bin', binary=True)

# Find the vector for a word
vector = model['python']
print(vector)

# Find similarity between two words
similarity = model.similarity('python', 'programming')
print(similarity)
```

In this example, the Google News Word2Vec model is used, which contains word vectors for 3 million words trained on a large corpus of Google News data.

3. TF-IDF vs. Word Embeddings

Both TF-IDF and word embeddings are used to represent text numerically, but they have key differences:

TF-IDF is a statistical approach based on word frequency and document importance, suitable for tasks where word occurrence is a strong indicator of meaning. It's simple, interpretable, and effective when context is less important.

Word embeddings, on the other hand, are dense, continuous vector representations that capture the semantic meaning of words. They are ideal for tasks where context and word relationships are important, such as sentiment analysis.

TF-IDF works best for tasks where the presence or absence of specific words is important, such as in document classification or spam detection. Word embeddings excel in tasks like sentiment analysis, where the meaning and relationship of words within the context of the sentence matter more.

Both TF-IDF and word embeddings are indispensable tools in the world of text processing for NLP tasks like sentiment analysis. TF-IDF is simple and efficient, especially for sparse data, while word embeddings provide a richer, more nuanced representation of text, capturing word meanings and relationships.

When performing sentiment analysis on social media or other textual data, choosing between TF-IDF and word embeddings depends on the nature of the task, the amount of data available, and the importance of semantic relationships in the analysis. In many advanced sentiment analysis projects, a combination of both methods—such as using TF-IDF features alongside word embeddings—can help improve the model's performance.

6.4 Training ML models for sentiment classification

In sentiment analysis, the goal is to automatically classify text into predefined sentiment categories, such as positive, negative, or neutral. For example, in a social media context, we might want to classify tweets as expressing positive, negative, or neutral sentiments toward a specific topic. Training a machine learning (ML) model for sentiment classification involves several key steps, including selecting the appropriate model, training it on labeled data, and evaluating its performance.

In this sub-chapter, we will walk through the process of training ML models for sentiment classification using techniques such as logistic regression, support vector machines (SVMs), naive Bayes, and deep learning models. We will also discuss the key steps of data preparation, feature extraction, model selection, and evaluation.

1. Preparing the Data

Before training any machine learning model, it is essential to prepare your data. This includes gathering labeled sentiment data, preprocessing it, and extracting useful features from the text.

1.1 Labeled Data

Sentiment analysis models require labeled datasets, where each instance (text) is associated with a sentiment label. For example:

Positive: "I love this product!"
Negative: "This product is terrible."
Neutral: "The product is okay."

There are several publicly available sentiment datasets you can use for training models, such as:

- **IMDb Movie Reviews**: Contains positive and negative reviews.
- **Twitter Sentiment Analysis Dataset**: Contains tweets labeled with sentiments.
- **Amazon Product Reviews**: Provides reviews and corresponding ratings, which can be used for sentiment classification.

If labeled data is not readily available, you may need to collect and label your own data manually or use unsupervised methods to automatically label the data.

1.2 Preprocessing the Data

Once the data is collected, you need to preprocess it before training. This involves tasks such as:

- **Tokenization**: Splitting the text into tokens (words or sentences).
- **Stopword Removal**: Eliminating common words (e.g., "the," "is," "in") that do not contribute much to sentiment.
- **Lowercasing**: Converting all text to lowercase to avoid treating the same word as different due to case sensitivity.
- **Stemming/Lemmatization**: Reducing words to their root form (e.g., "running" to "run").
- **Vectorization**: Converting text into numerical representations using techniques like TF-IDF or word embeddings.

These steps help to transform the raw text into a structured format that can be input into a machine learning model.

2. Feature Extraction for Sentiment Analysis

Machine learning algorithms cannot process raw text, so we need to convert text data into numerical vectors that can represent the content of the text. There are two main approaches for feature extraction in sentiment analysis:

2.1 TF-IDF Vectorization

As discussed earlier, TF-IDF (Term Frequency-Inverse Document Frequency) is a commonly used method for transforming text data into numerical vectors. Each word in the text is assigned a weight that reflects its importance in the given document and across the entire corpus. This method works well for capturing the importance of words in the context of the document.

2.2 Word Embeddings

Alternatively, you can use word embeddings, such as Word2Vec, GloVe, or fastText, to convert words into continuous vector representations. Word embeddings capture the semantic relationships between words, meaning that words with similar meanings will have similar vector representations. Word embeddings are often used when you need more contextual understanding of the text and are especially useful when dealing with large datasets and complex language.

In both cases, the goal is to convert each document (e.g., a sentence or tweet) into a fixed-length vector that represents the important features of the text.

3. Selecting and Training ML Models

With the features extracted from the text data, the next step is to train a machine learning model. Below are some of the most popular ML algorithms used for sentiment classification:

3.1 Logistic Regression

Logistic Regression is a simple and effective classification algorithm often used for binary sentiment classification (positive vs. negative). It works well with TF-IDF features and can be extended to multi-class classification for tasks such as positive, neutral, and negative sentiment classification.

Here's an example of using Logistic Regression for sentiment classification with TF-IDF features:

```
from sklearn.model_selection import train_test_split
from sklearn.feature_extraction.text import TfidfVectorizer
from sklearn.linear_model import LogisticRegression
from sklearn.metrics import accuracy_score, classification_report
```

```
# Sample corpus and labels
corpus = ["I love this product!", "This is terrible.", "Best purchase I've made."]
labels = [1, 0, 1]  # 1: Positive, 0: Negative

# Split the dataset
X_train, X_test, y_train, y_test = train_test_split(corpus, labels, test_size=0.2,
random_state=42)

# TF-IDF Vectorization
vectorizer = TfidfVectorizer()
X_train_tfidf = vectorizer.fit_transform(X_train)
X_test_tfidf = vectorizer.transform(X_test)

# Train Logistic Regression
model = LogisticRegression()
model.fit(X_train_tfidf, y_train)

# Predict on test data
y_pred = model.predict(X_test_tfidf)

# Evaluate the model
print("Accuracy:", accuracy_score(y_test, y_pred))
print("Classification Report:")
print(classification_report(y_test, y_pred))
```

Logistic regression provides an easy-to-interpret model and is a good baseline for sentiment analysis tasks.

3.2 Support Vector Machines (SVM)

Support Vector Machines are powerful classifiers that are particularly effective in high-dimensional spaces, such as text data. SVM tries to find a hyperplane that maximizes the margin between classes, making it a robust model for sentiment analysis, especially when the data is not linearly separable.

Here's an example of training an SVM classifier for sentiment classification:

```
from sklearn.svm import SVC
```

```
# Train SVM model
svm_model = SVC(kernel='linear')
svm_model.fit(X_train_tfidf, y_train)

# Predict on test data
y_pred_svm = svm_model.predict(X_test_tfidf)

# Evaluate the model
print("Accuracy:", accuracy_score(y_test, y_pred_svm))
print("Classification Report:")
print(classification_report(y_test, y_pred_svm))
```

SVM is effective for high-dimensional feature spaces, like those generated by TF-IDF, and works well in many sentiment analysis tasks.

3.3 Naive Bayes

Naive Bayes is a probabilistic classifier based on Bayes' Theorem, commonly used for text classification. It assumes that the features (words) are independent given the class, making it simple yet effective for sentiment classification tasks, especially with smaller datasets.

Here's an example of using Naive Bayes for sentiment classification:

```
from sklearn.naive_bayes import MultinomialNB

# Train Naive Bayes model
nb_model = MultinomialNB()
nb_model.fit(X_train_tfidf, y_train)

# Predict on test data
y_pred_nb = nb_model.predict(X_test_tfidf)

# Evaluate the model
print("Accuracy:", accuracy_score(y_test, y_pred_nb))
print("Classification Report:")
print(classification_report(y_test, y_pred_nb))
```

Naive Bayes works well when the features are not highly correlated and is particularly fast to train.

3.4 Deep Learning Models (LSTM, CNN)

For more complex sentiment analysis tasks, especially when working with large datasets, deep learning models like Long Short-Term Memory (LSTM) networks and Convolutional Neural Networks (CNNs) have shown great performance. These models can capture long-term dependencies in text data and understand complex language patterns.

3.5 Hyperparameter Tuning

Regardless of the model, tuning hyperparameters can significantly improve performance. Techniques like grid search or random search can help you find the optimal hyperparameters for your model. For example, tuning the regularization strength in logistic regression or the kernel parameters in SVMs can improve your model's accuracy.

4. Evaluating the Model

Once you have trained your sentiment classification model, it's essential to evaluate its performance using metrics like accuracy, precision, recall, and F1-score. These metrics help you understand how well the model is classifying sentiment:

- **Accuracy**: The proportion of correctly predicted instances.
- **Precision**: The proportion of true positive predictions out of all positive predictions.
- **Recall**: The proportion of true positive predictions out of all actual positives.
- **F1-score**: The harmonic mean of precision and recall.

The confusion matrix can also provide a visual representation of how well your model is performing by showing the number of true positives, false positives, true negatives, and false negatives.

Training machine learning models for sentiment classification involves several key steps: preparing the data, selecting an appropriate model, and evaluating the performance. Whether you choose traditional models like logistic regression, SVM, or Naive Bayes, or move to more advanced deep learning techniques, the ability to classify sentiment accurately can offer significant insights, especially in contexts like social media, customer feedback, and brand monitoring.

By understanding the basics of machine learning models for sentiment analysis and leveraging powerful feature extraction methods like TF-IDF and word embeddings, you can develop robust models that accurately predict sentiment in text data.

6.5 Deploying as a Twitter sentiment analysis app

Deploying a machine learning model as a web application is an essential step to making your project accessible to users and allowing them to interact with it. In this sub-chapter, we will walk you through deploying a sentiment analysis model for Twitter data using Flask, a lightweight Python web framework, and demonstrate how to interact with the model via a simple web application.

This example will show how to create a web-based sentiment analysis tool that allows users to input a Twitter username, fetch recent tweets, and analyze the sentiment of those tweets in real time. We'll break the process down into clear steps: preparing the model, setting up the Flask application, integrating Twitter API access, and deploying the application.

1. Preparing the Sentiment Analysis Model

Before deploying your model, you need to ensure that it is fully trained and ready for predictions. In the previous sections, we explored how to train sentiment analysis models using TF-IDF and machine learning algorithms like Logistic Regression or Random Forest. Once you have your trained model, the next step is to save it so that it can be used for prediction during deployment.

In Python, you can save your trained models using libraries such as joblib or pickle. Here's an example of how to save your trained model using joblib:

import joblib

 # Assuming your model is trained and stored in a variable called 'model'
joblib.dump(model, 'sentiment_model.pkl')

You can later load this model during the Flask app runtime to make predictions.

2. Setting Up the Flask Application

Now that we have our sentiment analysis model ready, we can begin building the Flask application to serve it to users. Flask is an excellent choice because it's lightweight and simple to set up for small projects like this one. You will also need Flask-Cors to allow cross-origin requests if you're running the app from a different domain.

2.1 Install Dependencies

To get started, you'll need to install Flask and other dependencies:

pip install flask flask-cors tweepy joblib

- **Flask**: The web framework for creating the API and serving the app.
- **Flask-Cors**: For handling cross-origin resource sharing (CORS) issues.
- **Tweepy**: For interacting with the Twitter API to fetch tweets.
- **Joblib**: To load the trained machine learning model.

2.2 Create the Flask Application

Next, create a file called app.py and set up the basic Flask application. This will include loading your pre-trained sentiment analysis model, connecting to the Twitter API, and defining routes for handling user input.

```
from flask import Flask, request, jsonify
from flask_cors import CORS
import tweepy
import joblib
import re
import string

# Initialize Flask app
app = Flask(__name__)
CORS(app)

# Load the pre-trained sentiment analysis model
model = joblib.load('sentiment_model.pkl')

# Twitter API credentials (use your own credentials from Twitter Developer Account)
consumer_key = 'YOUR_CONSUMER_KEY'
consumer_secret = 'YOUR_CONSUMER_SECRET'
access_token = 'YOUR_ACCESS_TOKEN'
access_token_secret = 'YOUR_ACCESS_TOKEN_SECRET'

# Authenticate to the Twitter API
auth = tweepy.OAuthHandler(consumer_key, consumer_secret)
```

```python
auth.set_access_token(access_token, access_token_secret)
api = tweepy.API(auth)

# Function to preprocess text (same as we did during training)
def preprocess_text(text):
    text = text.lower()
    text = re.sub(r'http\S+', '', text)  # Remove URLs
    text = re.sub(r'@\S+', '', text)  # Remove mentions
    text = re.sub(r'#\S+', '', text)  # Remove hashtags
    text = re.sub(r'[^a-zA-Z\s]', '', text)  # Remove non-alphabet characters
    return text

# Route to handle sentiment analysis of tweets
@app.route('/analyze', methods=['GET'])
def analyze_sentiment():
    # Get Twitter username from the query string
    username = request.args.get('username', None)

    if not username:
        return jsonify({"error": "Please provide a Twitter username"}), 400

    try:
        # Fetch the latest 10 tweets from the user's timeline
        tweets = api.user_timeline(screen_name=username, count=10,
tweet_mode='extended')
        tweet_texts = [tweet.full_text for tweet in tweets]

        # Preprocess the tweets and make predictions
        cleaned_tweets = [preprocess_text(tweet) for tweet in tweet_texts]

        # Convert the cleaned text to TF-IDF features (assuming the model was trained
with TF-IDF)
        tfidf_vectorizer = joblib.load('tfidf_vectorizer.pkl')  # Load the TF-IDF vectorizer
        tweet_features = tfidf_vectorizer.transform(cleaned_tweets)

        # Predict sentiment (Assume binary classification: 0 = Negative, 1 = Positive)
        predictions = model.predict(tweet_features)

        # Create a response dictionary with tweet text and sentiment
        response = [{"tweet": tweet, "sentiment": "Positive" if pred == 1 else "Negative"}
```

```
                 for tweet, pred in zip(tweet_texts, predictions)]

        return jsonify(response)

    except tweepy.TweepError as e:
        return jsonify({"error": f"Failed to fetch tweets: {str(e)}"}), 500

# Run the Flask app
if __name__ == '__main__':
    app.run(debug=True)
```

2.3 Explanation of Code

- **Twitter Authentication**: The Tweepy library is used to authenticate and interact with the Twitter API. You'll need to create a Twitter Developer account and obtain your API keys and tokens to access Twitter data.
- **Text Preprocessing**: The preprocess_text function removes URLs, mentions, hashtags, and non-alphabetic characters from the tweets, similar to what we did when training the model.
- **Sentiment Prediction**: The /analyze route takes the Twitter username as input, fetches the latest tweets, preprocesses them, converts them into features using the TF-IDF vectorizer, and then predicts the sentiment using the trained machine learning model.
- **Response Format**: The app returns the original tweets along with their predicted sentiment (positive or negative) in a JSON format.

3. Testing the App Locally

Once your Flask app is set up, you can test it locally by running the following command in your terminal:

```
python app.py
```

This will start a local server (typically on http://127.0.0.1:5000/), and you can make GET requests to the /analyze route with a Twitter username.

For example, to analyze the sentiment of tweets from a user called elonmusk, you can open a browser or use Postman to visit:

```
http://127.0.0.1:5000/analyze?username=elonmusk
```

The response will contain the tweets and their sentiment:

```
[
    {"tweet": "I love Tesla's new battery tech!", "sentiment": "Positive"},
    {"tweet": "SpaceX is a game changer!", "sentiment": "Positive"},
    ...
]
```

4. Deploying the App to the Cloud

To make the app accessible to users globally, you need to deploy it to a cloud service. Popular options include Heroku, AWS, and Google Cloud. For simplicity, we will deploy the app to Heroku:

4.1 Create a Procfile

To deploy to Heroku, you need a Procfile that tells Heroku how to run your app. In the root directory of your project, create a Procfile with the following content:

web: python app.py

4.2 Deploy to Heroku

Follow these steps to deploy to Heroku:

- Install the Heroku CLI: Heroku CLI Installation
- Log in to Heroku: heroku login
- Initialize a Git repository if you haven't already: git init
- Create a new Heroku app: heroku create
- Push the code to Heroku: git push heroku master

Heroku will automatically detect your Python app and install the necessary dependencies listed in requirements.txt. After deployment, Heroku will provide a URL where your app is live.

In this section, we've covered how to deploy a Twitter sentiment analysis application using Flask. By integrating the Tweepy library for fetching tweets and leveraging a trained sentiment analysis model, you can create a real-time, interactive application that analyzes

Twitter data. Deploying this application on platforms like Heroku makes it accessible to users, enabling you to share your machine learning models with the world.

This deployment process can be adapted for other use cases as well, such as analyzing product reviews, customer feedback, or any other textual data where sentiment classification is valuable.

7. Fraud Detection in Financial Transactions

In this chapter, we tackle the critical problem of fraud detection in financial transactions using machine learning. Fraud detection requires identifying anomalous patterns in large volumes of transaction data, often with highly imbalanced datasets. You'll learn how to use unsupervised learning techniques like Isolation Forest and Autoencoders, as well as supervised models like Random Forests and Gradient Boosting, to detect fraudulent activities. We'll cover essential topics such as feature engineering, handling imbalanced classes, and evaluating model performance with metrics like precision, recall, and ROC-AUC. By the end of this project, you will have a robust fraud detection system capable of identifying suspicious behavior in real-time, enhancing security and preventing financial losses. 💳

7.1 Understanding fraud detection challenges

Fraud detection in financial transactions is one of the most critical applications of machine learning (ML) in real-world settings. As the digital landscape expands, fraudsters continuously develop more sophisticated methods to exploit vulnerabilities in financial systems, posing significant threats to businesses, consumers, and the overall integrity of financial systems. Despite advancements in technology and the growth of machine learning tools, detecting fraudulent transactions remains an ongoing challenge. In this section, we will delve into the main challenges associated with fraud detection, explore how they impact financial institutions, and discuss the unique characteristics of financial data that complicate the development of effective fraud detection models.

1. The Evolving Nature of Fraud

One of the most significant challenges in fraud detection is the constantly evolving tactics employed by fraudsters. Fraud is not a static problem; it evolves as quickly as new security measures and machine learning models are implemented. Criminals are often quick to identify and exploit weaknesses in financial systems, adapting their strategies to bypass traditional rule-based systems or even machine learning models.

For example, fraudsters may use stolen payment information to make small, seemingly legitimate transactions to avoid triggering fraud detection systems. Over time, these techniques can become more sophisticated, utilizing identity theft, social engineering, and account takeover strategies that may evade detection by traditional methods. This dynamic and evolving nature of fraud is one of the primary reasons that fraud detection systems need to be continually updated and refined. Building a model that can adapt to new fraud patterns is one of the most significant challenges faced by machine learning practitioners working in this space.

2. Imbalanced Data

A core challenge in fraud detection lies in the imbalanced nature of the data. In a typical financial transaction dataset, fraudulent transactions make up only a tiny fraction of the total number of transactions. This extreme class imbalance creates significant challenges when training machine learning models. Standard algorithms often struggle to detect fraud because they are biased toward predicting the majority class (non-fraudulent transactions) simply due to its overwhelming presence in the dataset.

This imbalance results in a high number of false negatives (non-fraudulent transactions incorrectly classified as fraudulent) and an overrepresentation of true negatives (genuine transactions marked as legitimate). Additionally, due to the scarcity of fraudulent transactions in comparison to the legitimate ones, models may not get enough examples of fraud to learn from, making it difficult to generalize well to new, unseen fraudulent behaviors.

Several techniques can be used to handle this issue, such as undersampling, oversampling, SMOTE (Synthetic Minority Over-sampling Technique), or using algorithms designed specifically for imbalanced data, like Random Forests and XGBoost. However, despite these methods, the imbalance problem remains a significant hurdle that requires careful consideration during model training.

3. Lack of Labeled Data

For supervised learning techniques to work effectively in fraud detection, a large amount of labeled data is required. This data should ideally consist of transactions that are clearly labeled as either fraudulent or non-fraudulent. However, one of the major challenges in the domain of fraud detection is the lack of comprehensive labeled datasets.

Financial institutions and organizations may have an extensive amount of transactional data, but labeling these transactions accurately is often time-consuming, costly, and prone to human error. Additionally, fraud detection models rely on accurately identifying instances of fraud, which can be complicated due to the ever-changing tactics used by fraudsters. As a result, many datasets may have incomplete or ambiguous labels, which can reduce the effectiveness of the model. This challenge also extends to the process of annotating new data after the system has been deployed. Continuous monitoring and labeling of transactions are essential for maintaining an up-to-date and accurate model, but they require substantial human resources and time.

To overcome this challenge, unsupervised or semi-supervised learning methods can be useful, as they do not require labeled data. Anomaly detection, for instance, can help identify suspicious transactions by flagging those that deviate significantly from normal patterns. However, this approach is not without its challenges, and combining supervised and unsupervised learning techniques might offer a more comprehensive solution.

4. Feature Engineering and Data Complexity

Another challenge is the complexity of the data itself. In fraud detection, transactions are not isolated events. They occur within a broader context of customer behavior, including historical transactions, geolocation, device information, and account usage patterns. Identifying which features (or variables) are the most relevant to detecting fraud is a difficult and ongoing task.

Commonly used features for fraud detection include:

- **Transaction Amount**: Extremely high or low transaction amounts may indicate fraudulent activity.
- **Transaction Frequency**: Multiple transactions in a short period can signal potential fraud.
- **Location**: A transaction occurring in a location far from the customer's typical geographic area could be suspicious.
- **Device Information**: Fraudsters often use different devices to execute fraudulent transactions. Identifying discrepancies in device usage is important.

However, this list is far from exhaustive, and the variety of features available across different datasets can be overwhelming. Feature engineering becomes a key aspect of fraud detection because the choice of features directly impacts the performance of machine learning models. Fraud detection systems must be able to handle multidimensional and heterogeneous data, which includes numerical, categorical, and textual information. Additionally, time-series data, such as transaction timestamps, is another layer of complexity that must be managed effectively.

Effective feature engineering can involve transforming raw data into meaningful attributes, aggregating data over time, and identifying patterns of behavior that may signal fraud. Time windows and rolling averages are commonly used methods in feature extraction for fraud detection, as they help to capture patterns in transaction frequency and amounts over specific time periods.

5. Real-Time Processing and Latency

Fraud detection systems must be able to process transactions in real time to prevent financial loss. Delays in detecting fraudulent transactions can have devastating consequences for financial institutions, as well as for the customers affected by the fraud. For this reason, the ability to make accurate, timely predictions is paramount.

Machine learning models need to be integrated with transaction processing systems in real-time. This creates another challenge—handling large volumes of data and making predictions quickly without causing delays or latency in the transaction process. Financial institutions must strike a delicate balance between model accuracy and the ability to provide immediate feedback. Fraud detection systems are expected to flag potentially fraudulent transactions without slowing down the user experience or creating friction in the payment process.

One solution to mitigate latency is to use online learning or incremental learning techniques, where the model is trained continuously, learning from new data as it arrives. This approach can help improve both the performance and responsiveness of the fraud detection system.

6. Interpretability and Explainability

Machine learning models, particularly complex ones like neural networks and ensemble methods (e.g., Random Forests or XGBoost), are often criticized for being "black boxes." That is, their decision-making process is not easily interpretable or understandable by humans. In fraud detection, especially when the model flags a transaction as fraudulent, it is crucial for financial institutions to understand why the model made that decision.

Regulatory frameworks and internal auditing often require transparency in how models arrive at predictions. This explains why fraud detection models need to not only be accurate but also interpretable. In particular, financial institutions must be able to explain flagged transactions to stakeholders, customers, and regulators, which calls for models with transparent decision-making.

Tools like SHAP (SHapley Additive exPlanations) and LIME (Local Interpretable Model-Agnostic Explanations) are widely used to interpret complex models. They help highlight which features most influenced a particular prediction, offering insights that can improve model trust and compliance.

Fraud detection in financial transactions presents a set of unique challenges that require sophisticated machine learning models and approaches. From the evolving tactics used by fraudsters to the imbalanced, noisy, and complex nature of the data, the landscape for fraud detection is dynamic and ever-changing. Addressing these challenges requires ongoing refinement of models, an understanding of the limitations of data, and the careful balance of accuracy and real-time processing. As financial systems continue to digitize, the role of machine learning in fraud detection will only grow, offering an opportunity to enhance security, build trust, and reduce fraud-related losses.

7.2 Data imbalance and handling rare events

One of the most pressing challenges in fraud detection is the imbalance of data. Fraudulent transactions typically make up a very small fraction of total transactions, often less than 1%. This class imbalance presents a significant obstacle for machine learning models, as they are often biased toward predicting the majority class (non-fraudulent transactions). In this section, we will explore the impact of data imbalance on fraud detection systems and delve into strategies for handling rare events like fraudulent transactions to improve model accuracy and efficiency.

1. The Nature of Data Imbalance in Fraud Detection

Data imbalance is a fundamental challenge in fraud detection. In any financial system, the number of legitimate transactions far exceeds fraudulent transactions. The stark imbalance in the classes creates a situation where the model encounters far more "non-fraudulent" examples than "fraudulent" examples during training. As a result, traditional machine learning algorithms tend to be biased toward predicting the majority class (non-fraudulent transactions) and often fail to adequately detect rare fraudulent events.

For instance, let's consider a dataset where only 0.1% of transactions are fraudulent. If the model simply learns to predict "non-fraudulent" for every transaction, it would achieve an overall accuracy of 99.9%. While this accuracy seems impressive, the model would be ineffective in identifying fraud, which is the main objective. Therefore, traditional accuracy is not a reliable metric for evaluating fraud detection models. A more insightful approach involves focusing on metrics that account for the detection of rare events, such as Precision, Recall, and F1-Score.

The key issue here is that fraud detection is a rare event detection problem, where the goal is to identify the small percentage of fraudulent transactions while minimizing false negatives (i.e., non-fraudulent transactions wrongly classified as fraudulent).

2. Consequences of Class Imbalance

The class imbalance in fraud detection systems can result in several detrimental outcomes:

High False Negative Rate: Since fraudulent transactions are rare, models can easily predict all transactions as non-fraudulent. However, this leads to a high number of false negatives, meaning that fraudulent transactions are not detected and processed properly.

Skewed Model Performance: Machine learning models tend to perform poorly on rare events due to the overrepresentation of the majority class in the training data. This reduces the model's ability to generalize to unseen fraud cases.

Ineffective Evaluation Metrics: In an imbalanced dataset, relying on accuracy alone to evaluate a model is misleading. As discussed earlier, a model that predicts every transaction as legitimate can still appear accurate, but it wouldn't fulfill the purpose of fraud detection.

3. Strategies for Handling Imbalanced Data

To overcome these challenges, a variety of techniques can be employed to handle imbalanced datasets and improve the performance of fraud detection models. These strategies can be categorized into data-level techniques (modifying the dataset) and algorithm-level techniques (modifying the learning process).

3.1 Resampling Techniques

Resampling involves modifying the dataset to address class imbalance by either reducing the majority class (undersampling) or increasing the minority class (oversampling). Both techniques aim to balance the class distribution and allow the model to learn more effectively from rare events.

Oversampling the Minority Class (Fraudulent Transactions): In this approach, we duplicate or synthetically generate fraudulent transactions to increase the proportion of fraud instances. SMOTE (Synthetic Minority Over-sampling Technique) is a popular method that creates synthetic examples of the minority class by interpolating between existing data points. This helps provide a more balanced representation of both classes, allowing the model to focus on detecting fraud.

Undersampling the Majority Class (Non-fraudulent Transactions): Alternatively, undersampling reduces the number of non-fraudulent transactions to match the number of fraudulent transactions. However, this approach risks losing valuable information about legitimate transactions. If the undersampling is too aggressive, the model may not learn enough about normal transaction behavior.

Hybrid Approaches: A combination of oversampling and undersampling can be used to mitigate the drawbacks of each individual approach, balancing the dataset without excessively distorting either class.

3.2 Cost-Sensitive Learning

Rather than resampling the data, cost-sensitive learning adjusts the learning process to make the model more sensitive to rare events. In this approach, different costs are assigned to false positives (non-fraudulent transactions flagged as fraudulent) and false negatives (fraudulent transactions classified as legitimate). The model is then trained to minimize these costs rather than traditional classification errors.

For example, fraudulent transactions could be assigned a higher cost, reflecting the higher importance of correctly detecting fraud. This approach encourages the model to prioritize minimizing false negatives, thus improving the detection of fraudulent transactions.

Cost-sensitive learning techniques can be implemented using cost-sensitive classifiers (like Cost-Sensitive SVMs) or by modifying the loss function during training to account for the unequal cost of errors.

3.3 Anomaly Detection

Anomaly detection is an approach that doesn't explicitly rely on a labeled dataset. Instead, it focuses on identifying rare or abnormal patterns in the data that deviate from the norm. Fraudulent transactions, by nature, are anomalies—they deviate from the usual patterns of consumer behavior.

Algorithms for anomaly detection include:

- **Isolation Forest**: A popular algorithm that isolates anomalies instead of profiling normal data points.
- **One-Class SVM**: A model that learns the boundaries of the normal class and flags anything outside as anomalous.
- **Autoencoders**: Neural networks designed to learn compressed representations of normal transactions, which can then be used to identify anomalies based on reconstruction errors.

Anomaly detection works well in situations where fraud is not easily definable by specific features or when labeled data is scarce. However, its effectiveness depends heavily on the ability to characterize "normal" transactions accurately.

3.4 Ensemble Methods

Ensemble methods combine multiple models to improve predictive performance. In fraud detection, ensemble learning methods like Random Forests, Boosting (e.g., XGBoost, LightGBM), and Bagging can be very effective for handling imbalanced datasets.

Random Forests: This ensemble method works by building multiple decision trees and combining their results. Random Forests can handle imbalanced datasets well, as each individual tree can focus on different parts of the feature space, thus improving the overall robustness and generalization of the model.

Boosting: Boosting methods like XGBoost and LightGBM build models sequentially, with each new model correcting the errors of the previous one. These methods tend to perform well on imbalanced datasets because they place more emphasis on misclassified instances (i.e., fraudulent transactions).

Ensemble methods help in reducing variance and bias, and when combined with strategies like cost-sensitive learning or resampling, they become highly effective at detecting fraud.

4. Evaluation Metrics for Imbalanced Data

As mentioned earlier, accuracy is not an appropriate evaluation metric in imbalanced datasets. Instead, metrics that focus on the detection of rare events are more useful:

Precision: The proportion of predicted fraudulent transactions that are truly fraudulent. High precision ensures that the model is good at detecting actual fraud without incorrectly flagging too many legitimate transactions.

Recall: The proportion of actual fraudulent transactions that were correctly identified. High recall ensures that the model is able to detect as many fraudulent transactions as possible, minimizing false negatives.

F1-Score: The harmonic mean of precision and recall. The F1-score balances the trade-off between false positives and false negatives, providing a single metric to evaluate performance in imbalanced datasets.

Area Under the Precision-Recall Curve (PR-AUC): In imbalanced data scenarios, precision-recall curves provide a better understanding of how well the model performs at different thresholds than ROC curves.

Dealing with data imbalance in fraud detection is one of the most complex challenges machine learning practitioners face. Fraudulent transactions are rare, and detecting them within a sea of legitimate transactions requires specialized techniques. Resampling methods, cost-sensitive learning, anomaly detection, ensemble methods, and evaluation metrics that focus on rare events are all critical tools for overcoming the data imbalance problem in fraud detection. By carefully addressing these challenges, financial institutions can develop more robust and accurate fraud detection systems that minimize losses, improve customer trust, and secure digital transactions.

7.3 Implementing anomaly detection techniques

Anomaly detection plays a crucial role in the domain of fraud detection in financial transactions. As fraudulent transactions tend to deviate significantly from the norm, anomaly detection algorithms are designed to flag unusual behavior that could signify fraud. This approach does not require labeled data and is particularly effective when fraud patterns are not clearly defined or when labeled fraud cases are rare. In this section, we will explore the various techniques used in anomaly detection for fraud detection, with practical steps for implementing these methods.

1. Understanding Anomaly Detection

Anomaly detection is the process of identifying patterns in data that do not conform to expected behavior. In fraud detection, these "anomalies" typically represent fraudulent activities. Since fraudsters often manipulate transaction data to make it appear legitimate, these anomalies often manifest as unusual behavior that deviates from typical patterns observed in legitimate transactions.

Anomaly detection techniques can be broadly categorized into supervised and unsupervised methods:

Supervised Methods: These techniques rely on labeled data to train the model, identifying both legitimate and fraudulent transactions. However, supervised methods are less common in fraud detection because labeled data is often scarce and difficult to obtain.

Unsupervised Methods: These methods do not rely on labeled data and instead aim to identify outliers or anomalies in a dataset based on the statistical characteristics of the data. Unsupervised anomaly detection is more suitable for fraud detection, as fraudulent transactions are inherently rare and novel.

In this sub-chapter, we will focus on the unsupervised anomaly detection techniques and demonstrate how to implement them effectively.

2. Popular Anomaly Detection Techniques

2.1 Statistical Methods

Statistical methods are based on the assumption that most of the data follows a specific distribution, and deviations from that distribution indicate anomalies. These methods are simple to implement and effective for detecting clear outliers.

Z-Score (Standard Score): The Z-score measures how many standard deviations a data point is away from the mean. For each transaction, the Z-score is calculated based on features like transaction amount, frequency, and time of day. If the Z-score exceeds a certain threshold, the transaction is considered an anomaly.

Formula:

$$Z = \frac{X - \mu}{\sigma}$$

where:

- X is the feature value,

- μ is the mean of the feature,

- σ is the standard deviation of the feature.

Boxplots and IQR (Interquartile Range): Boxplots can be used to visualize the distribution of features, with outliers being detected as points outside the 1.5*IQR range. IQR is the range between the 25th and 75th percentiles, and any data point outside this range is considered an anomaly.

2.2 Clustering-Based Methods

Clustering techniques group similar data points together, and outliers are considered those that do not belong to any cluster or are far away from the center of a cluster. These methods are effective when fraudulent transactions behave differently than normal transactions in terms of feature space.

K-Means Clustering: K-means is one of the most widely used clustering algorithms. It works by partitioning the dataset into K clusters based on the similarity between data points. After clustering, points that are far away from any cluster centroid can be flagged as anomalies. In fraud detection, outliers from the centroids may represent suspicious transactions.

DBSCAN (Density-Based Spatial Clustering of Applications with Noise): DBSCAN is a density-based algorithm that groups together closely packed points and labels points in low-density regions as anomalies. Unlike K-means, DBSCAN does not require specifying the number of clusters and works well with noisy datasets. Fraudulent transactions that are outliers in terms of density can be easily detected using DBSCAN.

2.3 Isolation Forest

Isolation Forest is a tree-based anomaly detection algorithm that isolates anomalies rather than profiling normal data points. It randomly selects a feature and splits the data based on that feature, creating smaller and smaller subsets. Anomalies are easier to isolate because they are fewer in number and more different from the rest of the data.

This technique is particularly effective for fraud detection because it can handle large datasets and is well-suited for imbalanced data.

The algorithm works by generating multiple decision trees (called isolation trees), where each tree attempts to isolate anomalies by creating random partitions. The number of partitions needed to isolate a data point is used as a measure of its "anomaly score."

Steps to Implement Isolation Forest:

- Initialize an Isolation Forest model.
- Fit the model on transaction data.
- Score each transaction based on its anomaly score.
- Flag transactions with high anomaly scores as potential fraud.

In Python, this can be implemented using the sklearn.ensemble.IsolationForest class:

```
from sklearn.ensemble import IsolationForest

# Initialize the model
isolation_forest = IsolationForest(contamination=0.01)  # Contamination rate for the outlier fraction

# Fit the model
isolation_forest.fit(transaction_data)  # transaction_data is the preprocessed dataset

# Predict anomalies
anomaly_scores = isolation_forest.predict(transaction_data)
anomalies = transaction_data[anomaly_scores == -1]  # -1 indicates anomalies
```

2.4 One-Class SVM

One-Class Support Vector Machine (SVM) is an unsupervised learning algorithm designed to detect outliers. One-Class SVM works by finding a hyperplane that best separates the normal data from the origin in a high-dimensional feature space. This method assumes that most of the data points are normal and that anomalies lie far from the norm.

One-Class SVM models the "normal" class and flags points that do not belong to this class as outliers. It is particularly effective in fraud detection when the majority of the data consists of legitimate transactions.

Steps to Implement One-Class SVM:

- Fit a One-Class SVM on the dataset, assuming the majority of the data is legitimate.
- The model learns the decision boundary that separates normal transactions from potential fraud.
- Use the model to predict whether new transactions are anomalous.

Python implementation using sklearn.svm.OneClassSVM:

```
from sklearn.svm import OneClassSVM

# Initialize the One-Class SVM model
svm_model = OneClassSVM(nu=0.05, kernel="rbf", gamma="auto")  # nu controls the fraction of anomalies

# Fit the model on normal transactions
svm_model.fit(transaction_data)

# Predict anomalies
anomaly_scores = svm_model.predict(transaction_data)
anomalies = transaction_data[anomaly_scores == -1]  # -1 indicates anomalies
```

3. Evaluation and Tuning of Anomaly Detection Models

Once an anomaly detection model is implemented, it is crucial to evaluate its performance and fine-tune it to improve accuracy. In the case of fraud detection, the following steps can be followed:

3.1 Evaluation Metrics

Given the imbalanced nature of fraud detection, traditional metrics like accuracy are not ideal. Instead, focus on the following metrics:

- **Precision**: Measures the proportion of correctly detected anomalies (fraudulent transactions) among all flagged anomalies.
- **Recall**: Measures the proportion of actual fraudulent transactions that are correctly identified.

- **F1-Score**: The harmonic mean of precision and recall, providing a single score for model performance.
- **Area Under the ROC Curve (AUC-ROC):** Provides insight into the model's ability to distinguish between normal and fraudulent transactions.

3.2 Hyperparameter Tuning

Anomaly detection models, especially tree-based algorithms like Isolation Forest, have hyperparameters that can be tuned to optimize performance. Common parameters include the contamination rate (which defines the expected proportion of anomalies) and n_estimators (the number of trees in the model). Fine-tuning these parameters can significantly impact the performance of the model.

For example, in Isolation Forest, adjusting the contamination rate can help the model detect fraud more effectively:

```
from sklearn.model_selection import GridSearchCV

# Hyperparameter grid search
param_grid = {'contamination': [0.01, 0.05, 0.1], 'n_estimators': [100, 200, 300]}
grid_search = GridSearchCV(IsolationForest(), param_grid, cv=3)
grid_search.fit(transaction_data)
best_model = grid_search.best_estimator_
```

Implementing anomaly detection techniques for fraud detection is an essential step in protecting financial systems from fraudsters. The ability to detect unusual patterns of behavior without relying on labeled data makes anomaly detection particularly useful in real-world applications, where labeled data is scarce or continuously changing. Techniques such as Isolation Forest, One-Class SVM, and clustering-based methods can be highly effective in identifying fraudulent transactions that deviate from the norm. However, fine-tuning these models and evaluating them using appropriate metrics are crucial to improving performance. By leveraging anomaly detection techniques, organizations can build more resilient and adaptive fraud detection systems that can quickly respond to new and emerging fraud patterns.

7.4 Using autoencoders and isolation forests

In fraud detection, identifying fraudulent transactions involves recognizing patterns that deviate significantly from the normal behavior of legitimate transactions. While methods like statistical techniques, clustering, and anomaly detection with decision trees or SVMs are effective, more advanced techniques such as autoencoders and isolation forests can provide better performance, particularly in the context of high-dimensional data or when fraud patterns are complex and non-linear. This section explores how to use these two powerful methods—Autoencoders and Isolation Forests—in combination to detect fraud in financial transactions.

1. Introduction to Autoencoders

An autoencoder is a type of artificial neural network that learns to encode data into a compressed representation (latent space) and then decode it back to its original form. The key idea behind autoencoders is that the network learns to reconstruct the input data while minimizing the error between the original input and the reconstructed output. This ability to learn compressed representations makes autoencoders ideal for anomaly detection, as they can identify patterns in data that deviate from the norm by reconstructing data that does not fit well into the learned latent space.

How Autoencoders Work in Anomaly Detection:

Training: Autoencoders are trained on normal data (i.e., legitimate transactions). During this training, the autoencoder learns to compress and reconstruct normal transaction data efficiently. It learns the underlying patterns of the data.

Anomaly Detection: Once the model is trained, it is used to reconstruct new transactions. If a transaction is normal, the reconstruction error will be low, as the autoencoder has learned to represent such transactions well. However, if the transaction is fraudulent, the model will fail to reconstruct it accurately, leading to a high reconstruction error. These high-errors are flagged as anomalies or potential frauds.

Advantages of Autoencoders for Fraud Detection:

- **Handling High-Dimensional Data**: Autoencoders are particularly useful for detecting fraud in datasets with many features. The encoder-decoder architecture can learn complex, non-linear relationships in data.
- **Unsupervised Learning**: Autoencoders do not require labeled data, which is advantageous when fraudulent transactions are rare and hard to label.
- **Outlier Detection**: Since autoencoders focus on reconstruction errors, they are naturally inclined to detect outliers or anomalies—such as fraudulent transactions.

Steps to Implement an Autoencoder for Fraud Detection:

Preprocess the Data:

- Normalize the dataset so that the features have similar scales. This is essential for the neural network to learn effectively.
- Handle missing values and ensure the data is cleaned.

Design the Autoencoder:

The architecture of an autoencoder consists of an encoder (which compresses the input) and a decoder (which reconstructs the input).

For example, use a simple architecture like:

- **Encoder**: Dense layer (input -> hidden units)
- **Decoder**: Dense layer (hidden units -> output layer)

Train the Autoencoder:

Train the autoencoder on the normal transaction data. The goal is to minimize the reconstruction error, typically using Mean Squared Error (MSE).

Detect Anomalies:

- For each new transaction, pass it through the autoencoder and calculate the reconstruction error.
- If the reconstruction error exceeds a certain threshold, classify the transaction as anomalous (fraudulent).

Example: Using Keras for Autoencoder Implementation:

```
from keras.models import Model
from keras.layers import Input, Dense
from sklearn.preprocessing import StandardScaler
import numpy as np

# Preprocessing data
scaler = StandardScaler()
transaction_data = scaler.fit_transform(transaction_data)  # Normalize the data
```

```
# Define the autoencoder model
input_layer = Input(shape=(transaction_data.shape[1],))
encoded = Dense(64, activation='relu')(input_layer)  # Encoder
decoded = Dense(transaction_data.shape[1], activation='sigmoid')(encoded)  # Decoder

autoencoder = Model(input_layer, decoded)
autoencoder.compile(optimizer='adam', loss='mean_squared_error')

# Train the autoencoder
autoencoder.fit(transaction_data, transaction_data, epochs=50, batch_size=256,
shuffle=True, validation_split=0.1)

# Reconstruction error
reconstructed = autoencoder.predict(transaction_data)
reconstruction_error = np.mean(np.power(transaction_data - reconstructed, 2), axis=1)

# Detect anomalies based on reconstruction error
threshold = np.percentile(reconstruction_error, 95)  # set threshold based on domain
knowledge or experimentation
anomalies = transaction_data[reconstruction_error > threshold]
```

2. Introduction to Isolation Forests

The Isolation Forest (iForest) algorithm is a powerful technique specifically designed for anomaly detection. It works by isolating observations through random partitioning of the data. Since anomalies are few and different from the majority of the data, they require fewer partitions to be isolated, making them easier to detect.

How Isolation Forest Works:

Random Partitioning: The algorithm creates multiple decision trees by randomly selecting features and values to split the data. This process results in "isolation" of the points.

Scoring Anomalies: Anomalies, being sparse and distinct, are isolated faster than normal points. The number of splits required to isolate a point is calculated, and this becomes the anomaly score.

A lower score indicates that the point is more likely to be an anomaly (fraudulent).

A higher score indicates that the point is similar to the normal data distribution.

Advantages of Isolation Forests for Fraud Detection:

- **Efficiency**: Isolation Forests are very efficient, especially when dealing with large datasets. The algorithm's time complexity is linear with respect to the number of data points and the number of trees.
- **No Assumptions on Data Distribution**: Unlike traditional statistical methods, Isolation Forest does not assume any specific distribution of the data.
- **Scalability**: Isolation Forests scale well to high-dimensional datasets, making them ideal for fraud detection in financial systems where multiple features (transaction amount, frequency, location, etc.) are involved.

Steps to Implement Isolation Forest for Fraud Detection:

Preprocess the Data:

Normalize or standardize the data to bring all features to the same scale.

Train the Isolation Forest Model:

- Fit the Isolation Forest model on the normal transaction data, which allows the model to learn the typical patterns of legitimate transactions.

Score and Detect Anomalies:

- The model assigns anomaly scores to each transaction. Transactions with lower scores are flagged as anomalous.

Example: Using Scikit-Learn's Isolation Forest:

```
from sklearn.ensemble import IsolationForest
from sklearn.preprocessing import StandardScaler

# Preprocess the data
scaler = StandardScaler()
transaction_data = scaler.fit_transform(transaction_data)

# Train the Isolation Forest model
```

```
iso_forest = IsolationForest(contamination=0.01, random_state=42)  # Assuming 1% of
transactions are fraudulent
iso_forest.fit(transaction_data)

# Predict anomalies
anomaly_scores = iso_forest.predict(transaction_data)
anomalies = transaction_data[anomaly_scores == -1]  # -1 indicates anomalies
```

3. Combining Autoencoders and Isolation Forests

In practice, combining autoencoders with Isolation Forests can significantly improve the performance of fraud detection models. This combination leverages the strengths of both methods—autoencoders can effectively capture complex, non-linear patterns in data, while Isolation Forests are designed to efficiently detect anomalies.

How to Combine Autoencoders and Isolation Forests:

- **Step 1: Train the Autoencoder**: First, train an autoencoder to learn the normal transaction data.
- **Step 2: Compute Reconstruction Errors**: For each transaction, compute the reconstruction error using the trained autoencoder.
- **Step 3: Use Isolation Forest**: Use the reconstruction errors as features and train an Isolation Forest on the error values.
- **Step 4: Detect Anomalies**: Transactions with both high reconstruction errors and low Isolation Forest scores can be flagged as anomalies (potential fraud).

Advantages of Combining the Two:

- **Robustness**: Combining autoencoders and Isolation Forests provides complementary strengths, leading to more accurate and reliable fraud detection.
- **Flexibility**: This combination can handle a wide range of transaction data, including data with complex relationships and non-linear patterns.

Example Workflow:

```
# Step 1: Train autoencoder
autoencoder.fit(transaction_data, transaction_data, epochs=50, batch_size=256,
shuffle=True)

# Step 2: Compute reconstruction errors
```

```
reconstructed = autoencoder.predict(transaction_data)
reconstruction_error = np.mean(np.power(transaction_data - reconstructed, 2), axis=1)

# Step 3: Train Isolation Forest on reconstruction errors
iso_forest = IsolationForest(contamination=0.01, random_state=42)
iso_forest.fit(reconstruction_error.reshape(-1, 1))

# Step 4: Detect anomalies
anomalies = iso_forest.predict(reconstruction_error.reshape(-1, 1))
```

Combining autoencoders with Isolation Forests is a powerful approach to detecting fraud in financial transactions. Autoencoders are effective at learning the inherent patterns in normal data and detecting deviations through reconstruction errors, while Isolation Forests efficiently identify anomalies in high-dimensional datasets. Together, these methods provide a robust solution for detecting fraud in complex and noisy financial data. By leveraging these advanced techniques, organizations can enhance their ability to detect and mitigate fraudulent activities in real-time, ensuring safer financial systems.

7.5 Deploying fraud detection in a real-time pipeline

Once fraud detection models, such as autoencoders and Isolation Forests, have been trained and validated, the next critical step is deploying them into a real-time fraud detection pipeline. Fraud detection in real time is a vital requirement for financial institutions, e-commerce platforms, and any system where fraudulent transactions could lead to significant losses. A real-time system needs to continuously monitor transactions as they occur, flag suspicious activity instantly, and respond to alerts or actions.

In this sub-chapter, we will walk through the essential steps to deploy a fraud detection system into a real-time pipeline, ensuring that fraud can be detected and mitigated as soon as it happens.

1. The Components of a Real-Time Fraud Detection Pipeline

A real-time fraud detection pipeline typically consists of the following key components:

- **Data Ingestion**: This is the process of collecting real-time transaction data from various sources, such as payment gateways, transaction logs, and APIs.

- **Data Preprocessing**: Raw transaction data often needs to be cleaned, transformed, and preprocessed before it can be passed into the machine learning models.
- **Fraud Detection Models**: These models, like the ones discussed in earlier sections (Autoencoders, Isolation Forests, etc.), are responsible for identifying fraudulent transactions based on the features extracted from the incoming data.
- **Scoring & Alerting**: The fraud detection models score each transaction, and those with a higher likelihood of being fraudulent are flagged and escalated for manual review or automated action.
- **Integration & Feedback Loop**: Real-time systems require efficient integration with downstream systems such as alerting systems, user interfaces, and external databases. Feedback loops ensure that new fraudulent patterns are incorporated into model retraining processes.

2. Real-Time Data Ingestion and Stream Processing

The first step in a real-time fraud detection pipeline is data ingestion. It's essential to handle incoming transaction data efficiently and ensure it's delivered with minimal delay. Typically, this involves streaming data from sources like payment systems, mobile apps, or online banking systems.

Technologies for Real-Time Data Ingestion:

- **Apache Kafka**: A distributed event streaming platform that allows real-time data collection from various sources. Kafka can manage the high throughput of real-time transaction data and pass it on to processing engines.
- **Apache Flink**: A stream processing framework that can handle real-time data processing, making it suitable for fraud detection pipelines. Flink supports low-latency processing and can handle high volumes of data efficiently.
- **AWS Kinesis**: A cloud service by Amazon Web Services that can collect, process, and analyze real-time data streams.

In a fraud detection system, incoming transaction data is typically consumed by one of these stream processing systems, which sends the data to the model for scoring.

3. Real-Time Data Preprocessing

Once transaction data is ingested, it must be processed in real time before being passed into the fraud detection model. Preprocessing steps in real-time systems need to be lightweight, efficient, and able to handle high-velocity data streams.

Common Real-Time Data Preprocessing Tasks:

- **Feature Extraction**: As transactions come in, relevant features such as transaction amount, frequency, user location, device ID, and time of the transaction should be extracted or computed in real time.
- **Normalization and Scaling**: Ensuring features are normalized or standardized in real-time is critical to the model's performance. For example, scaling transaction amounts and timestamps helps prevent issues during prediction.
- **Handling Missing Data**: In a real-time environment, missing values can occur, so predefined strategies for imputation or ignoring missing features are required.
- **Categorical Encoding**: If categorical features are present (such as transaction type or country), they should be encoded into numeric values using techniques like one-hot encoding or label encoding.
- **Anomaly Detection on Features**: It may be helpful to run feature-specific anomaly detection, especially when a certain feature behaves outside expected parameters (e.g., a large transaction at an odd hour).

This data processing must be completed in real time, meaning the preprocessing system must be highly optimized to keep up with the data stream and deliver clean data as quickly as possible.

4. Scoring with Fraud Detection Models

The heart of the fraud detection pipeline is the model used to score incoming transactions. For real-time fraud detection, this requires models to be deployed in a way that they can quickly process individual transactions and return a fraud score in milliseconds.

Deploying the Model:

- **Model Export**: After training fraud detection models (like Autoencoders or Isolation Forests), the trained models are exported and converted into a format that is optimized for real-time use. For example, models can be saved in formats such as pickle for Python or ONNX for cross-platform compatibility.
- **Model Serving**: The model is typically served using model serving tools like:
- TensorFlow Serving: A framework for serving machine learning models in production environments.
- **Flask API**: A simple web framework in Python that can expose your machine learning models as REST APIs for real-time inference.

- **FastAPI**: A high-performance framework for building APIs that can serve models with minimal latency.

Batch vs. Online Scoring:

- Batch Processing is ideal when incoming data can be processed in groups (e.g., daily transaction summaries).
- Online Scoring refers to scoring each transaction in real time. This is typically necessary for fraud detection because fraud patterns can be highly dynamic.

In real-time fraud detection, the model evaluates each transaction and returns a fraud score (usually between 0 and 1), where a higher score indicates a higher likelihood of fraud.

5. Alerting and Actionable Insights

Once a transaction is scored by the fraud detection model, the next step is to generate alerts if the model predicts fraudulent activity. In a real-time system, alerting and action-taking should be immediate and effective.

Real-Time Alerting:

Thresholds: A predefined threshold is set based on fraud scores. If the score is higher than the threshold (indicating potential fraud), the transaction is flagged for manual review or further action.

Alerting Channels: Alerts can be sent via various channels:

- Emails to system administrators or fraud analysts.
- SMS or push notifications for immediate action from customer support teams.
- Integration with a fraud detection dashboard to give analysts visibility into flagged transactions.

Actions Post-Alert:

- **Manual Review**: Analysts can review flagged transactions and decide whether they are truly fraudulent.
- **Automated Action**: In some cases, fraudulent transactions can be automatically rejected, blocked, or flagged for further verification (e.g., two-factor authentication requests).

6. Real-Time Model Monitoring and Retraining

Fraud patterns are dynamic, and the models deployed for fraud detection need to evolve to detect new fraud techniques. A feedback loop is necessary to monitor the model's performance continuously and retrain the model as new fraud cases emerge.

Monitoring Model Performance:

Performance Metrics: It's essential to continuously track metrics such as precision, recall, F1-score, and ROC-AUC to evaluate the model's effectiveness in detecting fraud. Model Drift: Monitoring for concept drift (changes in the underlying data distribution) is critical to maintaining model accuracy. If the model's performance drops, retraining may be required.

Automated Retraining:

- **Retraining Pipelines**: Set up a scheduled retraining process based on updated transaction data. This process involves collecting new fraudulent and non-fraudulent data, retraining the model, and redeploying the updated version.
- **Continuous Learning**: More advanced setups involve using techniques such as online learning, where the model continues to learn from new data in real time.

Deploying fraud detection in a real-time pipeline is a complex but necessary task for detecting fraudulent activities as soon as they happen. By utilizing technologies like stream processing platforms, efficient model serving, and continuous monitoring, organizations can ensure that they are always up to date with emerging fraud patterns. This real-time detection system provides immediate benefits, including enhanced security, reduced fraud risk, and the ability to take swift corrective actions. Real-time fraud detection is essential to maintaining the integrity of financial transactions and ensuring a secure environment for users and businesses alike.

8. Demand Forecasting for Retail

In this chapter, we delve into the essential task of demand forecasting for retail businesses. Accurate forecasting enables companies to optimize inventory, improve supply chain efficiency, and avoid overstocking or understocking products. You will learn how to build time series forecasting models using techniques such as ARIMA, Exponential Smoothing, and LSTM networks. We'll guide you through the process of data preparation, handling seasonality, and evaluating model performance with metrics like mean absolute error (MAE) and root mean square error (RMSE). By the end of this project, you'll be able to forecast product demand with high accuracy, empowering retailers to make data-driven decisions and streamline operations. 🎁

8.1 Introduction to time-series forecasting

Time-series forecasting is one of the most widely used techniques in the retail industry for predicting future demand, sales, inventory needs, and customer behavior based on historical data. It plays a crucial role in helping businesses optimize stock levels, reduce costs, and enhance customer satisfaction by ensuring that products are available when needed. Time-series forecasting allows businesses to predict how certain variables will evolve over time, making it an indispensable tool for decision-making in the retail sector.

In this sub-chapter, we will explore the fundamentals of time-series forecasting, its relevance to retail, and how it can be effectively utilized to predict demand. We will also touch upon various forecasting models, their applications, and the factors that need to be considered to create accurate and reliable forecasts.

1. What is Time-Series Forecasting?

Time-series forecasting refers to the process of using historical data to make predictions about future values. Time-series data consists of observations recorded at specific time intervals, which could be daily, weekly, monthly, or even in real-time. The primary goal of time-series forecasting is to understand the underlying patterns or trends in the data and use that information to predict future outcomes.

For example, in the context of retail, time-series forecasting can be applied to predict the future demand for a product based on past sales data. Retailers can then use this information to plan inventory, manage supply chains, and avoid stockouts or overstocking.

2. Importance of Time-Series Forecasting in Retail

Time-series forecasting offers significant advantages for retail businesses, making it an essential tool in the industry. Here's how time-series forecasting impacts retail operations:

Optimizing Inventory Management: Retailers must strike a balance between having enough stock to meet customer demand and avoiding excess inventory that can lead to high storage costs. Time-series forecasting enables accurate predictions of demand for products, helping businesses optimize their inventory levels.

Improving Customer Satisfaction: Accurate demand forecasts ensure that popular products are available when customers want them. This helps reduce lost sales opportunities and increases customer satisfaction by minimizing the chances of stockouts.

Cost Reduction: By aligning inventory levels with predicted demand, retailers can reduce the costs associated with overstocking, such as excess storage and waste due to perishable goods.

Enhancing Supply Chain Efficiency: Time-series forecasting can help retailers align their supply chain processes with demand. Predicting demand patterns allows retailers to plan and coordinate with suppliers to ensure that products are delivered on time and in the right quantities.

Strategic Planning: Long-term demand forecasting enables retailers to make strategic decisions related to product launches, promotions, pricing strategies, and market expansion.

3. Key Concepts in Time-Series Data

Time-series forecasting is built on the understanding of various components and concepts that drive the data. These components are critical for interpreting patterns in historical data and generating accurate forecasts.

1. Trend

A trend represents the long-term movement or direction in a time-series dataset. It indicates whether the values are increasing, decreasing, or remaining constant over time. For example, a growing trend in sales may suggest increasing customer interest or product popularity.

2. Seasonality

Seasonality refers to repetitive and predictable patterns in data that occur at regular intervals due to external factors such as holidays, weather, or annual events. Retail businesses often experience seasonal demand spikes during specific times of the year (e.g., holiday seasons, summer sales, or back-to-school promotions).

3. Cyclical Patterns

Unlike seasonality, cyclical patterns occur over irregular periods. These fluctuations are often tied to economic conditions, market cycles, or business cycles. For example, during an economic downturn, demand for luxury goods may decline, while in a booming economy, sales might increase.

4. Noise

Noise refers to random fluctuations or irregularities in the data that cannot be attributed to any specific trend, seasonality, or cyclical patterns. Noise can be caused by data collection errors or other unpredictable factors.

5. Level

The level represents the baseline value around which data fluctuates. It serves as a reference point for understanding the overall magnitude of the data and trends.

4. Time-Series Forecasting Models

There are various forecasting models and techniques available for time-series prediction. Below are some of the most common models used in retail for demand forecasting:

1. Autoregressive Integrated Moving Average (ARIMA)

ARIMA is a popular time-series forecasting model that combines three components:

- **Autoregressive (AR):** This component uses the relationship between an observation and several lagged observations (previous time steps).
- **Integrated (I):** This component involves differencing the series to make it stationary (i.e., to remove trends).
- **Moving Average (MA):** This component models the error term as a linear combination of previous error terms.

ARIMA is effective for forecasting linear trends but may not be suitable for complex or nonlinear data.

2. Exponential Smoothing Methods

Exponential smoothing is another widely used technique in time-series forecasting. It assigns exponentially decreasing weights to past observations, with more recent data points receiving greater weight.

Common types of exponential smoothing include:

- **Simple Exponential Smoothing (SES):** Suitable for data without trend or seasonality.
- **Holt's Linear Trend Method**: Extends SES to capture linear trends in the data.
- **Holt-Winters Seasonal Method**: Accounts for both trend and seasonality in the data.

Exponential smoothing is computationally efficient and works well for short-term demand forecasting in retail.

3. Prophet

Prophet is a forecasting tool developed by Facebook designed to handle seasonal effects and holidays in time-series data. Prophet can handle missing data and outliers and is highly flexible, making it ideal for retail demand forecasting where seasonality is significant.

4. Long Short-Term Memory (LSTM) Networks

LSTM, a type of recurrent neural network (RNN), is highly effective for forecasting complex time-series data with long-term dependencies. LSTM models can capture both short-term and long-term patterns in demand, making them useful for forecasting in retail, particularly when dealing with high-volume, multivariate data.

5. Seasonal Autoregressive Integrated Moving Average (SARIMA)

SARIMA is an extension of ARIMA that includes seasonal components. SARIMA models are ideal for time-series data with strong seasonality, making them well-suited for forecasting retail demand during peak seasons (e.g., holiday sales or summer promotions).

5. Key Considerations in Time-Series Forecasting for Retail

While time-series forecasting provides powerful tools for demand prediction, there are several important factors to consider when implementing a forecasting model in retail:

1. Data Quality

Accurate demand forecasting depends on the quality of the historical data. Missing values, outliers, and inconsistent data can significantly affect the performance of the forecasting model. Data preprocessing and cleaning steps are crucial to ensure reliable predictions.

2. Model Selection

Choosing the right forecasting model is critical to the success of demand forecasting. Retailers must evaluate the characteristics of their data (e.g., seasonality, trends, or noise) and choose an appropriate model accordingly. For instance, if the data exhibits strong seasonal patterns, models like Holt-Winters or SARIMA may perform better than simpler approaches.

3. Hyperparameter Tuning

Many forecasting models require the tuning of hyperparameters to optimize their performance. For example, the ARIMA model requires selecting the appropriate order for the autoregressive and moving average components. Hyperparameter optimization can significantly improve forecasting accuracy.

4. External Factors

Retail demand can be influenced by various external factors such as marketing campaigns, promotions, weather conditions, and economic events. Incorporating these factors into the model through additional features can enhance forecasting accuracy.

5. Real-Time Forecasting

For many retailers, the ability to make real-time predictions is crucial. Real-time forecasting systems can adjust inventory levels and trigger replenishment orders based on live sales data, ensuring a seamless supply chain.

Time-series forecasting is a powerful technique that can significantly improve demand forecasting accuracy in the retail industry. By understanding the key components of time-series data and selecting the right forecasting model, businesses can better predict future demand, optimize inventory management, and enhance overall supply chain efficiency. Whether using traditional models like ARIMA or more advanced methods like LSTM, time-series forecasting offers invaluable insights for retailers looking to stay competitive in an ever-evolving market.

8.2 Preparing sales data for forecasting

Data preparation is a critical step in time-series forecasting, as the quality of the data directly influences the accuracy and reliability of the predictions. When it comes to sales forecasting for retail, the process of preparing the sales data involves several key steps that ensure the data is clean, organized, and ready for analysis. These steps can include handling missing values, removing outliers, transforming data, feature engineering, and making the data stationary. Each of these processes is essential to ensure that the time-series model can effectively capture the underlying patterns and make accurate predictions.

In this sub-chapter, we will explore how to properly prepare sales data for time-series forecasting, covering the essential techniques and best practices for each step in the data preparation process.

1. Understanding the Structure of Sales Data

Sales data in a retail context typically consists of several components, such as:

- **Time stamps**: The date or time at which the sales data point was recorded (daily, weekly, monthly).
- **Sales figures**: The quantity of products sold or the revenue generated during that specific time period.

- **Product details**: Information about the product being sold, including product category, SKU (stock keeping unit), and brand.
- **Store or location data**: Details about the store or region where the sales occurred, especially important for multi-location retailers.
- **Promotional data**: Flags or information about whether any discounts, promotions, or sales events were active during the period.

The first step in preparing sales data for forecasting is to ensure that the data is structured in a way that is suitable for time-series analysis. Typically, this involves organizing the data by time and ensuring that the sales figures are aligned with the correct timestamps.

2. Handling Missing Data

Missing data is a common issue in real-world sales data and can arise from various sources, such as system failures, human errors, or gaps in reporting. Handling missing values appropriately is crucial to avoid introducing bias into the forecasting model.

Techniques for Handling Missing Data:

Forward Fill: If sales data is missing for a specific time period, you can use the last available value to fill the missing spot. This approach works well in situations where sales do not fluctuate dramatically from one period to another.

Backward Fill: Similar to forward fill, backward fill uses the next available value to fill missing data points. This method can be useful if there's a reasonable assumption that future sales data may reflect previous trends.

Interpolation: For numerical data, linear interpolation can be used to estimate missing values by fitting a line between known values and predicting the missing data point.

Removing Rows: In some cases, it may be best to remove rows with missing data, especially if the missing values are sparse and their removal won't affect the overall analysis.

Imputation: Imputation methods involve predicting missing values based on other variables in the dataset. For example, if sales are missing for a particular store or product, machine learning models can be used to predict those values based on historical trends or similar stores/products.

The approach you choose should depend on the nature of the sales data and the amount of missing data.

3. Removing Outliers

Outliers are data points that deviate significantly from the expected pattern and can distort forecasting models. In the context of retail sales, outliers can arise due to promotions, stockouts, holidays, or data entry errors.

Techniques for Detecting and Handling Outliers:

Visual Inspection: A quick way to identify outliers is by plotting the sales data over time (e.g., using line plots or scatter plots). Outliers will appear as points that lie far outside the expected trend or seasonal patterns.

Statistical Methods: Common statistical techniques for detecting outliers include:

- **Z-Score**: A z-score above a certain threshold (e.g., 3 or -3) indicates that the data point is an outlier.
- **IQR (Interquartile Range):** Data points that fall outside the range of 1.5 times the IQR (between the first and third quartiles) can be considered outliers.

Contextual Identification: In retail, outliers may be due to events like promotions, holidays, or unexpected sales spikes. If an outlier is a legitimate part of the business cycle (e.g., increased sales during Black Friday), it should be kept in the dataset. However, if the outlier results from data entry errors or anomalies that do not reflect actual sales behavior, it should be removed or corrected.

4. Resampling the Data

Time-series data can be recorded at different time frequencies: daily, weekly, monthly, etc. Depending on the forecasting model and the granularity of the forecast, you may need to resample the data.

Types of Resampling:

Downsampling: Aggregating data from a higher frequency (e.g., daily) to a lower frequency (e.g., monthly). This can be done by summing, averaging, or taking the maximum value within each period.

Upsampling: If you need to forecast at a higher frequency (e.g., predicting sales at a daily level), you may upsample your data by interpolating between existing values.

It's important to ensure that resampling methods preserve the underlying patterns, such as trends and seasonality, which are critical for accurate forecasting.

5. Transforming and Scaling Data

Transforming and scaling data is essential to ensure that the time-series model can effectively learn patterns and trends. This process is particularly important when working with machine learning algorithms that are sensitive to the scale of the data.

Common Data Transformation Techniques:

Log Transformation: If sales data contains large fluctuations or a long-tailed distribution, applying a log transformation (taking the logarithm of the sales figures) can stabilize variance and make the data more suitable for modeling.

Differencing: Time-series data often exhibits trends that make it non-stationary (i.e., its statistical properties change over time). Differencing is a technique used to remove trends by subtracting the previous period's value from the current period's value. This process can help make the data stationary, which is required for models like ARIMA.

Seasonal Differencing: If the data exhibits strong seasonality (e.g., monthly sales with yearly patterns), you may need to apply seasonal differencing, where the current period's value is subtracted by the value from the same period in the previous season.

Scaling: Standardizing or normalizing the sales data can help certain models, like neural networks, perform better by bringing all features to a similar scale. Common scaling techniques include Min-Max scaling and Z-score normalization.

6. Feature Engineering for Time-Series

Feature engineering is the process of creating new features from the existing data to improve model performance. In time-series forecasting, additional features can help capture patterns that may not be evident in the raw sales data alone.

Common Features for Sales Data:

Lag Features: Lag features involve creating new columns that represent the sales from previous time steps (e.g., sales from one day ago, one week ago, or one month ago). These features help the model capture dependencies between past and future sales.

Rolling Statistics: Rolling mean, rolling standard deviation, and rolling sums over a window of time (e.g., 7 days, 30 days) can capture short-term trends and patterns in sales.

Holiday Indicators: Flags that indicate whether a particular date is a holiday or part of a promotional event (e.g., Black Friday, Christmas) can significantly improve forecast accuracy by accounting for unusual spikes in demand.

Price Features: Including information about product prices, discounts, or promotions as additional features can help the model understand how pricing affects sales.

7. Making the Data Stationary

For many time-series models (like ARIMA), the data must be stationary, meaning its statistical properties do not change over time. This includes having a constant mean, variance, and autocovariance structure.

Stationarity can be achieved through differencing, as mentioned earlier, or by transforming the data. Non-stationary data may lead to poor model performance, as the underlying assumptions of many forecasting models are based on the data being stationary.

Preparing sales data for time-series forecasting is a critical process that requires careful attention to detail. From handling missing values and outliers to transforming and scaling the data, each step plays a significant role in ensuring that the forecasting model has the best chance of making accurate predictions. By using proper techniques like resampling, feature engineering, and stationarity testing, retailers can create a solid foundation for their demand forecasting models. This preparation ultimately leads to more reliable forecasts, helping retailers optimize their inventory management and improve overall business performance.

8.3 Implementing ARIMA, Prophet, and LSTMs

When forecasting demand in retail, selecting the right model is essential for obtaining accurate predictions. In this sub-chapter, we will explore three popular methods used for time-series forecasting: ARIMA, Prophet, and Long Short-Term Memory (LSTM) networks. Each of these models has its own strengths and is suitable for different types of data. We'll dive into their implementation, use cases, and considerations for choosing the right approach depending on the characteristics of the demand data.

1. ARIMA (AutoRegressive Integrated Moving Average)

ARIMA is one of the most widely used statistical models for time-series forecasting. It is suitable for data that shows patterns like trends and seasonality. ARIMA is a linear model that works by combining three components:

- **AR (AutoRegressive):** A model that uses the relationship between an observation and several lagged observations (previous time steps).
- **I (Integrated):** The differencing of raw observations to make the time series stationary.

MA (Moving Average): A model that uses the relationship between an observation and a residual error from a moving average model applied to lagged observations.

Steps to Implement ARIMA for Demand Forecasting:

- **Check for Stationarity**: Before using ARIMA, ensure the data is stationary. If the series shows trends or seasonality, perform differencing (first-order or seasonal differencing) to stabilize the mean and variance.

Determine ARIMA Parameters (p, d, q):

- **p**: Number of lag observations in the autoregressive model.
- **d**: Degree of differencing needed to make the series stationary.
- **q:** Size of the moving average window.

You can use tools like the ACF (Autocorrelation Function) and PACF (Partial Autocorrelation Function) plots to identify the values for p and q. The d parameter can typically be set based on the number of differencing operations needed to achieve stationarity.

Fit the ARIMA Model: Once the parameters are set, the ARIMA model is trained on the historical sales data. The goal is to find the model coefficients that minimize the error.

Forecasting: After training the ARIMA model, you can use it to forecast future sales for the next periods. The forecast is based on the past values and is typically combined with confidence intervals.

Example in Python:

```
from statsmodels.tsa.arima.model import ARIMA
import pandas as pd

# Load data
data = pd.read_csv('sales_data.csv', parse_dates=True, index_col='date')

# Differencing to make the series stationary (if necessary)
data_diff = data.diff().dropna()

# Fit ARIMA model (p, d, q)
model = ARIMA(data_diff, order=(1, 1, 1))  # AR(1), I(1), MA(1)
model_fit = model.fit()

# Make forecast
forecast = model_fit.forecast(steps=30)
```

Advantages of ARIMA:

- Simple and interpretable.
- Works well for stationary data without complex patterns or seasonality.

Limitations:

- Requires data to be stationary (or transformed to be stationary).
- Struggles with data that has significant seasonal effects.

2. Prophet

Prophet, developed by Facebook, is a forecasting tool designed to handle data that exhibits strong seasonal effects and holiday patterns. Unlike ARIMA, Prophet is capable of handling missing data, large outliers, and irregular time intervals. Prophet is based on an additive model that includes components for trends, seasonality, and holidays.

Steps to Implement Prophet for Demand Forecasting:

Prepare the Data: Prophet requires the data to be in a specific format, where the time column is labeled as ds and the sales data column is labeled as y.

Train the Model: Prophet automatically detects daily, weekly, and yearly seasonality. You can also specify additional seasonalities or holiday effects.

Make Predictions: Once the model is trained, Prophet can generate forecasts with uncertainty intervals, making it useful for planning purposes.

Fine-tune the Model: You can adjust the seasonalities, add holidays, and fine-tune hyperparameters for better predictions.

Example in Python:

```python
from fbprophet import Prophet
import pandas as pd

# Prepare the data
data = pd.read_csv('sales_data.csv')
data = data.rename(columns={'date': 'ds', 'sales': 'y'})

# Initialize and train the model
model = Prophet(yearly_seasonality=True, weekly_seasonality=True,
daily_seasonality=False)
model.fit(data)

# Make forecast for the next 30 days
future = model.make_future_dataframe(data, periods=30)
forecast = model.predict(future)

# Plot the forecast
model.plot(forecast)
```

Advantages of Prophet:

- Handles seasonality and holiday effects well.
- Can accommodate missing values and outliers.
- Simple to use and doesn't require data transformation (like stationarity checks in ARIMA).

Limitations:

- It may not perform well for data that doesn't show significant seasonal effects or trends.
- Can be too simplistic for more complex forecasting tasks.

3. LSTMs (Long Short-Term Memory Networks)

LSTMs, a type of Recurrent Neural Network (RNN), are designed to capture long-term dependencies in sequential data. Unlike ARIMA and Prophet, LSTMs are deep learning models that can model non-linear relationships in time-series data and are particularly useful for forecasting when there are complex patterns, such as non-linear trends, multi-seasonality, and interactions between features.

LSTMs are highly powerful for time-series forecasting, but they require more data and computational resources compared to traditional methods like ARIMA or Prophet.

Steps to Implement LSTMs for Demand Forecasting:

Prepare the Data: LSTMs require the data to be formatted in sequences. You will need to create rolling windows or lag features to convert the time-series data into supervised learning format.

Normalize the Data: Neural networks are sensitive to the scale of input data, so it's essential to normalize or standardize the features before training the model.

Create LSTM Model: Define an LSTM architecture using deep learning libraries such as TensorFlow or Keras. The architecture typically includes one or more LSTM layers followed by dense layers.

Train the Model: Use historical sales data to train the LSTM model and validate it using a holdout set.

Make Predictions: Once trained, the LSTM model can be used to forecast future sales.

Example in Python using Keras:

import numpy as np
import pandas as pd

```python
from sklearn.preprocessing import MinMaxScaler
from tensorflow.keras.models import Sequential
from tensorflow.keras.layers import LSTM, Dense

# Load data
data = pd.read_csv('sales_data.csv', parse_dates=True, index_col='date')
sales = data['sales'].values.reshape(-1, 1)

# Normalize the data
scaler = MinMaxScaler(feature_range=(0, 1))
sales_scaled = scaler.fit_transform(sales)

# Prepare data for LSTM (create rolling windows)
def create_dataset(data, time_step=1):
    X, y = [], []
    for i in range(len(data) - time_step - 1):
        X.append(data[i:(i + time_step), 0])
        y.append(data[i + time_step, 0])
    return np.array(X), np.array(y)

time_step = 30  # Use the last 30 days to predict the next day
X, y = create_dataset(sales_scaled, time_step)

# Reshape input to be [samples, time steps, features]
X = X.reshape(X.shape[0], X.shape[1], 1)

# Build LSTM model
model = Sequential()
model.add(LSTM(units=50, return_sequences=True, input_shape=(X.shape[1], 1)))
model.add(LSTM(units=50, return_sequences=False))
model.add(Dense(units=1))
model.compile(optimizer='adam', loss='mean_squared_error')

# Train the model
model.fit(X, y, epochs=20, batch_size=32)

# Make predictions
predictions = model.predict(X)
predictions = scaler.inverse_transform(predictions)  # Reverse the scaling
```

Advantages of LSTM:

- Can model complex, non-linear relationships.
- Captures long-term dependencies, making it suitable for forecasting tasks with long sequences.
- Highly flexible and can handle multivariate time-series data.

Limitations:

- Requires large datasets for training.
- Computationally expensive and time-consuming.
- Needs a significant amount of data preprocessing and tuning.

Each of the models—ARIMA, Prophet, and LSTM—has its unique advantages, and the choice of model depends largely on the characteristics of the sales data. For simple, trend-based forecasting with stationary data, ARIMA is a great choice. If the data exhibits strong seasonality and holiday effects, Prophet might be the most effective. However, for complex, non-linear patterns with longer-term dependencies, LSTMs are the best option. Ultimately, understanding the data and experimenting with multiple models will help you select the most appropriate one for accurate demand forecasting in retail.

8.4 Handling seasonality and external factors

In retail demand forecasting, accurate prediction hinges not only on understanding past trends but also on accounting for seasonality and external factors that can significantly impact sales patterns. Seasonality refers to regular fluctuations in demand at specific intervals (e.g., monthly, quarterly, or annually), while external factors include variables such as promotions, economic conditions, weather, and holidays. Both of these elements must be properly modeled to improve forecast accuracy. In this section, we will explore how to handle seasonality and external factors in time-series forecasting.

1. Understanding Seasonality

Seasonality refers to predictable and recurring patterns within a time-series dataset. For example, retailers might observe higher sales during the holiday season, or certain products may experience higher demand during specific times of the year (e.g., winter clothing in colder months). Seasonality can have different periodicities depending on the nature of the data. Retailers often encounter both annual and weekly seasonality in their sales.

To model seasonality, we can leverage various methods depending on the model used, and each method will treat seasonality in different ways:

ARIMA: ARIMA itself can handle seasonality by including seasonal differencing (S) along with the regular differencing (d). This makes the model better suited for data with periodic fluctuations. However, ARIMA's ability to model seasonality is limited to simpler patterns, and it might not capture complex seasonalities (such as those due to holidays or special events).

Prophet: Prophet explicitly incorporates seasonality into its structure. By default, Prophet captures yearly, weekly, and daily seasonal patterns, but it also allows users to define custom seasonalities to capture more complex cycles. Prophet's additive model is perfect for handling scenarios where seasonality and trends can be adjusted separately.

LSTM: Long Short-Term Memory (LSTM) networks can also account for seasonality, but it requires proper data preprocessing. By segmenting the data into time windows (e.g., daily, weekly), and encoding seasonal patterns as features (using sine and cosine transformations), LSTM can learn the periodic behavior in the data. The flexibility of neural networks like LSTM allows them to capture more complex seasonal patterns.

2. External Factors and Exogenous Variables

In real-world retail forecasting, external factors can play a crucial role in driving demand. These factors often cannot be captured directly from historical sales data alone. Including exogenous variables (or external variables) can greatly enhance the predictive power of the model. Common external factors include:

- **Promotions and Discounts**: Sales during promotional periods are often much higher than regular sales. Modeling promotions as external factors can help adjust predictions accordingly.
- **Economic Indicators**: Economic conditions, such as consumer confidence, inflation rates, or unemployment, can affect spending patterns.
- **Weather**: Extreme weather events or seasonal temperature changes can impact the demand for certain products, such as jackets or air conditioners.
- **Holidays and Special Events**: Major holidays (Christmas, Black Friday) and events (sports events, festivals) can cause significant spikes in sales.

Incorporating these external factors into your forecasting models can help create more accurate and realistic predictions. Below are some strategies to consider when adding exogenous variables to forecasting models:

Prophet: Prophet is particularly adept at handling external factors because it allows users to input custom holidays and special events that can affect demand. By providing Prophet with a list of dates and holiday labels, it can adjust for spikes in demand during those times. Additionally, Prophet supports custom seasonalities, so it can be adjusted for events like yearly sales periods or cyclical patterns.

For instance, to model promotions or holidays in Prophet:

```
from fbprophet import Prophet
import pandas as pd

# Prepare the data with holidays
data = pd.read_csv('sales_data.csv')
data = data.rename(columns={'date': 'ds', 'sales': 'y'})

# Define holidays
holidays = pd.DataFrame({
  'holiday': 'promotion',
  'ds': pd.to_datetime(['2025-11-25', '2025-12-15']),
  'lower_window': 0,
  'upper_window': 1,
})

# Initialize Prophet with holidays
model = Prophet(holidays=holidays)
model.fit(data)

# Make predictions
future = model.make_future_dataframe(data, periods=30)
forecast = model.predict(future)

# Plot forecast
model.plot(forecast)
```

ARIMA with Exogenous Variables (ARIMAX): ARIMAX is an extension of ARIMA that allows for the inclusion of external variables as predictors. For example, when forecasting retail sales, you can incorporate weather data or promotional data into the model by using the ARIMAX formulation:

- The model is fit as: ARIMAX(y, exog=X) where y is the sales series, and X is the external variable matrix.
- This method works well when you have data that can directly influence the sales (e.g., promotions, holidays) but doesn't capture complex interactions.

Example using ARIMAX in Python:

```
from statsmodels.tsa.arima.model import ARIMA
import pandas as pd

# Load sales data and external factors
data = pd.read_csv('sales_data.csv')
weather_data = pd.read_csv('weather_data.csv')

# Define exogenous variable (e.g., temperature)
exog = weather_data['temperature']

# Fit ARIMAX model
model = ARIMA(data['sales'], order=(1, 1, 1), exog=exog)
model_fit = model.fit()

# Forecast with external variable
forecast = model_fit.forecast(steps=30, exog=exog[-30:])
```

LSTM with External Factors: When using LSTM, external factors like promotions, weather, and holidays can be fed into the model as additional features. This requires proper preprocessing to align external variables with the time-series data.

Example of preparing data for LSTM with external variables:

```
import numpy as np
import pandas as pd
from sklearn.preprocessing import MinMaxScaler
from tensorflow.keras.models import Sequential
from tensorflow.keras.layers import LSTM, Dense

# Load data and external factors (e.g., promotions, weather)
```

```
sales_data = pd.read_csv('sales_data.csv')
weather_data = pd.read_csv('weather_data.csv')

# Normalize sales and external features
scaler_sales = MinMaxScaler(feature_range=(0, 1))
sales_scaled = scaler_sales.fit_transform(sales_data['sales'].values.reshape(-1, 1))

scaler_weather = MinMaxScaler(feature_range=(0, 1))
weather_scaled =
scaler_weather.fit_transform(weather_data['temperature'].values.reshape(-1, 1))

# Prepare data for LSTM
def create_dataset(sales, weather, time_step=1):
    X, y = [], []
    for i in range(len(sales) - time_step - 1):
        X.append(np.column_stack((sales[i:(i + time_step), 0], weather[i:(i + time_step),
0])))
        y.append(sales[i + time_step, 0])
    return np.array(X), np.array(y)

time_step = 30
X, y = create_dataset(sales_scaled, weather_scaled, time_step)

# LSTM model
model = Sequential()
model.add(LSTM(units=50, return_sequences=True, input_shape=(X.shape[1],
X.shape[2])))
model.add(LSTM(units=50, return_sequences=False))
model.add(Dense(units=1))
model.compile(optimizer='adam', loss='mean_squared_error')
model.fit(X, y, epochs=20, batch_size=32)
```

3. Conclusion: Leveraging Seasonality and External Factors for Accurate Forecasting

Handling seasonality and external factors is crucial for making accurate demand forecasts in retail. While ARIMA and Prophet offer flexible ways to handle seasonality and exogenous variables, LSTM models provide powerful tools for capturing more complex, non-linear patterns. Retailers should experiment with different models and external factors to choose the best approach for their specific needs. Understanding how these factors influence demand is essential for creating robust forecasting systems that can help businesses optimize inventory, improve sales strategies, and plan for future demand more effectively.

8.5 Deploying a forecasting model with a visualization dashboard

Once a forecasting model for retail demand is developed and trained, the next crucial step is to deploy it in a way that enables stakeholders to interact with it easily and gain actionable insights. A common approach for this is to integrate the model into a visualization dashboard, which not only allows users to view predictions but also provides visual representations of trends, seasonality, and forecasting accuracy. In this section, we'll explore the steps involved in deploying a forecasting model and integrating it with a real-time visualization dashboard.

1. Overview of Model Deployment

Model deployment is the process of making a machine learning model accessible for use in production environments. This involves taking the trained model and ensuring it can accept new inputs, generate predictions, and provide results to the end-users in an efficient manner. In the case of demand forecasting, deployment involves ensuring the model can handle real-time data, integrate seamlessly with existing business processes, and generate actionable insights.

The key objectives of deploying a forecasting model are:

- **Provide real-time or near-real-time predictions**: Business decision-makers need up-to-date information to act quickly, especially when making decisions about inventory management, marketing strategies, and promotions.
- **Enable user-friendly interactions**: A visualization dashboard allows users to query the model, interpret its results, and make data-driven decisions without needing technical expertise.
- **Integrate external data sources**: In real-world applications, the forecasting model should accept not only historical sales data but also external factors like promotions, holidays, and economic conditions.

2. Choosing the Right Tools for Deployment

To deploy a demand forecasting model with a visualization dashboard, you will need several components:

- **Backend Model Hosting**: A backend service will serve the trained model and handle incoming requests. Common choices for this include:
- **Flask or FastAPI** (Python-based frameworks) for lightweight web applications and model serving.
- **Django** (Python web framework) if the application requires more complex features or integration with databases.
- **AWS SageMaker, Google AI Platform, or Azure Machine Learning** for cloud-based model hosting and scaling.
- **Dashboard Framework**: A dashboard for visualizing forecasting results can be built using several tools. The most common tools for building interactive dashboards are:
- **Plotly Dash**: A Python framework that allows you to create interactive web-based dashboards easily.
- **Streamlit**: Another Python framework focused on making it simple to deploy machine learning models with interactive visualizations.
- **Tableau or Power BI**: While more complex to integrate with machine learning models, these enterprise-level tools offer high-quality visualizations and can connect to model APIs for real-time data visualization.

3. Steps for Deploying a Forecasting Model with a Dashboard

Step 1: Prepare the Forecasting Model for Deployment

Before you can deploy a model, you must ensure that it's ready to serve predictions. This involves serializing the trained model and ensuring it is packaged in a way that allows it to be loaded efficiently. Popular Python libraries for model serialization include:

Pickle: A simple method for saving and loading Python objects, including trained models.

```
import pickle

# Save the trained model
with open('forecasting_model.pkl', 'wb') as f:
    pickle.dump(model, f)

# Load the trained model
with open('forecasting_model.pkl', 'rb') as f:
```

```python
        loaded_model = pickle.load(f)
```
Joblib: Optimized for storing large models like machine learning models.

```python
python
Copy
Edit
import joblib

# Save the model
joblib.dump(model, 'forecasting_model.joblib')

# Load the model
model = joblib.load('forecasting_model.joblib')
```

Step 2: Build the API for Model Inference

After serializing the model, you'll need to create an API endpoint to serve the model and handle incoming requests for predictions. Flask is a popular choice for serving machine learning models due to its simplicity.

First, you'll create a Flask application to load the model and expose an API endpoint for real-time forecasting.

Example of a simple Flask API:

```python
from flask import Flask, request, jsonify
import pickle
import pandas as pd

# Load the forecasting model
with open('forecasting_model.pkl', 'rb') as f:
    model = pickle.load(f)

app = Flask(__name__)

@app.route('/predict', methods=['POST'])
def predict():
    # Get data from POST request
    data = request.get_json()
    sales_data = pd.DataFrame(data)
```

```
# Generate forecast using the model
forecast = model.predict(sales_data)

# Return the forecast as JSON response
return jsonify({'forecast': forecast.tolist()})

if __name__ == '__main__':
    app.run(debug=True)
```

This basic API receives POST requests with new sales data and returns the forecasted demand.

Step 3: Build the Visualization Dashboard

Now that your model is deployed as a web service, you can build the visualization dashboard. Plotly Dash and Streamlit both offer easy-to-use methods to display forecasts in an interactive manner. Here's how you can create a dashboard with Streamlit.

Install Streamlit:

```
pip install streamlit
```

Create a simple dashboard: In this step, we will use Streamlit to build an interactive dashboard that fetches predictions from the Flask API and visualizes them.

Example code:

```
import streamlit as st
import requests
import pandas as pd
import matplotlib.pyplot as plt

# API endpoint
api_url = 'http://localhost:5000/predict'

# User inputs
st.title("Retail Demand Forecasting")
st.write("Enter the sales data for the next few days to get demand predictions.")
```

```
# Get user input for future data (e.g., next 30 days)
future_data = st.text_area("Enter sales data", value="['2025-03-01', 100, 20, 5]")

# Convert text input to a DataFrame
future_df = pd.read_json(future_data)

if st.button('Get Forecast'):
    # Send data to the Flask API
    response = requests.post(api_url, json=future_df.to_dict(orient='records'))

    # Get the forecasted demand from the response
    if response.status_code == 200:
        forecast = response.json()['forecast']
        forecast_df = pd.DataFrame(forecast, columns=["Predicted Sales"])

        # Plot the forecast
        st.write("Predicted Sales for the next 30 days")
        plt.figure(figsize=(10, 6))
        plt.plot(forecast_df['Predicted Sales'])
        plt.title("Sales Forecast")
        plt.xlabel("Days")
        plt.ylabel("Predicted Sales")
        plt.show()
        st.pyplot(plt)
    else:
        st.error("Error fetching data from API")
```

Step 4: Deploy the Dashboard and API

Once your model API and dashboard are ready, you can deploy them for production. Here are some options:

- **Heroku**: A simple platform-as-a-service (PaaS) that allows you to deploy Flask APIs and Streamlit applications.
- **AWS EC2**: Host the Flask API and dashboard on an EC2 instance.
- **Azure**: Use Azure Web Services or App Services for deploying web apps and APIs.
- **Google Cloud**: Google Cloud's App Engine or Compute Engine can also be used for deployment.

For real-time updates and predictions, the dashboard will need to periodically query the API, and the API will need to be robust enough to handle high traffic in production environments.

4. Conclusion: Bringing Forecasting to Life with Visualization

Deploying a forecasting model with a visualization dashboard is a powerful way to provide stakeholders with actionable insights into future retail demand. By integrating model predictions with user-friendly visualization tools, business leaders can make informed decisions about inventory management, promotions, and sales strategies. The combination of a predictive model with a dynamic dashboard helps bridge the gap between complex data analysis and practical, real-time decision-making, ultimately driving better business outcomes.

9. Image Classification with CNNs

In this chapter, we dive into the world of image classification using Convolutional Neural Networks (CNNs), one of the most powerful techniques in computer vision. You'll learn how to build a model capable of classifying images into predefined categories by leveraging CNN architectures that automatically extract hierarchical features from images. We'll guide you through the process of data augmentation, training models with TensorFlow or PyTorch, and fine-tuning the architecture to optimize performance. Additionally, we'll explore techniques like transfer learning to improve model accuracy with limited data. By the end of this project, you'll have the skills to build and deploy an image classification system, solving real-world visual recognition problems. 🖼️

9.1 Understanding convolutional neural networks

Convolutional Neural Networks (CNNs) have become one of the most widely used architectures for image classification tasks in deep learning. Their ability to automatically learn spatial hierarchies of features from raw images has revolutionized fields such as computer vision, autonomous driving, and medical imaging. In this section, we'll explore the fundamental concepts of CNNs, their unique components, and why they are particularly well-suited for image classification tasks.

1. What Are Convolutional Neural Networks?

At their core, Convolutional Neural Networks (CNNs) are a class of deep learning algorithms designed to analyze visual data such as images or videos. They are a type of neural network that is specifically designed to process grid-like data, such as pixel values in an image. A CNN is composed of several layers that automatically learn hierarchical representations of images, with lower layers capturing simple features (like edges and textures) and deeper layers capturing complex features (such as object parts or entire objects).

CNNs are highly effective because they can automatically extract relevant features from raw images, making them particularly suited for tasks like image classification, object detection, facial recognition, and more.

2. How Do CNNs Work?

The CNN architecture is built around a few key components that allow it to process images efficiently and effectively. Below are the primary layers that make up a CNN:

2.1. Convolutional Layer

The convolutional layer is the core building block of a CNN. It applies a convolution operation to the input image, which involves passing a filter (also known as a kernel) over the image. The filter slides over the image, and at each position, it computes the dot product between the filter and the section of the image it is currently covering. This process produces a feature map, which contains the detected features (such as edges or textures).

- **Filters (Kernels):** Filters are small matrices (e.g., 3x3 or 5x5) that scan across the image. Each filter is responsible for detecting different types of features. Early layers might use filters that detect edges, while deeper layers might detect more complex patterns like shapes, textures, or objects.
- **Stride**: The stride refers to the number of pixels by which the filter moves across the image. A larger stride means the filter moves more quickly, which reduces the spatial dimensions of the output feature map.
- **Padding**: Padding involves adding extra pixels around the border of the input image, often to preserve the size of the output feature map after the convolution operation.

2.2. Activation Function

After the convolution operation, an activation function is applied to the resulting feature map. The most commonly used activation function is the ReLU (Rectified Linear Unit) function, which introduces non-linearity to the network. ReLU replaces all negative values in the feature map with zero, which helps the network learn more complex patterns and improves training efficiency.

ReLU is widely used because it is computationally efficient and helps mitigate the vanishing gradient problem that can occur with other activation functions like the sigmoid or tanh.

2.3. Pooling Layer

The pooling layer is responsible for reducing the spatial dimensions (height and width) of the feature maps while retaining important information. This downsampling process helps reduce the number of parameters in the network and prevents overfitting. There are two main types of pooling:

- **Max Pooling**: In max pooling, the maximum value from a set of pixels within a defined window (e.g., 2x2) is selected. This operation helps retain the most important feature in each region of the image.
- **Average Pooling**: In average pooling, the average value of the pixels within a defined window is taken. Max pooling is typically preferred, but average pooling can sometimes be used depending on the problem.

Pooling reduces the dimensionality of the feature maps and increases computational efficiency.

2.4. Fully Connected Layer

After several convolutional and pooling layers, the output feature maps are flattened into a one-dimensional vector. This vector is then passed through a series of fully connected layers (also known as dense layers), which perform the final classification. In these layers, each neuron is connected to every neuron in the previous layer, allowing the network to make decisions based on the extracted features.

The fully connected layers are typically followed by a softmax activation function when the task is classification. Softmax converts the network's output into probability values that sum up to one, allowing the model to predict the likelihood of an image belonging to each class.

3. Advantages of CNNs for Image Classification

CNNs are particularly effective for image classification tasks for several reasons:

3.1. Local Receptive Fields

The convolutional operation ensures that each neuron only looks at a small portion of the image at a time, known as a local receptive field. This local processing helps the model focus on local patterns, such as edges or textures, which are crucial for image classification.

Additionally, each filter detects a specific feature in the image, and as we move through the layers, the network learns increasingly complex features that represent higher-level structures in the image.

3.2. Parameter Sharing

In a CNN, the same filter is applied across different parts of the image. This parameter sharing means that the network learns fewer parameters compared to fully connected networks, making CNNs less computationally expensive and less prone to overfitting. Instead of learning a different set of weights for each pixel in the image, CNNs learn a small set of weights (the filters), which are shared across the entire image.

3.3. Translation Invariance

CNNs are naturally translation invariant, meaning that the network can recognize an object in an image regardless of its position. This is due to the way the filters slide across the image, detecting features at different spatial locations. As a result, CNNs are robust to small shifts, rotations, or translations of objects within the image.

3.4. Hierarchical Feature Learning

One of the most powerful features of CNNs is their ability to learn a hierarchy of features. In the early layers, CNNs learn simple features like edges, colors, and textures. As the data moves through deeper layers, the model combines these simple features into more complex representations, such as object parts and even entire objects. This hierarchical learning allows CNNs to classify objects in images effectively.

4. CNNs in Action: Real-World Applications

CNNs are used in a wide range of applications, with some of the most notable being in the field of image classification. Below are some of the ways CNNs have transformed industries:

4.1. Object Recognition

CNNs are widely used in object recognition tasks, where the goal is to detect and classify objects within an image. For example, self-driving cars use CNNs to recognize pedestrians, vehicles, traffic signs, and other critical elements of the environment.

4.2. Medical Image Analysis

In healthcare, CNNs are used to analyze medical images, such as MRI scans or X-rays, to detect conditions like tumors, fractures, or abnormalities. CNNs can automatically detect subtle patterns in these images, helping doctors make more accurate diagnoses.

4.3. Facial Recognition

CNNs are also used in facial recognition systems, where the network is trained to recognize and match human faces. This technology is employed in security systems, social media platforms, and even mobile phone unlocking systems.

Convolutional Neural Networks (CNNs) are a powerful class of neural networks that have revolutionized the field of image classification and computer vision. By leveraging layers such as convolutional, pooling, and fully connected layers, CNNs can automatically extract hierarchical features from raw image data and make predictions with remarkable accuracy. Their ability to process images efficiently, combined with advantages like parameter sharing, translation invariance, and hierarchical feature learning, make them ideal for a wide range of image-related tasks, including object recognition, medical image analysis, and facial recognition.

As image classification tasks become more complex and real-world datasets continue to grow, CNNs remain one of the most important and widely adopted techniques in deep learning.

9.2 Collecting and augmenting image datasets

When building machine learning models for image classification, one of the critical steps is obtaining and preparing a suitable dataset. The quality and quantity of data directly impact the performance of the model, making it essential to gather comprehensive, high-quality image data. Additionally, image datasets are often limited or imbalanced, meaning augmentation techniques can be crucial in overcoming these challenges. This chapter will guide you through the process of collecting image datasets, sourcing data, and applying augmentation techniques to improve model generalization.

1. Collecting Image Datasets

1.1. Sourcing Datasets

There are several approaches to collecting image data, depending on your specific use case and the resources available. Below are the common methods for obtaining image datasets:

1.1.1. Publicly Available Datasets

For many common image classification tasks, such as object recognition or facial detection, publicly available datasets can be a great starting point. These datasets are often labeled and ready for use, saving time and resources. Some popular sources for public image datasets include:

- **ImageNet**: A massive collection of over 14 million labeled images in 21,000 categories. It has been widely used in object recognition challenges.
- **COCO (Common Objects in Context)**: A large-scale dataset with over 300,000 labeled images containing objects from 80 categories.
- **MNIST**: A dataset of handwritten digits used for digit classification. It is often used as a benchmark for evaluating new machine learning algorithms.
- **CIFAR-10 and CIFAR-100**: Datasets of 60,000 images in 10 and 100 classes, respectively, commonly used for image classification tasks.
- **Kaggle**: A platform that hosts a variety of datasets for machine learning and computer vision tasks, including specific datasets for niche applications.

1.1.2. Web Scraping

If no suitable dataset exists for your particular problem, or if you need a customized dataset, you can collect data using web scraping techniques. Web scraping involves programmatically extracting images from websites and social media platforms. Popular tools and libraries for web scraping include:

- **BeautifulSoup and Selenium**: These Python libraries allow for scraping and extracting images from HTML web pages.
- **Google Custom Search API**: Allows you to retrieve images from the web based on specific keywords and criteria.
- **Scrapy**: An open-source web crawling framework for scraping images from multiple sources.

While scraping, it's important to follow the terms of service of the websites you are collecting data from and ensure ethical considerations regarding data ownership and copyright.

1.1.3. Capturing Your Own Data

In some cases, the best option might be to collect images yourself. For example, if you are building a model for recognizing specific products, animals, or environments that are not widely available in public datasets, you might need to capture your own images. This can be done using cameras or smartphones and involves both manually taking photos and organizing them into categories.

This approach provides flexibility in obtaining images tailored to your project but requires more time and resources. Additionally, you may need to manually label and annotate the images, which can be a time-consuming process.

2. Image Data Annotation and Labeling

Once you have a collection of images, the next step is to label them appropriately. Labeling, or annotation, involves tagging each image with the correct class or category it represents. Depending on your project, the annotation task may vary:

- **Single-label classification**: Each image belongs to exactly one category.
- **Multi-label classification**: Each image can belong to multiple categories at once.
- **Object detection**: You will need to annotate the location and boundaries of objects within the image (often using bounding boxes or polygons).

Segmentation: Pixel-level annotations for object boundaries (commonly used in tasks like medical imaging).

There are various tools available to assist with labeling:

- **Labelbox**: A popular tool for managing image annotation tasks.
- **VGG Image Annotator (VIA):** A free tool for image annotation, useful for tasks like bounding boxes and segmentation.
- **RectLabel**: A tool for image classification, object detection, and segmentation annotations.

For larger datasets, you can also consider crowd-sourcing platforms like Amazon Mechanical Turk to speed up the labeling process.

3. Image Augmentation Techniques

In the real world, gathering a large, high-quality labeled dataset can be expensive and time-consuming. Moreover, even with large datasets, models may not generalize well on unseen data if the data is too homogeneous or lacks diversity. This is where image augmentation comes into play.

Image augmentation involves applying transformations to existing images in the dataset, creating new variations of the same image to simulate real-world variability. Augmentation helps improve the model's ability to generalize and enhances robustness to different input conditions.

Here are some commonly used image augmentation techniques:

3.1. Geometric Transformations

3.1.1. Rotation

Rotating images by a certain angle (e.g., 90°, 180°, or random degrees) simulates the effect of viewing an object from different angles. This transformation is beneficial for object detection tasks where objects might appear at different orientations.

3.1.2. Scaling

Scaling involves resizing an image, either by zooming in or zooming out. This transformation ensures that the model can recognize objects at various sizes. Scaling can also help improve the model's invariance to object scale.

3.1.3. Flipping

Flipping images horizontally or vertically mirrors the image, creating new variations. Flipping is particularly useful in tasks where the orientation of objects does not affect classification (e.g., animal recognition).

3.2. Color and Lighting Adjustments

3.2.1. Brightness and Contrast Adjustment

Changing the brightness and contrast of an image can simulate lighting changes or different times of the day. This transformation is crucial for making the model more resilient to varying environmental conditions, such as images captured in low-light or bright conditions.

3.2.2. Color Jittering

Color jittering involves randomly changing the color balance in an image. By slightly altering the hue, saturation, or saturation levels, you can simulate different lighting conditions and camera settings.

3.3. Noise and Distortion

3.3.1. Adding Noise

Adding random noise (such as Gaussian noise) to an image introduces random pixel variations. This helps make the model more robust to imperfections and noise present in real-world data.

3.3.2. Elastic Transformations

Elastic transformations simulate random distortions that resemble deformations caused by slight movements of the camera or objects. This technique is especially useful in medical imaging or hand-writing recognition.

3.4. Cropping and Padding

3.4.1. Random Cropping

Random cropping involves cutting a portion of the image and using only that part for training. This forces the model to focus on relevant features even if parts of the object are cut off.

3.4.2. Padding

Padding involves adding extra pixels (e.g., black or white space) around the image. This is useful when images have different aspect ratios, and it helps standardize the input size for the model.

4. Data Augmentation with Deep Learning Frameworks

Many popular deep learning frameworks have built-in functions for performing image augmentation. Some of the widely used libraries include:

- **Keras ImageDataGenerator**: A simple-to-use utility in Keras that can apply real-time augmentations while training the model.
- **TensorFlow Image API**: TensorFlow also provides various utilities for image preprocessing and augmentation, such as tf.image for resizing, rotating, and flipping.
- **Albumentations**: A Python library that offers highly efficient and flexible image augmentation techniques.
- **PyTorch Transforms**: PyTorch provides several transformation functions for augmentation through its torchvision library.

Collecting and augmenting image datasets are essential steps in any computer vision project. While publicly available datasets are a valuable resource, creating custom datasets through web scraping or capturing your own data may be necessary for specific use cases. Once you have your dataset, applying augmentation techniques such as rotation, scaling, and noise addition can help create a more diverse and robust dataset, enabling the model to generalize better. By using these strategies, you can enhance the performance of your image classification models and prepare them for real-world applications, where data variability is a significant challenge.

9.3 Training a CNN model using TensorFlow/PyTorch

In this section, we'll walk through the process of training a Convolutional Neural Network (CNN) model using two of the most popular deep learning frameworks: TensorFlow and PyTorch. CNNs are highly effective for image classification tasks, as they can learn hierarchical features from raw pixel data, making them ideal for applications such as object recognition, facial recognition, and scene analysis.

We'll break down the steps to create, train, and evaluate a CNN model using both TensorFlow (Keras) and PyTorch, giving you the flexibility to choose the framework that fits your needs.

1. Overview of CNN Architecture

A typical Convolutional Neural Network (CNN) consists of several layers that are designed to process images in a hierarchical manner:

- **Convolutional Layers**: These layers perform convolutions on the input image, applying filters (kernels) to extract feature maps. The filters are learned during training.

- **Activation Function (ReLU):** After convolution, an activation function (often ReLU) is applied to introduce non-linearity and enable the network to learn more complex patterns.
- **Pooling Layers**: These layers downsample the feature maps, reducing spatial dimensions and retaining important information. Max pooling is the most commonly used technique.
- **Fully Connected Layers (Dense Layers):** These layers flatten the feature maps and connect every neuron to every other neuron in the next layer. They are typically used for classification tasks.
- **Output Layer**: The output layer typically uses softmax activation for multi-class classification, which produces probabilities for each class.

2. Training CNN with TensorFlow/Keras

TensorFlow (with its Keras API) is one of the most widely used frameworks for deep learning. It offers an easy-to-use interface for creating and training CNN models.

2.1. Importing Required Libraries

To begin, you need to install TensorFlow. If it's not installed yet, you can do so using:

pip install tensorflow

Then, import the necessary libraries:

import tensorflow as tf
from tensorflow.keras import datasets, layers, models
import matplotlib.pyplot as plt

2.2. Load Dataset

We'll use the CIFAR-10 dataset for simplicity. CIFAR-10 contains 60,000 32x32 color images in 10 classes.

 # Load CIFAR-10 dataset
(train_images, train_labels), (test_images, test_labels) = datasets.cifar10.load_data()

2.3. Data Preprocessing

Preprocessing is essential to prepare the data for training. We'll normalize the images to the range of 0 to 1 by dividing by 255 (since pixel values range from 0 to 255).

```
# Normalize pixel values to be between 0 and 1
train_images, test_images = train_images / 255.0, test_images / 255.0
```

2.4. Define the CNN Architecture

Next, we define the architecture of our CNN. The network consists of convolutional layers, pooling layers, a flattening layer, and dense layers.

```
# Build the CNN model
model = models.Sequential([
    layers.Conv2D(32, (3, 3), activation='relu', input_shape=(32, 32, 3)),  # Convolutional layer
    layers.MaxPooling2D((2, 2)),  # Pooling layer
    layers.Conv2D(64, (3, 3), activation='relu'),  # Convolutional layer
    layers.MaxPooling2D((2, 2)),  # Pooling layer
    layers.Conv2D(64, (3, 3), activation='relu'),  # Convolutional layer
    layers.Flatten(),  # Flatten the output for the fully connected layers
    layers.Dense(64, activation='relu'),  # Fully connected layer
    layers.Dense(10)  # Output layer for classification (10 classes)
])
```

2.5. Compile the Model

Now, we need to compile the model. This involves selecting a loss function, an optimizer, and evaluation metrics.

```
# Compile the model
model.compile(optimizer='adam',
        loss=tf.keras.losses.SparseCategoricalCrossentropy(from_logits=True),
        metrics=['accuracy'])
```

2.6. Train the Model

We can now train the model using the training data. We specify the number of epochs and batch size. For CIFAR-10, we'll train for 10 epochs.

```
# Train the model
```

```
history   =   model.fit(train_images,   train_labels,   epochs=10,   batch_size=64,
validation_data=(test_images, test_labels))
```

2.7. Evaluate the Model

Once the model has been trained, we can evaluate it on the test data.

```
# Evaluate the model on the test set
test_loss, test_acc = model.evaluate(test_images, test_labels)
print(f"Test accuracy: {test_acc}")
```

2.8. Visualize the Training Process

It's often helpful to visualize how the model's accuracy and loss evolve over time during training.

```
# Plot training and validation accuracy
plt.plot(history.history['accuracy'], label='Training accuracy')
plt.plot(history.history['val_accuracy'], label='Validation accuracy')
plt.xlabel('Epoch')
plt.ylabel('Accuracy')
plt.legend(loc='lower right')
plt.show()
```

3. Training CNN with PyTorch

PyTorch is another powerful deep learning framework, known for its dynamic computation graph and ease of debugging. Here's how you can train a CNN using PyTorch.

3.1. Install PyTorch

If you haven't already installed PyTorch, you can do so with:

```
pip install torch torchvision
```

3.2. Import Libraries

```
import torch
import torch.nn as nn
import torch.optim as optim
```

```
from torch.utils.data import DataLoader
from torchvision import datasets, transforms
import matplotlib.pyplot as plt
```

3.3. Load Dataset

PyTorch offers convenient tools to load popular datasets like CIFAR-10.

```
# Define transformations (e.g., normalizing images)
transform = transforms.Compose([transforms.ToTensor(),
                transforms.Normalize((0.5, 0.5, 0.5), (0.5, 0.5, 0.5))])

# Load CIFAR-10 dataset
trainset    =    datasets.CIFAR10(root='./data',    train=True,    download=True,
transform=transform)
testset    =    datasets.CIFAR10(root='./data',    train=False,    download=True,
transform=transform)

trainloader = DataLoader(trainset, batch_size=64, shuffle=True)
testloader = DataLoader(testset, batch_size=64, shuffle=False)
```

3.4. Define CNN Architecture

We define a CNN using PyTorch's nn.Module class.

```
class CNN(nn.Module):
    def __init__(self):
        super(CNN, self).__init__()
        self.conv1 = nn.Conv2d(3, 32, kernel_size=3, padding=1)
        self.pool = nn.MaxPool2d(kernel_size=2, stride=2, padding=0)
        self.conv2 = nn.Conv2d(32, 64, kernel_size=3, padding=1)
        self.conv3 = nn.Conv2d(64, 128, kernel_size=3, padding=1)
        self.fc1 = nn.Linear(128 * 4 * 4, 512)
        self.fc2 = nn.Linear(512, 10)

    def forward(self, x):
        x = self.pool(torch.relu(self.conv1(x)))
        x = self.pool(torch.relu(self.conv2(x)))
        x = self.pool(torch.relu(self.conv3(x)))
        x = x.view(-1, 128 * 4 * 4)
```

```
x = torch.relu(self.fc1(x))
x = self.fc2(x)
return x
```

3.5. Instantiate Model, Loss, and Optimizer

```
model = CNN()
criterion = nn.CrossEntropyLoss()
optimizer = optim.Adam(model.parameters(), lr=0.001)
```

3.6. Training Loop

Now we can train the model using a standard training loop.

```
epochs = 10
for epoch in range(epochs):
    running_loss = 0.0
    correct = 0
    total = 0
    for inputs, labels in trainloader:
        optimizer.zero_grad()
        outputs = model(inputs)
        loss = criterion(outputs, labels)
        loss.backward()
        optimizer.step()

        running_loss += loss.item()
        _, predicted = torch.max(outputs, 1)
        total += labels.size(0)
        correct += (predicted == labels).sum().item()

    print(f"Epoch    {epoch+1},    Loss:    {running_loss/len(trainloader)},    Accuracy:
{correct/total}")
```

3.7. Evaluation

Evaluate the model's performance on the test set.

```
correct = 0
total = 0
```

```
with torch.no_grad():
    for inputs, labels in testloader:
        outputs = model(inputs)
        _, predicted = torch.max(outputs, 1)
        total += labels.size(0)
        correct += (predicted == labels).sum().item()

print(f"Test Accuracy: {100 * correct / total}%")
```

Training a Convolutional Neural Network (CNN) for image classification is a rewarding process, especially with the power of frameworks like TensorFlow/Keras and PyTorch. TensorFlow offers high-level abstractions for quick prototyping, while PyTorch provides more control with its dynamic graph structure. Regardless of the framework you choose, the key steps—such as defining a CNN architecture, preprocessing the data, compiling the model, and evaluating performance—remain the same. By mastering these techniques, you can successfully tackle real-world image classification tasks using CNNs.

9.4 Transfer learning with pre-trained models

In this section, we'll explore the concept of transfer learning, a powerful technique that leverages pre-trained models to accelerate the training process, improve model performance, and overcome the challenges of limited data. Transfer learning is especially useful in image classification tasks, where large datasets (such as ImageNet) have been used to train deep neural networks. By transferring knowledge from a pre-trained model, you can reduce the amount of time and resources required to train your own model while still achieving high performance.

We'll walk through the steps of using pre-trained models in TensorFlow (Keras) and PyTorch for transfer learning, focusing on the benefits and practical applications of this approach.

1. What is Transfer Learning?

Transfer learning involves taking a model that has been trained on one task (usually with a large dataset) and reusing its learned features for a new, but related task. Instead of training a model from scratch, which can be computationally expensive and time-consuming, transfer learning allows you to fine-tune the model to your specific dataset with relatively little data.

The key idea is that the early layers of a CNN learn low-level features (e.g., edges, textures), while deeper layers capture more abstract and task-specific features. By reusing the initial layers of a pre-trained model and adjusting the later layers to suit your task, you can save significant training time and still achieve state-of-the-art performance.

2. How Transfer Learning Works

Transfer learning typically works in one of two ways:

Feature Extraction: In this approach, you use the pre-trained model as a fixed feature extractor. The pre-trained model's layers are frozen, and only the final layers are trained on your specific dataset. This method is useful when your dataset is small and similar to the data the model was trained on.

Fine-Tuning: Fine-tuning involves unfreezing some of the pre-trained model's layers and continuing the training on your dataset. This approach is more computationally expensive but can lead to better performance, especially when your dataset is significantly different from the original data.

3. Transfer Learning with TensorFlow/Keras

In TensorFlow/Keras, pre-trained models like VGG16, ResNet, InceptionV3, and MobileNet are available in the tensorflow.keras.applications module. Here's how you can use these models for transfer learning.

3.1. Importing Required Libraries

import tensorflow as tf
from tensorflow.keras import datasets, layers, models
from tensorflow.keras.applications import VGG16
from tensorflow.keras.preprocessing import image
from tensorflow.keras import Model

3.2. Loading a Pre-trained Model (VGG16)

We'll use VGG16, a popular CNN architecture pre-trained on the ImageNet dataset. To use it for transfer learning, we'll remove the top layers (fully connected layers) and add our own classifier.

 # Load the pre-trained VGG16 model (without the top layers)

```
base_model = VGG16(weights='imagenet', include_top=False, input_shape=(224, 224,
3))

# Freeze the layers of the base model (so they won't be trained)
base_model.trainable = False
```

3.3. Adding Custom Layers

Once the base model is set up, you can add your own layers for classification.

```
# Add custom layers on top of the pre-trained model
model = models.Sequential([
    base_model,
    layers.GlobalAveragePooling2D(),    # Global average pooling layer to reduce
dimensionality
    layers.Dense(128, activation='relu'),  # Fully connected layer with ReLU activation
    layers.Dense(10, activation='softmax')  # Output layer for 10 classes
])
```

3.4. Compile and Train the Model

Next, you compile and train the model. Since the base model is frozen, only the new layers will be trained.

```
# Compile the model
model.compile(optimizer=tf.keras.optimizers.Adam(),
        loss='categorical_crossentropy',
        metrics=['accuracy'])

# Train the model (using your own dataset)
model.fit(train_images,        train_labels,        epochs=10,        batch_size=64,
validation_data=(val_images, val_labels))
```

3.5. Fine-Tuning the Model

After training the new layers, you can unfreeze some layers of the base model and fine-tune them.

```
# Unfreeze some layers of the base model
base_model.trainable = True
```

```
for layer in base_model.layers[:15]:  # Freeze all but the last 15 layers
    layer.trainable = False
```

```
# Re-compile the model (this step is important when unfreezing layers)
model.compile(optimizer=tf.keras.optimizers.Adam(learning_rate=1e-5),  # Use a low
learning rate
        loss='categorical_crossentropy',
        metrics=['accuracy'])
```

```
# Fine-tune the model
model.fit(train_images, train_labels, epochs=5, batch_size=64,
validation_data=(val_images, val_labels))
```

4. Transfer Learning with PyTorch

In PyTorch, transfer learning is also easy to implement using pre-trained models from the torchvision.models module. Here's how you can use a pre-trained ResNet18 model for transfer learning.

4.1. Importing Required Libraries

```
import torch
import torch.nn as nn
import torch.optim as optim
from torch.utils.data import DataLoader
from torchvision import datasets, transforms, models
import matplotlib.pyplot as plt
```

4.2. Load Pre-trained Model (ResNet18)

In PyTorch, you can load a pre-trained ResNet model and replace the final fully connected layers with your own classifier.

```
# Load the pre-trained ResNet18 model
model = models.resnet18(pretrained=True)
```

```
# Freeze the layers of the pre-trained model
for param in model.parameters():
    param.requires_grad = False
```

```
# Replace the fully connected layer with a custom one for our specific task
model.fc = nn.Linear(model.fc.in_features, 10)  # Assume 10 output classes
```

4.3. Define Loss Function and Optimizer

Next, define the loss function and optimizer. Since we've frozen most of the model's layers, we'll only train the newly added layers.

```
# Define loss function and optimizer
criterion = nn.CrossEntropyLoss()
optimizer = optim.Adam(model.fc.parameters(), lr=0.001)
```

4.4. Training the Model

Train the model using the same process as training any PyTorch model, focusing on the newly added layers.

```
# Training loop
for epoch in range(10):
    model.train()  # Set the model to training mode
    running_loss = 0.0
    for inputs, labels in trainloader:
        optimizer.zero_grad()  # Clear previous gradients
        outputs = model(inputs)  # Forward pass
        loss = criterion(outputs, labels)  # Compute the loss
        loss.backward()  # Backpropagation
        optimizer.step()  # Update the weights

        running_loss += loss.item()
    print(f"Epoch {epoch+1}, Loss: {running_loss/len(trainloader)}")
```

4.5. Fine-Tuning the Model

After training the custom layers, you can fine-tune the entire model by unfreezing some layers.

```
# Unfreeze some layers of the pre-trained model
for param in model.layer4.parameters():  # Unfreeze the last layer block
    param.requires_grad = True
```

```
# Re-define the optimizer to update all parameters
optimizer = optim.Adam(model.parameters(), lr=1e-5)

# Fine-tune the model
for epoch in range(5):
    model.train()
    running_loss = 0.0
    for inputs, labels in trainloader:
        optimizer.zero_grad()
        outputs = model(inputs)
        loss = criterion(outputs, labels)
        loss.backward()
        optimizer.step()

        running_loss += loss.item()
    print(f"Epoch {epoch+1}, Loss: {running_loss/len(trainloader)}")
```

Transfer learning is a powerful method for leveraging pre-trained models to improve the performance of your image classification tasks. Both TensorFlow/Keras and PyTorch make it easy to apply transfer learning by providing a variety of pre-trained models, such as VGG16, ResNet, and InceptionV3. Whether you freeze the base model and only train the custom layers, or fine-tune the entire model, transfer learning can significantly reduce training time and improve the performance of your model, especially when you have limited data or computational resources.

By using transfer learning, you can tap into the vast amount of knowledge embedded in pre-trained models and apply it to a wide variety of real-world problems in image classification, object detection, and beyond.

9.5 Deploying an image classification API

Once you have trained your Convolutional Neural Network (CNN) model for image classification, the next step is to make it accessible to users or applications for real-world use. This involves deploying the model as a web service, typically through an API (Application Programming Interface). In this section, we will discuss how to deploy your image classification model using Flask, a lightweight web framework for Python. Flask allows you to easily build APIs, while tools like TensorFlow or PyTorch handle the model inference.

We will guide you through the process of setting up the environment, creating the Flask app, and serving the image classification model as an API endpoint. This will enable users to send images to the API, get predictions, and receive results in a standardized format.

1. Setting Up the Environment

Before we start, ensure that you have the necessary libraries installed. If you haven't already, you can install Flask and other required packages using pip:

```
pip install flask
pip install tensorflow   # If using TensorFlow
# OR
pip install torch torchvision  # If using PyTorch
pip install pillow       # For image processing
pip install numpy        # For numerical operations
```

Once you have the required libraries, ensure that your trained model (either in TensorFlow/Keras or PyTorch format) is saved in a format that can be loaded for inference. If you're using TensorFlow/Keras, you might save your model as an H5 file. For PyTorch, the model will be saved in the .pth format.

2. Create a Flask Application

Next, we will create a Flask application that serves the image classification model.

2.1. Import Required Libraries

First, import the necessary libraries for Flask and model loading.

```
from flask import Flask, request, jsonify
from tensorflow.keras.preprocessing import image
import numpy as np
import tensorflow as tf
from PIL import Image
import io
```

If you're using PyTorch, you would instead import the corresponding libraries, like so:

```
import torch
from torchvision import transforms
```

from PIL import Image

2.2. Load the Pre-Trained Model

Now, we'll load the trained image classification model. This can be a TensorFlow/Keras model or a PyTorch model.

For TensorFlow/Keras:

```
# Load the pre-trained Keras model
model = tf.keras.models.load_model('path_to_your_model.h5')
```

For PyTorch:

```
# Load the pre-trained PyTorch model
model = torch.load('path_to_your_model.pth')
model.eval()  # Set the model to evaluation mode
```

2.3. Initialize Flask App

Next, create the Flask application.

```
app = Flask(__name__)
```

2.4. Image Preprocessing Function

Regardless of whether you're using TensorFlow or PyTorch, you'll need to preprocess the incoming image before passing it to the model. This involves resizing the image, normalizing it, and possibly expanding its dimensions.

For TensorFlow/Keras:

```
def preprocess_image(image_path):
    img = Image.open(image_path).resize((224, 224))  # Resize image to fit model input size
    img = np.array(img) / 255.0  # Normalize image to range [0,1]
    img = np.expand_dims(img, axis=0)  # Add batch dimension
    return img
```

For PyTorch:

```
def preprocess_image(image_path):
    transform = transforms.Compose([
        transforms.Resize((224, 224)),
        transforms.ToTensor(),
        transforms.Normalize(mean=[0.485, 0.456, 0.406], std=[0.229, 0.224, 0.225])  #
ImageNet normalization
    ])
    img = Image.open(image_path)
    img = transform(img).unsqueeze(0)  # Add batch dimension
    return img
```

2.5. Define Prediction Endpoint

Now, define the API endpoint where users can send images for predictions.

```
@app.route('/predict', methods=['POST'])
def predict():
    if 'file' not in request.files:
        return jsonify({'error': 'No file part'}), 400

    file = request.files['file']

    if file.filename == '':
        return jsonify({'error': 'No selected file'}), 400

    try:
        # Preprocess the image
        img = preprocess_image(file)

        # Make a prediction using the model
        if isinstance(model, tf.keras.Model):  # For TensorFlow/Keras
            prediction = model.predict(img)
            class_idx = np.argmax(prediction, axis=1)[0]
        else:  # For PyTorch
            with torch.no_grad():
                img = img.to(device)  # Send image to GPU if available
                prediction = model(img)
                class_idx = torch.argmax(prediction, dim=1).item()
```

```
    # Return the prediction as a JSON response
    response = {'prediction': int(class_idx)}
    return jsonify(response)

except Exception as e:
    return jsonify({'error': str(e)}), 500
```

2.6. Run the Flask App

Finally, run the Flask application.

```
if __name__ == '__main__':
    app.run(debug=True, host='0.0.0.0', port=5000)
```

When you run the script, your model will be available for predictions at http://localhost:5000/predict.

3. Testing the API

Once the Flask application is running, you can test it by sending a POST request with an image file. You can use a tool like Postman or write a simple script to send the image using requests in Python.

Here's an example of how to send an image to the API using requests:

```
import requests

url = 'http://localhost:5000/predict'
image_path = 'path_to_test_image.jpg'

files = {'file': open(image_path, 'rb')}
response = requests.post(url, files=files)

print(response.json())
```

If everything is set up correctly, you should get a JSON response with the predicted class index (or label) for the input image.

4. Deploying to the Cloud

Once the model is serving predictions locally, you may want to deploy it to a production environment. For production deployment, cloud platforms like Heroku, AWS, Google Cloud, and Azure provide services to deploy Flask APIs seamlessly. Here's an overview of how you can deploy the model using Heroku:

Prepare the app for Heroku:

- Create a requirements.txt file containing all dependencies.
- Create a Procfile to tell Heroku how to run the app (e.g., web: python app.py).

Deploy to Heroku:

- Commit the code to a Git repository.
- Push the repository to Heroku using git push heroku master.

Access the API: Once deployed, you can access your model through the public URL provided by Heroku.

Deploying an image classification model as an API enables real-world applications to interact with your model easily. By using Flask, we were able to set up a simple yet robust API for making predictions. Whether you're using TensorFlow or PyTorch, the steps remain similar: preprocess the input image, use the model for inference, and return the results as a JSON response. Additionally, by deploying the API to the cloud, you can scale your model and make it available to a wider audience. This is a critical step in transitioning from a model in development to a model that is deployed and actively used in real-world scenarios.

10. Recommender System for E-Commerce

In this chapter, we explore how to build a recommender system to personalize user experiences in e-commerce platforms. You'll learn how to design and implement both collaborative filtering and content-based filtering techniques to recommend products to users based on their preferences and browsing history. We'll cover essential topics such as matrix factorization, user-item interaction data, and the use of nearest neighbor algorithms to suggest relevant products. Additionally, we'll dive into hybrid models that combine both approaches for more accurate recommendations. By the end of this project, you'll have the knowledge to create a personalized product recommendation system that can enhance user engagement and drive sales for e-commerce businesses. □

10.1 Understanding collaborative and content-based filtering

Recommender systems have become an integral part of e-commerce platforms, guiding users to products that match their preferences, ultimately improving user experience and driving sales. These systems are designed to predict the items a user might be interested in, based on their past behavior or the preferences of similar users. Broadly speaking, recommender systems can be divided into two main approaches: Collaborative Filtering (CF) and Content-Based Filtering (CBF). In this sub-chapter, we will explore these two types of filtering techniques, their differences, and how they work in the context of building a recommender system for e-commerce platforms.

1. Collaborative Filtering (CF)

Collaborative filtering is one of the most widely used methods in recommender systems. It works by analyzing patterns of user interactions, focusing on how users have rated, purchased, or interacted with items. The core idea behind collaborative filtering is that users who agreed in the past will agree in the future. For instance, if User A and User B have a similar history of interacting with products, collaborative filtering would recommend products that User B liked to User A, assuming they might like them too.

1.1 Types of Collaborative Filtering

There are two main approaches to collaborative filtering:

User-Based Collaborative Filtering (UBCF): This method finds users who are similar to the target user and recommends products that these similar users have liked or interacted with. If User A and User B have similar purchasing histories, the system would recommend products that User B bought but User A hasn't yet interacted with. This method is based on the assumption that if users share preferences, they will likely continue to share similar preferences in the future.

- **Pros**: Simple and intuitive; can provide diverse recommendations based on user behavior.
- **Cons**: Computationally expensive when scaling to large datasets; difficult to generate recommendations for new users (cold start problem).

Item-Based Collaborative Filtering (IBCF): In this approach, the system finds items that are similar to those the user has already interacted with and recommends those items. If User A purchased or liked a certain product, the system will recommend products that are similar to the one User A interacted with. This approach focuses on finding similarities between items based on user interactions and the assumption that items with similar purchase patterns will appeal to similar users.

- **Pros**: Easier to scale compared to user-based CF; provides better recommendations for users who have interacted with many items.
- **Cons**: Can be biased towards popular items and may have trouble with niche or new items.

1.2 Collaborative Filtering Challenges

Cold Start Problem: One of the significant challenges of collaborative filtering is the cold start problem. This problem arises when a new user or item enters the system with insufficient interaction history. Without enough data, the system struggles to provide accurate recommendations.

Sparsity: In real-world e-commerce systems, the user-item interaction matrix tends to be very sparse. Many users have only interacted with a small subset of items, making it difficult to identify similarities and generate recommendations.

Scalability: As the number of users and items increases, collaborative filtering can become computationally expensive. The need to calculate similarities between users or items and to store the user-item interaction matrix can strain system resources.

2. Content-Based Filtering (CBF)

Content-based filtering works on a fundamentally different principle. Instead of relying on user interactions or behaviors, it makes recommendations based on the attributes of items and the user's past preferences. In a content-based recommender system, each item is described by a set of features, such as category, brand, price, and description. The system matches these features with a user's historical behavior and recommends items with similar attributes to the ones the user has shown interest in.

2.1 How Content-Based Filtering Works

Item Representation: Every item in the system is represented by a set of features or metadata. In the case of an e-commerce platform, items could be represented by features such as product category, description, price, brand, color, and other relevant attributes.

User Profile: Content-based filtering uses the user's past preferences or behaviors to build a profile. For example, if a user frequently purchases electronics, the system builds a profile based on the features of electronics (e.g., brands, product types, price ranges, etc.).

Recommendation Generation: Once the user profile is established, the system compares the features of available items to the user profile and recommends items that share similar attributes to what the user has previously interacted with. For example, if a user has bought a lot of smartphones, the system might recommend new smartphones from the same or similar brands, with similar specifications.

2.2 Content-Based Filtering Challenges

Limited Exploration: Since content-based filtering is based on the user's past behavior, it tends to recommend items that are very similar to what the user has already seen. This could lead to a lack of diversity in the recommendations, where the user is only exposed to a narrow range of products.

Feature Engineering: The success of content-based filtering depends heavily on how well the items are represented by their features. If the features do not adequately capture the items' characteristics, or if there are too many irrelevant features, the quality of recommendations can suffer.

Cold Start Problem: Although content-based filtering does not suffer from the same cold start problem as collaborative filtering, it still faces challenges when it comes to recommending items for a new user. Without sufficient user interaction data, building an effective user profile can be difficult.

3. Hybrid Approaches

Both collaborative filtering and content-based filtering have their advantages and challenges, and often the best solution for an e-commerce recommender system is a hybrid approach, which combines elements of both techniques. A hybrid model can leverage the strengths of collaborative filtering to make diverse recommendations based on user interactions, while also using content-based filtering to personalize recommendations based on item attributes.

For instance, a hybrid recommender system might:

- Combine collaborative filtering's ability to provide recommendations based on user behavior with content-based filtering's focus on item features.
- Use collaborative filtering for initial recommendations and content-based filtering for refining the suggestions by adding personal attributes that the user cares about (such as price, brand, or category).
- Apply hybrid techniques to handle the cold start problem more effectively, by using content-based filtering to recommend items to new users while collaborative filtering can suggest similar items once the user has interacted with enough products.

4. Choosing the Right Filtering Approach for E-Commerce

When designing a recommender system for an e-commerce platform, the choice between collaborative filtering and content-based filtering largely depends on the business objectives, the nature of the data, and the user behavior.

Collaborative filtering is ideal when you have a large volume of user interaction data and want to capture the collective preferences of users. It works well for recommending items that are popular or have been highly rated by similar users.

Content-based filtering is useful when the items have rich metadata and attributes that can be leveraged to make personalized recommendations. This approach works well when you want to recommend niche items, or when there is limited interaction history available for new users or items.

Collaborative and content-based filtering are two cornerstone techniques in building recommender systems, each with its strengths and limitations. Collaborative filtering excels in capturing user preferences through historical data, making it powerful in recommending popular items. However, it is hindered by the cold start problem and scalability issues. Content-based filtering, on the other hand, offers a more personalized approach by analyzing the features of items, but it may lack diversity in recommendations and is dependent on the quality of item metadata. By understanding both approaches, you can make informed decisions when designing a recommender system for e-commerce platforms, ensuring that users receive relevant and personalized product suggestions. A hybrid model, which integrates both techniques, can often provide the best of both worlds, overcoming individual limitations and delivering more effective recommendations.

10.2 Data preparation and feature engineering

In the process of building a recommender system for e-commerce, data preparation and feature engineering are essential steps that directly influence the quality of recommendations. Without the right data and well-engineered features, even the best algorithm may fail to generate meaningful recommendations. This chapter will cover key techniques for preparing and engineering data to optimize the performance of collaborative and content-based filtering models.

1. Importance of Data Preparation

Data preparation is the process of cleaning, transforming, and structuring raw data into a usable format for analysis and modeling. In the context of a recommender system, the raw data typically includes user interactions, item metadata, and sometimes external factors, such as demographic or contextual data. The goal of data preparation is to ensure the system has reliable, accurate, and relevant data to generate meaningful predictions.

1.1 Collecting and Cleaning Data

The first step in data preparation is gathering all the relevant data. This includes both user interactions (e.g., purchases, clicks, ratings, etc.) and item information (e.g., product details like category, price, and brand). For a comprehensive recommender system, it is essential to collect a variety of user-item interaction data, such as:

- User-item interaction data: Transactions, clicks, ratings, reviews, etc.
- Item metadata: Category, brand, description, price, stock, etc.
- User data (optional): Demographics, location, behavior history, etc.

Once the data is collected, it must be cleaned and preprocessed. Data cleaning includes:

- **Removing duplicates**: Ensuring there are no redundant records, especially in user-item interaction data.
- **Handling missing values**: If there are missing interactions, either impute the missing values or discard the incomplete data, depending on its importance.
- **Filtering out noise**: Filtering out irrelevant or erroneous data points (e.g., users who have interacted with only one item or items with no user interactions).

1.2 Data Transformation

Transforming data into a format suitable for modeling is another important part of data preparation. For example, the user-item interaction matrix is typically sparse and not directly usable in its raw form. It must be transformed into a format that works for your recommender system approach.

Collaborative Filtering: In the case of collaborative filtering, user-item interactions are often represented in a user-item matrix where each row represents a user, and each column represents an item. The values in this matrix could represent ratings, purchase frequencies, or interaction counts.

For example, if User A purchased Item X, the interaction matrix will have a value at the intersection of User A's row and Item X's column.

Content-Based Filtering: In content-based filtering, items are typically represented by a feature matrix, where each row corresponds to an item and each column corresponds to a feature (e.g., brand, category, price range, etc.). The features are often encoded in numerical form.

2. Feature Engineering for Recommender Systems

Feature engineering is the process of creating new features from the raw data that will help the model better understand patterns and relationships within the data. The features used in a recommender system can be classified into item-based and user-based features, depending on whether they are related to the item being recommended or the user receiving the recommendation.

2.1 Item-Based Features

For content-based filtering, the features of the item play a crucial role in generating recommendations. Examples of item-based features include:

Product Category: Items with similar categories may be recommended to users who have interacted with other products in the same category (e.g., electronics, clothing, home appliances).

Brand: Users who have purchased items from a particular brand may be more likely to purchase items from the same brand in the future.

Price Range: Users may have preferences for certain price ranges, so including price as a feature helps filter recommendations based on the user's price sensitivity.

Product Description: Textual descriptions of items can be processed to create features like keywords or topics that can help match similar products based on content. For example, using Natural Language Processing (NLP) techniques to extract product attributes from the description.

Ratings or Reviews: The average user rating or sentiment extracted from reviews can be used as features in the recommendation system, influencing the likelihood that a user will be interested in an item.

Availability/Stock: Items that are frequently out of stock might not be recommended to users, whereas items with ample availability can be prioritized.

Sales History: The number of sales of an item can provide an indication of its popularity, helping to recommend best-sellers to new users.

2.2 User-Based Features

In collaborative filtering, user-specific features are important in identifying similar users and generating personalized recommendations. User-based features include:

User Demographics: Basic demographic information such as age, gender, location, and income level can help in generating recommendations based on similarities between users with the same characteristics.

Behavioral Data: A user's interaction history, such as items they have purchased, clicked on, rated, or added to their cart, plays a critical role in shaping personalized recommendations.

Engagement History: How often a user interacts with the platform, the types of products they engage with, and how much time they spend browsing can be indicative of their preferences.

Social Influences: Users' social networks (e.g., followers, friends) can also influence recommendations. If a user's social circle has interacted with certain products, the system might suggest those products as well.

User Intent: Understanding a user's intent (e.g., shopping for a gift vs. purchasing for personal use) can be derived from behavior patterns and enhance the relevance of recommendations.

2.3 Combining Item-Based and User-Based Features

While item-based and user-based features are distinct, they can be combined in hybrid models to improve recommendation performance. For example:

User-Item Interaction Matrix: In collaborative filtering, item-based features can be used to refine the similarities between items, while user-based features can help further personalize the recommendations based on demographic information.

Cross-Filtering: Combining collaborative and content-based filtering can lead to a more robust system by balancing item similarity with user profile data. For example, if collaborative filtering suggests an item based on user similarity, content-based filtering can ensure the item is consistent with the user's past preferences.

3. Feature Transformation and Encoding

Once features have been identified, they need to be transformed into a numerical format that can be processed by machine learning algorithms. Common techniques for feature transformation and encoding include:

One-Hot Encoding: For categorical features like product category or brand, one-hot encoding is commonly used. This technique converts each category into a binary vector, where each dimension corresponds to a unique category.

Numerical Encoding: For features like price or ratings, numerical encoding can be directly applied, ensuring that these values are in a format suitable for mathematical models.

TF-IDF (Term Frequency-Inverse Document Frequency): For textual data such as product descriptions, TF-IDF is often used to quantify the relevance of words or phrases. This helps create a vectorized representation of items based on their textual content.

Normalization: Features such as price, ratings, or age may have different scales. Normalizing these features ensures they are treated equally in models, preventing any one feature from dominating the others.

Embedding Representations: For more complex data, like images or long text, embedding techniques such as Word2Vec for text or CNN-based embeddings for images can help transform raw data into more useful representations.

4. Handling Data Sparsity

Data sparsity is a common issue in recommender systems, especially for collaborative filtering. It arises when a large portion of the user-item interaction matrix is empty (i.e., users have interacted with only a small fraction of items). To address this issue:

Matrix Factorization: Techniques like Singular Value Decomposition (SVD) and Alternating Least Squares (ALS) can be used to factorize the interaction matrix into lower-dimensional representations that capture latent factors, thus reducing sparsity.

Neighborhood Methods: In item-based collaborative filtering, finding items with similar characteristics (based on feature vectors) helps alleviate sparsity by recommending items that are similar in feature space, even if they have not been interacted with yet.

Data preparation and feature engineering are foundational steps in building an effective recommender system for e-commerce. By carefully preparing and transforming raw data into useful features, businesses can ensure that their recommender system delivers personalized, accurate, and relevant product suggestions to users. Whether it's through collaborative filtering or content-based filtering, well-engineered features can help overcome challenges like data sparsity and cold-start problems, enhancing the system's overall performance.

10.3 Building a basic recommender system

Building a basic recommender system involves selecting the right algorithm, processing the data, and implementing a solution that can provide personalized recommendations to users. This chapter will walk you through the steps required to build a simple yet effective recommender system using collaborative filtering techniques, and it will also touch on content-based filtering. We will use Python along with popular libraries like Pandas, NumPy, and Scikit-learn, as well as a few others, to implement and evaluate the model.

1. Choosing the Type of Recommender System

Recommender systems can be broadly classified into three categories: collaborative filtering, content-based filtering, and hybrid approaches. In this section, we'll focus on building a basic recommender system using collaborative filtering techniques. Collaborative filtering is based on the idea of recommending items by leveraging the preferences of similar users or items.

We will build a user-based collaborative filtering system, but the principles of item-based collaborative filtering can also be applied in a similar way. To keep things simple, we will use the nearest neighbors algorithm to identify similar users.

2. Dataset Preparation

Before building the recommender, we need a dataset that contains user-item interactions. In a typical e-commerce platform, this would be data about customers (users) and their interactions with products (items). Common interaction data includes ratings, clicks, purchases, etc. For this example, we will assume the dataset has the following columns:

- **UserID**: The identifier of the user.
- **ItemID**: The identifier of the item (e.g., product ID).
- **Rating**: The user's rating or interaction score with the item (this can be purchase frequency, rating, etc.).

Let's consider the following basic format of the data:

UserID	ItemID	Rating
1	101	5
1	102	3
2	101	4
2	103	5
3	102	5
3	103	4
4	101	2

This dataset indicates how users have rated or interacted with various products. We can use this data to recommend products to users based on their past interactions and the interactions of similar users.

3. Data Preprocessing

The first step in building any machine learning model is preprocessing the data. In collaborative filtering, we need to transform the raw user-item interaction data into a user-item matrix, also known as the interaction matrix. This matrix will have users as rows, items as columns, and the values corresponding to the ratings or interactions between them.

For example, the user-item matrix for the above data would look like this:

UserID	101	102	103
1	5	3	NaN
2	4	NaN	5
3	NaN	5	4
4	2	NaN	NaN

Where:

- The rows represent users.
- The columns represent items.
- The NaN values represent missing ratings (i.e., the user has not interacted with that item).

We can use the pivot_table() function from Pandas to create this matrix. We can also handle missing values by filling them with zeros or using imputation techniques, but for simplicity, we'll leave them as NaN for now.

```
import pandas as pd

# Sample user-item interaction data
data = {'UserID': [1, 1, 2, 2, 3, 3, 4],
        'ItemID': [101, 102, 101, 103, 102, 103, 101],
        'Rating': [5, 3, 4, 5, 5, 4, 2]}

df = pd.DataFrame(data)

# Create the user-item interaction matrix
interaction_matrix = df.pivot_table(index='UserID', columns='ItemID', values='Rating')

# Show the interaction matrix
print(interaction_matrix)
```

4. Building the Collaborative Filtering Model

We can now move on to implementing the collaborative filtering model. One of the simplest algorithms for collaborative filtering is K-Nearest Neighbors (KNN). This algorithm identifies the most similar users (neighbors) to a target user and recommends items that those neighbors have liked or interacted with.

We will use the KNeighborsClassifier from scikit-learn to find the nearest neighbors based on the user-item matrix.

First, we need to fill in the NaN values (missing ratings) in the interaction matrix. For simplicity, we will use the mean imputation strategy, where missing values are replaced with the average rating for that item.

```
from sklearn.impute import SimpleImputer

# Fill NaN values with the mean value of each column (i.e., each item)
imputer = SimpleImputer(strategy='mean')
interaction_matrix_filled = imputer.fit_transform(interaction_matrix)
```

```
# Show the filled matrix
print(interaction_matrix_filled)
```

Once the matrix is ready, we can use KNN to find similar users:

```
from sklearn.neighbors import NearestNeighbors

# Create the KNN model
knn = NearestNeighbors(metric='cosine', algorithm='brute')

# Fit the model on the interaction matrix
knn.fit(interaction_matrix_filled)

# Find the 3 nearest neighbors for user 1
distances, indices = knn.kneighbors([interaction_matrix_filled[0]], n_neighbors=3)

# Show the indices of the nearest neighbors
print("Nearest Neighbors for User 1:", indices)
```

5. Making Recommendations

Now that we have identified the nearest neighbors for a given user, we can recommend items based on what similar users have interacted with. For example, if User 1 is similar to User 2 and User 3, we can recommend items that these users have rated highly but that User 1 has not yet interacted with.

To make this process automatic, we can use the following approach:

- Find the neighbors of the target user.
- Collect the items rated by these neighbors that the target user has not rated.
- Recommend the top-rated items among the ones not yet interacted with.

Here's how to implement this:

```
# Get the items rated by nearest neighbors
def get_recommendations(user_index, num_neighbors=3):
    neighbors = indices[0]
    recommended_items = []

    for neighbor in neighbors:
```

```
    # Get the items rated by the neighbor
    items_rated_by_neighbor = interaction_matrix.iloc[neighbor].dropna().index.tolist()

    # Add the items that user has not rated yet
    for item in items_rated_by_neighbor:
        if pd.isna(interaction_matrix.iloc[user_index][item]):
            recommended_items.append(item)

    return recommended_items[:num_neighbors]

# Get recommendations for User 1
recommended_items = get_recommendations(0)
print("Recommended items for User 1:", recommended_items)
```

This function will return the top N recommended items for the given user.

6. Evaluation of the Model

Evaluating a recommender system is an important step to ensure it provides useful recommendations. Common evaluation metrics include Precision, Recall, and Mean Squared Error (MSE).

For simplicity, let's use the Mean Absolute Error (MAE) to measure the performance:

```
from sklearn.metrics import mean_absolute_error

# Actual ratings for User 1
actual_ratings = interaction_matrix.iloc[0].dropna()

# Predicted ratings (for simplicity, let's assume we predict the items using the neighbors)
predicted_ratings = [interaction_matrix.iloc[indices[0][0]][item] for item in actual_ratings.index]

# Calculate MAE
mae = mean_absolute_error(actual_ratings, predicted_ratings)
print("Mean Absolute Error:", mae)
```

In this section, we walked through the process of building a basic recommender system using collaborative filtering. We covered data preparation, building the interaction matrix, creating the model with K-Nearest Neighbors, making recommendations, and evaluating the system.

This basic recommender system can be improved and extended with techniques like matrix factorization, hybrid models, and deeper learning approaches. However, this example serves as a strong foundation for understanding how to approach building recommender systems for e-commerce platforms.

10.4 Implementing a hybrid recommendation engine

A hybrid recommendation engine combines different recommendation techniques to improve the accuracy and robustness of recommendations. By leveraging both collaborative filtering and content-based filtering, hybrid systems aim to take the best of both worlds, thus mitigating the limitations that each technique may have when used independently.

While collaborative filtering relies on user-item interactions to recommend products based on similarity between users or items, content-based filtering recommends items by comparing the features or attributes of items. A hybrid model incorporates both these techniques, offering a more personalized and diverse set of recommendations.

In this section, we will walk through how to build a simple hybrid recommendation engine using weighted hybridization. This involves combining the results of collaborative filtering and content-based filtering, where we assign weights to each recommendation technique and combine them to make the final recommendations.

1. Revisit the Collaborative Filtering Model

As discussed in earlier sections, collaborative filtering works by finding users who are similar to the target user and recommending items they have liked. This is done through a similarity matrix built from the user-item interaction data.

Let's assume we have already created a user-item interaction matrix and have implemented a collaborative filtering technique (such as K-Nearest Neighbors or Matrix Factorization) that returns the top-N recommended items for a user. For simplicity, let's say the collaborative filtering model yields the following top 5 recommendations for User 1:

Collaborative Filtering Recommendations (Top 5): Item 101, Item 102, Item 103, Item 105, Item 106

These items are based on the preferences and behaviors of similar users.

2. Revisit the Content-Based Filtering Model

Content-based filtering recommends items based on the features of the items themselves. In the case of an e-commerce platform, item features could include product categories (e.g., "Electronics," "Clothing"), price range, brand, color, etc. Content-based filtering uses these attributes to identify items that are similar to what a user has interacted with in the past.

Let's assume we have a dataset of item features for each product, and we calculate the similarity between items based on their features using a cosine similarity measure. The content-based filtering model for User 1 might yield the following recommendations:

Content-Based Filtering Recommendations (Top 5): Item 104, Item 107, Item 102, Item 109, Item 110

These items are recommended based on the similarity in features to the items User 1 has interacted with previously.

3. Combining Collaborative Filtering and Content-Based Filtering

Now that we have the recommendations from both collaborative filtering and content-based filtering, the next step is to combine them to create a hybrid recommendation list. The most straightforward way to do this is through weighted hybridization, where we assign weights to the recommendations from both models and combine them to form a final ranked list.

To implement this, we will first create a function to assign a weight to each technique. For example, we can give a higher weight to collaborative filtering if it is more reliable or better suited for the current data. After that, we will merge the recommendations from both models and sort them according to the assigned weights.

4. Assigning Weights and Merging the Recommendations

Let's assume the following weights for the two techniques:

- **Collaborative Filtering Weight**: 0.7
- **Content-Based Filtering Weight**: 0.3

We'll create a simple function that combines the recommendations from both models, keeping the weighted contributions in mind. Here's how to implement this:

```python
import pandas as pd
import numpy as np

# Sample collaborative filtering recommendations
collaborative_recommendations = ['Item101', 'Item102', 'Item103', 'Item105', 'Item106']

# Sample content-based filtering recommendations
content_based_recommendations = ['Item104', 'Item107', 'Item102', 'Item109', 'Item110']

# Assign weights to both recommendation systems
collaborative_weight = 0.7
content_based_weight = 0.3

# Create a combined list with item names and weights
combined_recommendations = []

# Create a function to combine recommendations with weights
def combine_recommendations(collab_recs, content_recs, collab_weight, content_weight):
    for item in collab_recs:
        combined_recommendations.append((item, collab_weight))  # Add the item with the collaborative filtering weight

    for item in content_recs:
        combined_recommendations.append((item, content_weight))  # Add the item with the content-based filtering weight

    # Convert to DataFrame for easy sorting
    recommendations_df = pd.DataFrame(combined_recommendations, columns=['Item', 'Weight'])

    # Group by Item, sum the weights, and sort by the combined weight
    recommendations_df = recommendations_df.groupby('Item').agg({'Weight': 'sum'}).reset_index()
```

recommendations_df = recommendations_df.sort_values(by='Weight',
ascending=False)

return recommendations_df

 # Combine the recommendations and print the final ranked list
final_recommendations = combine_recommendations(collaborative_recommendations,
content_based_recommendations, collaborative_weight, content_based_weight)

 # Show the final recommendations
print(final_recommendations)

The combine_recommendations function does the following:

- Merges the items from both recommendation systems with their respective weights.
- Groups by item name and sums the weights of each item.
- Sorts the items by the combined weight to determine the final ranking.

Here's an example of how the final sorted recommendations could look:

Item	Weight
Item101	0.7
Item102	0.6
Item104	0.3
Item103	0.7
Item107	0.3
Item105	0.7
Item106	0.7
Item109	0.3
Item110	0.3

5. Evaluating the Hybrid Model

Once the hybrid recommender system is built, it's important to evaluate its performance. You can use metrics such as Precision, Recall, and F1-Score to evaluate how well your system is making relevant recommendations. These metrics can be calculated by comparing the items recommended by the hybrid system to a ground truth list (e.g., the items the user actually purchased or interacted with).

For example, you can calculate Precision as the fraction of recommended items that are relevant to the user, and Recall as the fraction of relevant items that are recommended by the system.

```
from sklearn.metrics import precision_score, recall_score

# Assume ground truth for relevant items
ground_truth = ['Item101', 'Item102', 'Item105']

# Predict the top-N recommendations (say top 3)
top_n_recommendations = final_recommendations.head(3)['Item'].tolist()

# Calculate Precision and Recall
precision = precision_score(ground_truth, top_n_recommendations, average='binary')
recall = recall_score(ground_truth, top_n_recommendations, average='binary')

print("Precision:", precision)
print("Recall:", recall)
```

By implementing a hybrid recommendation engine, we've significantly improved the quality and reliability of the recommendations compared to using a single recommendation technique. Collaborative filtering captures the wisdom of similar users, while content-based filtering offers item-specific insights based on their features. Combining these techniques using weighted hybridization ensures that we are leveraging the strengths of both approaches.

In practice, hybrid recommendation systems are highly effective for e-commerce platforms, streaming services, and other applications where personalized recommendations are crucial. Further refinements, such as using more advanced algorithms like Matrix Factorization, Deep Learning-based approaches, or incorporating user demographics as additional features, can further enhance the performance of hybrid recommender systems.

10.5 Deploying a recommender system on a web app

Deploying a recommender system in a web application enables real-time personalized recommendations for users as they interact with the platform. This involves creating a robust backend that serves the recommendation model, connecting it with a frontend interface that users can interact with, and ensuring scalability and efficiency for high traffic applications. In this sub-chapter, we will walk through the steps involved in deploying a recommender system using a popular framework such as Flask (for the backend) and HTML/CSS (for the frontend).

By the end of this section, you'll have a working web app that provides personalized product recommendations to users based on the recommender system we've built earlier.

1. Preparing the Recommender System for Deployment

Before deployment, ensure that your recommender system is fully trained and tested. This means:

- Fine-tuning the recommendation model (whether collaborative filtering, content-based filtering, or hybrid).
- Validating the model using metrics like Precision, Recall, or F1-score.
- Saving the model to disk so it can be loaded in the web application (for example, using pickle or joblib).

Here's an example of how to save a trained model using joblib:

import joblib

 # Save the trained recommender system model
joblib.dump(final_recommendations, 'recommender_model.pkl')

This will create a file recommender_model.pkl that can be loaded later in the Flask application.

2. Setting Up the Flask Backend

Flask is a lightweight web framework for Python that can serve as the backend for our web application. It will handle the logic of loading the recommender model and making real-time predictions based on user input.

2.1 Installing Flask

To get started, you need to install Flask. You can do this using pip:

pip install Flask

2.2 Creating the Flask App

Once Flask is installed, you can create a simple app that loads the saved recommender model and serves recommendations.

Let's create the following structure for your project:

```
/recommender_web_app
   /templates
      index.html
   app.py
   recommender_model.pkl
```

- **app.py**: This will contain the main logic for serving recommendations.
- **/templates/index.html**: This is the HTML page that the user will see.
- **recommender_model.pkl**: The saved model that contains your recommender system.

Here's how app.py might look:

```
from flask import Flask, render_template, request
import joblib

# Initialize Flask app
app = Flask(__name__)

# Load the saved recommender model
recommender_model = joblib.load('recommender_model.pkl')

# Define the function to get recommendations
def get_recommendations(user_input):
    # In this example, we're using a simple list of recommendations
    # In a real scenario, use your trained recommender system logic here
    return
recommender_model[recommender_model['Item'].str.contains(user_input)]['Item'].tolist()
```

```
@app.route('/', methods=['GET', 'POST'])
def index():
    recommendations = []
    if request.method == 'POST':
        user_input = request.form['user_input']
        recommendations = get_recommendations(user_input)
    return render_template('index.html', recommendations=recommendations)

# Run the app
if __name__ == '__main__':
    app.run(debug=True)
```

In this example:

- The model is loaded using joblib.load().
- The get_recommendations function takes the user's input (e.g., the category of items they are interested in) and filters the items from the model based on that input.
- The index() function is the route that handles both the initial page load (GET) and when a user submits a search query (POST).

2.3 Creating the Frontend (index.html)

The frontend will provide an interface where users can input their preferences (such as a product category or keyword) and get recommendations. This will be implemented in the index.html file.

Here's an example of how to set up a simple HTML form to collect user input:

```
<!DOCTYPE html>
<html lang="en">
<head>
    <meta charset="UTF-8">
    <meta name="viewport" content="width=device-width, initial-scale=1.0">
    <title>Recommender System</title>
</head>
<body>
    <h1>Product Recommendation System</h1>
    <form method="POST">
        <label for="user_input">Enter your preference (e.g., product category):</label>
```

```
<input type="text" id="user_input" name="user_input" required>
<button type="submit">Get Recommendations</button>
</form>

{% if recommendations %}
<h2>Top Recommendations:</h2>
<ul>
    {% for item in recommendations %}
    <li>{{ item }}</li>
    {% endfor %}
</ul>
{% endif %}
</body>
</html>
```

This simple HTML page includes:

A form where the user can enter their preference (such as a product name or category).
A section that displays the recommended products once the form is submitted.
When the user submits the form, the input is sent to the Flask backend, which returns the recommendations based on the model. These recommendations are then displayed dynamically on the page.

3. Running the Web App

Once everything is set up, you can start the Flask development server by running the following command in your terminal:

python app.py

By default, Flask will run on http://127.0.0.1:5000/. When you navigate to this URL in your browser, you should see the input form where you can submit your preferences. After submitting the form, the recommended items based on your input will be shown on the same page.

4. Making the App Production-Ready

While the above implementation works for development, it's not suitable for production. In a production environment, you need to ensure that your application is optimized for performance and scalability. Here are some key considerations for deploying a web app in a production environment:

4.1 Using a Production Web Server

In production, you should use a production-ready web server like Gunicorn instead of Flask's built-in server, which is not optimized for production use. You can install Gunicorn with pip:

pip install gunicorn

Then, to run your app with Gunicorn, use the following command:

gunicorn -w 4 app:app

This will start the server with 4 worker processes to handle multiple requests simultaneously.

4.2 Hosting the App

To make your web app accessible to users around the world, you need to deploy it to a cloud service provider such as Heroku, AWS, or Google Cloud. Each platform provides simple tools and documentation to help you deploy your Flask application.

For example, to deploy to Heroku, you would:

Create a Heroku account and install the Heroku CLI.

Create a Procfile in your project directory, which tells Heroku how to run your app:

web: gunicorn app:app

Commit your changes to Git and push to Heroku:

```
git init
heroku create my-recommender-app
git add .
git commit -m "Initial commit"
git push heroku master
```

Heroku will take care of provisioning servers and deploying your application to a public URL.

Deploying a recommender system to a web app enables real-time personalized recommendations for users, enhancing user engagement and satisfaction. In this chapter, we learned how to:

- Prepare and save a recommender model.
- Build a Flask backend to serve recommendations.
- Create a simple frontend to display the recommendations.
- Deploy the app to a production environment.

With this knowledge, you can extend the app by incorporating advanced features such as real-time recommendation updates, user authentication, and data logging for model improvements. You can also scale it for large user bases by integrating it with cloud infrastructure and other performance optimization techniques.

11. Chatbot with NLP

In this chapter, we build a chatbot that uses Natural Language Processing (NLP) to interact with users in a conversational manner. You will learn how to process and understand text data through tokenization, part-of-speech tagging, and named entity recognition (NER). We'll guide you through using powerful NLP tools such as spaCy and Transformers for intent recognition and response generation. You'll also learn to build an intelligent conversational agent using techniques like seq2seq models and BERT for more context-aware conversations. By the end of this chapter, you'll be able to create a fully functional chatbot capable of engaging in meaningful conversations, solving customer queries, and delivering personalized experiences. □💬

11.1 Introduction to chatbots and conversational AI

Chatbots and conversational AI systems have transformed the way businesses interact with customers. By utilizing natural language processing (NLP) techniques, chatbots can understand and respond to user queries in a manner that mimics human conversation. These systems have become an essential tool in customer service, sales, and support, automating communication and improving user engagement. In this section, we will explore the fundamentals of chatbots, delve into conversational AI, and examine how these technologies are applied in real-world scenarios.

What Are Chatbots?

A chatbot is a software application designed to simulate human conversation through text or voice. They can be deployed on websites, messaging platforms like WhatsApp, Facebook Messenger, or even integrated into mobile applications. Chatbots are designed to answer specific questions, perform tasks, and even guide users through complex processes, offering a seamless and interactive user experience.

There are two main types of chatbots:

Rule-based (or Scripted) Chatbots: These are simple bots that follow pre-defined rules and respond to specific keywords or patterns in the user input. For example, if a user types "hello," the chatbot will respond with "Hi, how can I assist you today?" Rule-based bots are relatively easy to implement but are limited in their scope because they cannot handle variations in user input that do not match the predefined patterns.

AI-powered (Conversational) Chatbots: These bots leverage machine learning and NLP algorithms to understand context, meaning, and intent in user interactions. They can handle more complex queries, provide personalized responses, and learn over time through continuous interactions. These bots are more flexible and dynamic compared to rule-based bots, as they can adapt to new patterns in user input and provide more relevant, context-aware responses.

Conversational AI: The Backbone of Advanced Chatbots

While traditional chatbots rely on rule-based logic, conversational AI elevates chatbot interactions by enabling machines to understand and simulate human language. Conversational AI is a combination of NLP, machine learning, and deep learning models that empowers chatbots to engage in open-ended conversations. It allows chatbots to move beyond scripted interactions to handle ambiguous and varied inputs, making them capable of sophisticated and nuanced conversations.

Key technologies that drive conversational AI include:

Natural Language Processing (NLP): NLP is the field of artificial intelligence that focuses on enabling machines to understand, interpret, and generate human language. It involves several tasks, such as:

- **Text Classification**: Categorizing text into predefined categories (e.g., determining if a user's query is about a product or an account issue).
- **Named Entity Recognition (NER):** Identifying specific entities in text, such as names, dates, locations, etc.
- **Sentiment Analysis**: Determining the sentiment behind a user's message, such as whether it is positive, negative, or neutral.
- **Part-of-Speech Tagging**: Identifying grammatical components such as nouns, verbs, adjectives, etc.
- **Speech Recognition and Generation**: Converting spoken language into text and generating speech from text, which enables voice-enabled chatbots.

Machine Learning (ML): Machine learning algorithms are used to train the chatbot on large datasets of conversational data. This training allows the bot to improve over time by learning from previous interactions, identifying patterns in the data, and making predictions about how to respond to new inputs. Reinforcement learning and supervised learning are commonly used in chatbot training to optimize responses based on feedback.

Deep Learning: Deep learning techniques, such as neural networks, can be employed to create advanced models that understand the nuances of human language. These models, such as transformers (e.g., GPT, BERT), have significantly improved the ability of chatbots to generate coherent and contextually relevant responses. Deep learning models excel at handling more complex conversational tasks, making them ideal for sophisticated chatbot applications.

How Chatbots Are Used in Real-World Applications

Chatbots and conversational AI have been adopted across a wide range of industries to streamline operations, enhance customer experience, and increase efficiency. Some of the common use cases include:

Customer Support: Many businesses use chatbots to handle customer inquiries and provide 24/7 support. These bots can quickly resolve common issues like password resets, order tracking, and product FAQs, freeing up human agents to handle more complex problems. Chatbots can also be integrated with customer relationship management (CRM) systems to provide personalized assistance based on user data.

E-commerce: Chatbots in e-commerce assist users by recommending products, guiding them through the checkout process, and answering product-related questions. They can analyze customer behavior, provide tailored suggestions, and even handle payment transactions. Additionally, AI-driven chatbots can help with abandoned cart recovery by sending follow-up messages to users who left items in their carts without completing the purchase.

Healthcare: In the healthcare industry, chatbots can provide preliminary diagnosis based on symptoms, schedule appointments, remind patients about medication, and answer health-related questions. They can be used to triage patient concerns, ensuring that only more serious cases are escalated to human doctors.

Banking and Finance: Chatbots in banking can help users check balances, transfer funds, track spending, and answer general account inquiries. AI-driven bots can also detect unusual patterns in financial transactions, offering enhanced security by flagging potential fraud in real-time.

Human Resources: Many companies use chatbots to automate HR-related tasks such as recruiting, onboarding, and employee engagement surveys. These bots can answer FAQs related to company policies, help schedule interviews, and even assist with performance reviews.

Travel and Hospitality: In the travel industry, chatbots can assist with flight bookings, hotel reservations, and itinerary planning. They can provide recommendations for local attractions and help travelers with real-time updates regarding their flights, cancellations, and delays.

Benefits of Chatbots and Conversational AI

The rise of chatbots powered by conversational AI brings several benefits to both businesses and end-users:

Enhanced Customer Experience: Chatbots provide instant responses to customer queries, ensuring that users don't have to wait for long periods to get assistance. This improves customer satisfaction and engagement.

Cost-Effective: By automating routine customer service tasks, chatbots reduce the need for large teams of support agents, lowering operational costs for businesses. They also allow human agents to focus on more complex and valuable tasks.

Scalability: Chatbots can handle an unlimited number of interactions simultaneously, making them ideal for businesses experiencing high volumes of customer inquiries, especially during peak times (e.g., holidays, product launches).

Personalization: With the help of machine learning and NLP, chatbots can provide personalized responses based on user preferences and behavior, improving the relevance and value of interactions.

24/7 Availability: Chatbots don't require breaks, making them available around the clock. This is particularly beneficial for businesses that operate in different time zones or require constant support.

Challenges in Building Effective Chatbots

Despite their many advantages, building an effective chatbot can be challenging. Some of the common obstacles developers face include:

Understanding Context: Chatbots may struggle to maintain context across multiple interactions. If a user asks several questions in a single conversation, the chatbot may fail to connect them coherently.

Handling Ambiguity: Natural language is inherently ambiguous, and chatbots must be able to understand the intent behind a message, even when the language is vague or unclear. Developing this capability requires advanced NLP techniques and large datasets.

Data Privacy and Security: Chatbots often handle sensitive user data, and ensuring that this data is securely processed and stored is critical. Developers must implement robust security protocols to prevent data breaches.

Bias in AI Models: AI models, including those used in chatbots, may inherit biases present in training data. This can lead to unfair or discriminatory outcomes, so it's essential to carefully curate the training data and perform regular audits to detect and mitigate bias.

Chatbots and conversational AI are powerful tools that have revolutionized communication in many industries. By leveraging natural language processing, machine learning, and deep learning, these systems can understand, interpret, and respond to human language with remarkable accuracy. While there are challenges to developing effective chatbots, the benefits they offer—such as improved customer experience, cost savings, and scalability—make them indispensable in the modern digital landscape. In this book, we will explore how to build your own chatbot with NLP, guiding you through the process from data collection to deployment, ensuring that you can create intelligent, engaging, and functional chatbots.

11.2 Preprocessing and intent classification

In building a chatbot with natural language processing (NLP), preprocessing and intent classification are two essential steps that form the backbone of understanding user queries. Preprocessing ensures that the raw input data is clean and ready for analysis, while intent classification allows the chatbot to determine the user's purpose or intent from their message. These steps are crucial for creating an effective chatbot that can understand user inputs and provide meaningful, accurate responses.

In this section, we will explore the key aspects of preprocessing and intent classification, detailing the methods and tools used to implement these processes. Let's break these down to understand their significance and how to execute them effectively.

Preprocessing: Preparing Text for Analysis

Raw text data is often messy, and processing it before feeding it into a machine learning model is a crucial step. Text preprocessing involves cleaning and transforming the input data to ensure that the chatbot can better understand the user's message. Several techniques are commonly used during this phase, and each plays a vital role in making the text data suitable for model training.

1. Tokenization

Tokenization is the process of breaking down a string of text into smaller units, known as tokens. These tokens could be words, characters, or subwords. Tokenization is one of the first steps in text preprocessing because it transforms unstructured text into a format that a machine learning model can work with. For example, the sentence "I love machine learning" would be tokenized into ["I", "love", "machine", "learning"].

Tokenization can be either word-based or character-based, depending on the requirements of the model. Word-based tokenization works well for many NLP tasks, while character-based tokenization might be used for more nuanced language applications, like working with misspelled words or rare terms.

2. Lowercasing

Converting all the text to lowercase is another preprocessing step. The reason for this is to standardize the input, as the words "Chatbot" and "chatbot" should be treated as the same word. By lowering the case of all text, we avoid creating unnecessary distinctions between words that are essentially the same, making the model more robust.

3. Removing Stopwords

Stopwords are common words like "the", "is", "in", "and", "to", which appear frequently in a language but carry very little semantic meaning in the context of NLP tasks. Removing stopwords helps reduce the complexity of the text data and improves the performance of NLP models. However, in some cases, stopwords may be important, and it's crucial to assess whether they should be removed depending on the specific application.

4. Stemming and Lemmatization

Both stemming and lemmatization are techniques used to reduce words to their base or root form. These techniques help in handling different variations of a word and reduce the vocabulary size.

- Stemming removes suffixes from words, often resulting in stems that may not always be valid words (e.g., "running" becomes "run").
- Lemmatization, on the other hand, reduces words to their dictionary form (e.g., "running" becomes "run"), and it takes into account the context of the word, often resulting in more meaningful outputs.

Lemmatization is preferred in many cases as it preserves the meaning of the word, but stemming may be useful in some contexts when computational efficiency is the primary concern.

5. Removing Special Characters and Noise

Text data often contains special characters such as punctuation marks, symbols, or URLs that do not contribute to the chatbot's understanding of the input. Cleaning the text by removing these characters reduces noise and helps focus on the core content of the message. For example, if a user types "How much is $100?" the "$" symbol does not need to be considered for intent classification, so it would be removed.

6. Handling Synonyms and Variations

Handling variations in user input, such as synonyms, spelling mistakes, and slang, is another aspect of preprocessing. Users may phrase questions in various ways, using different terminology or abbreviations. A robust chatbot should be capable of understanding these variations and treating them as equivalent. For example, "What's the weather like?" and "How's the weather?" should be understood as the same query.

A technique like spell correction and the use of a synonym dictionary or word embeddings (discussed in the next section) can help handle variations and improve chatbot accuracy.

Intent Classification: Understanding User Intent

Once the data has been preprocessed, the next key step is intent classification—the task of determining the user's intent behind the message. The intent is what the user aims to achieve, and it drives the response that the chatbot will provide. This step is crucial because the chatbot must understand whether the user is asking for information, making a purchase, or asking a question about an existing product.

1. What is Intent Classification?

Intent classification is the process of categorizing a user's query into predefined classes or labels based on the purpose or goal behind the message. For instance, in a retail chatbot, user intents might include:

- **"Product Inquiry"** (e.g., "Tell me more about this phone.")
- **"Order Tracking"** (e.g., "Where is my order?")
- **"Customer Support"** (e.g., "I have a problem with my payment.")
- **"FAQs"** (e.g., "What is your return policy?")

These intents need to be defined based on the business needs and the user scenarios that the chatbot aims to address.

2. Labeling Data for Training

Intent classification is typically a supervised learning problem, meaning that the model must be trained on labeled data. Labeled data consists of user queries that are paired with their corresponding intent labels. For example:

- **Query**: "What is the status of my order?" → Intent: "Order Tracking"

- **Query**: "Can you help me with my payment issue?" → Intent: "Customer Support"

A large labeled dataset is required to train an accurate intent classifier. As the chatbot interacts with users, new queries can be labeled and added to the training data, enabling continuous improvement in the chatbot's ability to classify intent.

3. Machine Learning Models for Intent Classification

Several machine learning models can be used for intent classification, ranging from traditional models to deep learning approaches. The choice of model depends on the complexity of the task and the quality of the available data. Common approaches include:

Naive Bayes Classifier: A simple probabilistic classifier that is often used for text classification tasks. It works well for basic intent classification problems when you have a limited dataset.

Support Vector Machine (SVM): SVM is another popular model for text classification, particularly effective in high-dimensional spaces. It is a good choice when the dataset is more complex and contains multiple features.

Deep Learning Models: Advanced deep learning models, such as Recurrent Neural Networks (RNNs) or Convolutional Neural Networks (CNNs), are often used when dealing with large datasets. More recently, transformers like BERT and GPT have shown exceptional performance in intent classification tasks by capturing context and dependencies in language.

Pre-trained Models: If the dataset is limited, using pre-trained models such as BERT or GPT can provide a strong foundation for intent classification, as these models are already trained on massive text corpora and can be fine-tuned for specific tasks.

4. Feature Extraction for Intent Classification

Before training a model, the text data must be transformed into numerical representations that a machine learning algorithm can understand. The most common feature extraction techniques for text include:

Bag-of-Words (BoW): This approach represents text as a collection of words and their frequencies. While simple, it can be effective in many basic applications.

TF-IDF (Term Frequency-Inverse Document Frequency): TF-IDF is an improved version of BoW that weighs words based on their importance in the document relative to their frequency across the entire corpus.

Word Embeddings: Word embeddings such as Word2Vec and GloVe map words into dense, continuous vector spaces that capture semantic meaning. This representation helps in understanding the relationships between words and their context.

Contextual Embeddings: Modern NLP techniques like BERT use contextual embeddings, where the meaning of a word is determined by its surrounding words, making these representations more accurate for intent classification tasks.

Preprocessing and intent classification are fundamental components of building an effective chatbot with NLP capabilities. Preprocessing helps clean and normalize the user input, while intent classification enables the chatbot to understand and categorize user queries. By carefully selecting and applying preprocessing techniques and training an accurate intent classifier, developers can build a chatbot that effectively interacts with users, understands their needs, and provides valuable responses. These steps are the foundation for any NLP-based conversational AI system and directly impact the overall performance of the chatbot.

11.3 Implementing transformer-based NLP models

Transformer-based models have revolutionized the field of Natural Language Processing (NLP), making significant advancements in tasks such as machine translation, sentiment analysis, question answering, and chatbot development. In this section, we will dive into the details of implementing transformer-based models, specifically focusing on their application for chatbot development.

Transformers are powerful models that rely on self-attention mechanisms to capture long-range dependencies in text. They have become the go-to architecture for NLP tasks because of their ability to handle large amounts of data, learn contextual relationships, and outperform traditional models.

This chapter will guide you through understanding transformers, the architecture behind them, how to implement pre-trained models like BERT and GPT, and how to fine-tune them for specific tasks like intent classification, response generation, and improving the overall performance of your chatbot.

What Are Transformer Models?

Before diving into implementation, it's important to understand the basics of transformers. Transformers, introduced by Vaswani et al. in the paper Attention is All You Need (2017), shifted away from earlier sequence models like Recurrent Neural Networks (RNNs) and Long Short-Term Memory (LSTM) networks. The main innovation in transformers is the self-attention mechanism, which allows the model to weigh the importance of different words in a sentence when processing them.

Self-Attention Mechanism

Self-attention allows a transformer model to consider all words in the input sequence simultaneously and determine which words should be focused on to predict the next word in the sequence or to understand the meaning of a particular word in context. For example, in the sentence "The dog chased the ball," the model would pay attention to the relationship between "dog" and "chased," which are important for understanding the action of the sentence. This allows transformers to capture long-range dependencies in text effectively, even across long sentences.

The core components of the transformer architecture are:

- **Multi-head Self-attention Mechanism**: This allows the model to focus on different parts of a sentence simultaneously, capturing various aspects of relationships.
- **Positional Encoding**: Since transformers do not process sequences in a step-by-step manner (like RNNs), positional encoding helps the model keep track of the position of words in the sequence.
- **Feed-forward Neural Networks**: These networks are applied to each position separately and are used to process the output from the attention mechanism.
- **Layer Normalization**: This ensures stability and smooth learning during training.

The combination of these components enables transformers to perform exceptionally well in a wide range of NLP tasks, including intent classification and response generation for chatbots.

Popular Transformer-based Models for Chatbot Development

Several transformer-based models have been developed and fine-tuned for various NLP tasks. In the context of building chatbots, the most commonly used models are BERT (Bidirectional Encoder Representations from Transformers) and GPT (Generative Pre-trained Transformer). Let's explore both of these models and how to use them in chatbot development.

BERT: Bidirectional Contextual Representation

BERT, developed by Google, is a transformer-based model that revolutionized NLP by using bidirectional context. Unlike traditional models that read text in a left-to-right or right-to-left manner, BERT reads the text in both directions at once. This allows it to capture richer, more contextual information.

BERT is often used for tasks that require understanding and classification, such as:

- Intent classification
- Named entity recognition (NER)
- Question answering

BERT is typically fine-tuned for specific tasks by training it on labeled datasets. The model can be used as a feature extractor, where the output embeddings of the model are passed through a classifier to perform specific tasks such as intent detection.

GPT: Generative Pre-trained Transformer

GPT, developed by OpenAI, is a transformer-based model designed for text generation. Unlike BERT, which is used for understanding text, GPT focuses on generating coherent and contextually relevant responses. GPT has been trained on large amounts of text data and can generate human-like text based on a given prompt.

GPT excels in tasks that involve generating responses, such as:

- Conversational AI
- Text completion
- Dialogue generation

Chatbots powered by GPT can hold dynamic conversations and generate relevant responses to user inputs. GPT-3, in particular, has gained popularity for its ability to produce text that is remarkably close to human language, making it ideal for chatbot applications.

Implementing Transformer-based Models for Chatbots

Now that we understand the basic concepts and use cases for transformer-based models, let's move on to implementing these models in your chatbot. We will use Python and popular libraries such as Hugging Face Transformers to load and fine-tune pre-trained transformer models for specific chatbot tasks.

1. Setting Up the Environment

Before you begin, you need to set up your development environment. You will need the following packages:

- **Transformers**: The Hugging Face library provides pre-trained transformer models and easy-to-use interfaces for fine-tuning and inference.
- **Torch or TensorFlow**: Depending on which deep learning framework you prefer (PyTorch or TensorFlow), you'll need to install one of these.

pip install transformers
pip install torch

2. Loading Pre-trained Models

Once the environment is set up, you can load a pre-trained transformer model using Hugging Face's transformers library. Let's start by loading a pre-trained BERT model for intent classification.

```
from transformers import BertTokenizer, BertForSequenceClassification
import torch

# Load the pre-trained BERT model and tokenizer
tokenizer = BertTokenizer.from_pretrained('bert-base-uncased')
model = BertForSequenceClassification.from_pretrained('bert-base-uncased')

# Example input
text = "What is the weather like today?"

# Tokenize the input
inputs = tokenizer(text, return_tensors="pt")

# Make a prediction
with torch.no_grad():
    logits = model(**inputs).logits

# Get the predicted class
predicted_class = torch.argmax(logits)
print(f"Predicted Class: {predicted_class.item()}")
```

This simple script loads a pre-trained BERT model, tokenizes an example sentence, and predicts its intent class. In a chatbot scenario, you would extend this by fine-tuning the model on your labeled intent data.

3. Fine-tuning for Specific Tasks

For a chatbot, you will want to fine-tune the model for specific tasks such as intent classification or response generation. For intent classification, you can fine-tune BERT on your labeled dataset of user queries and their corresponding intents. For response generation, you can fine-tune GPT on conversation datasets.

Fine-tuning BERT for intent classification involves modifying the model to output the correct class (e.g., "Product Inquiry," "Order Status"). Here is a simplified version of how to fine-tune a model for intent classification:

```
from transformers import Trainer, TrainingArguments

# Prepare dataset (example)
train_dataset = ...  # Define your dataset here
val_dataset = ...  # Define validation dataset here

# Training Arguments
training_args = TrainingArguments(
    output_dir='./results',
    evaluation_strategy="epoch",
    per_device_train_batch_size=16,
    per_device_eval_batch_size=64,
    logging_dir='./logs',
    logging_steps=10,
)

# Trainer
trainer = Trainer(
    model=model,
    args=training_args,
    train_dataset=train_dataset,
    eval_dataset=val_dataset,
)

# Train the model
trainer.train()
```

Once fine-tuned, the model will be able to classify user intents more effectively based on the patterns it has learned from the training data.

4. Generating Responses with GPT

For generating chatbot responses, GPT is often the better choice because it is designed for generative tasks. Fine-tuning GPT on a conversational dataset allows the model to generate human-like responses in a dialogue context.

Here's how you might implement GPT-3 for response generation:

```
from transformers import GPT2LMHeadModel, GPT2Tokenizer
```

```
# Load the GPT-2 model and tokenizer
tokenizer = GPT2Tokenizer.from_pretrained('gpt2')
model = GPT2LMHeadModel.from_pretrained('gpt2')

# Encode input text
input_text = "Hello, how can I help you today?"
input_ids = tokenizer.encode(input_text, return_tensors='pt')

# Generate response
output = model.generate(input_ids, max_length=100, num_return_sequences=1)

# Decode the output text
response = tokenizer.decode(output[0], skip_special_tokens=True)
print(f"Response: {response}")
```

This code uses GPT-2 to generate a response based on the user's input. You can fine-tune GPT on a specific conversation dataset to make the responses more contextually relevant.

Implementing transformer-based models for chatbot development allows for more accurate intent classification and dynamic, context-aware responses. Whether using BERT for understanding user queries or GPT for generating human-like dialogue, transformer models are powerful tools in the NLP toolkit. By leveraging pre-trained models and fine-tuning them for your specific use cases, you can create a sophisticated chatbot that effectively engages with users, understands their needs, and provides valuable interactions. With tools like Hugging Face's Transformers library, implementing these models has become more accessible, enabling the development of advanced conversational AI systems.

11.4 Adding context and memory to chatbot interactions

One of the key challenges in building effective conversational AI is creating chatbots that can engage in more natural and meaningful conversations over multiple turns. Most basic chatbots, especially those relying on traditional rule-based systems or simple transformer models, may provide relevant responses to a single query but struggle to handle context across a conversation. As a result, the conversation often feels disjointed, and the bot may fail to recall prior exchanges, making it difficult for users to have coherent, ongoing dialogues.

To solve this issue, we need to introduce context and memory into the chatbot's architecture. In this section, we will explore how you can enhance your chatbot with mechanisms that allow it to remember past interactions, maintain context across conversations, and improve the overall user experience. We'll look at the methods used to capture context and memory, the benefits of doing so, and practical techniques for implementation.

Why Context and Memory Matter in Chatbots

Context and memory are essential for creating a more engaging and human-like chatbot experience. Context allows the chatbot to understand and remember what has been said earlier in the conversation, while memory helps it store relevant information over time for future use. Here's why they are so important:

Continuity in Conversation: Without context, chatbots would treat every user input as an isolated query, without understanding previous interactions. Context enables chatbots to follow the thread of the conversation, allowing them to answer follow-up questions effectively and offer coherent dialogue.

Personalization: Memory allows the chatbot to remember facts about individual users, such as their preferences, past interactions, or specific needs. This allows for a personalized user experience, where the bot can tailor its responses based on the user's history.

Improved Task Completion: For more complex tasks, such as booking a flight or troubleshooting an issue, maintaining context ensures that the bot doesn't need to ask the same questions repeatedly. This reduces user frustration and enhances the chatbot's efficiency.

Better User Experience: The ability to recall prior conversations or maintain context provides a more fluid, human-like interaction, ultimately improving user satisfaction.

Types of Context in Chatbots

Before diving into implementation, let's break down the types of context that can be used to enhance chatbot interactions:

Session Context: This is the most basic type of context and refers to the conversation history within a single session or interaction. For example, if a user asks a question like "What is the weather like today?" and later asks "What about tomorrow?", the chatbot can recall the original question and provide a relevant response for the following day. This is usually managed in memory for the duration of the session.

User Context: This is more long-term and relates to personalized information about the user, which may persist beyond a single session. For example, a chatbot could remember the user's name, preferences, or previous purchases and use that data to provide a more tailored response. This could involve storing user data in a database or using cloud storage.

Dialogue History: The dialogue history refers to a more structured memory system where the chatbot records important interactions and facts for long-term use. For example, the bot could remember that a user previously asked about a specific product and offer that product as a suggestion in the future, even if the interaction is happening weeks or months later.

External Context: This context could be based on factors outside the conversation itself. For example, the chatbot could take into account a user's location, time of day, or other external information (e.g., weather conditions or current events) to provide more relevant answers.

How to Add Context and Memory to a Chatbot

Now that we've established why context and memory are important, let's explore some practical methods for implementing them in your chatbot.

1. Short-Term Context (Session Memory)

For a chatbot to effectively maintain short-term context during a session, it must track the user's previous inputs within that session. This can be achieved by storing recent exchanges in memory, which the chatbot can use to generate more relevant responses.

Contextual Embeddings: One effective approach is to use contextual embeddings, such as those produced by transformer models like BERT or GPT, which encode the current query with information from previous exchanges in the conversation. This allows the chatbot to better understand the context of the conversation. You can feed the entire conversation history (or a window of recent exchanges) into the model, so it produces responses based on a larger body of context.

Dialogue History Management: A simpler approach for maintaining short-term memory involves storing recent messages in a list or a queue. This could be as basic as saving the last two or three turns in the conversation, allowing the bot to reference this information when answering follow-up questions.

For example, consider the following Python code to manage short-term memory in a chatbot:

```python
class ChatbotMemory:
    def __init__(self):
        self.history = []

    def update_history(self, user_input, bot_response):
        self.history.append(f"User: {user_input}")
        self.history.append(f"Bot: {bot_response}")

    def get_recent_context(self):
        return " ".join(self.history[-4:])  # Return the last 2 exchanges (4 lines)

# Example usage
bot_memory = ChatbotMemory()

user_input_1 = "What's the weather today?"
bot_response_1 = "It's sunny today."

# Update history
bot_memory.update_history(user_input_1, bot_response_1)

user_input_2 = "What about tomorrow?"
bot_response_2 = "Tomorrow will be cloudy."

# Update history
bot_memory.update_history(user_input_2, bot_response_2)

# Get recent context
print(bot_memory.get_recent_context())
```

This code snippet stores a brief conversation history, and when the user asks a follow-up question, the chatbot can access recent context to generate a relevant response.

2. Long-Term Context (Persistent Memory)

To create more personalized interactions, long-term memory is essential. This can include storing user preferences or maintaining a history of interactions over multiple sessions. There are various strategies for implementing long-term memory:

Database Integration: A chatbot can store user data (such as names, preferences, and past interactions) in a database. For example, if a user frequently asks about certain topics, the chatbot can retrieve this information and provide recommendations or suggestions based on previous queries.

User Profiles: The chatbot can create and update user profiles, which could include information like past orders, favorite products, or frequently asked questions. This profile can be updated in real-time as the user interacts with the bot.

For example, consider this pseudocode to store user preferences in a database:

```
import sqlite3

# Create a database connection
conn = sqlite3.connect('chatbot_memory.db')
cursor = conn.cursor()

# Create a table to store user preferences
cursor.execute('''CREATE TABLE IF NOT EXISTS user_preferences (
        user_id TEXT,
        preference_key TEXT,
        preference_value TEXT)''')

# Function to update user preferences
def update_user_preference(user_id, key, value):
    cursor.execute('''INSERT OR REPLACE INTO user_preferences
            (user_id, preference_key, preference_value)
            VALUES (?, ?, ?)''', (user_id, key, value))
    conn.commit()

# Example usage
user_id = 'user123'
update_user_preference(user_id, 'favorite_color', 'blue')
```

This would allow the chatbot to recall user preferences across sessions and provide personalized responses based on past interactions.

3. Handling Multiple Turns with Transformers

To further improve context retention, transformer models like GPT and BERT can be used to generate responses with awareness of prior turns in the conversation. For multi-turn conversations, you can concatenate the current user input with previous turns and use transformers to generate more coherent and contextually relevant replies.

For instance, feeding multiple turns into GPT-2 to maintain context:

```
input_text = "Hello, I'm looking for a product."
context = "User: Hello, I'm looking for a product.\nBot: Sure, I can help you with
that.\nUser: What kind of products do you recommend?"

# Generate response using GPT-2 model
input_ids = tokenizer.encode(context, return_tensors="pt")
output = model.generate(input_ids, max_length=100, num_return_sequences=1)
response = tokenizer.decode(output[0], skip_special_tokens=True)

print(response)
```

By providing the entire conversation context, the model generates more contextually relevant responses.

Adding context and memory to chatbot interactions is crucial for creating more dynamic, personalized, and human-like experiences. Short-term memory allows chatbots to manage conversation continuity within a session, while long-term memory enables them to recall user preferences and prior interactions over time. Implementing transformers like BERT and GPT further enhances context retention, allowing chatbots to generate more coherent and relevant responses. By integrating both session context and persistent memory, chatbots can provide an engaging and efficient user experience, leading to higher user satisfaction and greater task completion.

11.5 Deploying as a Telegram/WhatsApp chatbot

Once your chatbot is built and has passed testing for its basic functionality, the next critical step is deploying it in a live environment where real users can interact with it. Two of the most popular messaging platforms for deploying chatbots are Telegram and WhatsApp.

These platforms provide simple ways to integrate your chatbot, allowing you to take advantage of their vast user base, reach, and ease of interaction.

In this section, we will walk through the process of deploying your chatbot to both Telegram and WhatsApp. We will look at the specific requirements for each platform, how to integrate your chatbot, and the steps involved in setting up these bots to start accepting live user interactions.

Deploying a Telegram Chatbot

Telegram provides a robust Bot API that allows you to create bots and integrate them into their messaging platform. The Telegram Bot API is simple, and you can get started quickly with little overhead. Below are the steps to deploy your NLP-based chatbot on Telegram:

Step 1: Create a Bot on Telegram

To begin, you'll need to create your bot using the BotFather on Telegram, which is a built-in tool that allows you to create and manage bots.

- Open Telegram and search for BotFather in the search bar.
- Start a conversation with BotFather and send the /newbot command.
- Follow the prompts to choose a name for your bot and a unique username (it must end with "bot", e.g., weather_assistant_bot).
- Once created, you will receive an API token that is essential for authenticating and communicating with the Telegram Bot API.

Step 2: Set Up Your Development Environment

Make sure you have the necessary libraries and tools installed for integrating with the Telegram Bot API. You can use Python and the popular python-telegram-bot library to facilitate the integration.

To install the necessary library:

pip install python-telegram-bot

Step 3: Connect Your Chatbot to Telegram

Using the Telegram Bot API and the bot token provided by BotFather, you can connect your chatbot to Telegram. Here's a basic code snippet to integrate the chatbot with Telegram:

```python
from telegram.ext import Updater, CommandHandler, MessageHandler, Filters
import logging

# Set up logging
logging.basicConfig(format='%(asctime)s - %(name)s - %(levelname)s - %(message)s',
level=logging.INFO)

# Define the start command
def start(update, context):
    update.message.reply_text("Hi! I'm your chatbot. How can I assist you today?")

# Define a function to handle user messages
def handle_message(update, context):
    user_message = update.message.text
    bot_response = get_bot_response(user_message)  # Your function to generate a response from your chatbot model
    update.message.reply_text(bot_response)

# Function to initialize the bot
def main():
    updater = Updater("YOUR_BOT_API_TOKEN", use_context=True)

    dp = updater.dispatcher

    dp.add_handler(CommandHandler("start", start))
    dp.add_handler(MessageHandler(Filters.text & ~Filters.command, handle_message))

    updater.start_polling()
    updater.idle()

if __name__ == '__main__':
    main()
```

Here, the bot listens for any text message, passes it through your chatbot model to get the response, and sends it back to the user.

Step 4: Test and Deploy

After running the script, your chatbot will start interacting with users on Telegram. You can test it by searching for your bot using the username you set earlier, and initiating a conversation.

Once you've confirmed that the bot works correctly, you can deploy it on a cloud server (e.g., AWS, Heroku, or Google Cloud) to ensure continuous operation. If you're using a cloud service like Heroku, you can deploy your bot with ease by following the platform-specific deployment instructions.

Deploying a WhatsApp Chatbot

Deploying a chatbot on WhatsApp requires a bit more setup, as WhatsApp doesn't provide a bot API directly for free use. Instead, businesses can use the WhatsApp Business API, which is geared towards medium and large businesses that want to automate communication at scale. However, for individual developers or smaller use cases, third-party services like Twilio and 360dialog make it easier to integrate a chatbot with WhatsApp.

Let's look at the steps to deploy a WhatsApp chatbot using Twilio.

Step 1: Set Up Twilio Account and WhatsApp Sandbox

- Create a Twilio account by visiting Twilio.
- After signing up, navigate to the Twilio Console, and look for WhatsApp Sandbox under the "Messaging" section.
- Follow the instructions to connect your WhatsApp account to Twilio's sandbox environment. You'll receive a WhatsApp number from Twilio (sandbox environment) for testing.

Step 2: Install Twilio Python Library

To connect to WhatsApp through Twilio, you'll need to install the Twilio Python library:

pip install twilio

Step 3: Write Python Code to Handle WhatsApp Messages

Now that Twilio is set up, you can start writing Python code to handle WhatsApp messages. Here's a basic example that integrates your chatbot with WhatsApp using Twilio:

```python
from twilio.rest import Client
from flask import Flask, request
import logging

app = Flask(__name__)

# Set up Twilio client
account_sid = 'your_account_sid'
auth_token = 'your_auth_token'
client = Client(account_sid, auth_token)

# Flask route to handle incoming WhatsApp messages
@app.route('/whatsapp', methods=['POST'])
def reply_whatsapp():
    incoming_msg = request.values.get('Body', '').lower()
    response_msg = get_bot_response(incoming_msg)  # Generate response using your chatbot model

    # Send response back via WhatsApp
    message = client.messages.create(
        body=response_msg,
        from_='whatsapp:+14155238886',  # This is Twilio's WhatsApp sandbox number
        to='whatsapp:+YourPhoneNumber'  # Replace with your WhatsApp number
    )
    return '', 200

# Start Flask server
if __name__ == '__main__':
    app.run(debug=True)
```

This code creates a simple Flask web server that listens for incoming messages and responds with the chatbot's output. When a user sends a message to your Twilio WhatsApp number, Twilio will forward it to this Flask route, which then uses your model to generate a reply.

Step 4: Deploy and Go Live

Once the chatbot is working in your local environment, you can deploy it on a cloud server such as Heroku, AWS, or any other server that supports Flask. After deployment, your WhatsApp chatbot will be able to respond to user inquiries in real-time.

To use WhatsApp in production, you'll need to move beyond the sandbox environment. Twilio offers an easy upgrade process to a live environment, where you'll get a dedicated WhatsApp number for your chatbot.

Deploying a chatbot on messaging platforms like Telegram and WhatsApp allows you to provide real-time, interactive experiences to users. Telegram offers a simple and developer-friendly Bot API, while WhatsApp requires using the Business API (often via third-party services like Twilio). Regardless of the platform, both offer seamless ways to bring your chatbot into production and make it accessible to a wide audience.

In this section, we've covered the key steps for deploying a chatbot on Telegram and WhatsApp, from setting up your bot to writing the integration code and deploying it to the cloud. With these steps, you'll be able to reach users wherever they communicate, enhancing your chatbot's utility and engagement.

12. Autonomous Vehicle Simulation

In this chapter, we dive into the exciting world of autonomous vehicles and how machine learning can be used to train models for self-driving cars. You'll learn how to create and simulate reinforcement learning (RL) agents that can navigate virtual environments and make decisions such as lane changes, obstacle avoidance, and route optimization. We'll cover the fundamentals of RL algorithms like Q-learning and Deep Q-Networks (DQN), as well as the use of simulation environments like OpenAI Gym or CARLA to train your models. By the end of this chapter, you'll have a solid understanding of how autonomous systems learn and adapt to real-world driving challenges, and you'll be able to simulate intelligent vehicle behaviors in a controlled setting. 🚗💡

12.1 Basics of reinforcement learning in self-driving cars

Self-driving cars are one of the most exciting applications of Artificial Intelligence (AI) and Machine Learning (ML) today. At the heart of the technology behind autonomous vehicles is Reinforcement Learning (RL), which plays a crucial role in enabling the car to make decisions, navigate through the environment, and learn from its experiences in real-time. In this sub-chapter, we will explore the fundamentals of reinforcement learning and its application in self-driving cars.

What is Reinforcement Learning (RL)?

Reinforcement Learning is a branch of machine learning where an agent (in this case, the autonomous vehicle) learns how to take actions within an environment in order to maximize a reward signal. Unlike supervised learning, where a model learns from labeled data, RL involves an agent interacting with its environment and receiving feedback in the form of rewards or penalties based on the actions it takes.

The learning process in RL can be broken down into the following components:

- **Agent**: The learner or decision maker (the self-driving car in this case).
- **Environment**: Everything the agent interacts with (the road, other vehicles, traffic signs, etc.).
- **State**: A snapshot of the environment at a given time (e.g., the position of the car, speed, nearby obstacles).

- **Action**: The choices the agent can make (e.g., accelerating, braking, turning the steering wheel).
- **Reward**: The feedback the agent receives after taking an action (e.g., positive reward for reaching the destination, negative reward for collisions).
- **Policy**: A strategy used by the agent to decide which action to take in a given state.

In self-driving cars, reinforcement learning helps the vehicle decide what actions to take in various traffic situations and environments based on the state of the world and the reward feedback it receives after taking each action.

The Reinforcement Learning Process for Autonomous Vehicles

Let's dive deeper into how RL is used in the context of self-driving cars, particularly focusing on how these vehicles learn through interaction with their environment:

Step 1: Defining the Environment

The environment of an autonomous vehicle is complex, including road networks, traffic signals, pedestrians, other vehicles, road markings, and dynamic objects. The car's sensors, including cameras, LiDAR, and radar, feed data to the vehicle's perception system, which forms the car's state. The vehicle must learn to interpret and act on this state to drive safely.

For example, the state might include the current location of the car, its speed, the distance from nearby objects, traffic light signals, and the presence of pedestrians or other vehicles. Based on this state, the RL agent (self-driving car) must decide on the best course of action.

Step 2: Defining Actions

In reinforcement learning, actions represent what the agent can do in a given state. For a self-driving car, actions typically include:

- **Steering**: Adjusting the direction of the car (left or right).
- **Acceleration**: Increasing or decreasing speed.
- **Braking**: Reducing the car's speed.
- **Lane Changes**: Shifting lanes based on traffic flow or road conditions.

These actions must be carefully chosen to ensure the car can navigate safely and efficiently through the environment while respecting traffic laws and road conditions.

Step 3: Defining Rewards

A key component of reinforcement learning is the reward function. The car is rewarded for taking actions that bring it closer to the desired outcome, such as successfully reaching its destination without collisions or traffic violations. The reward function typically rewards the car for the following:

- **Positive rewards**: Reaching a goal (such as safely completing a route or correctly following a traffic light).
- **Negative rewards (penalties):** Colliding with an obstacle, running a red light, or driving outside of a lane.

In the beginning, the car will not know what actions lead to high rewards or low penalties. However, over time and with enough experience, it will learn which behaviors maximize its long-term reward.

Step 4: Exploration vs. Exploitation

One of the key challenges in reinforcement learning is the exploration vs. exploitation dilemma. Initially, the car will not know which actions are best for navigating the environment, so it must explore different strategies. Exploration means trying out different actions and learning from the feedback, even if the results are unknown or risky. However, too much exploration can lead to inefficient performance or accidents, especially in the case of self-driving cars.

Once the car starts receiving consistent feedback about which actions are beneficial, it will begin to exploit the knowledge it has gained by following the action strategies that yield the highest reward. The car aims to balance between exploration (trying new actions) and exploitation (using what it has learned).

Step 5: Training the RL Agent

Training the RL agent is where the actual learning happens. The autonomous vehicle performs actions in a simulated environment, receives rewards, and updates its strategy (policy) based on the outcome. The RL model typically uses one of the following approaches to learn from the environment:

Value-based methods: These methods involve estimating the value of each state or action, typically using algorithms such as Q-Learning or Deep Q-Networks (DQN). The agent learns a Q-table or Q-function that assigns values to state-action pairs. The agent then selects the actions with the highest Q-values.

Policy-based methods: These methods focus on learning the policy directly, i.e., a mapping from states to actions. One popular algorithm is Proximal Policy Optimization (PPO), which is widely used in autonomous driving.

Actor-Critic methods: A combination of value-based and policy-based methods, actor-critic models use two components: an actor, which chooses actions, and a critic, which evaluates the actions.

Step 6: Testing and Deployment

Once the model has been trained in simulation, the real-world deployment phase begins. Autonomous vehicles use reinforcement learning to continuously improve their decision-making abilities in real-time. After deploying the model, the vehicle continues to interact with the environment, refine its policy, and adapt to changing conditions.

Since real-world environments are highly dynamic and uncertain, it is crucial for autonomous vehicles to learn from every interaction. For instance, they must handle unpredictable events, such as pedestrians crossing the street or sudden traffic congestion. These scenarios must be learned in a safe and controlled manner using methods like safe exploration or reward shaping to prevent accidents during the training process.

Challenges in Using RL for Self-Driving Cars

While reinforcement learning has proven to be a powerful technique for teaching autonomous vehicles, it is not without its challenges:

Safety: Testing RL models in real-world environments can be dangerous, especially in the early stages. It is crucial to ensure that the agent does not make poor decisions, such as crashing or disobeying traffic laws, during the learning process. A combination of simulation environments and controlled testing is used to mitigate risks.

Sample Efficiency: Reinforcement learning typically requires large amounts of data to train models effectively. In the case of self-driving cars, collecting real-world data in such quantities is expensive and time-consuming. Researchers often rely on simulation platforms, such as CARLA or AirSim, to provide virtual environments that mimic real-world conditions.

Long-Term Rewards: Autonomous vehicles must plan for long-term rewards, such as avoiding accidents in the future rather than achieving short-term gains. This requires the vehicle to have a broader understanding of its actions and consequences.

Exploration vs. Exploitation: Finding the right balance between exploration and exploitation remains a difficult challenge. In some cases, the vehicle may need to explore dangerous situations to discover better strategies, but too much exploration can risk safety.

Reinforcement learning plays a critical role in developing intelligent, decision-making algorithms for self-driving cars. By interacting with the environment, an autonomous vehicle can learn to navigate, make safe driving decisions, and improve over time. While reinforcement learning offers promising solutions, the complexities of real-world driving make it a challenging domain to master. However, through careful training, simulation, and testing, RL has the potential to revolutionize the way we think about transportation and self-driving cars.

In the next chapters, we will explore more advanced RL techniques and how they are being implemented to solve real-world driving scenarios in autonomous vehicles.

12.2 Setting up a simulation environment (CARLA, AirSim)

As we dive deeper into the world of self-driving cars and reinforcement learning (RL), setting up a realistic simulation environment becomes a crucial step in training, testing, and deploying autonomous vehicle models. The real world is unpredictable and testing autonomous vehicles on public roads is expensive, risky, and not always feasible. Therefore, researchers and engineers often rely on simulation environments to model complex driving scenarios, providing a safe space to experiment with reinforcement learning algorithms.

In this sub-chapter, we will explore two widely used simulation environments for autonomous driving—CARLA and AirSim—and guide you through the process of setting them up. Both CARLA and AirSim provide realistic environments, high-quality graphics, and accurate vehicle dynamics, enabling developers to train autonomous vehicles safely and efficiently.

Why Use Simulation for Autonomous Vehicles?

Simulations offer several benefits when it comes to developing self-driving cars:

Safe Testing: Testing an autonomous vehicle on real roads can lead to accidents, especially when the system is still being trained. Simulation allows you to test your RL models in a virtual environment without the risk of causing harm to people or property.

Data Generation: It's challenging to gather enough data for training autonomous systems in the real world, especially in various traffic conditions. Simulations can generate vast amounts of training data for vehicle behaviors, sensor data, and different scenarios, which are essential for teaching an RL agent.

Cost-Effective: Real-world testing can be costly in terms of fuel, vehicle wear and tear, and safety protocols. Simulation is a more cost-effective alternative, requiring only computational resources.

Controlled Environments: Simulation environments give you full control over the road conditions, weather, traffic, and obstacles, allowing you to train models under ideal conditions or simulate rare events that are difficult to encounter in real life.

Let's dive into the specifics of setting up two of the most popular simulation environments used for autonomous vehicle research and RL training: CARLA and AirSim.

CARLA Simulator

CARLA is an open-source simulator designed specifically for autonomous driving research. It provides high-quality graphics, realistic physics, and supports various sensors, including cameras, LiDAR, GPS, and radar. The flexibility of CARLA makes it an ideal choice for training RL models for self-driving cars.

Installing CARLA

Prerequisites Before installing CARLA, make sure you have the following prerequisites installed:

- Ubuntu 20.04 (or another Linux distribution) or Windows 10
- Python 3.7+ and pip
- Unreal Engine 4.26 or later (CARLA uses Unreal Engine for rendering)
- NVIDIA drivers (if using GPU for rendering)

Installation Steps

Step 1: Download the CARLA release package from the official GitHub repository or the CARLA website.

- **GitHub**: https://github.com/carla-simulator/carla
- **Website**: https://carla.org/

Step 2: For Windows users, extract the downloaded ZIP file and run CarlaUE4.exe. For Linux users, follow the installation guide provided in the repository to build CARLA from source.

Step 3: Once the simulator is installed, you can start the server by running:

./CarlaUE4.sh

Step 4: Launch the Python API to interact with the simulator using:

python3 manual_control.py

This will allow you to control the car using a simple interface and begin testing your algorithms in CARLA.

CARLA API and Features

CARLA provides a Python API to interact with the simulation environment programmatically. You can control various aspects of the simulation, such as:

- Vehicle control (acceleration, steering, braking)
- Sensor simulation (cameras, LiDAR, GPS)
- Traffic control (stop signs, traffic lights, pedestrian behavior)
- Weather and lighting conditions (fog, rain, time of day)

The API also allows you to implement Reinforcement Learning (RL) agents and let them interact with the environment, observe states, and take actions to maximize rewards.

AirSim Simulator

AirSim is another popular open-source simulator developed by Microsoft for training autonomous vehicles. While it was originally designed for drones, AirSim has been extended to support autonomous cars. It integrates with Unreal Engine and offers highly realistic environments for training self-driving cars using sensors like cameras, LiDAR, and GPS.

Installing AirSim

Prerequisites Before installing AirSim, ensure you have:

- Windows 10 or Ubuntu 18.04+
- Unreal Engine 4.25 or later (AirSim is built on top of Unreal Engine)
- Python 3.6+
- Visual Studio 2019 (for Windows users)

Installation Steps

Step 1: Clone the AirSim repository from GitHub:

git clone https://github.com/microsoft/AirSim.git

Step 2: Navigate to the AirSim directory and build the project using the appropriate method for your operating system. For Windows, run the build.cmd script; for Linux, follow the build instructions in the repository.

Step 3: After the build is complete, launch the Unreal Engine project in AirSim:

./AirSim

Alternatively, you can run the car simulation in the Unreal Engine editor.

Step 4: Once the environment is running, use the Python API to interact with the simulation.

AirSim API and Features

AirSim offers a range of features for autonomous car training:

- **Vehicle Control**: You can control the car's throttle, brake, steering, and gearshift programmatically.
- **Sensors**: It supports various sensors such as RGB cameras, depth cameras, LiDAR, and IMU, which are essential for autonomous vehicle training.

- **Simulating Real-World Scenarios**: AirSim provides various maps, including cityscapes and rural roads, where you can train your models on real-world-like environments.
- **Reinforcement Learning**: Similar to CARLA, AirSim can be used to train reinforcement learning agents, allowing self-driving cars to learn policies for driving in a range of scenarios.

AirSim also includes built-in tools for simulating traffic, pedestrians, and dynamic objects, providing a highly dynamic environment for testing autonomous vehicle behaviors.

Setting Up RL in Simulation Environments

Both CARLA and AirSim are great platforms for integrating reinforcement learning models. Below are the general steps for setting up RL in these environments:

Define the State Space: The state space refers to the information the RL agent needs to make decisions. In a self-driving car, this may include the car's position, speed, traffic conditions, and sensor data.

Define the Action Space: The action space consists of the actions that the RL agent can take, such as steering the car, accelerating, braking, or changing lanes.

Design the Reward Function: In RL, the agent learns from feedback based on the rewards it receives. The reward function defines how the agent is rewarded for actions that lead to positive outcomes, such as staying on the road or avoiding collisions.

Train the RL Agent: Once the state, action, and reward functions are defined, the next step is training the RL model. This is done through trial and error, where the agent interacts with the simulation, takes actions, and adjusts its behavior based on the rewards received.

Evaluate and Refine: After training, evaluate the performance of your model in the simulation. If the agent's performance is unsatisfactory, adjust the reward function, state, or action space and retrain the model.

Simulators like CARLA and AirSim are indispensable tools in the development of autonomous vehicles, especially for training reinforcement learning agents. These environments provide realistic, controlled settings where autonomous cars can learn to navigate, make decisions, and adapt to new situations. By using these platforms, developers can ensure that their self-driving algorithms are safe, efficient, and ready for real-world deployment.

In the next chapter, we will explore how to implement Reinforcement Learning algorithms using these simulation environments and how they can be optimized for real-world autonomous driving tasks.

12.3 Implementing deep Q-learning and policy gradient methods

In this section, we will explore how to implement two of the most popular reinforcement learning (RL) techniques used for training self-driving cars in simulated environments: Deep Q-Learning (DQN) and Policy Gradient Methods. Both approaches are widely used for decision-making in continuous, dynamic environments such as autonomous driving, where the agent must navigate roads, avoid obstacles, and interact with other traffic entities.

These algorithms differ in their approach to learning policies, and understanding their strengths and weaknesses will enable you to choose the right method for your autonomous driving project.

1. Deep Q-Learning (DQN)

Deep Q-Learning (DQN) is a value-based reinforcement learning algorithm that uses deep neural networks to approximate the Q-function, which represents the expected cumulative future rewards for an agent in a given state and action. The agent uses this Q-function to make decisions, selecting the action that maximizes the expected future reward.

Key Concepts of DQN:

Q-function: The Q-function, or action-value function, represents the quality of an action taken in a particular state, as evaluated by the expected future rewards. Formally, it is represented as $Q(s, a)$, where s is the state, and a is the action.

Deep Neural Network: A deep neural network (DNN) is used to approximate the Q-function since the space of states and actions is often too large to compute or store Q-values directly.

Experience Replay: One of the key features of DQN is the use of experience replay, where the agent stores its past experiences (state, action, reward, next state) in a buffer. During training, it samples random mini-batches from this buffer to break the correlation between consecutive training samples, improving stability.

Target Network: Another important feature is the use of a target network, which is a copy of the Q-network that is updated less frequently. This helps reduce instability by preventing oscillations in Q-value updates.

Steps to Implement Deep Q-Learning:

Set Up the Environment: First, ensure that you have a simulation environment like CARLA or AirSim up and running. The environment should allow the agent (your self-driving car) to take actions (steering, accelerating, braking) and receive observations (sensor data such as camera images, speed, position).

Initialize the Q-Network: Define a neural network that takes the state (such as the vehicle's current position, speed, and surrounding environment) as input and outputs Q-values for each possible action.

The network architecture typically consists of convolutional layers (for image-based input) followed by fully connected layers that output the Q-values.

Example:

```
class DQN(nn.Module):
    def __init__(self):
        super(DQN, self).__init__()
        self.conv1 = nn.Conv2d(3, 32, kernel_size=8, stride=4)
        self.conv2 = nn.Conv2d(32, 64, kernel_size=4, stride=2)
        self.conv3 = nn.Conv2d(64, 64, kernel_size=3, stride=1)
        self.fc1 = nn.Linear(64 * 7 * 7, 512)
        self.fc2 = nn.Linear(512, 4)  # Assuming 4 possible actions

    def forward(self, x):
        x = F.relu(self.conv1(x))
        x = F.relu(self.conv2(x))
        x = F.relu(self.conv3(x))
        x = x.view(x.size(0), -1)  # Flatten the output for the fully connected layers
```

```
x = F.relu(self.fc1(x))
return self.fc2(x)
```

Define the Loss Function and Optimizer: DQN uses mean squared error (MSE) loss to update the Q-values. Use an optimizer like Adam or RMSProp to minimize the loss.

```
optimizer = optim.Adam(q_network.parameters(), lr=1e-4)
loss_fn = nn.MSELoss()
```

Experience Replay: Implement the experience replay buffer, where the agent stores its experiences as tuples of (state, action, reward, next_state). During training, randomly sample mini-batches from this buffer to update the Q-network.

```
class ReplayBuffer:
    def __init__(self, capacity):
        self.buffer = deque(maxlen=capacity)

    def push(self, experience):
        self.buffer.append(experience)

    def sample(self, batch_size):
        return random.sample(self.buffer, batch_size)
```

Training the Agent: During training, the agent interacts with the environment, collects experiences, and updates the Q-network by performing the Q-value updates using the Bellman equation:

$$Q(s_t, a_t) = r_t + \gamma \max_{a'} Q(s_{t+1}, a')$$

Here, γ is the discount factor, which determines the importance of future rewards.

Target Network Update: Periodically update the target network by copying the Q-network's weights.

Testing and Fine-Tuning: After training for a specified number of episodes, test the agent's performance in the simulation and adjust the model as needed (e.g., tuning the learning rate, reward function, etc.).

2. Policy Gradient Methods

Unlike value-based methods like DQN, Policy Gradient Methods directly optimize the policy (a mapping from states to actions), bypassing the need for estimating the Q-function. This approach is useful when dealing with continuous action spaces or environments where the state-action space is too large or complex to handle with value functions alone.

Key Concepts of Policy Gradient Methods:

Policy: The policy is a function $\pi(a|s)$ that gives the probability of taking action a given state s. In Policy Gradient methods, the goal is to optimize this function directly.

Stochastic Policy: The policy is often modeled as a stochastic function (usually a neural network) that outputs probabilities for different actions rather than deterministic values.

Objective Function: Policy Gradient methods aim to maximize the expected cumulative reward, typically using a reinforce algorithm, where the objective is:

$$J(\theta) = \mathbb{E}\left[\sum_{t=0}^{T} R_t \log \pi_\theta(a_t|s_t)\right]$$

Where R_t is the reward received at time step t, and $\pi_\theta(a_t|s_t)$ is the probability of taking action a_t in state s_t.

Steps to Implement Policy Gradient:

Set Up the Environment: Just like in DQN, use a simulation environment like CARLA or AirSim.

Define the Policy Network: Use a neural network to model the policy. The network should take the current state (such as the car's position and speed) as input and output a probability distribution over possible actions (e.g., steering angles, acceleration values).

Example:

```
class PolicyNetwork(nn.Module):
    def __init__(self):
        super(PolicyNetwork, self).__init__()
        self.fc1 = nn.Linear(state_size, 128)
```

```
self.fc2 = nn.Linear(128, 64)
self.fc3 = nn.Linear(64, action_space)  # Output a probability distribution

def forward(self, x):
    x = F.relu(self.fc1(x))
    x = F.relu(self.fc2(x))
    return F.softmax(self.fc3(x), dim=-1)
```

Define the Loss Function: In policy gradient methods, the loss is typically computed using the likelihood of the taken actions weighted by the rewards received.

Training the Policy: Sample actions based on the policy network's output, interact with the environment, and compute the policy gradient updates. Use stochastic gradient ascent to maximize the expected cumulative reward.

Testing and Fine-Tuning: Test the performance of the trained policy in the simulation, and make adjustments to the architecture, hyperparameters, or reward structure as needed.

Both Deep Q-Learning and Policy Gradient Methods are powerful reinforcement learning techniques that can be applied to autonomous driving tasks. DQN is particularly useful for discrete action spaces and when you can represent the problem with a Q-function, while Policy Gradient methods are ideal for continuous action spaces or complex environments.

By implementing these algorithms within simulation environments like CARLA and AirSim, you can train self-driving agents capable of handling a variety of road conditions and scenarios. As you gain experience with these methods, you will be able to refine your models to achieve more accurate and efficient autonomous driving systems.

12.4 Evaluating agent performance in simulations

Evaluating the performance of an agent, particularly in the context of autonomous vehicle simulations, is a critical step in reinforcement learning (RL) projects. As we move from theory to practical application, it's essential to have robust metrics and tools for assessing the effectiveness of our trained models. This section will guide you through the process of evaluating the performance of an RL agent in a simulated environment, highlighting key evaluation strategies and metrics commonly used in autonomous driving simulations.

Why Performance Evaluation Matters

Performance evaluation in RL is essential for understanding how well an agent is able to perform tasks such as navigating through traffic, avoiding obstacles, and making intelligent driving decisions. In the case of autonomous vehicle simulations, performance evaluation helps ensure that the agent behaves safely, efficiently, and robustly in different simulated environments. Moreover, evaluations help refine models, identify issues, and improve real-world deployment.

1. Key Performance Metrics

To evaluate how well an RL agent has learned to perform its tasks, we need to track several metrics that reflect different aspects of its behavior. Below are some of the most commonly used performance metrics:

1.1 Cumulative Reward

In RL, the agent is typically rewarded (or penalized) for performing certain actions. Cumulative reward is the total reward accumulated by the agent over the course of an episode. A higher cumulative reward suggests that the agent is making decisions that align with the goal of the task.

Formula:

$$R_{total} = \sum_{t=0}^{T} r_t$$

Where r_t is the reward at time step t, and T is the length of the episode.

Interpretation: A higher cumulative reward generally indicates that the agent is performing well by reaching its goal (e.g., safely navigating to a destination).

1.2 Average Speed

In autonomous driving simulations, the average speed of the vehicle is a crucial factor. The agent must balance between driving efficiently (fast enough to reach a destination in time) and safely (not speeding, avoiding collisions, and following traffic rules).

Formula:

$$v_{avg} = \frac{1}{T} \sum_{t=0}^{T} v_t$$

Where v_t is the speed of the vehicle at time step t, and T is the total time of the episode.

Interpretation: If the vehicle consistently drives at a reasonable average speed, it indicates that the agent has learned how to maintain a balance between speed and caution.

1.3 Collision Rate

The collision rate measures how often the agent crashes into obstacles (such as other cars, pedestrians, or barriers). High collision rates typically indicate poor decision-making and failure to learn safe driving behaviors. Conversely, a low collision rate signifies that the agent is cautious and aware of potential hazards.

Formula:

$$C = \frac{\text{Number of collisions}}{\text{Total number of episodes}}$$

Interpretation: A lower collision rate is an indication that the agent has successfully learned to avoid obstacles and operate within the boundaries of the environment.

1.4 Success Rate

The success rate is the percentage of episodes in which the agent successfully completes its task, such as reaching a destination without colliding or violating any traffic rules. A high success rate indicates that the agent has learned an effective policy for completing the task.

$$S = \frac{\text{Successful episodes}}{\text{Total episodes}} \times 100$$

Interpretation: A higher success rate means the agent is successfully reaching its destination with fewer errors, demonstrating that it has learned a reliable strategy.

1.5 Time to Goal

The time to goal measures how long it takes the agent to complete its task, such as reaching the destination or completing a lap in a given environment. This metric provides insight into the agent's efficiency in accomplishing its objectives. It is important to note that faster completion does not always mean better performance, especially if it results in more collisions or other negative outcomes.

Formula:

$$T_{goal} = \text{Time taken to reach the goal}$$

Interpretation: A shorter time to goal indicates that the agent has learned an efficient driving policy. However, this must be balanced with safety (low collision rate) and adherence to traffic rules.

1.6 Fuel Efficiency / Resource Utilization

For self-driving cars, especially when simulating in environments with resource constraints (such as limited fuel or battery), fuel efficiency or resource utilization may be an important performance metric. An agent should aim to complete the task while minimizing resource consumption, making it more sustainable and cost-effective.

Formula:

$$E = \frac{\text{Total energy used}}{\text{Distance traveled}}$$

Interpretation: A more fuel-efficient agent uses fewer resources to achieve the same goal, reflecting both the efficiency and strategic planning of the agent.

2. Testing Scenarios and Environments

The evaluation of an agent's performance depends heavily on the scenarios and environments in which it is tested. In the context of autonomous vehicle simulations, various environmental factors and road conditions can impact agent behavior. Some key scenarios to consider during performance evaluation include:

2.1 Normal Road Conditions

Testing the agent in standard, ideal conditions with predictable traffic and weather. This scenario tests the agent's basic driving capabilities.

2.2 Adverse Weather Conditions

Simulating heavy rain, fog, snow, or other weather-related challenges tests the agent's ability to operate under low-visibility or slippery conditions.

2.3 Complex Traffic Scenarios

Introducing multiple vehicles, pedestrians, and obstacles in a dynamic environment with traffic signals, intersections, and pedestrians. This helps evaluate how well the agent handles interactions with other road users.

2.4 Unpredictable Obstacles

Testing the agent in environments where obstacles such as pedestrians, animals, or fallen objects appear unpredictably. This tests the agent's ability to make real-time decisions under uncertainty.

2.5 Off-Road or Challenging Terrain

Testing the agent's ability to navigate off-road, such as through dirt paths, rocky terrain, or hilly areas. This scenario challenges the agent's ability to handle difficult and unstructured environments.

2.6 Real-Time Stress Testing

Simulating environments where time-sensitive decisions are required, such as when a car must make a sudden stop to avoid a collision or navigate a congested road quickly.

3. Visualization and Logging

To gain insights into how well the agent performs, visualization and logging play a vital role. Some of the tools commonly used for evaluating the performance of RL agents include:

Visualizing the Agent's Trajectory: This involves plotting the path of the self-driving car within the environment, allowing you to visually inspect the agent's actions, decision-making process, and errors (such as collisions).

Reward and Loss Curves: These graphs show the cumulative reward and loss over time, helping you identify trends in agent learning and whether it is converging to an optimal policy.

Logging Key Metrics: Logging metrics such as collision rate, average speed, and time to goal during each episode helps you track the agent's performance over time and identify areas for improvement.

4. Final Evaluation and Fine-Tuning

Once the agent has been trained and evaluated, the final step is to fine-tune the model. This can involve:

Hyperparameter Tuning: Experimenting with different learning rates, batch sizes, and other hyperparameters to improve training performance.

Reward Shaping: Modifying the reward function to provide better incentives for desired behaviors. For instance, penalizing harsh acceleration or sharp turns can help improve safety.

Regularization and Robustness: Ensuring that the model is robust and can generalize well to unseen scenarios by applying techniques like dropout or adding noise to the environment during training.

Evaluating the performance of an autonomous vehicle agent in simulations is a complex but essential task to ensure safety, efficiency, and reliability before real-world deployment. By tracking key performance metrics such as cumulative reward, collision rate, time to goal, and efficiency, and by testing the agent under a variety of environmental scenarios, we can gain valuable insights into the agent's capabilities and make the necessary adjustments to improve its performance.

Ultimately, successful evaluation ensures that the RL model is well-equipped to navigate the challenges of the real world and can perform the tasks for which it was designed.

12.5 Real-world applications and limitations

The field of autonomous vehicles, fueled by advancements in reinforcement learning (RL), has grown significantly in recent years. As we continue to simulate, train, and deploy RL-based agents for self-driving cars, the ultimate goal is to transition from controlled, simulated environments to complex, real-world scenarios. This section will explore the real-world applications of RL in autonomous vehicles, while also addressing the challenges and limitations that come with deploying such systems in the physical world.

Real-World Applications of RL in Autonomous Vehicles

Autonomous vehicles (AVs) powered by reinforcement learning have vast potential in numerous sectors. Below are some key areas where RL-driven self-driving cars are being applied:

1. Urban Mobility and Ride-Sharing Services

RL can be used to enhance the operations of ride-sharing services like Uber and Lyft. By enabling self-driving cars to learn and adapt to urban traffic conditions, RL-powered vehicles can optimize routes, reduce ride times, and increase overall efficiency. These vehicles can adapt to dynamic urban environments by learning from traffic patterns, customer preferences, and other real-time factors.

Real-world benefit: Improved ride efficiency, reduced traffic congestion, and enhanced customer satisfaction through optimized routing.

2. Logistics and Delivery Services

Autonomous delivery vehicles are being designed to handle packages, food, and other goods. RL can help these vehicles optimize delivery routes, avoid roadblocks, and adjust their paths according to traffic conditions or road closures. Logistics companies, such as Amazon, have been experimenting with drones and autonomous delivery vehicles to ensure faster and more efficient deliveries.

Real-world benefit: Increased efficiency in supply chain management, reduced delivery times, and lower operational costs.

3. Public Transport Systems

Autonomous buses and shuttles powered by RL can improve public transportation systems by adapting to passenger demand, optimizing stops, and avoiding traffic congestion. These vehicles can communicate with each other and adjust their speeds, routes, and schedules based on real-time data. This kind of RL-driven dynamic scheduling ensures that public transportation becomes more accessible and efficient for urban residents.

Real-world benefit: Increased frequency, reduced wait times, and lower operational costs for public transit authorities.

4. Autonomous Trucking

Self-driving trucks, powered by RL, are revolutionizing freight transportation. With RL, autonomous trucks can learn how to navigate highways, adjust for weather conditions, and optimize fuel consumption. By reducing the need for human drivers, these trucks can operate more efficiently, driving longer hours and improving the consistency of deliveries.

Real-world benefit: Reduced transportation costs, increased operational hours, and minimized human error.

5. Testing and Training Autonomous Systems

Autonomous vehicles can also use RL for self-testing and continuous learning in real-world conditions. By deploying vehicles in varied environments, they can learn new driving strategies and improve their robustness. RL-based testing can speed up the development of safe and reliable AV systems by allowing vehicles to test new algorithms in real-time on the road.

Real-world benefit: Continuous improvement of self-driving systems through real-world learning, enhancing safety and reliability.

Limitations and Challenges of RL in Autonomous Vehicles

Despite the promising applications of RL in autonomous driving, several challenges and limitations must be addressed to bring these systems from simulation to real-world deployment. Below are some of the key limitations that engineers and researchers must overcome:

1. Safety and Reliability

Safety is paramount when it comes to autonomous vehicles. RL agents are trained to maximize rewards based on their environment, but they may not always account for all potential risks, such as unpredictable human behavior or rare scenarios that don't occur often in simulations. In the real world, safety-critical situations—such as accidents or severe weather—can lead to catastrophic consequences if the vehicle makes incorrect decisions.

Challenge: Ensuring that RL agents can handle edge cases and make safe, reliable decisions in unpredictable environments.

2. High Computational Costs

Training RL models for self-driving cars requires significant computational resources, especially when the agent needs to process large amounts of data in real-time. The high computational cost of training RL models, which involves continuous trial-and-error learning in dynamic environments, can be a significant barrier. Furthermore, real-time processing during driving demands low-latency decision-making, which requires powerful onboard systems that can be costly and resource-intensive.

Challenge: Managing the computational complexity and latency involved in real-time decision-making on autonomous vehicles.

3. Generalization to Unseen Environments

One of the major limitations of RL models in autonomous vehicles is the ability to generalize. RL agents are often trained in specific simulated environments, which means they may perform well under conditions similar to those they were trained on. However, in the real world, there are a vast number of variables, including changes in weather, road conditions, and unpredictable human drivers. The agent needs to adapt to new, unforeseen scenarios, but this can be difficult to achieve without substantial retraining.

Challenge: Ensuring that RL agents can generalize well to unseen or rare situations, thus improving their ability to operate in diverse environments.

4. Data Privacy and Security

Autonomous vehicles rely on large amounts of real-time data for navigation, decision-making, and system performance. This data often includes sensitive information about passengers, traffic conditions, and personal preferences. Handling this data responsibly, ensuring privacy, and protecting it from cyberattacks are significant concerns when deploying RL-based AVs in the real world.

Challenge: Implementing robust data protection protocols and ensuring privacy compliance, especially when operating in urban environments with numerous external data sources.

5. Interaction with Human Drivers and Pedestrians

Autonomous vehicles must be able to interact with human drivers, cyclists, pedestrians, and other road users who may not follow predictable patterns. While RL agents can be trained to navigate around other vehicles, they may struggle to predict and react appropriately to the actions of human drivers, who can be erratic and unpredictable. These interactions add a layer of complexity that goes beyond what is typically encountered in simulations.

Challenge: Ensuring smooth and safe interaction with human drivers, pedestrians, and other road users who do not necessarily behave according to predefined rules.

6. Ethical and Legal Considerations

The deployment of RL-based autonomous vehicles raises significant ethical and legal questions, particularly concerning decision-making in life-or-death scenarios. For example, if a self-driving car must choose between avoiding a pedestrian or swerving into another vehicle, how should the decision be made? Additionally, there are concerns about liability—if an autonomous vehicle is involved in an accident, who is held responsible?

Challenge: Addressing ethical dilemmas and establishing clear legal frameworks around liability, accountability, and insurance for self-driving vehicles.

While reinforcement learning holds great promise in transforming autonomous vehicles, it also comes with its fair share of challenges and limitations. Real-world applications, such as urban mobility, logistics, and autonomous trucking, highlight the potential benefits of RL in making transportation safer, more efficient, and more cost-effective. However, as we move toward widespread deployment, careful attention must be paid to ensuring the safety, reliability, and ethical integrity of these systems.

In the long term, overcoming these challenges and addressing the limitations will pave the way for more robust, intelligent, and safer autonomous vehicles, ultimately reshaping the future of transportation. Nonetheless, as we continue to evolve these systems, a thoughtful approach to testing, real-time monitoring, and continual learning will be essential for the successful integration of RL in real-world autonomous vehicles.

13. Edge AI with TinyML

In this chapter, we explore the world of Edge AI by using TinyML to deploy machine learning models on resource-constrained devices like microcontrollers, Raspberry Pi, and Arduino. You'll learn how to build lightweight models that can run directly on edge devices, enabling real-time decision-making without the need for cloud computing. We'll cover essential topics such as model quantization, data preprocessing, and optimizing models for low-power, high-efficiency operations. You'll also gain hands-on experience in deploying TinyML models on hardware and setting up sensors for applications like environmental monitoring, gesture recognition, and predictive maintenance. By the end of this chapter, you'll be equipped to bring machine learning to the edge, creating powerful solutions with minimal hardware requirements. □⚡

13.1 Introduction to ML on embedded systems

The intersection of machine learning (ML) and embedded systems, often referred to as Edge AI, has opened up a wealth of opportunities for building intelligent devices that operate independently of cloud infrastructure. The concept of Edge AI with TinyML is a breakthrough that allows machine learning models to run directly on small, resource-constrained devices such as microcontrollers, sensors, wearables, and IoT (Internet of Things) devices. This shift toward localized processing enables faster, more efficient decision-making, with applications ranging from healthcare monitoring to smart homes and industrial automation.

In this section, we will explore what ML on embedded systems is, how it works, and the key factors that differentiate it from traditional ML models. We will also touch on some of the benefits, challenges, and real-world applications of TinyML in embedded systems.

What is ML on Embedded Systems?

Embedded systems are specialized computing systems that perform specific functions within a larger system, often with limited processing power, memory, and storage. They are typically designed to be power-efficient and highly reliable, making them ideal for real-time applications.

When machine learning is deployed on these embedded systems, it enables devices to make decisions locally, often without relying on cloud-based computing resources. This is where TinyML comes into play—a specialized subset of machine learning that focuses on optimizing ML models to run on small, resource-constrained devices, such as microcontrollers and edge devices.

Machine learning on embedded systems involves the following key components:

- **Data Collection**: Embedded systems are equipped with sensors or data acquisition units that gather information from the environment, such as temperature, motion, or sound. This data forms the basis of the learning process.
- **Model Training**: Traditional ML models are often trained on powerful servers or cloud infrastructure, where large datasets can be processed efficiently. In Edge AI, the models are trained on more resource-intensive platforms before being deployed to the embedded device.
- **Inference on the Edge**: Once a model is trained, it is deployed to the embedded system where it performs inference (prediction or decision-making) in real-time. This local inference allows the device to process data and generate results without needing to communicate with a cloud server.

Why Edge AI and TinyML?

As the demand for real-time, low-latency processing grows, there is an increasing need for devices that can operate autonomously and make intelligent decisions without being tethered to centralized cloud servers. This is where Edge AI powered by TinyML comes into play. There are several compelling reasons why ML on embedded systems is gaining traction:

1. Latency Reduction

In traditional cloud-based ML applications, data must be transmitted to a cloud server for processing, and the results must then be sent back to the device. This round-trip communication introduces latency, which can be problematic for time-sensitive applications such as autonomous vehicles, robotics, and healthcare monitoring. By moving the processing to the edge, inference can happen almost instantaneously, reducing latency and improving response time.

2. Privacy and Security

By processing data locally, edge devices avoid sending sensitive information to the cloud, reducing the risk of data breaches and privacy concerns. This is particularly important in fields like healthcare and finance, where the security of personal data is paramount.

3. Bandwidth and Cost Efficiency

Transmitting large volumes of data to the cloud can be costly and bandwidth-intensive, especially for devices in remote or rural locations. By performing computations on the device, Edge AI minimizes the amount of data that needs to be sent to the cloud, reducing costs and alleviating bandwidth congestion.

4. Power Efficiency

Embedded systems are often battery-powered or designed to operate in environments where power consumption is a major concern. TinyML enables models to run on devices with minimal energy consumption, making it possible for edge devices to function for extended periods without needing frequent recharging.

5. Robustness and Reliability

Edge devices are often deployed in environments where connectivity to the cloud is intermittent or unreliable. By enabling local processing, Edge AI ensures that devices can continue to operate effectively even when cloud access is unavailable.

Key Challenges in ML for Embedded Systems

While the benefits of deploying ML on embedded systems are clear, there are several challenges that need to be addressed to make Edge AI a practical and scalable solution.

1. Resource Constraints

Embedded systems are typically designed with limited resources in terms of memory, processing power, and storage. Traditional ML models, especially deep learning models, are resource-intensive and require significant computational power. As a result, TinyML focuses on simplifying and optimizing models so that they can run efficiently on microcontrollers with as little as a few kilobytes of memory and limited processing power.

2. Model Optimization

Optimizing machine learning models to run efficiently on embedded devices requires a different approach compared to traditional cloud-based ML. For TinyML to work on embedded systems, models must be compressed, quantized, and pruned to fit within the limited hardware constraints. Tools like TensorFlow Lite, Edge Impulse, and PyTorch

Mobile provide libraries that help streamline the process of optimizing and deploying ML models on edge devices.

3. Real-Time Constraints

Embedded systems are often used in real-time applications, where decisions must be made quickly to avoid negative outcomes. Ensuring that ML models can run in real-time with low latency, while still providing high accuracy, can be challenging. Optimization techniques like model pruning and quantization, as well as hardware accelerators like specialized microcontrollers and FPGAs (Field-Programmable Gate Arrays), are critical to meeting real-time requirements.

4. Limited Data

Embedded systems frequently operate in isolated or remote environments, where collecting large datasets for training may be difficult. In some cases, data may only be available in small quantities or with limited diversity. Techniques like transfer learning, data augmentation, and federated learning are becoming increasingly important to train models with limited data on the edge.

5. Maintenance and Updates

Once deployed, embedded systems with machine learning models need to be updated and maintained. Since these devices often operate in remote locations or in mission-critical environments, ensuring that models can be updated without physical intervention or downtime is essential. Techniques like over-the-air (OTA) updates allow developers to push new model versions or bug fixes to edge devices without needing to bring them back to a central location.

Key Tools and Frameworks for Edge AI

The development of ML models for embedded systems requires specialized tools and frameworks designed to handle the constraints and requirements of edge computing. Some key tools for TinyML include:

- **TensorFlow Lite for Microcontrollers**: TensorFlow Lite is an open-source framework that enables developers to deploy lightweight ML models on embedded systems. It supports a wide range of devices, from microcontrollers to mobile devices, and optimizes models for low-latency inference.

- **Edge Impulse**: This platform simplifies the development of TinyML applications by offering a complete solution for collecting sensor data, training models, and deploying them on embedded systems. Edge Impulse is widely used for edge AI applications like predictive maintenance, anomaly detection, and health monitoring.
- **PyTorch Mobile**: PyTorch Mobile enables the deployment of PyTorch-based models on mobile and embedded devices, allowing developers to build high-performance applications for real-time inference at the edge.
- **Arduino and Raspberry Pi**: These open-source hardware platforms are commonly used for building and prototyping embedded systems. They support integration with various ML libraries, enabling developers to bring ML models to edge devices efficiently.

Applications of TinyML in Embedded Systems

TinyML is transforming industries by bringing intelligence to embedded systems. Some key applications of TinyML include:

1. Healthcare

TinyML can be used in wearable devices to monitor vital signs such as heart rate, temperature, and activity levels. These devices can use ML models to detect anomalies or predict health conditions in real time, sending alerts to users or medical professionals when needed.

2. Smart Homes

Edge AI makes it possible to build smarter homes where devices like thermostats, lights, and security cameras learn from their environment and make decisions without needing constant cloud interaction. For example, a smart thermostat can learn your preferences and adjust the temperature based on your behavior, optimizing comfort and energy efficiency.

3. Industrial Automation

TinyML plays a critical role in predictive maintenance and process optimization in industrial environments. By embedding machine learning into factory machines and sensors, businesses can predict equipment failures, reduce downtime, and increase operational efficiency.

4. Environmental Monitoring

Edge AI enables real-time monitoring of environmental conditions using small, low-power sensors. TinyML models can detect anomalies, such as changes in air quality or soil moisture levels, and trigger alerts for proactive interventions.

Machine learning on embedded systems, particularly with TinyML, is revolutionizing the way intelligent devices are deployed in the real world. By enabling devices to make autonomous, real-time decisions locally, TinyML provides substantial benefits in terms of latency, privacy, cost efficiency, and power consumption. As the demand for intelligent, connected devices continues to grow, the applications of TinyML will expand, transforming industries ranging from healthcare to industrial automation.

However, despite its potential, challenges such as resource constraints, model optimization, and real-time performance must be carefully addressed. As technology continues to advance and new tools and frameworks emerge, the integration of ML into embedded systems will become more seamless, allowing for more intelligent, robust, and efficient edge devices across various sectors.

13.2 Model compression and optimization techniques

Machine learning models, particularly deep learning models, can be quite resource-intensive, requiring substantial memory, storage, and computational power. However, when deploying machine learning (ML) models on embedded systems with limited resources, like microcontrollers, wearables, and IoT devices, these resource constraints must be overcome. This is where model compression and optimization techniques come into play.

Model compression refers to the process of reducing the size of a machine learning model while maintaining its accuracy and performance. Optimization techniques ensure that the model runs efficiently on the target device without compromising on inference speed or power consumption. In this sub-chapter, we will explore the various strategies for compressing and optimizing machine learning models to make them suitable for deployment in resource-constrained environments, such as embedded systems.

Why Model Compression and Optimization are Critical for Embedded Systems

The primary goal of applying model compression and optimization techniques is to make ML models feasible for embedded systems, which are often constrained by factors such as:

- **Limited Memory**: Embedded devices typically have a few kilobytes or megabytes of memory available, which means that large deep learning models need to be reduced to fit within this space.
- **Limited Storage**: The storage space on embedded systems can be minimal. Large models may not fit within the available storage, which can make it difficult to deploy models without extensive optimization.
- **Computational Power**: Embedded systems are not designed for high-performance computation. Without optimization, models may be too slow to run on these devices.
- **Energy Consumption**: Many embedded systems are battery-powered. Running resource-intensive models can drain power quickly, making it difficult to achieve prolonged operation times.

Key Techniques for Model Compression and Optimization

There are several techniques that can be applied to machine learning models to reduce their size and optimize their performance. Below, we explore some of the most commonly used techniques.

1. Pruning

Pruning is a technique that involves removing certain parts of the model, such as weights or entire neurons, that contribute little to the model's performance. This can be particularly useful for neural networks, which often contain a large number of redundant connections. By pruning these unnecessary weights, the model becomes smaller and faster to compute while retaining most of its accuracy.

Types of Pruning:

- **Weight Pruning**: This involves removing individual weights in a neural network that have minimal impact on the output. Weights are typically pruned based on their magnitude; weights with small absolute values are less important and can be removed.
- **Neuron Pruning**: Neurons that do not significantly affect the model's output can also be pruned. This results in a model with fewer layers or units and, thus, a reduced complexity.

Benefits of Pruning:

- Reduced model size and memory footprint
- Faster inference time on embedded systems
- Lower computational resource usage

2. Quantization

Quantization is the process of reducing the precision of the weights and activations in a model, typically from 32-bit floating-point precision to lower bit-width formats, such as 8-bit integers. This reduction in precision allows models to be stored in less memory and executed more efficiently without losing significant accuracy.

Types of Quantization:

- **Weight Quantization**: The weights of the model are reduced to lower precision. For example, 32-bit floating-point weights might be reduced to 8-bit integers.
- **Activation Quantization**: The activations (the output of neurons) can also be quantized to lower precision during the inference phase.
- **Post-training Quantization**: This is the process of quantizing a model after it has been trained, which can be applied to pretrained models without requiring retraining.
- **Quantization-Aware Training (QAT):** This technique involves training the model with quantization in mind, allowing the model to adapt to lower precision during training.

Benefits of Quantization:

- Reduced memory and storage requirements
- Faster model inference with lower computational cost
- Lower power consumption on embedded devices

3. Knowledge Distillation

Knowledge distillation is a technique in which a smaller, more efficient model (the "student") is trained to replicate the performance of a larger, more complex model (the "teacher"). The teacher model is typically a deep neural network with a high number of parameters and complexity, while the student model is simpler and smaller, designed to run on resource-constrained devices.

The process works by transferring the "knowledge" (probabilities, activations, or intermediate representations) from the teacher to the student model. By mimicking the teacher's outputs, the student model can achieve near-similar performance while being significantly smaller and more efficient.

Benefits of Knowledge Distillation:

- Reduced model size with similar performance to the larger model
- Smaller models can be deployed on devices with limited resources
- Effective for transferring the performance of large models to smaller embedded systems

4. Tensor Decomposition

Tensor decomposition involves breaking down high-dimensional tensors (which are common in deep learning models) into lower-dimensional components, effectively reducing the number of parameters in the model. Techniques such as Singular Value Decomposition (SVD) or Tucker decomposition can help simplify complex tensors, leading to smaller and more efficient models.

Benefits of Tensor Decomposition:

- Significant reduction in model size
- Lower computational cost
- Preservation of important features for high accuracy

5. Low-Rank Factorization

Low-rank factorization is a method of approximating a matrix or tensor by breaking it into lower-rank matrices. This technique is useful for models with large weight matrices (such as fully connected layers in neural networks). By approximating these matrices with lower-rank versions, the model becomes more efficient while retaining much of its original performance.

Benefits of Low-Rank Factorization:

- Reduced number of parameters and computational load
- Efficient for models with dense layers or large weight matrices
- Lower memory and storage requirements

6. Huffman Coding

Huffman coding is a lossless compression technique often used for compressing model weights. It involves assigning shorter codes to frequently occurring values and longer codes to rarer values. This method helps reduce the storage required for the model without losing any information.

Benefits of Huffman Coding:

- Reduced storage requirements for model weights
- No loss of model accuracy, as it is a lossless technique

7. Model Simplification and Architecture Modifications

Sometimes, reducing the complexity of the model architecture itself can lead to significant improvements in resource efficiency. This can be done by:

- **Reducing the number of layers or units**: Simplifying the model architecture by removing unnecessary layers or neurons can reduce the number of computations required during inference.
- **Using lightweight architectures**: For example, using MobileNet or SqueezeNet instead of traditional deep neural networks can reduce the number of parameters and computations required for tasks like image classification and object detection.

Benefits of Model Simplification:

- Reduced inference time
- Lower memory and storage requirements
- Faster deployment of models on embedded systems

Tools and Frameworks for Model Compression and Optimization

Several tools and frameworks have been developed to facilitate model compression and optimization for embedded systems. These tools automate many of the techniques discussed above and make it easier to deploy ML models on resource-constrained devices.

- **TensorFlow Lite**: This open-source framework helps optimize and deploy models on mobile and embedded systems. It supports model quantization, pruning, and other optimizations for running machine learning models on edge devices.
- **Edge Impulse**: Edge Impulse is a platform that provides tools for developing, training, and deploying TinyML models on embedded devices. It supports various compression and optimization techniques, such as quantization, pruning, and model simplification.
- **NNAPI (Android Neural Networks API):** NNAPI is designed to provide low-level access to machine learning acceleration hardware on Android devices. It supports model optimization for edge devices by offloading certain operations to specialized hardware.
- **PyTorch Mobile**: PyTorch Mobile provides an efficient way to deploy machine learning models on mobile and embedded devices. It includes tools for quantization, pruning, and optimizing model performance for edge devices.

Model compression and optimization are essential for deploying machine learning models on embedded systems with limited resources. Techniques such as pruning, quantization, knowledge distillation, tensor decomposition, and low-rank factorization enable the creation of efficient models that run effectively on resource-constrained devices. By applying these techniques, developers can deploy high-performance machine learning models in real-time applications while minimizing the computational and storage overhead.

As the demand for edge AI and TinyML solutions grows, further advances in model optimization will continue to unlock the potential of machine learning in embedded systems. Optimized models will enable a new wave of intelligent, autonomous devices that can operate in various fields, including healthcare, agriculture, manufacturing, and smart homes.

13.3 Training models for microcontrollers (TensorFlow Lite)

As the world moves toward a more connected, intelligent future, embedded systems like microcontrollers are playing an increasingly important role. These low-power, low-cost devices are at the heart of many everyday applications, such as wearables, smart sensors, home automation, and IoT (Internet of Things) devices. However, due to their limited memory, storage, and computational power, deploying machine learning (ML) models on microcontrollers requires specialized approaches.

In this sub-chapter, we will focus on training models for microcontrollers using TensorFlow Lite, a lightweight solution designed to run machine learning models efficiently on mobile and embedded devices. TensorFlow Lite (TFLite) is a version of TensorFlow optimized for edge devices, enabling developers to run ML models on microcontrollers and other constrained hardware.

Understanding TensorFlow Lite for Microcontrollers

TensorFlow Lite is an open-source deep learning framework that is optimized for running models on mobile, embedded, and IoT devices. TensorFlow Lite allows developers to create and deploy ML models on a wide range of hardware, from powerful smartphones to low-power microcontrollers. With its focus on performance, memory efficiency, and cross-platform compatibility, TensorFlow Lite has become the go-to solution for deploying machine learning models on edge devices.

For microcontrollers—tiny, low-cost embedded processors designed for simple tasks—TensorFlow Lite provides TensorFlow Lite for Microcontrollers (TFLite Micro), a minimal version of TensorFlow Lite that can run models with very small memory footprints (often as low as 16 KB of RAM).

Key Features of TensorFlow Lite for Microcontrollers:

- **Low Memory Footprint**: TensorFlow Lite is designed to minimize memory usage. This is crucial for microcontrollers, which may have limited storage and memory resources.
- **Optimized Inference**: The inference process is optimized for low-power and low-latency execution, making it ideal for real-time applications.
- **Cross-platform Compatibility**: TensorFlow Lite for Microcontrollers supports a variety of hardware, including popular microcontroller families such as ARM Cortex-M, ESP32, and others.
- **Tiny Model Support**: TFLite Micro is designed for small models with fewer parameters, suitable for running on microcontrollers with limited computation resources.
- **Model Conversion**: Models trained using TensorFlow or Keras can be converted to TFLite format to run on microcontrollers.

Steps for Training Models for Microcontrollers with TensorFlow Lite

The process of training and deploying models for microcontrollers typically involves several stages, from data preparation and model training to conversion and deployment.

Below are the steps for training a machine learning model suitable for microcontrollers using TensorFlow Lite:

1. Preparing the Dataset

The first step in any machine learning project is collecting and preparing data. For embedded systems and microcontrollers, it is crucial to consider the characteristics of the dataset and the specific problem you want to solve.

Dataset Considerations:

- **Size and Complexity**: Microcontrollers have limited memory and processing power, so models trained on large datasets may need to be reduced in size. Focus on simplifying the problem and using smaller, high-quality datasets.
- **Daa tPreprocessing**: Depending on the application, you might need to preprocess the data. For example, in sensor data processing (such as temperature, humidity, or accelerometer readings), you may need to normalize or standardize the input features.
- **Feature Selection**: Select only the most relevant features for the problem at hand to reduce model complexity and avoid overfitting.

For instance, if you are developing a simple motion detection system with an accelerometer, the dataset might include time-series sensor data with three accelerometer readings (x, y, z) and corresponding labels indicating the presence or absence of movement.

2. Training the Model

Once you have prepared the dataset, you can train a machine learning model. For models targeting microcontrollers, simpler architectures with fewer parameters tend to work best. The goal is to achieve reasonable accuracy without overwhelming the microcontroller's limited resources.

Model Selection:

- **Use Lightweight Models**: Simpler architectures like decision trees, support vector machines (SVMs), or shallow neural networks are ideal for microcontroller deployment. Convolutional Neural Networks (CNNs) and Recurrent Neural Networks (RNNs) might be overkill, depending on the application.

- **Use Quantization**: Quantization reduces the precision of model weights and activations, converting them from 32-bit floating-point to lower bit-width formats, such as 8-bit integers. This reduces the memory footprint of the model and speeds up inference. TensorFlow Lite supports post-training quantization for further optimization.
- **Avoid Overfitting**: Since the dataset and model are small, overfitting can be a risk. Apply regularization techniques, such as dropout or L2 regularization, to avoid overfitting.

In TensorFlow, you can train the model as you normally would for a standard application. For example:

```
import tensorflow as tf

# Example: Simple dense neural network for sensor data classification
model = tf.keras.Sequential([
    tf.keras.layers.Dense(128, activation='relu', input_shape=(input_shape,)),
    tf.keras.layers.Dense(64, activation='relu'),
    tf.keras.layers.Dense(2, activation='softmax')
])

model.compile(optimizer='adam', loss='categorical_crossentropy', metrics=['accuracy'])
model.fit(X_train, y_train, epochs=10, batch_size=32, validation_data=(X_val, y_val))
```

3. Convert the Model to TensorFlow Lite Format

Once the model is trained, the next step is to convert it into a TensorFlow Lite (TFLite) format. TensorFlow Lite models are optimized to run on mobile and embedded devices with limited resources.

The model is converted using the TFLiteConverter tool:

```
import tensorflow as tf

# Convert the trained model to TensorFlow Lite format
converter = tf.lite.TFLiteConverter.from_keras_model(model)
tflite_model = converter.convert()

# Save the converted model
with open('model.tflite', 'wb') as f:
```

f.write(tflite_model)

TensorFlow Lite also supports quantization during the conversion process, further reducing the model size.

4. Model Optimization for Microcontrollers

To make the model fit and perform efficiently on microcontrollers, you must optimize the converted TensorFlow Lite model. The following optimization techniques are commonly applied:

Post-Training Quantization

Quantization reduces the bit-width of model weights and activations from floating-point precision (32-bit) to lower precision (8-bit integers). This makes the model smaller and faster without significant loss in accuracy.

You can apply post-training quantization directly in TensorFlow Lite:

 # Apply post-training quantization
converter.optimizations = [tf.lite.Optimize.DEFAULT]
converter.target_spec.supported_ops = [tf.lite.OpsSet.TFLITE_BUILTINS_INT8]
tflite_model_quantized = converter.convert()

Pruning

Pruning removes the least important weights in the model, reducing its size and improving computational efficiency.

Efficient Architectures

Choose efficient model architectures that are tailored for embedded systems. Lightweight models, such as MobileNet, SqueezeNet, or custom small neural networks, are optimized for edge devices and microcontrollers.

5. Deploying the Model to a Microcontroller

Now that the model is converted and optimized for microcontrollers, the next step is deployment. The TensorFlow Lite for Microcontrollers (TFLite Micro) library is used to run TensorFlow Lite models on embedded systems with extremely limited resources. TFLite

Micro supports a range of microcontroller platforms such as ARM Cortex-M, ESP32, and others.

Steps for Deployment:

- **Set Up Development Environment**: Install the required toolchains for your specific microcontroller (e.g., ARM GCC for ARM-based microcontrollers).
- **Integrate TensorFlow Lite for Microcontrollers**: You can use the TensorFlow Lite for Microcontrollers library to load and run your .tflite model on the target device.
- **Run Inference**: Once the model is deployed, you can run inference on your microcontroller by loading the TensorFlow Lite model and making predictions based on input data, such as sensor readings or user inputs.

Example code for running inference on a microcontroller (simplified):

```
#include "tensorflow/lite/micro/micro_interpreter.h"
#include "tensorflow/lite/model.h"

// Load the model
const tflite::Model* model = tflite::GetModel(model_data);

// Set up the interpreter
tflite::MicroInterpreter interpreter(model, tensor_arena, kTensorArenaSize);

// Run inference
interpreter.Invoke();
```

6. Testing and Iteration

After deploying the model on the microcontroller, it's essential to test it on real-world data. Evaluate the model's performance in terms of accuracy, speed, and power consumption. Fine-tuning may be necessary to improve performance or reduce power consumption.

Training and deploying models on microcontrollers using TensorFlow Lite is an essential part of the growing trend of edge AI and TinyML. TensorFlow Lite for Microcontrollers enables the development of lightweight models that can run efficiently on embedded devices with limited computational resources. By following best practices like model selection, quantization, and pruning, and using TensorFlow Lite's model conversion tools, you can deploy machine learning models on microcontrollers to power intelligent, real-time applications in resource-constrained environments.

13.4 Deploying ML models on Raspberry Pi and Arduino

As the demand for intelligent edge devices grows, deploying machine learning models on small, low-cost hardware platforms like the Raspberry Pi and Arduino has become increasingly popular. These platforms, known for their versatility and widespread use in DIY and embedded systems projects, provide an excellent foundation for deploying machine learning (ML) models in real-world applications. In this sub-chapter, we will explore how to deploy ML models on two of the most popular platforms: Raspberry Pi and Arduino.

1. Why Use Raspberry Pi and Arduino for Edge ML?

Raspberry Pi and Arduino are widely recognized for their ease of use and accessibility, making them ideal platforms for deploying ML models in a variety of projects. Both devices provide unique advantages:

Raspberry Pi: The Raspberry Pi is a powerful single-board computer that runs a full operating system (usually Raspberry Pi OS, based on Debian Linux). It offers more processing power, memory, and storage than typical microcontrollers. This makes it well-suited for more complex ML tasks such as image classification, speech recognition, and real-time processing of sensor data. It supports both TensorFlow Lite (TFLite) and other machine learning libraries, enabling it to run a wide range of models.

Arduino: On the other hand, Arduino is a microcontroller platform with far more limited resources compared to the Raspberry Pi. It's ideal for simpler ML models or tasks requiring minimal computational overhead. Arduino is excellent for projects with minimal power consumption, such as sensor data collection, simple classification tasks, or other embedded systems applications. Deploying ML models on Arduino typically involves using more lightweight frameworks, such as TensorFlow Lite for Microcontrollers.

2. Deploying ML Models on Raspberry Pi

The Raspberry Pi's larger memory and processing capabilities make it a powerful platform for deploying machine learning models. The process involves several steps, from setting up the device to running ML inference using pre-trained models.

Steps for Deploying ML Models on Raspberry Pi

Set Up Raspberry Pi

- Install the Raspberry Pi OS on an SD card and boot up the Raspberry Pi.
- Ensure the Raspberry Pi is connected to the internet and has access to the required software repositories.

Update the system using the following commands:

sudo apt update
sudo apt upgrade

Install Required Libraries

For ML tasks, you may need to install libraries such as TensorFlow, TensorFlow Lite, or OpenCV for image processing tasks. The installation steps may vary depending on your requirements:

sudo apt-get install python3-pip

pip3 install tensorflow

If you're working with TensorFlow Lite models, install the TensorFlow Lite runtime:

pip3 install tflite-runtime

Prepare the Model

Train and convert your model into the TensorFlow Lite format using the TensorFlow Lite converter. If you're working with a non-TensorFlow model, use the relevant conversion tools for other frameworks (e.g., PyTorch to ONNX, then ONNX to TensorFlow Lite). Example for converting a trained Keras model:

import tensorflow as tf

model = tf.keras.models.load_model('model.h5')
converter = tf.lite.TFLiteConverter.from_keras_model(model)
tflite_model = converter.convert()
with open('model.tflite', 'wb') as f:

```
f.write(tflite_model)
```

Load and Run the Model on Raspberry Pi

Now, load the TensorFlow Lite model on the Raspberry Pi and run inference. Here's an example of how you can do this using Python:

```
import tensorflow as tf
import numpy as np

# Load the TFLite model
interpreter = tf.lite.Interpreter(model_path="model.tflite")
interpreter.allocate_tensors()

# Get input and output tensor details
input_details = interpreter.get_input_details()
output_details = interpreter.get_output_details()

# Example: Prepare input data (for image classification)
input_data = np.array([input_image], dtype=np.float32)

# Run inference
interpreter.set_tensor(input_details[0]['index'], input_data)
interpreter.invoke()

# Get the output
output_data = interpreter.get_tensor(output_details[0]['index'])
print(f'Prediction: {output_data}')
```

Optimizing for Performance

For real-time or low-latency applications, consider optimizing your model further with post-training quantization to reduce model size and improve inference speed:

```
converter.optimizations = [tf.lite.Optimize.DEFAULT]
converter.target_spec.supported_ops = [tf.lite.OpsSet.TFLITE_BUILTINS_INT8]
tflite_model_quantized = converter.convert()
```

Deploy the Model in Real-Time Applications

Once your model is running, you can integrate it with sensors (such as cameras or microphones) for tasks like object detection or speech recognition. Use libraries like OpenCV to process image or video inputs and feed them to the model for inference.

Use Cases for Raspberry Pi in ML Projects

- **Image Classification**: Use the Raspberry Pi's camera module to classify objects in real-time.
- **Voice Recognition**: Implement speech-to-text or voice command recognition using pre-trained models.
- **IoT Integration**: Connect sensors and devices to the Raspberry Pi to build intelligent IoT systems.
- **Robotics**: Utilize Raspberry Pi for autonomous robots by running object detection, navigation, and control models.

3. Deploying ML Models on Arduino

While the Arduino platform is much more constrained than the Raspberry Pi, it is still possible to deploy machine learning models on it, especially when you are working with simple ML tasks. Since Arduino lacks the power of a full operating system or the memory and processing capabilities of the Raspberry Pi, the approach here involves simplifying the models as much as possible and using TensorFlow Lite for Microcontrollers to deploy models that are small enough to fit into Arduino's limited resources.

Steps for Deploying ML Models on Arduino

Set Up Arduino

- Install the Arduino IDE on your computer and ensure that you have the correct board and libraries installed.
- Make sure your Arduino board (e.g., Arduino Nano 33 BLE Sense) is connected via USB for programming.

Train and Convert the Model

- Since Arduino has very limited resources, you will typically need to use smaller models, such as decision trees, SVMs, or lightweight neural networks.
- After training a model in TensorFlow or Keras, convert the model to TensorFlow Lite format using the TFLiteConverter tool.

Use TensorFlow Lite for Microcontrollers

- Download the TensorFlow Lite for Microcontrollers library and include it in your Arduino project. This allows you to run your model on the microcontroller.
- Write code to integrate the model with Arduino sensors, and make sure to optimize the model to use minimal RAM and processing power.

Upload the Model to Arduino

Once the model is converted, use the TensorFlow Lite interpreter for microcontrollers to deploy the model. Here's an example of loading a TensorFlow Lite model on an Arduino board:

```
#include "tensorflow/lite/micro/micro_interpreter.h"
#include "tensorflow/lite/model.h"

// Load the TFLite model (binary data)
const tflite::Model* model = tflite::GetModel(model_data);
tflite::MicroInterpreter interpreter(model, tensor_arena, kTensorArenaSize);

void setup() {
  // Initialize the Arduino sensor
  pinMode(A0, INPUT);
  Serial.begin(9600);
}

void loop() {
  // Read data from sensor and run inference
  float sensor_input = analogRead(A0);
  interpreter.SetInput(0, &sensor_input);
  interpreter.Invoke();

  // Retrieve and process inference output
  float* output = interpreter.GetOutput(0);
  Serial.println(*output);

  delay(1000);  // Run inference every second
}
```

Deploy and Monitor

- After uploading the model, connect your Arduino to the sensors and deploy the application.
- Monitor the performance and ensure the model runs within the limited resources of the Arduino platform.

Use Cases for Arduino in ML Projects

- **Sensor Classification**: Deploy models that classify sensor data, such as temperature or motion data, into different categories.
- **Gesture Recognition**: Use accelerometer data to classify gestures or actions, ideal for wearables or remote controls.
- **Anomaly Detection**: Run lightweight anomaly detection algorithms on Arduino to identify unusual behavior or faults in sensor data.

Deploying machine learning models on Raspberry Pi and Arduino brings AI to the edge, allowing for intelligent decision-making in real time without relying on cloud processing. The Raspberry Pi, with its powerful hardware, is capable of running more complex models, while Arduino is best suited for simpler, low-power applications. With tools like TensorFlow Lite and TensorFlow Lite for Microcontrollers, developers can efficiently deploy models on both platforms, making them ideal for a wide variety of edge AI applications such as robotics, IoT, and embedded systems.

13.5 Real-world applications of Edge AI

Edge AI refers to the deployment of artificial intelligence (AI) models directly on edge devices, such as smartphones, wearables, sensors, and microcontrollers, without the need to rely on a central server or cloud infrastructure for processing. By executing AI algorithms closer to the data source, Edge AI enables real-time decision-making, reduces latency, and conserves bandwidth. This approach is increasingly becoming a key enabler of a wide range of applications across industries, from healthcare and agriculture to automotive and smart cities.

In this section, we will explore various real-world applications of Edge AI, highlighting how machine learning models are deployed on edge devices like Raspberry Pi, Arduino, and other low-power, resource-constrained hardware. We will also look at how these applications contribute to innovation, improve efficiency, and address challenges in everyday life.

1. Smart Cameras and Computer Vision

Edge AI is particularly useful in the domain of computer vision, where real-time processing and fast decision-making are crucial. With smart cameras and embedded vision systems powered by edge AI, industries can automate tasks that would traditionally require human intervention. These applications include:

Security and Surveillance: Smart cameras equipped with AI capabilities can perform real-time object detection, face recognition, and motion tracking. This enables automated monitoring of premises, reducing the need for human oversight while improving security. For instance, edge AI-powered cameras can identify intruders or track the movement of people in a particular area and alert security teams instantly.

Retail Analytics: In retail environments, edge AI is used to analyze customer behavior, detect anomalies, and track inventory. Smart cameras placed on shelves can monitor how customers interact with products, provide insights on popular items, and even trigger alerts when products are out of stock.

Automated Quality Control: In manufacturing, edge AI can help in quality control by analyzing images of products as they are produced. AI models can detect defects, ensuring only high-quality items move to the next stage in the production line. This reduces errors and waste, improving efficiency.

2. Healthcare and Medical Devices

The healthcare industry is one of the most promising sectors for Edge AI applications, especially when it comes to real-time health monitoring and diagnostic systems. Some key use cases include:

Wearables for Health Monitoring: Edge AI is deployed in wearables such as fitness trackers and smartwatches to continuously monitor vital signs such as heart rate, blood oxygen levels, and activity levels. These devices can perform basic AI-driven analysis (e.g., detecting irregular heart rhythms) and alert users or medical professionals if abnormalities are detected, enabling timely interventions.

Diagnostic Tools: In medical imaging, edge AI models can analyze X-rays, MRIs, or CT scans on-site, without the need to send large image files to the cloud for processing. This not only speeds up diagnoses but also reduces bandwidth usage and ensures privacy. For instance, AI models can detect tumors or fractures in medical images, providing doctors with insights faster.

Personalized Treatment: Devices embedded with AI algorithms can also personalize patient care by monitoring symptoms in real-time. For example, smart inhalers for asthma patients can use edge AI to track usage patterns and provide feedback to the patient and healthcare provider, ensuring better disease management.

3. Autonomous Vehicles

The automotive industry has embraced edge AI to enhance safety, improve navigation, and drive autonomous vehicle development. Autonomous vehicles rely on real-time decision-making, where processing speed and low latency are critical. Some key areas where edge AI plays a vital role in autonomous vehicles include:

Self-Driving Cars: Autonomous vehicles use multiple sensors, such as cameras, LiDAR, and radar, to perceive their environment. AI models running on edge devices in the vehicle process sensor data in real-time, enabling the vehicle to make decisions on actions like steering, braking, and accelerating. These models ensure the car can avoid obstacles, navigate complex traffic situations, and make real-time decisions without relying on cloud-based servers.

Driver Assistance Systems: Even in non-autonomous vehicles, edge AI is used in advanced driver-assistance systems (ADAS). For example, lane-keeping assist, collision detection, and adaptive cruise control rely on edge AI to process sensor data and make immediate decisions to improve driver safety.

Fleet Management: Edge AI is used for managing fleets of vehicles by tracking vehicle health, monitoring driver behavior, and optimizing routes in real time. This reduces fuel consumption, enhances driver safety, and improves operational efficiency.

4. Industrial IoT (IIoT) and Predictive Maintenance

Edge AI is transforming the Industrial Internet of Things (IIoT) by enabling smarter factories, warehouses, and supply chains. Machine learning models can be deployed on edge devices to analyze sensor data in real time, allowing for improved efficiency and predictive maintenance.

Predictive Maintenance: One of the key applications of Edge AI in industrial settings is predictive maintenance. Sensors installed on machines collect data related to vibration, temperature, and other indicators. Edge AI models process this data to predict potential failures before they occur. By detecting anomalies early, companies can avoid costly downtime and perform maintenance when it is actually needed, rather than relying on fixed schedules.

Smart Manufacturing: Edge AI allows manufacturers to optimize production processes by analyzing data from machines and production lines. Real-time analysis of equipment performance, energy consumption, and product quality helps improve operational efficiency. AI-powered robots and machines can adjust their operations autonomously, resulting in faster production cycles and lower operational costs.

5. Smart Homes and IoT

Edge AI is revolutionizing the concept of smart homes, where various devices are connected and can autonomously perform tasks based on user behavior and environmental conditions. Some notable applications include:

Voice Assistants: Devices such as smart speakers (e.g., Amazon Echo, Google Home) use edge AI to process voice commands locally, allowing them to respond to users quickly and without latency. The voice recognition models can be fine-tuned to each user's voice, enabling more personalized interactions.

Smart Thermostats: AI-powered smart thermostats use machine learning to learn a user's temperature preferences over time and adjust heating or cooling systems autonomously. These devices use edge AI to analyze environmental data (e.g., temperature, humidity) and optimize energy usage, contributing to cost savings and sustainability.

Home Security Systems: Smart cameras and motion sensors powered by edge AI can detect intruders, recognize familiar faces, or identify unusual activity. These devices can alert homeowners in real-time, enabling faster responses to security threats.

6. Agriculture and Environmental Monitoring

Edge AI is also transforming industries such as agriculture and environmental monitoring by enabling real-time analysis of vast amounts of data collected from sensors, drones, and satellites. Some applications include:

Precision Agriculture: Edge AI models can be deployed on drones or IoT sensors to analyze soil moisture, crop health, and environmental factors. This allows farmers to make data-driven decisions about irrigation, fertilization, and harvesting, optimizing yields and reducing resource consumption.

Wildlife Monitoring: Edge AI is used in remote wildlife monitoring systems to analyze data from cameras and sensors placed in forests or nature reserves. AI-powered models can detect and track wildlife in real-time, helping conservationists monitor endangered species or prevent illegal poaching.

Air Quality Monitoring: Edge AI enables real-time air quality monitoring by analyzing sensor data from environmental stations. This is critical for early warnings about pollution levels, helping city authorities take immediate actions to protect public health.

7. Retail and Customer Engagement

Edge AI is increasingly being used in retail environments to enhance customer experience and optimize store operations. Examples include:

In-Store Personalization: Retailers use edge AI to analyze customer data in real-time to offer personalized recommendations, discounts, and promotions. AI models can identify shopping patterns and tailor experiences based on individual preferences.

Inventory Management: AI-powered cameras and sensors in stores can track product availability, predict demand, and automate restocking. Edge AI enables real-time inventory updates, preventing stockouts and reducing waste.

Edge AI has opened up new possibilities for deploying machine learning models in real-world applications. From smart devices in homes and vehicles to industrial IoT and healthcare, Edge AI is enabling faster decision-making, reducing latency, and making AI more accessible and efficient. With continued advancements in hardware and software, Edge AI will become even more integrated into our everyday lives, providing smarter, more responsive systems that can learn and adapt in real time. The potential for Edge AI to revolutionize industries is vast, and its applications are only beginning to scratch the surface of what is possible.

14. MLOps & Model Deployment

In this chapter, we focus on the critical topic of MLOps—the practice of deploying, managing, and scaling machine learning models in production environments. You'll learn how to implement a seamless model deployment pipeline that integrates with continuous integration (CI) and continuous delivery (CD) frameworks. We'll walk you through the best practices for model versioning, model monitoring, and scalability, ensuring that your models perform optimally in real-world applications. Additionally, you'll gain hands-on experience with deployment tools such as Docker, Kubernetes, and cloud platforms like AWS and Google Cloud. By the end of this chapter, you'll have the skills to take machine learning models from development to production, ensuring they are robust, maintainable, and scalable in any environment. 🚀

14.1 Introduction to MLOps and CI/CD for ML

Machine learning (ML) has evolved significantly over the last decade, and the complexity of deploying and maintaining ML models in production has also increased. In this era of AI-driven applications, businesses and developers face the challenge of ensuring that ML models are not only developed successfully but also maintained and updated efficiently in live environments. This is where MLOps (Machine Learning Operations) and Continuous Integration/Continuous Deployment (CI/CD) come into play. These practices are crucial for automating the entire lifecycle of ML models, from development to deployment, and ensuring that they remain accurate, efficient, and adaptable to changing data.

In this section, we will explore the concept of MLOps, its importance in the ML pipeline, and how CI/CD practices can be applied to machine learning workflows. By adopting MLOps and CI/CD strategies, teams can address key challenges such as model versioning, automation of deployment pipelines, scalability, and the overall quality of their ML models.

What is MLOps?

MLOps is a set of practices, tools, and techniques that combine the principles of DevOps (Development Operations) with machine learning. The goal of MLOps is to automate and streamline the process of building, deploying, monitoring, and managing ML models in production environments. Similar to DevOps, which is focused on the automation and integration of software development and IT operations, MLOps ensures that machine learning models can be consistently delivered, maintained, and improved in production systems.

MLOps involves various stages of the ML lifecycle, including:

- **Model Development**: Building the machine learning model using different algorithms, techniques, and data sources.
- **Model Training**: Training the model on datasets and evaluating its performance using validation techniques.
- **Model Deployment**: Moving the trained model into a live production environment where it can interact with real-world data and generate predictions.
- **Model Monitoring**: Continuously tracking the model's performance and behavior to detect any degradation or drift in its predictive capabilities.
- **Model Retraining and Maintenance**: Updating and retraining the model as new data becomes available or the model's performance begins to decline.

The goal of MLOps is to create a collaborative environment between data scientists, developers, and IT operations teams, ensuring that the ML model lifecycle is optimized for productivity and scalability.

Why is MLOps Important?

The need for MLOps has become critical in the AI industry for several reasons:

Scaling Machine Learning: Traditional software development practices cannot handle the scale and complexity of modern ML applications. As the number of ML models grows, automating the deployment and management of these models becomes necessary to ensure they operate efficiently and at scale.

Collaboration Across Teams: MLOps facilitates collaboration between data scientists, engineers, and IT teams, creating an environment where each group can focus on their areas of expertise without being bogged down by the complexities of the others' responsibilities. This collaboration is key to delivering robust ML solutions that work effectively in production environments.

Continuous Improvement: In the fast-paced world of data, machine learning models can become obsolete quickly. MLOps ensures that ML models can be continuously updated, retrained, and redeployed to adapt to new data and changing environments. This process ensures that models stay relevant and continue to provide value over time.

Automation of Pipelines: Automating the ML pipeline, from data collection and model training to deployment and monitoring, allows for faster iterations and reduces the chances of human error. With automated pipelines, the development process becomes more efficient, and the risk of model drift and errors can be minimized.

Model Governance and Compliance: MLOps ensures that models are managed and tracked throughout their lifecycle. This is particularly important in industries where regulatory compliance and model transparency are critical, such as healthcare, finance, and insurance. Proper model governance ensures that models are auditable and meet necessary standards.

Continuous Integration and Continuous Deployment (CI/CD) for ML

CI/CD is a set of modern software development practices aimed at automating and streamlining the process of integrating, testing, and deploying code changes. While CI/CD is most often used in traditional software development, it has become equally important in machine learning, especially when managing models in production. Let's break down what CI/CD means in the context of ML and why it is vital.

Continuous Integration (CI) for ML

Continuous Integration refers to the practice of integrating new code changes into the main branch of a project's repository frequently, usually multiple times a day. In traditional software development, this involves integrating updates to the source code. However, in the context of machine learning, CI refers to the process of integrating data, code, and model changes together in a version-controlled system. Here's how it works in ML:

Version Control for Code and Models: Just like software developers use version control systems (e.g., Git), data scientists can use version control to track the source code, model configurations, and even datasets used for training. This ensures that the models can be easily updated, and previous versions can be restored if needed.

Automated Testing: In CI, automated tests are run whenever a new change is made to the codebase or model. For ML, these tests can include unit tests for data preprocessing pipelines, model validation, and performance metrics like accuracy, F1 score, etc. This ensures that code and model changes don't break the system or negatively impact model performance.

Data Validation: In addition to testing the models themselves, CI pipelines in ML also validate the data. This step checks the integrity of data sources and ensures that the data is in the correct format and free of errors or inconsistencies before being fed into models.

Continuous Deployment (CD) for ML

Continuous Deployment takes the CI process a step further by automating the process of deploying model changes to production. Once a model has passed all validation tests, it is automatically deployed to the production environment. This is a key practice in MLOps as it allows for rapid iteration and seamless updates to the deployed model. Here's how CD works in the context of ML:

Model Deployment Automation: With CD pipelines, after successful testing and validation, models can be deployed to the production environment automatically. This eliminates the need for manual intervention and ensures that the latest version of the model is always available for inference.

Monitoring and Logging: Once deployed, CD pipelines incorporate monitoring tools that track the performance of the model in real-time. Key metrics, such as response times, accuracy, or prediction latency, are continuously monitored. In case of a model failure or significant drop in performance, the system can trigger alerts and rollback the deployment to a previous stable version.

Model Rollback: A unique challenge in ML deployments is model drift, which occurs when a model's performance deteriorates due to changing data patterns. CD pipelines can automatically detect these issues and initiate a rollback to a previous version of the model to ensure stability.

Model Retraining and Updates: As new data becomes available, MLOps pipelines allow for periodic retraining of models, ensuring that the deployed model stays up to date. This can be integrated into the CD pipeline, so models are retrained with fresh data and then redeployed with minimal manual effort.

Tools for MLOps and CI/CD in ML

There are several tools and platforms that assist in implementing MLOps and CI/CD practices. Some of the most popular include:

Kubeflow: An open-source platform designed for deploying and managing ML workflows on Kubernetes. Kubeflow provides an integrated suite of tools for data ingestion, model training, deployment, and monitoring.

MLflow: A platform for managing the ML lifecycle, from experimentation to deployment. It helps with versioning models, tracking experiments, and managing deployment pipelines.

TensorFlow Extended (TFX): A production-ready platform for deploying ML pipelines, TFX focuses on integrating ML models into production environments efficiently.

Jenkins: A popular open-source automation server used to set up CI/CD pipelines for software development. Jenkins can also be extended to handle ML-specific workflows, such as model training, testing, and deployment.

GitLab and GitHub Actions: These platforms support CI/CD pipelines and can be customized to manage ML workflows, enabling version control, automated testing, and continuous deployment for ML models.

MLOps and CI/CD are essential for managing the full lifecycle of machine learning models, from development to deployment and continuous monitoring. By automating the ML workflow, teams can ensure that models are consistently delivered, maintained, and updated, improving efficiency, scalability, and model accuracy. As the demand for AI and machine learning grows, implementing effective MLOps and CI/CD practices will be key to successfully scaling ML applications and ensuring that models remain accurate and relevant in the ever-evolving real-world data environments. By adopting MLOps, organizations can unlock the full potential of machine learning while mitigating risks associated with model degradation and deployment complexities.

14.2 Dockerizing ML models for production

In modern software development, Docker has emerged as a pivotal tool for ensuring consistency across different computing environments. It simplifies the process of packaging applications and their dependencies into containers, which can be deployed across any machine running Docker. This is particularly beneficial for machine learning (ML) models, as they often require specific versions of libraries, frameworks, and tools that may vary between development and production environments.

In this sub-chapter, we will explore how Docker can be used to containerize machine learning models for production. We will cover the benefits of Docker in machine learning, the steps to Dockerize ML models, and how Docker can facilitate smoother deployment, scalability, and maintenance of models in production environments.

Why Docker for ML Models?

Machine learning models are typically developed in controlled environments where data scientists and engineers work with specific versions of libraries, frameworks, and operating systems. However, when these models are deployed to production, they may face compatibility issues or behave unpredictably due to differences between development and production environments. Docker solves this issue by creating lightweight, reproducible, and isolated containers that can run any application consistently, regardless of where they are deployed.

Some of the main reasons Docker is ideal for ML models are:

Environment Consistency: Docker guarantees that the ML model will run in the exact same environment it was developed in. The container encapsulates all dependencies, eliminating version mismatches, missing libraries, and other inconsistencies.

Portability: Docker containers are platform-independent. You can develop your ML model in a local environment, test it, and then deploy it to a production environment, whether it's on a cloud server, on-premises hardware, or a personal machine.

Scalability: Docker containers can be orchestrated using tools like Kubernetes, which makes it easy to scale up ML models as the application demand grows. Multiple instances of the same container can run in parallel, ensuring that the model can handle increased traffic and compute requirements.

Efficient Resource Utilization: Containers are lightweight and share the underlying host operating system, so they use fewer resources compared to traditional virtual machines. This allows organizations to run more instances of models or other services on the same infrastructure.

Simplified Deployment: Docker can automate the deployment process and create reproducible pipelines, making it easier to deploy ML models in a consistent, error-free manner.

Version Control and Rollback: Docker images can be versioned and stored in a registry (like Docker Hub or a private registry), which allows teams to track changes and rollback to previous versions if needed. This is especially useful for ML models, as updates may be frequent, and previous versions may need to be restored to ensure stability.

Steps to Dockerize ML Models

The process of Dockerizing an ML model involves packaging the model, its dependencies, and a suitable runtime environment into a Docker container. Below are the key steps to Dockerize your ML model:

1. Prepare Your ML Model

Before you can Dockerize your model, it must be ready for deployment. This means having a trained model and a script to load the model and handle inference (prediction) tasks. The most common formats for saving ML models include:

- **TensorFlow/Keras**: .h5 or .savedmodel
- **PyTorch**: .pth or .pt
- **Scikit-learn**: Pickle files (.pkl)
- **XGBoost**: .model

Ensure that your model is trained and saved in a format that is compatible with the libraries you will use inside the Docker container.

2. Create a Dockerfile

A Dockerfile is a script that contains the instructions for creating a Docker image. This file specifies the base image (operating system), installs dependencies, copies necessary files (including the model), and sets up the environment for the ML model to run.

A basic Dockerfile for Dockerizing an ML model might look like this:

 # Step 1: Use an official Python runtime as a base image
FROM python:3.8-slim

 # Step 2: Set environment variables (optional)
ENV PYTHONUNBUFFERED 1

 # Step 3: Install necessary system dependencies

```
RUN apt-get update && apt-get install -y \
    build-essential \
    libpq-dev \
    && rm -rf /var/lib/apt/lists/*

# Step 4: Create a working directory
WORKDIR /app

# Step 5: Copy the model file and inference script
COPY model.h5 /app/model.h5
COPY inference.py /app/inference.py

# Step 6: Install required Python packages
COPY requirements.txt /app/requirements.txt
RUN pip install --no-cache-dir -r /app/requirements.txt

# Step 7: Expose the port (if running a web API)
EXPOSE 5000

# Step 8: Command to run the model for inference
CMD ["python", "/app/inference.py"]
```

In this example, the Dockerfile:

- Uses the official Python base image (python:3.8-slim) for the container.
- Installs necessary dependencies such as build-essential and libpq-dev.
- Copies the pre-trained ML model file (model.h5) and the Python script (inference.py) that will handle inference requests.
- Installs Python packages listed in requirements.txt.
- Exposes port 5000 for communication (if deploying through a web API).
- Specifies the command to run when the container starts, which is the inference.py script.

3. Write the Inference Script

The inference script (inference.py) is responsible for loading the model and performing predictions. For example, in Python, you could use the following script to load the model and make predictions on new data:

```
import tensorflow as tf
```

```
import numpy as np

# Load the trained model
model = tf.keras.models.load_model('model.h5')

# Define the function to make predictions
def predict(input_data):
    # Preprocess input_data (e.g., scaling, reshaping)
    processed_data = np.array(input_data).reshape(1, -1)
    prediction = model.predict(processed_data)
    return prediction

# Test the model with a sample input
sample_input = [5.1, 3.5, 1.4, 0.2]
prediction = predict(sample_input)
print(f"Prediction: {prediction}")
```

This script loads the pre-trained model and uses it to make predictions on input data.

4. Build the Docker Image

After creating the Dockerfile and the inference script, the next step is to build the Docker image. To do this, navigate to the directory where your Dockerfile is located and run the following command:

```
docker build -t ml-model .
```

This command will build the Docker image and tag it as ml-model. Docker will execute the steps in the Dockerfile, which include installing dependencies, copying files, and setting up the container.

5. Run the Docker Container

Once the Docker image has been built, you can run the container locally to test the ML model. Use the following command to start the container:

```
docker run -p 5000:5000 ml-model
```

This command will start the container and expose port 5000, which allows communication with the running container through a web API. If you plan to deploy the model via a web interface (e.g., Flask, FastAPI), this port will be the entry point for making prediction requests.

6. Deploy to Production

Once the Docker image has been tested and validated locally, it can be deployed to a production environment. Popular cloud platforms like AWS, Google Cloud, and Azure all support Docker containers, and many provide specialized services to simplify container deployment, such as:

- AWS Elastic Container Service (ECS)
- Google Kubernetes Engine (GKE)
- Azure Kubernetes Service (AKS)

You can upload the Docker image to a container registry (e.g., Docker Hub, Amazon ECR, Google Container Registry) and deploy it to your chosen production environment.

Dockerizing ML models provides a powerful approach to ensuring that machine learning applications can be reliably and efficiently deployed across different environments. By containerizing the model and its dependencies, you can avoid compatibility issues, streamline deployment, and scale your application to meet growing demand. Moreover, Docker's flexibility, coupled with CI/CD pipelines, enables continuous updates, testing, and optimization of your models in production. Whether you are deploying a small model for personal use or a large-scale system for enterprise applications, Docker is an essential tool for managing and delivering machine learning models.

14.3 Kubernetes for scaling ML applications

As machine learning (ML) models evolve and become more integral to real-world applications, the demand for efficient deployment, scaling, and management of ML applications has risen dramatically. Traditional methods of deploying ML models often struggle to handle large volumes of data, computational resources, and traffic spikes effectively. This is where Kubernetes, an open-source container orchestration platform, plays a pivotal role.

Kubernetes simplifies the management and scaling of applications by automating deployment, scaling, and operations of containerized applications. For machine learning applications, Kubernetes provides a robust and scalable solution that can handle everything from model training to real-time inference at scale. It enables ML teams to manage, deploy, and scale ML models in a consistent, efficient, and reproducible manner. In this sub-chapter, we will explore how Kubernetes can be leveraged for scaling ML applications, including its features, benefits, and practical implementation strategies.

Why Kubernetes for ML Applications?

Kubernetes has become a critical tool for deploying containerized applications in production, especially for machine learning workloads, due to the following advantages:

Automated Scaling: ML applications often need to scale dynamically based on incoming data, the number of user requests, or other variables. Kubernetes allows for both horizontal and vertical scaling of ML applications to ensure optimal resource allocation. For instance, Kubernetes can automatically spin up more replicas of a model-serving container when the traffic increases and scale them down during low-traffic periods.

Resource Management: ML workloads, particularly training and inference, can be computationally intensive. Kubernetes efficiently manages resources, including CPU, GPU, and memory, by automatically allocating resources to containers based on availability and demand. This ensures that ML models get the necessary resources without overloading the system.

Efficient Experimentation and Versioning: As ML models continuously evolve, versioning becomes crucial to ensure reproducibility and traceability of experiments. Kubernetes simplifies the management of multiple model versions by enabling easy deployment, rollback, and continuous updates to models, making experimentation and version control streamlined.

Fault Tolerance and High Availability: In production environments, it's critical to ensure that ML models are available and running without interruptions. Kubernetes' self-healing capabilities, including automatic restarts and failover, ensure high availability and fault tolerance. This is crucial when models are serving real-time predictions and need to be operational 24/7.

Support for Distributed ML: Many ML applications require distributed training across multiple nodes to process large datasets or train complex models. Kubernetes facilitates the orchestration of distributed ML frameworks like TensorFlow, PyTorch, and Horovod, making it easier to manage large-scale ML training jobs across a cluster.

Continuous Integration and Delivery (CI/CD): Kubernetes is often used in conjunction with CI/CD pipelines to streamline the deployment and monitoring of ML models in production. It allows for the continuous delivery of new versions of models while ensuring minimal downtime, which is particularly valuable in dynamic environments like e-commerce, healthcare, or financial services.

Isolation of Components: Kubernetes enables the isolation of various components of the ML pipeline (data preprocessing, training, evaluation, inference, etc.) into distinct containers. This modular architecture allows for better management of resources and scaling of each component independently.

How Kubernetes Works for ML Applications

Kubernetes works by abstracting infrastructure resources and managing the deployment, scaling, and networking of containerized applications through a set of core components. Let's look at how these components apply specifically to machine learning:

1. Pods

At the heart of Kubernetes is the concept of "pods," which represent the smallest deployable unit in Kubernetes. A pod can contain one or more containers. In the context of ML applications, each pod might represent a different component of the ML pipeline, such as a model-serving container, a data pre-processing container, or a training container.

For example:

- **Model serving pod**: A pod that serves the trained ML model for inference requests.
- **Training pod**: A pod that runs the training script and processes large datasets.

Multiple pods can be created to run replicas of the ML models for load balancing and failover.

2. Deployments

Deployments in Kubernetes allow for the declaration and management of applications running in pods. With Kubernetes deployments, ML applications can be easily scaled, updated, and rolled back to previous versions. For instance, if a new version of the ML model has been trained and needs to be deployed, a new deployment can be created without affecting the existing production system. Kubernetes will automatically update the deployment and handle the transition smoothly.

3. Services

Kubernetes services abstract the communication between pods and other external systems. For ML applications, services make it easy to expose model endpoints for inference via RESTful APIs or other protocols. A service can be used to expose the model to external clients, ensuring stable and reliable communication with the model-serving containers. Kubernetes services also help load-balance incoming requests, ensuring that no single container is overwhelmed.

4. Horizontal Pod Autoscaler (HPA)

The Horizontal Pod Autoscaler automatically scales the number of pod replicas based on observed CPU utilization, memory usage, or custom metrics such as response time. For an ML application, this can be especially useful when serving predictions at scale. If there is a sudden spike in incoming requests for predictions, Kubernetes can spin up more pod replicas to handle the load, ensuring low latency and high availability.

5. Persistent Volumes

Training ML models, especially on large datasets, requires significant storage capacity. Kubernetes' persistent volumes (PVs) allow for the separation of storage and compute. This ensures that data remains accessible to the containers even when the containers are restarted or rescheduled to different nodes. For ML models, persistent storage is crucial for storing datasets, model weights, logs, and configurations.

6. StatefulSets

In cases where ML models need to maintain a consistent state (e.g., when running long-term inference), Kubernetes' StatefulSets allow you to manage stateful applications. StatefulSets are particularly useful for managing ML models that require consistent, stable identities (such as a running version of the model or a distributed training process).

Implementing Kubernetes for ML Applications

To demonstrate how Kubernetes can be used to scale ML applications, let's break down the process of deploying an ML model on Kubernetes.

Step 1: Containerize Your Model

The first step is to Dockerize the ML model, as explained in the previous section. After you have a working Docker container for your model, the next step is to upload the Docker image to a container registry, such as Docker Hub, Google Container Registry (GCR), or Amazon Elastic Container Registry (ECR).

Step 2: Create Kubernetes Deployment

Once the model is containerized, you need to create a Kubernetes deployment that specifies how many replicas of the model to run, the resources (CPU, GPU, memory) required, and the container image to use.

Here is an example of a basic Kubernetes deployment configuration for an ML model serving container:

```
apiVersion: apps/v1
kind: Deployment
metadata:
  name: ml-model-deployment
spec:
 replicas: 3
 selector:
  matchLabels:
    app: ml-model
 template:
  metadata:
   labels:
     app: ml-model
  spec:
   containers:
   - name: ml-model
     image: your-container-registry/ml-model:latest
     ports:
     - containerPort: 5000
     resources:
      limits:
        cpu: "1"
        memory: "2Gi"
```

This configuration sets up three replicas of the model serving container and allocates 1 CPU core and 2 GB of memory per replica. Kubernetes will automatically manage the scaling of these containers.

Step 3: Create a Kubernetes Service

To expose the ML model, you need to create a Kubernetes service. This service will allow external applications or users to interact with the model via APIs.

Here is an example of a Kubernetes service configuration:

```
apiVersion: v1
kind: Service
metadata:
  name: ml-model-service
spec:
  selector:
    app: ml-model
  ports:
    - protocol: TCP
      port: 80
      targetPort: 5000
  type: LoadBalancer
```

This service exposes the ML model on port 80 and maps it to port 5000, where the model is serving predictions.

Step 4: Autoscaling and Resource Management

To enable autoscaling, you can use the Horizontal Pod Autoscaler (HPA) to automatically scale the number of pods based on resource utilization.

Here is an example of an HPA configuration:

```
apiVersion: autoscaling/v2
kind: HorizontalPodAutoscaler
metadata:
  name: ml-model-hpa
spec:
  scaleTargetRef:
```

```
apiVersion: apps/v1
kind: Deployment
name: ml-model-deployment
minReplicas: 1
maxReplicas: 10
metrics:
- type: Resource
  resource:
    name: cpu
    target:
      type: Utilization
      averageUtilization: 80
```

This HPA configuration automatically scales the ML model deployment between 1 and 10 replicas based on CPU utilization.

Kubernetes is a powerful tool for scaling and managing machine learning applications in production. With Kubernetes, teams can automate the deployment, scaling, and monitoring of ML models, ensuring they run reliably and efficiently at scale. Kubernetes' features like resource management, autoscaling, and version control provide ML teams with the flexibility and control they need to deliver robust and performant AI-powered applications. Whether you're deploying a simple model-serving endpoint or managing a complex distributed training pipeline, Kubernetes can streamline the process and enhance the scalability of your ML applications.

14.4 Monitoring deployed ML models

Once machine learning (ML) models are deployed into production, the work doesn't stop at the deployment phase. In fact, monitoring deployed models is an essential aspect of maintaining high-quality, robust, and reliable ML systems. Effective monitoring ensures that the models continue to perform as expected and allows teams to quickly detect and mitigate issues such as model drift, degraded performance, or data quality problems. Without proper monitoring, even the most sophisticated ML systems can fail to deliver consistent results over time.

In this sub-chapter, we will explore how to monitor deployed ML models, the key performance indicators (KPIs) to track, and the tools and techniques used to ensure continuous model performance.

Why Monitoring is Critical for Deployed ML Models

ML models operate in dynamic environments where various factors can impact their performance. These include:

Data Drift: Over time, the underlying data distribution may shift, which can lead to a reduction in model accuracy. This phenomenon is called data drift (or concept drift). For example, in a fraud detection model, fraudulent patterns may evolve, causing the model to miss new types of fraud.

Model Drift: Even if the data distribution stays the same, the model might deteriorate over time. This happens when the model's assumptions no longer hold, or the model's performance on unseen data declines due to changes in the environment.

Real-time Performance Issues: As more data flows into the system, performance issues such as latency and throughput can arise, particularly when the model is handling high volumes of requests in real-time.

Business Impact: If an ML model fails to perform well, it can negatively impact business outcomes. For instance, inaccurate predictions in a recommendation engine could result in poor customer satisfaction, or incorrect financial predictions could lead to wrong business decisions.

Compliance and Ethical Concerns: Many industries require regular checks and audits to ensure that the deployed models adhere to regulatory and ethical standards. Monitoring can ensure compliance and highlight any biases or unethical outcomes generated by the model.

Key Aspects of Monitoring Deployed ML Models

Effective monitoring of ML models involves tracking a range of metrics, including performance-related indicators, resource usage, and business metrics. Below are some of the critical areas to monitor:

1. Performance Metrics

The most fundamental aspect of model monitoring is tracking the performance of the deployed model. Some important performance metrics include:

Accuracy: The most basic metric that measures how often the model makes correct predictions.

Precision, Recall, and F1-Score: These metrics are essential in classification problems, especially when dealing with imbalanced datasets. Precision tells us how many of the predicted positive cases are actually positive, while recall indicates how many of the actual positive cases were correctly identified. F1-score balances precision and recall.

AUC-ROC Curve: The Area Under the Receiver Operating Characteristic curve helps assess the trade-off between sensitivity and specificity. It's commonly used in binary classification tasks.

Mean Absolute Error (MAE) and Root Mean Squared Error (RMSE): These are common metrics in regression tasks. MAE measures the average magnitude of the errors in predictions, while RMSE penalizes large errors more heavily.

Model Loss: Monitoring the loss function value during inference helps detect if the model's predictions are diverging from expected outcomes.

Latencies: Monitoring the time it takes for the model to generate predictions (inference latency) is critical, especially in real-time systems. For example, in financial trading systems or autonomous vehicles, a delay of even a few milliseconds can have significant consequences.

2. Data Drift and Concept Drift

Over time, the data used to make predictions may change, and this is particularly true for dynamic environments. To ensure that your model remains effective, you need to track:

Feature Distribution: Monitor the distributions of input features and compare them with the distributions used during training. Significant changes in feature distributions can indicate data drift. Tools such as WhyLabs and Evidently can help visualize and monitor these shifts.

Model Performance on New Data: It's important to evaluate model performance on a regular basis with fresh, live data to see how the model is performing compared to when it was initially deployed.

Prediction Errors: Track prediction errors, and especially track cases where the model performs significantly worse than expected. This might indicate that the model has started making erroneous predictions due to changing data distributions.

3. Business Metrics

The ultimate goal of deploying an ML model is to solve a business problem. Therefore, it is crucial to monitor metrics that reflect the business impact of the model. These metrics depend on the use case and may include:

Customer Engagement: For recommendation systems or personalization engines, monitor how the recommendations or predictions affect customer engagement, such as click-through rates, conversion rates, or retention rates.

Revenue Impact: Track the financial outcomes of the predictions, such as the increase in sales for a demand forecasting model or the amount of fraud detected in a fraud detection system.

Operational Efficiency: In cases where ML models are used for process optimization (e.g., supply chain management), monitor how the predictions improve operational metrics like cost savings, on-time delivery rates, or resource utilization.

4. Resource Usage

Deployed models consume computational resources such as CPU, GPU, memory, and storage. Efficient resource management ensures that the system remains responsive and scalable. Important metrics to monitor include:

CPU and Memory Usage: Track the utilization of CPU and memory resources to ensure that the model isn't using too many resources or overloading the system.

GPU Usage: In deep learning models, monitoring GPU usage is crucial, particularly when handling large-scale inference or when running models on specialized hardware.

Throughput: This metric measures how many requests are processed by the model in a given time period. Monitoring throughput helps determine if the system can handle the expected load.

Infrastructure Scaling: Ensure that the infrastructure is scaled appropriately to meet demand. With Kubernetes, for example, the Horizontal Pod Autoscaler (HPA) can automatically scale up or down based on resource usage.

5. Alerting and Notifications

Setting up proper alerting mechanisms is crucial in a production environment. Automated alerts allow you to proactively address issues before they escalate. For instance, if model performance drops below a certain threshold or if resource usage spikes, the system should notify the relevant team.

Some common alerting strategies include:

Threshold Alerts: Set performance thresholds for accuracy, latency, and other metrics, so that when a value exceeds or falls below a certain threshold, an alert is triggered.

Anomaly Detection: Use anomaly detection algorithms to identify unusual patterns in model performance or data. This can include sudden spikes in prediction errors or unusual latencies in real-time inference.

Logging and Audit Trails: Log all model predictions, inputs, and errors to build an audit trail. This is especially useful for compliance, troubleshooting, and future analysis.

Tools for Monitoring ML Models

Several tools are available to help manage and monitor deployed ML models. Some popular ones include:

Prometheus & Grafana: Prometheus is an open-source tool that collects and stores metrics in a time-series database. Grafana is commonly used for visualizing and monitoring these metrics. Both tools can be integrated into Kubernetes to monitor deployed models.

MLflow: An open-source platform for managing the end-to-end machine learning lifecycle, MLflow provides tools for experiment tracking, model versioning, and monitoring.

Evidently AI: This tool provides an easy-to-use interface to track and visualize data and model drift, model performance, and other KPIs over time.

WhyLabs: WhyLabs is an AI observability platform that helps monitor and explain ML model performance, data drift, and business metrics.

Seldon: An open-source platform for deploying and monitoring machine learning models. It provides detailed tracking of model predictions, serving metrics, and integration with monitoring tools like Prometheus.

Monitoring deployed ML models is a continuous and crucial process that ensures models remain effective, reliable, and aligned with business goals. By tracking the right performance metrics, detecting data and model drift, and monitoring business impact, teams can quickly identify issues and improve their models. Additionally, with the right set of tools and infrastructure in place, ML systems can be scaled and maintained effectively in production, providing long-term value to the organization. Effective monitoring not only helps in detecting problems early but also fosters trust in the deployed models, ensuring they deliver optimal results over time.

14.5 Automating model retraining pipelines

In the dynamic world of machine learning (ML), models can degrade over time as they encounter new patterns in data or as underlying trends evolve. This phenomenon, often referred to as model drift or data drift, can cause deployed models to lose their effectiveness. To combat this, automated model retraining pipelines are essential for ensuring that models remain accurate, relevant, and perform well in real-time environments.

Automating retraining processes is vital in large-scale systems, where manually retraining models would be time-consuming and impractical. In this sub-chapter, we will delve into the importance of automating retraining, how to build an efficient retraining pipeline, the tools and frameworks that facilitate automation, and how to ensure the pipeline can be deployed in production.

Why Automate Model Retraining?

As the world around us changes, so too does the data that our models rely on. Here are several reasons why automating model retraining is necessary:

1. Data Drift and Concept Drift

Over time, the statistical properties of the input data may change. This is referred to as data drift. For example, in a recommendation system, user behavior may change, or in a fraud detection system, new types of fraudulent activity may emerge. This can cause the model to underperform, as it may no longer be trained on data that reflects the current patterns.

Concept drift, on the other hand, refers to a shift in the relationship between the input and the output. For example, in a predictive maintenance system, machinery may begin to fail due to new operating conditions that were not present when the model was initially trained.

Both data drift and concept drift require periodic retraining to keep the model's performance stable and relevant.

2. New Data Availability

As more data becomes available over time, the model may benefit from new patterns and insights. Retraining the model with fresh data allows it to learn from the most current information, potentially improving its predictive power.

3. Continuous Improvement

Automating retraining creates an environment where the model can continuously improve without manual intervention. Retraining on new data can allow the model to incorporate more complex patterns, learn from mistakes, and deliver better performance.

4. Minimizing Human Intervention

Manually retraining models requires human intervention, which can be error-prone, time-consuming, and inconsistent. By automating this process, we ensure consistency, minimize human error, and free up resources for other important tasks.

Building an Automated Model Retraining Pipeline

An automated retraining pipeline involves several steps that can be executed without manual intervention. These steps typically include the following:

1. Data Monitoring

The first step in an automated retraining pipeline is monitoring the data that the model processes in real time. This includes tracking the distribution of input features, target variables, and prediction errors. The goal is to detect when significant shifts in data or performance occur, signaling the need for retraining.

Data Drift Monitoring: Tools such as WhyLabs and Evidently AI can monitor and alert when data distribution shifts beyond a predefined threshold, signaling potential drift that may require retraining.

Performance Monitoring: Metrics like accuracy, precision, recall, or other custom KPIs can be tracked. If performance drops below a certain threshold, this indicates that retraining might be necessary.

2. Data Collection and Preprocessing

Once drift or performance degradation is detected, the next step is to collect and preprocess the new data for model retraining. This step involves:

Gathering New Data: This may include scraping fresh data from databases, APIs, or logs.

Preprocessing Data: Similar to the initial model training process, new data needs to be preprocessed. This includes cleaning the data, handling missing values, and performing transformations (such as scaling, encoding, and feature engineering).

3. Model Selection

The retraining pipeline should be flexible enough to experiment with different model types. This may involve:

Training a New Model: When fresh data is available, you may choose to retrain an existing model using the new dataset.

Model Selection Algorithms: Sometimes, rather than just retraining the current model, it may be beneficial to try different algorithms (e.g., switching from a decision tree to a random forest or testing a deep learning model). AutoML frameworks like TPOT, H2O.ai, or Google Cloud AutoML can assist in automatically selecting the best model for the data.

Model Versioning: As new versions of models are trained, it's important to keep track of which versions are being used in production. MLflow and DVC (Data Version Control) are popular tools that support model versioning, making it easier to track different model versions and configurations.

4. Model Evaluation

Before the new model can be deployed, it should be thoroughly evaluated to ensure that it performs better or at least as well as the existing model. Model evaluation typically includes:

Cross-validation: Use techniques such as cross-validation to assess how well the new model generalizes to unseen data.

Performance Metrics: Use appropriate metrics (e.g., accuracy, AUC, RMSE, etc.) to evaluate the model's performance on test data or a validation set.

A/B Testing: In some cases, it may be beneficial to run A/B tests where the new model is deployed alongside the existing model for a period to compare performance in a real-world environment.

5. Model Deployment

Once the retrained model has been evaluated and meets performance standards, the next step is to deploy it into production. The deployment pipeline should be automated to handle the transition from the model training phase to deployment. This includes:

Dockerization: Packaging the model in a Docker container ensures that it is portable and can be easily deployed to different environments. Docker allows for consistent deployment, regardless of the underlying infrastructure.

CI/CD Pipelines: Continuous Integration (CI) and Continuous Deployment (CD) pipelines can automate the entire process, from model training to deployment. Jenkins, GitLab CI, and CircleCI are popular tools for automating CI/CD pipelines.

Model Monitoring: Post-deployment, continuous monitoring of the model's performance ensures that it continues to deliver accurate predictions. If performance drops, the pipeline can automatically trigger a retraining process.

6. Retraining Triggers

The retraining pipeline must include automated triggers to ensure that it only retrains when necessary. These triggers may include:

Threshold-based Triggers: For instance, if the model's performance metrics (e.g., accuracy or F1-score) fall below a certain threshold, the retraining process is initiated.

Time-based Triggers: Retraining can also be scheduled periodically (e.g., monthly, quarterly) to ensure that the model is always up-to-date.

Data-based Triggers: Retraining could be triggered when a certain amount of new data has been processed or when new data that significantly deviates from previous data is detected.

Tools for Automating Model Retraining

Several tools and frameworks can help automate the retraining pipeline, including:

MLflow: MLflow is an open-source platform for managing the ML lifecycle, from experimentation to deployment. It supports model versioning, tracking, and automation of retraining pipelines.

Kubeflow: Kubeflow is a Kubernetes-based open-source platform that automates the deployment, scaling, and management of ML workflows. It includes tools for building end-to-end retraining pipelines.

TFX (TensorFlow Extended): TFX is a production-ready ML pipeline framework that supports automated retraining. It's tailored for TensorFlow-based applications and integrates with tools like Apache Airflow.

Seldon: Seldon is an open-source platform for deploying, monitoring, and managing machine learning models. It offers features for model versioning, monitoring, and retraining.

DVC (Data Version Control): DVC is a version control system for machine learning projects. It helps automate the process of data versioning, model retraining, and deployment.

Automating model retraining pipelines is a critical step in maintaining high-performance machine learning models in production. By setting up efficient, flexible, and scalable retraining systems, organizations can ensure that their models stay relevant and continue to deliver value over time. With the right tools and processes in place, automation minimizes human intervention, reduces the time to react to changes in data, and ensures that models perform optimally in a rapidly evolving environment. By combining monitoring, model versioning, and continuous integration/deployment practices, teams can deliver more reliable, accurate, and robust machine learning systems.

15. Monitoring and Maintenance of ML Models

In this chapter, we delve into the crucial aspect of monitoring and maintaining machine learning models once they are deployed in production. Machine learning models can degrade over time due to changes in data, shifts in business goals, or evolving environments. You'll learn how to set up automated monitoring to track model performance, detect issues like concept drift, and trigger model retraining when necessary. We'll explore tools and frameworks for log management, model performance tracking, and automated alerts to ensure your models stay reliable. Additionally, we'll cover the importance of A/B testing, version control, and model rollback strategies to maintain the quality and accuracy of your models over time. By the end of this chapter, you'll be equipped with the knowledge to proactively monitor and maintain your ML models, ensuring they continue to deliver high value and remain aligned with business objectives. ⚒️

15.1 Concept drift and model performance decay

Machine learning (ML) models are not static systems; their performance can degrade over time due to changes in real-world data. This phenomenon, known as concept drift, can lead to inaccurate predictions, poor decision-making, and ultimately a loss of trust in ML-based systems. In this section, we will explore what concept drift is, how it affects model performance, methods for detecting it, and strategies for mitigating its impact.

Understanding Concept Drift

Concept drift occurs when the statistical properties of input features and their relationship with target variables change over time. When this happens, models trained on historical data may become outdated and fail to make accurate predictions. There are several types of concept drift:

1. Sudden Drift

- A sharp change in data distribution happens in a short period.
- **Example**: A new regulation in the banking industry changes the criteria for loan approvals, making past data obsolete overnight.

2. Gradual Drift

- Data distribution changes slowly over time.
- **Example**: Customer preferences shift gradually, causing a recommendation engine to become less effective.

3. Recurring Drift

- Data patterns change periodically, only to return to their previous state later.
- **Example**: Retail sales fluctuate based on seasonal trends, causing changes in purchasing behavior throughout the year.

4. Incremental Drift

- Small, continuous changes in data distribution accumulate over time.
- **Example**: Social media sentiment gradually shifts as cultural opinions evolve.

Understanding the nature of concept drift in an application helps determine the best approach to detect and handle it.

Why Does Concept Drift Happen?

Several real-world factors contribute to concept drift:

- **Evolving User Behavior** – In applications like recommendation systems, fraud detection, and customer churn prediction, user preferences and behaviors change over time.
- **Regulatory Changes** – New laws or policies can alter the rules governing financial transactions, medical diagnoses, or hiring decisions.
- **Market Dynamics** – Economic conditions, competitor strategies, and industry trends shift the way businesses operate.
- **Technology Advancements** – The introduction of new technologies (e.g., new payment methods) can alter the way data is generated.

Ignoring concept drift can lead to model performance decay, meaning the model's accuracy and reliability will deteriorate over time.

How Concept Drift Affects Model Performance

1. Declining Accuracy and Precision

- As data distributions change, models trained on old data fail to generalize well to new patterns.
- **Example**: A spam filter may misclassify legitimate emails due to evolving spam techniques.

2. Increased False Positives/Negatives

In fraud detection, an outdated model may incorrectly flag legitimate transactions as fraud or fail to detect real fraudulent activity.

3. Poor Business Decision-Making

A pricing model based on outdated demand patterns may set incorrect prices, leading to lost revenue.

4. Loss of Trust in AI Systems

If predictions become unreliable, users may stop using the ML-powered system and revert to manual decision-making.

To prevent these issues, it is crucial to detect and mitigate concept drift as early as possible.

Detecting Concept Drift

Concept drift detection methods fall into two categories:

1. Statistical Methods

These methods monitor changes in the input data distribution over time:

- **Kolmogorov-Smirnov Test** – Measures the difference between two probability distributions.
- **Kullback-Leibler Divergence** – Quantifies how much a probability distribution differs from another.
- **Wasserstein Distance** – Computes the shift in distributions between two datasets.

2. Performance-Based Methods

These methods monitor the model's predictions and compare them with actual outcomes:

- **Sliding Window Approach** – Tracks model performance over time and detects deviations.
- **Population Stability Index (PSI)** – Measures the stability of variable distributions.
- **Adaptive Windowing (ADWIN)** – Dynamically detects changes by comparing recent and past performance.

For example, if a credit risk model suddenly starts approving riskier loans more frequently, a performance monitoring tool should trigger a warning to investigate potential drift.

Handling Concept Drift and Model Performance Decay

1. Periodic Model Retraining

- Schedule regular retraining using fresh data to keep the model relevant.
- **Example**: A fraud detection model may be retrained every six months using recent transaction data.

2. Online Learning & Adaptive Models

- Use models that continuously learn and update themselves as new data arrives.
- **Example**: Online random forests and reinforcement learning can adjust to changes without requiring complete retraining.

3. Data Augmentation

- If past data is still partially relevant, mix it with new data to maintain a balanced dataset.

4. Model Monitoring and Drift Alerts

- Set up automated monitoring systems to detect drift early.
- **Example**: Deploying Evidently AI or WhyLabs to track data drift in real-time.

5. Hybrid Approaches

- Use a combination of retraining, monitoring, and adaptive learning to create a robust ML system.

Tools for Concept Drift Detection and Prevention

Several tools can help automate drift detection and retraining pipelines:

- **Evidently AI** – Monitors data and concept drift in real-time.
- **MLflow** – Helps track model performance and versioning.
- **Alibi Detect** – Provides real-time outlier and drift detection for ML models.
- **TensorFlow Data Validation** – Used for detecting dataset shifts in TensorFlow-based ML pipelines.
- **River (Scikit-Multiflow)** – A Python library for online learning and drift detection.

Using these tools, teams can maintain ML models in production without manual intervention.

Case Study: Concept Drift in a Loan Approval Model

Consider a bank using an ML model to approve or reject loan applications. Initially, the model was trained on historical data, but after a few months, it starts to underperform. Upon investigation, analysts find that:

- The economic landscape has changed, affecting customers' creditworthiness.
- New regulations have altered lending criteria.
- Customer behavior has shifted, with more applicants seeking loans for different purposes.

To fix the issue, the bank:

- Retrains the model with the latest loan application data.
- Implements a monitoring system to track key model performance metrics.
- Deploys adaptive learning to adjust predictions based on real-time trends.

With these strategies, the model regains its accuracy, improving loan approval decisions.

Concept drift is an inevitable challenge in machine learning, but proactive monitoring and maintenance can prevent model performance decay. By implementing automated drift detection, regular retraining, and adaptive learning techniques, organizations can ensure that their models remain reliable, accurate, and aligned with changing data patterns.

By using the right tools and strategies, ML practitioners can minimize the risks associated with concept drift and build resilient AI-driven systems. In the next section, we will explore the best practices for maintaining and scaling ML models in production environments.

15.2 A/B testing in machine learning models

A/B testing, also known as split testing, is a fundamental approach to evaluating the effectiveness of machine learning (ML) models in real-world applications. It helps measure the impact of new models, algorithms, or system changes by comparing their performance against a baseline. This ensures that any modifications lead to measurable improvements before full deployment.

In this section, we will explore the core principles of A/B testing in ML, the steps involved in running an experiment, best practices, and real-world applications.

What is A/B Testing?

A/B testing is a controlled experiment where two variants, A (control group) and B (test group), are compared to determine which performs better based on predefined metrics. In ML, it helps evaluate:

- **New vs. old models** (e.g., comparing a newly trained recommendation model to an existing one).
- **Feature engineering changes** (e.g., testing the impact of adding a new input feature).
- **Hyperparameter tuning** (e.g., evaluating two versions of a model with different hyperparameters).
- **User experience changes** (e.g., testing different ranking algorithms in search engines).

A/B testing ensures that ML model updates lead to actual performance improvements rather than relying solely on offline evaluations (e.g., test dataset accuracy).

Why is A/B Testing Important for ML Models?

Prevents Performance Regressions

- Deploying an untested model can lead to unintended consequences (e.g., increased false positives in fraud detection).
- A/B testing provides data-driven evidence before full rollout.

Validates Model Generalization

- Models that perform well in training environments may not generalize well in production.
- A/B testing assesses real-world performance on live data.

Reduces Business Risks

- Rolling out untested changes can negatively impact revenue, customer experience, or system reliability.
- Controlled experimentation helps mitigate risks.

Optimizes Decision-Making

- ML models are continuously evolving; A/B testing ensures that changes lead to measurable improvements.

How to Conduct A/B Testing for ML Models

Step 1: Define Success Metrics

- Establish key performance indicators (KPIs) to measure model performance.

Example metrics:

- **Accuracy, Precision, Recall**, F1-score (for classification models).
- **Mean Squared Error (MSE),** R^2 score (for regression models).
- **Click-through rate (CTR),** conversion rate (for recommendation engines).

Step 2: Split Traffic into Control and Test Groups

- Randomly assign users, transactions, or samples into two groups:
- Control Group (A): Uses the current model.
- Test Group (B): Uses the new model.
- Traffic split can be 50/50 or adjusted based on risk (e.g., 90/10 for initial testing).

Step 3: Run the Experiment in Parallel

- Both models operate simultaneously, receiving live inputs.
- Predictions from each model are logged and compared over time.

Step 4: Collect and Analyze Results

- Monitor real-time performance metrics.
- Perform statistical analysis to ensure results are statistically significant using:
- t-tests (for comparing continuous outcomes).
- Chi-square tests (for categorical outcomes).
- Bayesian analysis (for probabilistic inference).

Step 5: Interpret Results and Make Deployment Decisions

- If the new model outperforms the control, deploy it fully.
- If results are inconclusive, extend the test period or refine the model.
- If the new model underperforms, investigate errors and iterate.

Best Practices for A/B Testing in ML

1. Ensure Sufficient Sample Size

- Small datasets can lead to misleading results.
- Use power analysis to determine the required sample size for statistical confidence.

2. Control for External Factors

- Ensure that seasonality, market trends, or external events do not bias the experiment.

3. Run Tests for an Appropriate Duration

- Short tests may capture noise, while long tests delay decision-making.
- A good rule of thumb: Run tests until results reach 95% statistical confidence.

4. Log Predictions and User Interactions

- Store results for further analysis and debugging.

5. Monitor for Model Bias

- A/B testing should check for unintended biases (e.g., disproportionate impact on certain user groups).

Challenges in A/B Testing ML Models

Delayed Outcomes

Some ML applications (e.g., churn prediction) require long-term observation, making A/B testing slow.

Data Leakage

Test and control groups must be completely independent to avoid bias.

Cold Start Problem

New models may initially perform poorly due to lack of historical data.

Interference Effects

Users influenced by multiple models (e.g., different recommendations) can distort results.

Case Study: A/B Testing in a Recommender System

A leading e-commerce platform wants to improve its recommendation engine.

Experiment Setup

- **Control Group (A):** Uses the existing collaborative filtering model.
- **Test Group (B):** Uses a new hybrid recommendation model.
- **Success Metric**: Click-through rate (CTR) and conversion rate.
- **Traffic Split**: 50% of users see Model A, 50% see Model B.

Results After 2 Weeks

- Model A CTR: 12.5%
- Model B CTR: 14.2% (statistically significant improvement).
- Conversion Rate: Model B leads to a 6% revenue increase.

Decision

- Model B is fully deployed, replacing Model A.

- This demonstrates how A/B testing prevents unnecessary risks while optimizing business outcomes.

A/B Testing Tools for ML

Several tools help automate A/B testing for ML models:

- **Google Optimize** – A/B testing platform for web-based applications.
- **Optimizely** – Advanced experimentation tool for ML-driven products.
- **FeatureFlags.io** – Enables controlled rollouts of ML models.
- **AWS SageMaker Model Monitor** – Tracks ML model performance in production.
- **Evidently AI** – Provides real-time performance drift detection.

Using these tools, ML teams can run experiments efficiently without disrupting production systems.

A/B testing is an essential practice in ML model deployment, ensuring that changes lead to real-world improvements before full rollout. By defining clear success metrics, controlling for biases, and using statistical methods for evaluation, teams can make data-driven decisions confidently.

As ML applications continue to evolve, continuous A/B testing will remain a crucial strategy for maintaining high-performing, reliable models in production environments.

In the next section, we will explore advanced monitoring techniques to track ML models post-deployment and ensure their long-term success.

15.3 Logging and monitoring ML pipelines

Machine learning models do not exist in isolation; they operate within pipelines that continuously process data, make predictions, and impact real-world applications. To ensure reliability, performance, and accuracy over time, logging and monitoring ML pipelines are crucial. These practices help detect issues such as data drift, model degradation, and unexpected failures before they affect business decisions or user experiences.

In this section, we will explore the importance of logging and monitoring in ML workflows, the best practices for implementing them, and tools that help automate the process.

Why Logging and Monitoring Matter in ML Pipelines

Unlike traditional software, ML models depend on dynamic data, and their performance can degrade over time due to various factors, such as:

- **Concept Drift** – The relationship between input features and the target variable changes.
- **Data Drift** – The input data distribution changes from what the model was trained on.
- **Feature Distribution Shift** – Specific features start behaving differently over time.
- **Model Decay** – Performance metrics decline due to changing patterns in the data.
- **Unexpected Anomalies** – Errors due to pipeline failures, missing data, or incorrect model updates.

Proper logging and monitoring help detect these issues early, allowing teams to retrain models or adjust pipelines before significant performance drops occur.

Key Aspects of Logging in ML Pipelines

1. Model Training Logs

- Capture metadata related to training runs, including:
- Hyperparameters (learning rate, batch size, number of layers, etc.)

Model architecture

- Training dataset versions
- Training loss and validation accuracy over epochs
- Compute resource usage (CPU, GPU, memory)

Example Logging in Python:

```
import logging

logging.basicConfig(filename='training.log', level=logging.INFO)

def log_training_run(model_name, hyperparams, accuracy):
    logging.info(f"Model: {model_name}, Hyperparameters: {hyperparams}, Accuracy: {accuracy}")
```

```
log_training_run("RandomForestClassifier", {"n_estimators": 100, "max_depth": 5}, 0.89)
```

2. Data Pipeline Logs

- Log when data is ingested, processed, and cleaned.
- Detect missing values, outliers, or incorrect formatting early.

Example:

```
import pandas as pd

def log_data_quality(df):
    missing_values = df.isnull().sum().sum()
    duplicate_rows = df.duplicated().sum()
    print(f"Missing Values: {missing_values}, Duplicates: {duplicate_rows}")

data = pd.read_csv("customer_data.csv")
log_data_quality(data)
```

3. Prediction Logs

- Log real-time model predictions, confidence scores, and latency.
- Helps track model behavior in production.

Example:

```
import json
from datetime import datetime

def log_prediction(input_data, prediction, confidence):
    log_entry = {
        "timestamp": str(datetime.utcnow()),
        "input": input_data,
        "prediction": prediction,
        "confidence": confidence
    }
    with open("prediction_logs.json", "a") as f:
        f.write(json.dumps(log_entry) + "\n")

log_prediction({"age": 30, "income": 50000}, "Approved", 0.92)
```

4. Model Performance Logs

- Track key performance metrics such as accuracy, precision, recall, F1-score, RMSE, and ROC-AUC.
- Helps detect concept drift when performance starts degrading.

Monitoring ML Pipelines

Logging is useful, but real-time monitoring takes it a step further by providing alerts and dashboards when problems arise.

1. Data Drift Monitoring

- Compare live data distribution with the original training dataset.
- Identify significant deviations that may require retraining.

Tools for Data Drift Monitoring:

- **Evidently AI** – Monitors changes in feature distributions.
- **WhyLabs AI** – Tracks data drift with alerts.

2. Model Performance Monitoring

- Continuously measure model accuracy and precision on fresh data.
- Detect performance degradation due to evolving patterns.

Example Workflow:

- Set up a baseline model performance (e.g., 85% accuracy).
- Define an alert threshold (e.g., alert if accuracy drops below 80%).
- Log daily or hourly model predictions and compare them with ground truth labels.

3. Latency and Availability Monitoring

- Monitor model response times to ensure low latency in production.
- Detect API failures, slow responses, or resource bottlenecks.

Example Tools:

- **Prometheus & Grafana** – For real-time API monitoring.
- **Datadog** – Tracks model serving infrastructure health.

4. Anomaly Detection in ML Pipelines

- Use anomaly detection algorithms to identify outliers in predictions.
- Helps prevent biased predictions due to sudden data shifts.

Example:

Using Isolation Forest to detect anomalies in real-time predictions.

```
from sklearn.ensemble import IsolationForest
import numpy as np

model = IsolationForest(contamination=0.05)
data = np.random.rand(100, 5)
model.fit(data)

anomalies = model.predict(data)  # Identify outliers (-1 indicates anomaly)
```

Best Practices for ML Logging and Monitoring

Standardize Logging Formats

Use JSON or structured logs for consistency.

Example log entry:

```
{
    "timestamp": "2025-02-05T12:34:56",
    "event": "model_prediction",
    "model_name": "churn_classifier",
    "input_features": {"age": 30, "subscription_length": 12},
    "prediction": "churn",
    "confidence": 0.88
}
```

Set Up Alerts for Critical Failures

Send alerts when accuracy drops, latency spikes, or data anomalies occur.

Automate Model Retraining

Use pipelines that trigger retraining when data drift is detected.

Monitor Feature Importance

Track changes in feature importance over time using SHAP values.

Case Study: Monitoring a Fraud Detection Model

A fintech company deploys a fraud detection model that processes thousands of transactions per minute.

Challenges Faced:

- The fraud detection rate dropped from 92% to 85% over six months.
- A sudden increase in false positives led to unnecessary transaction blocks.

Solution Implemented:

- **Data Drift Monitoring** – Tracked changes in transaction patterns using Evidently AI.
- **Prediction Logging** – Logged real-time fraud predictions and compared them with human-labeled fraud cases.
- **Performance Alerts** – Set up alerts when recall dropped below 88%.
- **Automated Retraining** – Scheduled monthly retraining on the latest transaction data.

Outcome:

- Model performance improved from 85% back to 91% recall after retraining.
- False positives reduced by 30%, improving customer experience.

Logging and monitoring ML pipelines are essential for maintaining reliable, efficient, and high-performing models in production. By implementing structured logging, real-time monitoring, and automated alerts, ML teams can detect issues early, reduce business risks, and ensure models remain effective over time.

In the next section, we will explore concept drift detection techniques to further enhance model maintenance strategies.

15.4 Building a feedback loop for continuous improvement

In the real world, machine learning models are not static; they continuously interact with new data and user behavior. Over time, models can experience performance degradation, bias shifts, and data drift, making it essential to have a feedback loop that allows continuous learning and improvement.

A well-designed feedback loop ensures that ML models remain relevant, accurate, and effective by incorporating new insights, retraining on fresh data, and adapting to changing conditions. In this chapter, we will explore how to design and implement a robust feedback loop for continuous improvement in ML models.

1. Why Feedback Loops Matter in ML

Feedback loops allow ML systems to evolve based on real-world data and user interactions. Without feedback, models can become outdated and unreliable. The primary benefits of a feedback loop in ML include:

- **Early Detection of Concept Drift** – Identifies when data patterns change, affecting model performance.
- **Automatic Model Retraining** – Ensures models stay up to date with the latest trends.
- **Error Reduction** – Helps improve model accuracy by learning from incorrect predictions.
- **User Adaptation** – Adjusts recommendations, predictions, or classifications based on user behavior.

Real-World Examples of Feedback Loops

- **Google Search Autocomplete** – Learns from user input corrections to refine suggestions.
- **Netflix Recommendations** – Adjusts movie suggestions based on user viewing habits.
- **Fraud Detection Systems** – Updates risk models based on newly detected fraudulent transactions.

2. Key Components of an ML Feedback Loop

A robust ML feedback loop consists of the following stages:

- **Data Collection & Logging** – Continuously collect real-time predictions and user feedback.
- **Error Detection & Monitoring** – Identify incorrect or low-confidence predictions.
- **Data Annotation & Labeling** – Validate new data to ensure it is correctly labeled.
- **Model Retraining & Updating** – Use updated data to improve model performance.
- **Model Deployment & Evaluation** – Deploy the updated model and track its impact.

Each of these components works together to create a cycle of improvement, ensuring that the model remains effective.

3. Implementing a Feedback Loop in ML Pipelines

Step 1: Collect Real-World Feedback

To improve an ML model, we must gather real-world data about its performance. This can be done through:

- User interactions (clicks, ratings, corrections, etc.)
- Human labeling (for fraud detection, medical diagnoses, etc.)
- Prediction confidence scores (low-confidence predictions trigger review)

Example: Logging Model Predictions for Feedback

```python
import json
from datetime import datetime

def log_prediction_feedback(input_data, prediction, confidence, user_feedback=None):
    log_entry = {
        "timestamp": str(datetime.utcnow()),
        "input": input_data,
        "prediction": prediction,
        "confidence": confidence,
        "user_feedback": user_feedback  # User validation of the prediction
    }
```

```
with open("feedback_logs.json", "a") as f:
    f.write(json.dumps(log_entry) + "\n")

# Example: Logging a recommendation system's prediction and collecting feedback
log_prediction_feedback({"user_id": 123, "movie": "Inception"}, "Liked", 0.85, "Disliked")
```

Step 2: Identify & Analyze Incorrect Predictions

Once feedback is collected, we need to analyze model failures and identify trends:

- Are certain data segments leading to high error rates?
- Are specific features becoming less relevant?
- Is there a pattern in misclassified cases?

Example: Analyzing Incorrect Predictions in Python

```
import pandas as pd

# Load feedback log
df = pd.read_json("feedback_logs.json", lines=True)

# Check incorrect predictions
incorrect_preds = df[df["user_feedback"] != df["prediction"]]
print(incorrect_preds)
```

Step 3: Retraining the Model with New Data

Newly collected and labeled data must be incorporated into the training pipeline.

- Define a retraining threshold (e.g., retrain when 5,000 new samples are collected).
- Add new labeled data to the training set.
- Re-train and evaluate model performance before deploying updates.

Example: Automating Model Retraining

```
from sklearn.ensemble import RandomForestClassifier
import joblib

def retrain_model(new_data, labels, model_path="model.pkl"):
    model = RandomForestClassifier(n_estimators=100)
```

```
model.fit(new_data, labels)
joblib.dump(model, model_path)  # Save updated model

# Load new training data
new_data = pd.read_csv("new_training_data.csv")
labels = new_data.pop("label")

# Retrain model
retrain_model(new_data, labels)
```

Step 4: Deploying and Monitoring the Updated Model

Once a model is retrained, it must be deployed and monitored for improvements. Key actions include:

- Versioning models to track improvements.
- A/B Testing the new model vs. the old model to measure performance gains.
- Monitoring key metrics such as precision, recall, and inference latency.

Example: Versioning Models Using MLflow

```
import mlflow

mlflow.start_run()
mlflow.log_param("model_version", "1.2")
mlflow.log_metric("accuracy", 0.92)
mlflow.end_run()
```

4. Case Study: Feedback Loop in Customer Churn Prediction

Problem

A telecom company deploys an ML model to predict customer churn, but over time, its accuracy drops.

Solution

- **Collect real-time user feedback** – Whenever a model predicts that a customer will churn, an email survey is sent to confirm if they actually left.

- **Analyze incorrect predictions** – Customer responses are analyzed to find misclassified cases.
- **Retrain the model with fresh data** – Monthly retraining is scheduled using new labeled data.
- **Deploy and monitor performance** – A/B testing is used to ensure the updated model performs better.

Results

- Churn prediction accuracy improved by 8%.
- False positive churn predictions reduced by 25%, leading to fewer unnecessary retention offers.

5. Best Practices for Continuous Model Improvement

✓ **Automate Feedback Collection** – Use APIs, user interactions, and logging mechanisms to collect real-world feedback.

✓ **Regularly Monitor Model Performance** – Set up dashboards to track accuracy, precision, recall, and F1-score.

✓ **Establish a Retraining Schedule** – Define when and how often the model should be updated.

✓ **Validate New Models Before Deployment** – Use A/B testing and performance benchmarks.

✓ **Keep Track of Model Versions** – Maintain historical records of model changes and improvements.

A feedback loop is a critical component of any production ML system, enabling continuous improvement and adaptation to changing conditions. By collecting real-world feedback, identifying errors, retraining with fresh data, and monitoring performance, ML teams can ensure their models stay accurate, relevant, and impactful over time.

In the next section, we will discuss A/B testing techniques for evaluating new model versions to further refine ML performance.

15.5 Security challenges in ML deployment

Machine learning models are becoming an integral part of many real-world applications, from finance and healthcare to e-commerce and autonomous systems. However, deploying ML models in production environments comes with significant security risks. Threat actors can exploit vulnerabilities in ML systems, leading to data breaches, model theft, adversarial attacks, and biased decision-making.

In this chapter, we will explore the key security challenges in ML deployment, the different types of attacks, and best practices to safeguard ML systems against emerging threats.

1. Why is ML Security Critical?

Unlike traditional software, ML models learn from data and make autonomous decisions. This makes them more vulnerable to manipulation than rule-based systems. Security failures in ML deployments can lead to:

- Unauthorized access to sensitive data (e.g., healthcare records, financial transactions).
- Model theft where an attacker reverse-engineers a proprietary model.
- Adversarial attacks that manipulate model predictions.
- Data poisoning where bad actors inject misleading data to alter outcomes.
- Model bias exploitation, leading to discriminatory decisions.

Real-World ML Security Incidents

- **Deepfake Scams** – Attackers use AI to impersonate people for fraud (e.g., voice and video deepfakes).
- **Credit Scoring Attacks** – Hackers manipulate financial models to alter credit risk assessments.
- **Adversarial AI in Self-Driving Cars** – Researchers have demonstrated how small changes to road signs can mislead AI-powered autonomous vehicles.

Given these risks, securing ML models is essential for organizations deploying AI-driven applications.

2. Key Security Challenges in ML Deployment

2.1 Data Security Risks

ML models rely on large datasets, often containing sensitive user information. Poor data security can lead to:

- **Data breaches** – Exposing confidential user data.

- **Data poisoning** – Injecting malicious samples to mislead training.
- **Privacy violations** – Collecting and using personal data without consent.

Mitigation Strategies:

✓ Encrypt sensitive training data using AES-256 encryption.

✓ Implement differential privacy to anonymize user data.

✓ Use secure data access controls to prevent unauthorized modifications.

2.2 Model Theft & Reverse Engineering

Attackers can steal a trained model by querying it repeatedly (model extraction attack) or reverse-engineering the weights using side-channel attacks.

Mitigation Strategies:

✓ Deploy models on secure cloud environments with strict API rate limits.

✓ Use model watermarking to detect unauthorized copies.

✓ Implement homomorphic encryption to protect model computations.

2.3 Adversarial Attacks on ML Models

Adversarial attacks involve manipulating input data to deceive ML models.

Types of Adversarial Attacks:

- **Evasion Attacks** – Slightly altering inputs to mislead the model (e.g., modifying images to fool a classifier).
- **Trojan Attacks** – Injecting hidden triggers into models to cause incorrect predictions when activated.

Example: Adversarial Attack on an Image Classifier

```
import torch
import torchvision.models as models
import torchvision.transforms as transforms
from PIL import Image
```

```
# Load a pre-trained model
model = models.resnet18(pretrained=True)
model.eval()

# Load an image and apply an adversarial perturbation
def adversarial_attack(image_path, epsilon=0.02):
    image = Image.open(image_path)
    transform = transforms.Compose([transforms.Resize((224, 224)),
transforms.ToTensor()])
    image_tensor = transform(image).unsqueeze(0)

    # Create adversarial noise
    noise = torch.randn_like(image_tensor) * epsilon
    adversarial_image = image_tensor + noise
    return adversarial_image

# Generate an adversarial example
adv_image = adversarial_attack("dog.jpg")
```

Mitigation Strategies:

✓ Use adversarial training to make models robust to attacks.

✓ Apply input validation to detect manipulated data.

✓ Deploy AI firewalls that filter adversarial inputs.

2.4 Model Bias & Fairness Exploitation

ML models can develop biases based on imbalanced training data. Attackers can exploit these biases for unfair advantages, such as manipulating financial models for loan approvals.

Mitigation Strategies:

✓ Conduct bias audits before deployment.

✓ Use FairML and AI fairness tools to detect discrimination.

✓ Implement explainability techniques (SHAP, LIME) to ensure transparency.

2.5 Security in Model APIs & Endpoints

ML models are often deployed as APIs, making them vulnerable to injection attacks, unauthorized access, and denial-of-service (DoS) attacks.

Mitigation Strategies:

✓ Secure API endpoints using OAuth 2.0 authentication.

✓ Limit API access with rate limiting and request validation.

✓ Implement input sanitization to prevent injection attacks.

3. Secure ML Deployment Strategies

To protect ML models in production, organizations must adopt a multi-layered security approach.

Security Challenge	Solution Approach
Data Security	Encryption, Differential Privacy, Access Controls
Model Theft	Watermarking, Homomorphic Encryption, Rate Limiting
Adversarial Attacks	Robust Training, Input Validation, AI Firewalls
Bias Exploitation	Fairness Audits, Explainability Tools
API Vulnerabilities	OAuth 2.0, Rate Limiting, Logging & Monitoring

4. Case Study: Securing a Fraud Detection Model

Problem:

A financial institution deployed an ML-based fraud detection system, but hackers attempted to bypass the model by manipulating transaction data.

Solution:

- Implemented adversarial training to make the model resilient against manipulation.
- Encrypted the API communications using TLS 1.3.
- Deployed an AI firewall to detect unusual API query patterns.

- Monitored predictions for sudden shifts in fraud detection accuracy.

Results:

- Reduced fraudulent transactions by 37%.
- Prevented adversarial attacks from bypassing the fraud detection model.

5. Best Practices for Secure ML Deployment

✓ **Adopt Zero-Trust Architecture** – Assume every access request could be malicious and verify all interactions.

✓ **Implement Multi-Layer Security** – Protect data, models, APIs, and inference pipelines.

✓ **Regularly Update & Patch Models** – Security threats evolve, so models must be updated frequently.

✓ **Monitor for Anomalous Behavior** – Track unusual API calls, prediction patterns, and access logs.

✓ **Educate Teams on ML Security** – Engineers, data scientists, and DevOps teams must understand security risks.

ML models are increasingly targeted by cyberattacks, making security a top priority for organizations deploying AI solutions. By encrypting data, securing APIs, defending against adversarial attacks, and ensuring model fairness, businesses can protect their ML systems from exploitation.

In the next section, we will explore scalability challenges in ML and how to optimize models for big data environments.

16. Ethics & Bias in Machine Learning

In this chapter, we explore the ethical considerations and potential biases that can arise in machine learning models. As AI systems become increasingly integrated into society, it's essential to ensure they are fair, transparent, and accountable. You'll learn how to identify and mitigate biases in data and models, understanding how factors like historical inequalities, data collection methods, and algorithm design can lead to unintended consequences. We'll also discuss the importance of explainable AI (XAI) to make models more interpretable and accountable. Through case studies, you'll gain insight into the ethical dilemmas surrounding AI applications in areas such as hiring, finance, and criminal justice. By the end of this chapter, you'll have the tools to build more ethical, unbiased machine learning models and navigate the moral complexities of AI deployment in real-world scenarios. ⚖️□

16.1 Understanding bias in datasets and models

Machine learning (ML) has transformed industries by automating decision-making, improving efficiency, and uncovering insights from data. However, one of the most significant challenges in ML is bias—unintentional yet systematic errors in data and models that can lead to unfair or discriminatory outcomes. Bias in ML can impact hiring decisions, healthcare treatments, loan approvals, criminal justice predictions, and even content recommendations.

In this chapter, we will explore the sources of bias, how it manifests in datasets and models, and strategies to mitigate its effects to create fair and ethical AI systems.

1. What is Bias in Machine Learning?

Bias in ML refers to systematic errors in predictions that favor or disadvantage certain groups based on factors such as gender, race, age, socioeconomic status, or other sensitive attributes. It can arise at multiple stages of the ML pipeline, including data collection, feature engineering, model selection, and interpretation of results.

Bias can lead to unfair predictions, reinforcing societal inequalities. For example:

- Hiring Models may favor male candidates if trained on historical hiring data that reflects gender bias.

- Loan Approval Models may reject minority applicants due to biased credit history data.
- Facial Recognition Systems may perform poorly on darker-skinned individuals if trained on predominantly lighter-skinned datasets.

Understanding bias in ML is crucial to ensuring fairness, transparency, and accountability in AI-driven decision-making.

2. Types of Bias in ML Datasets and Models

2.1 Data Collection Bias

Bias can stem from how data is collected, labeled, and sampled. If the data does not represent the real-world population fairly, the resulting model will inherit and amplify these biases.

Examples:

✅ **Selection Bias** – Training data is not representative of all users. Example: A chatbot trained on English text struggles with non-native speakers.
✅ **Labeling Bias** – Human annotators introduce subjective opinions in labeling. Example: Sentiment analysis models trained on biased human labels may misinterpret neutral statements.
✅ **Historical Bias** – Data reflects past societal inequalities. Example: A resume-screening ML model favors male candidates because historical hiring patterns did.

Mitigation Strategies:

✓☐ Ensure data is diverse, balanced, and representative of all demographics.
✓☐ Conduct bias audits before training models.
✓☐ Use active learning to refine datasets with diverse examples.

2.2 Algorithmic Bias

Even if the dataset is unbiased, the ML model itself can introduce bias due to its design, optimization function, or underlying assumptions.

Examples:

✅ **Bias in Loss Function** – Many models minimize overall error, which can ignore disparities among different groups.

✅ **Feature Selection Bias** – If sensitive attributes (e.g., gender, race) influence predictions, the model can learn biased patterns.

✅ **Overfitting to Majority Groups** – If certain groups are underrepresented in training data, the model will perform worse on them.

Mitigation Strategies:

✓☐ Use fairness-aware algorithms that adjust model training to prevent discrimination.

✓☐ Regularly test models for disparate impact across demographic groups.

✓☐ Implement techniques like reweighing and adversarial debiasing.

2.3 Bias in Model Interpretation & Deployment

Even if a model appears fair during testing, biases can emerge in real-world deployment. This happens when models face unexpected data shifts, adversarial manipulation, or feedback loops.

Examples:

✅ **Dynamic Bias** – A model trained on historical hiring data might start reinforcing existing patterns of discrimination.

✅ **Automation Bias** – Users overly trust AI predictions, even when they are flawed. Example: Courts using predictive policing algorithms may rely too much on their outputs.

✅ **Feedback Loops** – Algorithmic decisions influence future data collection. Example: A search engine ranking certain news stories higher can reinforce misinformation.

Mitigation Strategies:

✓☐ Conduct ongoing monitoring of model performance in production.

✓☐ Implement explainable AI (XAI) techniques to interpret predictions transparently.

✓☐ Gather human feedback to refine model behavior.

3. How to Measure Bias in ML Models?

To mitigate bias, we must first detect and quantify it. Several fairness metrics help evaluate whether a model treats different groups equitably.

3.1 Common Fairness Metrics

Metric	Description	Example Use Case
Demographic Parity	Model outcomes should be independent of sensitive attributes.	Ensuring a loan approval model gives equal approval rates for different racial groups.
Equalized Odds	Model should have similar accuracy for different groups.	A medical diagnosis model should have the same false positive/negative rates across genders.
Disparate Impact	Measures the ratio of positive outcomes across groups.	Evaluating if a hiring model disproportionately favors one demographic.
Counterfactual Fairness	A prediction should not change if a sensitive attribute (e.g., race) changes.	Checking if changing a job applicant's gender alters the model's decision.

Example: Measuring Bias with Python

```
from sklearn.metrics import confusion_matrix

# Simulated model predictions
actual_labels = [1, 0, 1, 1, 0, 0, 1, 0]
predicted_labels = [1, 0, 1, 0, 0, 0, 1, 1]

# Confusion matrix to evaluate fairness
cm = confusion_matrix(actual_labels, predicted_labels)
print("Confusion Matrix:\n", cm)
```

By analyzing false positives and false negatives across groups, we can assess fairness disparities.

4. Strategies for Bias Mitigation

4.1 Fair Data Collection

✓ Ensure datasets are balanced and diverse.
✓ Use data augmentation to address underrepresented classes.
✓ Apply synthetic data generation for fairness.

4.2 Fair Algorithm Design

✓ Use fairness constraints during training (e.g., fairness-aware loss functions).

✓☐ Apply reweighing techniques to balance underrepresented groups.
✓☐ Implement adversarial debiasing to remove unwanted correlations.

4.3 Fair Model Deployment

✓☐ Conduct real-time fairness monitoring.
✓☐ Provide human oversight to review AI decisions.
✓☐ Enable user feedback loops to detect biases in production.

5. Ethical Considerations in ML Development

Beyond technical solutions, ethical AI development requires awareness, responsibility, and accountability. Key considerations include:

✓ **Transparency**: AI decisions should be interpretable and explainable.
✓ **Accountability**: Organizations must take responsibility for biased AI systems.
✓ **Regulation Compliance**: ML systems should follow ethical guidelines like GDPR, AI Act, and Equal Opportunity Laws.
✓ **Public Awareness**: Users should understand how AI impacts their lives.

6. Case Study: Mitigating Bias in a Loan Approval Model

Problem:

A bank's AI-driven loan approval system was disproportionately rejecting applicants from certain minority groups.

Solution:

- **Bias Audit**: Conducted fairness tests to identify disparities in loan approval rates.
- **Data Balancing**: Augmented training data to ensure diverse representation.
- **Fair Model Training**: Used adversarial debiasing techniques to remove bias.
- **Transparency Measures**: Implemented explainable AI to clarify decisions.

Results:

✓ Increased fairness in loan approvals while maintaining model accuracy.

✓ Compliance with fair lending regulations.

✓ Improved public trust in AI-driven financial decisions.

Bias in machine learning is a significant challenge that can lead to unfair and discriminatory outcomes. However, by understanding bias sources, implementing fairness metrics, and adopting ethical AI principles, we can build more equitable and trustworthy AI systems.

In the next section, we will explore the regulatory landscape of AI ethics and how organizations can align their ML models with global fairness standards.

16.2 Fairness-aware ML techniques

Ensuring fairness in machine learning (ML) models is a critical aspect of ethical AI development. Bias in ML models can lead to unintended discrimination, negatively impacting marginalized groups in areas such as hiring, healthcare, finance, and law enforcement. Fairness-aware ML techniques aim to mitigate bias and ensure equitable outcomes for all users.

In this chapter, we explore fairness-aware ML techniques, including pre-processing, in-processing, and post-processing approaches. We will also discuss practical tools and methods to ensure fairness in real-world applications.

1. Categories of Fairness-Aware ML Techniques

Fairness techniques in ML can be categorized into three main types:

Technique Type	Description	Example Use Cases
Pre-processing	Modify data before training to reduce bias	Balancing datasets by resampling
In-processing	Modify algorithms during training to promote fairness	Adding fairness constraints to loss functions
Post-processing	Adjust predictions after model training to ensure fairness	Calibrating model outputs to remove disparities

Each of these techniques has its strengths and weaknesses, and the right choice depends on the use case, data availability, and regulatory requirements.

2. Pre-Processing Techniques for Fair ML

Pre-processing techniques aim to reduce bias in datasets before training the model. If the training data itself is biased, then even a well-designed ML algorithm can produce unfair predictions.

2.1 Reweighting Data to Balance Representation

In many datasets, certain groups are underrepresented, leading to biased models. A simple pre-processing technique is to reweight data samples so that each group contributes equally to the model.

✅ **Example**: A loan approval dataset where female applicants are underrepresented. By assigning higher weights to female applicants during training, the model learns from a more balanced dataset.

Python Example: Reweighting Data

```python
from imblearn.over_sampling import SMOTE
from sklearn.utils.class_weight import compute_class_weight

# Compute class weights for balanced learning
classes = [0, 1]  # Example binary classification
class_weights = compute_class_weight('balanced', classes=classes, y=train_labels)
print("Class Weights:", class_weights)
```

2.2 Data Augmentation for Fairness

Another approach is to generate synthetic data for underrepresented groups. Techniques like SMOTE (Synthetic Minority Over-sampling Technique) create synthetic samples to balance datasets.

✅ **Example**: In a facial recognition dataset with fewer images of darker-skinned individuals, data augmentation (rotation, flipping, scaling) can artificially expand the dataset.

Python Example: SMOTE for Data Augmentation

```python
from imblearn.over_sampling import SMOTE
```

```
smote = SMOTE(sampling_strategy='auto')
X_resampled, y_resampled = smote.fit_resample(X_train, y_train)
```

2.3 Removing Sensitive Attributes

A straightforward approach to reducing bias is removing sensitive attributes (e.g., gender, race) from the dataset. However, this does not always ensure fairness, as proxy variables may still reveal biases.

✅ **Example**: Removing "race" from a hiring dataset may not remove bias if "ZIP code" acts as a proxy for race.

Alternative: Using Fair Representations

Instead of removing sensitive attributes, we can transform the dataset to ensure that sensitive attributes do not influence predictions. Adversarial debiasing (training a model to remove any learnable bias) is one such method.

3. In-Processing Techniques for Fair ML

In-processing techniques adjust the learning algorithm to improve fairness. This includes modifying loss functions, constraints, and optimization procedures to ensure fair treatment across groups.

3.1 Fairness Constraints in Model Training

A simple approach is to include fairness constraints in the model's optimization function.

✅ **Example**: In a loan approval model, we can add constraints ensuring that approval rates are equal across different demographic groups.

Python Example: Fairness-Aware Logistic Regression

```
from aif360.algorithms.inprocessing import AdversarialDebiasing
from tensorflow.keras.optimizers import Adam

# Train a fairness-aware classifier
adv_debias = AdversarialDebiasing(prot_attr="gender", adversary_loss_weight=0.1,
optimizer=Adam(0.001))
```

adv_debias.fit(X_train, y_train)

📌 The model learns not to use "gender" as a predictive factor, improving fairness.

3.2 Regularization for Fairness

Bias-aware regularization adds penalty terms in the loss function to discourage discrimination.

✅ **Example**: The Fairness Constraints (FC) method modifies standard ML loss functions to prevent disparate treatment.

Python Example: Fairness-Aware Loss Function

```python
import tensorflow as tf

def fairness_loss(y_true, y_pred, sensitive_attr):
    base_loss = tf.keras.losses.BinaryCrossentropy()(y_true, y_pred)
    fairness_penalty = tf.reduce_mean(tf.abs(tf.reduce_mean(y_pred[sensitive_attr==0])
- tf.reduce_mean(y_pred[sensitive_attr==1])))
    return base_loss + fairness_penalty
```

3.3 Adversarial Debiasing

Adversarial learning can remove biases by training the model to minimize discrimination while maximizing accuracy.

✅ **Example**: Train a neural network to classify customer creditworthiness while ensuring that gender does not influence predictions.

- Steps in Adversarial Debiasing
- Train a main model to predict outcomes.
- Train an adversarial model to predict sensitive attributes.

Adjust weights so that the adversary cannot guess the sensitive attribute, making the main model unbiased.

📌 This technique is useful in real-world applications such as AI hiring tools and credit scoring models.

4. Post-Processing Techniques for Fair ML

Post-processing techniques adjust predictions after training to reduce bias while preserving model accuracy.

4.1 Equalized Odds Adjustment

Ensures the model gives similar accuracy across different groups.

✅ **Example**: A healthcare AI must have similar false positive and false negative rates across racial groups.

Python Example: Post-Processing Bias Correction

```
from aif360.algorithms.postprocessing import EqualizedOddsPostprocessing

eq_odds = EqualizedOddsPostprocessing()
eq_odds.fit(y_train, y_pred_train)
y_pred_corrected = eq_odds.predict(y_pred_test)
```

4.2 Reject Option-Based Fairness

If the model has uncertain predictions, it defers to human decision-makers for fairness-sensitive cases.

✅ **Example**: In a hiring model, if the AI is uncertain about a female applicant, it sends the case to a human reviewer instead of making an automated decision.

5. Case Study: Fairness in Hiring Models

A company develops an AI hiring tool that screens candidates based on resumes. However, the model shows a higher rejection rate for women due to biased historical data.

Steps to Improve Fairness:

✓☐ **Pre-processing**: Balanced training data by oversampling female candidates.
✓☐ **In-processing**: Used adversarial debiasing to remove gender correlations.
✓☐ **Post-processing**: Applied equalized odds adjustments to ensure fair selection rates.

✓ **Result**: The new model eliminated gender bias while maintaining accuracy.

Fairness-aware ML techniques are essential for ethical AI development. By integrating pre-processing, in-processing, and post-processing methods, we can build AI systems that promote fairness while maintaining accuracy.

In the next section, we will explore AI ethics regulations and how businesses can align their ML models with global fairness standards.

16.3 Transparency and explainability in AI

As artificial intelligence (AI) systems become more integral to decision-making across industries, the need for transparency and explainability in machine learning (ML) models has grown significantly. Many AI-driven decisions impact high-stakes areas such as healthcare, finance, hiring, and law enforcement, making it crucial for stakeholders to understand how and why a model arrives at a particular outcome.

This chapter explores the concepts of AI transparency and explainability, discusses their importance, and introduces techniques to make ML models more interpretable.

1. Understanding Transparency and Explainability

While often used interchangeably, transparency and explainability in AI have distinct meanings:

Concept	Definition	Example
Transparency	The degree to which an AI system's workings are visible and understandable to users	Open-source AI models with clear documentation
Explainability	The ability to describe how an AI model arrives at a decision in human-understandable terms	A loan approval AI providing reasons for rejecting an applicant

A transparent AI system allows users to inspect its architecture, data sources, and training process, while explainability focuses on interpreting its decision-making process.

📌 **Example**: If an AI model rejects a loan application, transparency reveals how the model was trained, while explainability describes which factors contributed to the rejection (e.g., low credit score, unstable income).

2. Why Transparency and Explainability Matter

2.1 Regulatory Compliance

Governments worldwide are introducing AI regulations that require explainability.

- GDPR (General Data Protection Regulation) mandates that users have a "right to explanation" when AI makes automated decisions.
- The EU AI Act classifies AI systems based on risk and requires transparency for high-risk applications.
- The U.S. AI Bill of Rights promotes fairness and accountability in AI decision-making.

📌 **Example**: In Europe, an AI-based hiring tool must justify why it selects or rejects candidates.

2.2 Building Trust in AI

Users are more likely to trust AI if they understand its decisions.

- Doctors need explainability in AI-assisted diagnostics to verify medical predictions.
- Financial institutions require AI loan approval models to justify their decisions.

📌 **Example**: A doctor using an AI cancer detection tool must know why it flagged a tumor as malignant to confirm the diagnosis.

2.3 Identifying and Reducing Bias

Explainability helps detect and correct biases in AI models.

- If an AI hiring model favors certain demographics, explainability tools can identify biased features.
- AI bias in facial recognition can be exposed through transparency techniques.

📌 **Example**: A biased facial recognition model misclassifies dark-skinned individuals due to unbalanced training data. Explainability techniques help uncover and correct this issue.

3. Techniques for AI Explainability

3.1 Feature Importance Analysis

Feature importance techniques identify which input features most influence a model's predictions.

✅ **Example**: In a loan approval model, explainability methods reveal whether income, credit score, or employment history played a bigger role in the decision.

Python Example: Feature Importance with Random Forest

```python
from sklearn.ensemble import RandomForestClassifier
import pandas as pd

# Train a Random Forest model
model = RandomForestClassifier()
model.fit(X_train, y_train)

# Get feature importance
feature_importance = pd.Series(model.feature_importances_,
index=X_train.columns).sort_values(ascending=False)
print(feature_importance)
```

📌 This output ranks the most important features affecting the model's decisions.

3.2 SHAP (SHapley Additive Explanations)

SHAP values provide a detailed breakdown of how each feature contributes to a model's output.

✅ **Example**: In healthcare, SHAP can explain why an AI predicts high risk of heart disease by showing how each factor (e.g., age, cholesterol levels) contributes to the prediction.

Python Example: SHAP Explanation for a Model

```python
import shap

explainer = shap.TreeExplainer(model)
shap_values = explainer.shap_values(X_test)
```

```
# Visualize SHAP values
shap.summary_plot(shap_values, X_test)
```

📌 The SHAP summary plot shows which features push predictions higher or lower, providing clear insights.

3.3 LIME (Local Interpretable Model-Agnostic Explanations)

LIME explains individual predictions by approximating complex models with simpler, interpretable models.

✅ **Example**: If a fraud detection AI flags a transaction as fraudulent, LIME can highlight which factors (e.g., transaction amount, location) influenced the decision.

Python Example: Using LIME for Model Interpretation

```
import lime
import lime.lime_tabular

explainer = lime.lime_tabular.LimeTabularExplainer(X_train.values,
feature_names=X_train.columns, class_names=['No Fraud', 'Fraud'],
mode='classification')
exp = explainer.explain_instance(X_test.iloc[0].values, model.predict_proba)

# Show explanation
exp.show_in_notebook()
```

📌 LIME provides an easy-to-understand breakdown of how different features contributed to a specific decision.

3.4 Model Transparency with White-Box Models

Some ML models are naturally interpretable (white-box models), whereas complex deep learning models (black-box models) require additional explainability techniques.

Model Type	Transparency Level	Example
Linear Regression	High (Easy to interpret coefficients)	Salary prediction model
Decision Trees	Medium (Tree structure shows decision paths)	Customer churn prediction
Neural Networks (Deep Learning)	Low (Requires SHAP, LIME, etc.)	Image classification, NLP

✓ **Example**: If a bank wants full transparency, it may use a decision tree instead of a deep learning model for credit scoring.

4. Case Study: Explainability in Loan Approval AI

A bank deploys an AI loan approval system but faces complaints that rejections seem arbitrary and unfair.

Problems Identified:

✗ Customers don't understand why their loans were rejected.

✗ Regulators require an explanation for every decision.

Solution: Implement Explainability Techniques

✓ Used SHAP values to identify the most influential factors (credit score, income).
✓ Applied LIME to generate customer-friendly explanations.
✓ Created a dashboard to display transparent AI decisions.

✓ **Result**: Customers received clear explanations, and the bank complied with regulations.

Transparency and explainability in AI are crucial for building trust, ensuring fairness, and meeting regulatory requirements. Techniques like SHAP, LIME, and feature importance analysis can help make AI models more interpretable.

In the next section, we will explore how AI governance frameworks are evolving to address the challenges of transparency, bias, and fairness in machine learning models.

16.4 Ethical considerations in AI decision-making

As artificial intelligence (AI) systems become increasingly embedded in daily life, their ethical implications have come under intense scrutiny. From hiring and healthcare to criminal justice and finance, AI-driven decisions can significantly impact individuals and communities. While AI has the potential to drive efficiency and innovation, it also introduces risks such as bias, discrimination, privacy violations, and lack of accountability.

In this chapter, we explore the ethical considerations surrounding AI decision-making, examine real-world cases where ethical concerns have arisen, and discuss best practices for developing responsible AI systems.

1. Why Ethics Matter in AI

AI models are only as unbiased and fair as the data they are trained on and the assumptions they encode. Ethical concerns arise when:

- AI systems reinforce existing social biases (e.g., discriminatory hiring algorithms).
- Decisions lack transparency (e.g., black-box AI models in criminal sentencing).
- User privacy is compromised (e.g., mass surveillance through AI-powered facial recognition).
- Accountability is unclear (e.g., self-driving car accidents where responsibility is disputed).

📌 **Example**: A recruitment AI trained on historical hiring data might reject female candidates because past hiring decisions favored men. This bias is unintentionally baked into the algorithm.

2. Key Ethical Considerations in AI

2.1 Fairness & Bias in AI Models

Bias in AI can occur at multiple levels:

- **Data Bias**: Training data may reflect societal inequalities (e.g., facial recognition systems that perform poorly on darker skin tones).
- **Algorithmic Bias**: Models may learn correlations that lead to unfair predictions (e.g., predicting crime rates based on zip codes, which can correlate with race and socioeconomic status).

- **Deployment Bias**: AI may be used in ways that reinforce discrimination (e.g., AI resume screening systems disproportionately rejecting minority candidates).

📌 **Example**: COMPAS, a criminal risk assessment tool used in U.S. courts, was found to predict higher recidivism rates for Black defendants compared to White defendants, raising concerns about racial bias in AI-driven sentencing.

How to Mitigate Bias:

✓☐ Use diverse, representative datasets during training.
✓☐ Apply bias-detection techniques (e.g., fairness-aware ML algorithms).
✓☐ Regularly audit AI models for disparate impact on different demographic groups.

2.2 Transparency & Explainability

AI systems often function as black boxes, meaning their decision-making processes are opaque. This lack of transparency can lead to:

- Unfair decisions that users can't contest (e.g., being denied a loan without understanding why).
- Trust issues with AI adoption (e.g., doctors unwilling to rely on AI-driven medical diagnoses without clear explanations).
- Regulatory compliance risks (e.g., GDPR mandates a "right to explanation" for AI decisions affecting individuals).

📌 **Example**: In 2020, Apple's credit card algorithm faced backlash when women received lower credit limits than men with similar financial profiles, but Apple could not explain why due to its black-box AI model.

How to Improve Transparency:

✓☐ Use explainable AI techniques (e.g., SHAP, LIME) to clarify decision-making.
✓☐ Provide human oversight in critical AI decisions.
✓☐ Design AI systems that offer user-friendly explanations for their outputs.

2.3 Privacy & Data Security

AI systems require vast amounts of data to function effectively, raising serious concerns about privacy and security. Ethical AI development must balance data-driven insights with user protection.

Major privacy concerns include:

- **Mass surveillance**: AI-powered facial recognition has led to privacy invasions and wrongful arrests.
- **Data misuse**: Companies collecting AI training data may later use it for unintended purposes.
- **Lack of consent**: Many users unknowingly contribute personal data to AI systems.

📌 **Example**: In 2021, Clearview AI's facial recognition tool was banned in several countries for scraping billions of images from the internet without user consent.

How to Protect Privacy:

✓ Implement privacy-preserving AI (e.g., federated learning, differential privacy).
✓ Ensure compliance with data protection laws (e.g., GDPR, CCPA).
✓ Allow users to opt-in/opt-out of AI data collection.

2.4 Accountability & Responsibility

When AI systems make mistakes, who is responsible? Many AI failures involve blame shifting between developers, companies, and regulators.

Challenges in AI accountability include:

- **Lack of clear liability**: If a self-driving car causes an accident, is the fault with the manufacturer, software developer, or human operator?
- **Automated decision-making in life-critical fields**: AI-driven medical misdiagnoses can have life-threatening consequences.
- **Job displacement**: As automation replaces human workers, companies face ethical questions about job losses and workforce retraining.

📌 **Example**: Tesla's Autopilot feature has been involved in multiple accidents. Legal debates continue over whether Tesla, the driver, or regulators should be held accountable for failures.

How to Improve Accountability:

✓☐ Establish clear regulatory frameworks for AI liability.

✓☐ Require human-in-the-loop (HITL) systems for high-risk AI applications.

✓☐ Ensure AI systems align with ethical AI principles (e.g., IEEE Ethically Aligned Design).

3. Case Study: Ethical AI in Healthcare

AI in Cancer Diagnosis

AI-powered medical imaging tools can detect tumors, fractures, and diseases faster than human doctors. However, ethical concerns arise when:

✗ The AI model lacks transparency, making doctors hesitant to trust it.

✗ The system fails on diverse patient groups, leading to misdiagnoses.

✗ The hospital does not inform patients that an AI, not a human, made their diagnosis.

How Ethical AI Practices Were Applied:

✓☐ Developers trained the AI model on diverse, inclusive datasets to reduce bias.

✓☐ The system was made interpretable using explainability tools.

✓☐ A doctor-AI collaboration approach was adopted, ensuring final decisions were made by medical professionals.

✓ **Result**: The AI system improved cancer detection rates while maintaining ethical standards.

4. Ethical AI: Looking Ahead

As AI continues to evolve, governments, researchers, and organizations must collaborate to create frameworks that prioritize fairness, transparency, and accountability.

Key Takeaways:

✓☐ Bias and fairness must be actively addressed through diverse datasets and bias-mitigation techniques.

✓☐ Explainability is essential for trust, regulation, and ethical decision-making.

✓☐ Privacy protection must be a priority in AI development.

✓☐ Accountability mechanisms should be built into AI governance frameworks.

As we advance AI capabilities, ethics must evolve alongside technology to ensure AI systems serve humanity fairly, responsibly, and transparently.

16.5 Regulatory frameworks and compliance

As artificial intelligence (AI) becomes more deeply integrated into industries such as finance, healthcare, transportation, and law enforcement, governments and regulatory bodies worldwide are developing AI governance frameworks to ensure these technologies are deployed responsibly. These regulations and compliance standards aim to mitigate risks such as bias, privacy violations, security threats, and lack of accountability.

In this chapter, we will explore key AI regulations, global compliance efforts, and best practices for aligning machine learning (ML) projects with legal and ethical standards.

1. Why AI Regulation Matters

AI-powered systems make critical decisions in high-stakes environments—such as approving loans, diagnosing diseases, or predicting crime risk. Without proper oversight, these systems can lead to:

- Discrimination and bias (e.g., biased facial recognition misidentifying minority groups).
- Privacy violations (e.g., mass data collection without user consent).
- Lack of transparency (e.g., AI-driven decisions that users cannot challenge).
- Security vulnerabilities (e.g., adversarial attacks that manipulate AI models).

📌 **Example**: In 2020, the Dutch government faced backlash for an AI-driven fraud detection system used in welfare programs. The system disproportionately flagged low-income and minority families for fraud, leading to wrongful investigations and financial hardship.

Regulations help ensure AI systems are fair, explainable, privacy-conscious, and accountable.

2. Key AI Regulations Around the World

AI governance varies by country, but several major regulatory frameworks have emerged to address AI risks and standardize best practices.

2.1 European Union: AI Act

The EU AI Act, proposed in 2021, is one of the world's first comprehensive AI regulations. It categorizes AI applications into risk levels:

- **Unacceptable risk (banned AI):** Social scoring systems, real-time biometric surveillance.
- **High risk (strictly regulated AI):** AI in healthcare, hiring, and credit scoring.
- **Limited risk (transparency required):** AI chatbots, deepfake detection.
- **Minimal risk (no restrictions):** AI-powered video games, spam filters.

The AI Act requires companies to:

✓ Conduct risk assessments before deploying AI systems.
✓ Ensure data quality and fairness in AI models.
✓ Provide explainability and transparency in decision-making AI.

📌 **Example**: Under the AI Act, a hiring algorithm that disproportionately rejects female applicants would be classified as high-risk AI and subject to audits.

2.2 United States: Algorithmic Accountability Act & Executive Orders

The U.S. does not have a comprehensive AI law, but it has introduced sector-specific AI regulations and executive orders, including:

- **Algorithmic Accountability** Act (proposed): Requires companies to audit AI systems for bias and discrimination.
- **AI Bill of Rights (2022):** Guidelines to promote fairness, transparency, and accountability in AI.
- **Executive Orders on AI Safety (2023):** Mandates AI risk assessments for national security and critical infrastructure.

Additionally, the Federal Trade Commission (FTC) enforces AI compliance by penalizing companies for deceptive AI practices and privacy violations.

📌 **Example**: In 2021, the FTC warned AI companies against selling biased facial recognition software, threatening legal action for deceptive practices.

2.3 China: AI Ethics & Social Governance

China has implemented strict AI regulations, focusing on content moderation, biometric data control, and social responsibility. Key policies include:

- **AI Ethics Guidelines (2021):** Emphasize human oversight, fairness, and transparency.
- **Deepfake Regulations (2022):** Require clear labeling of AI-generated content.
- **Personal Information Protection Law (PIPL):** Protects user data from misuse by AI systems.

📌 **Example**: In 2022, Chinese regulators fined major tech companies for using AI-driven algorithms that manipulated consumer behavior (e.g., unfair pricing models).

2.4 Other Global AI Regulations

Country/Region	Key AI Regulations & Compliance Standards
UK	AI Regulation White Paper (2023) focusing on **proportionate AI governance**.
Canada	Artificial Intelligence and Data Act (AIDA) for **responsible AI use**.
Australia	AI Ethics Principles ensuring **human-centered AI development**.
India	AI Policy Framework promoting **fair and inclusive AI adoption**.

3. AI Compliance Best Practices

To ensure AI projects comply with legal and ethical standards, organizations should implement compliance strategies throughout the AI lifecycle.

3.1 Conduct AI Risk Assessments

✓☐ Identify high-risk AI applications (e.g., healthcare, hiring, financial decisions).
✓☐ Evaluate potential bias, privacy risks, and security threats.
✓☐ Document risk mitigation strategies for compliance reporting.

3.2 Implement AI Audits & Bias Testing

✓☐ Use bias-detection tools (e.g., Fairness Indicators, SHAP analysis).

✓☐ Regularly audit AI predictions for disparate impact across demographic groups.

✓☐ Maintain compliance documentation to track AI fairness efforts.

📌 **Example**: A bank using AI for loan approvals should test for racial bias and ensure fair lending practices.

3.3 Ensure Transparency & Explainability

✓☐ Use explainable AI models (e.g., SHAP, LIME) to make AI decisions interpretable.

✓☐ Provide clear AI disclosures to users (e.g., "This decision was made by AI").

✓☐ Design AI systems that allow human intervention when needed.

📌 **Example**: A medical AI predicting cancer diagnoses should provide explanations for its predictions to assist doctors.

3.4 Strengthen Data Privacy & Security

✓☐ Use privacy-preserving AI techniques (e.g., differential privacy, federated learning).

✓☐ Encrypt sensitive user data and ensure GDPR/CCPA compliance.

✓☐ Obtain informed consent before using personal data for AI training.

📌 **Example**: AI-powered chatbots collecting user conversations must ensure data encryption and anonymization.

3.5 Establish Accountability & Governance

✓☐ Define AI ethics policies within organizations.

✓☐ Assign AI ethics officers to oversee compliance.

✓☐ Regularly review AI decision impacts to address unintended consequences.

📌 **Example**: Companies developing AI-based facial recognition must ensure proper oversight to prevent misuse.

4. The Future of AI Regulation

As AI advances, governments and industries will continue shaping regulatory frameworks to balance innovation with ethical responsibility.

◆ **More transparency laws**: Regulations will likely mandate explainability for high-risk AI decisions.

◆ **Stronger data protection policies**: Stricter laws on AI data collection, storage, and usage will emerge.

◆ **AI liability laws**: Governments may define legal responsibility for AI failures and harms.

◆ **Industry-led AI standards**: Companies will develop self-regulatory guidelines for ethical AI.

📌 **Key Takeaway**: AI developers must proactively align with evolving global compliance standards to ensure responsible AI adoption.

AI regulation is no longer optional—governments worldwide are enforcing compliance measures to ensure AI systems are fair, transparent, and accountable. Developers and businesses must take a proactive approach to AI governance, adopting best practices in bias testing, privacy protection, and responsible deployment.

By aligning with regulatory frameworks like the EU AI Act, U.S. AI Bill of Rights, and GDPR, AI practitioners can build ethical AI systems that benefit society while maintaining compliance with evolving global laws.

17. Scaling ML for Big Data

In this chapter, we dive into the challenges and strategies for scaling machine learning models to handle big data effectively. As datasets grow larger and more complex, traditional machine learning techniques may struggle with performance and computational limitations. You'll learn how to leverage distributed computing frameworks like Apache Spark and Hadoop to process large volumes of data in parallel. We'll explore model parallelism and data parallelism to train models at scale and discuss techniques like batch processing and online learning for continuous data streams. Additionally, we'll cover the use of cloud platforms and GPU acceleration to speed up model training and reduce computational overhead. By the end of this chapter, you'll have the skills to efficiently scale machine learning solutions to handle big data, ensuring your models can operate seamlessly in real-world, data-heavy environments. 🚀💾

17.1 Distributed ML with Apache Spark and Dask

In the world of machine learning (ML), working with large datasets can present significant challenges. Whether you're processing vast amounts of sensor data, user-generated content, or millions of financial transactions, scaling your ML workflows to handle big data is essential for extracting valuable insights and creating robust models. Traditional single-machine learning techniques often fall short when it comes to handling these vast datasets, especially in terms of computational power, memory usage, and processing time. This is where distributed computing frameworks like Apache Spark and Dask come into play, offering the ability to process large-scale data in parallel across many machines, enabling scalable ML solutions.

In this sub-chapter, we will explore distributed machine learning using two popular frameworks, Apache Spark and Dask, and understand how they can help scale ML models for big data environments. By the end of this section, you will have a strong understanding of how these tools work and how to use them to process and model large datasets efficiently.

1. Introduction to Distributed Machine Learning

Distributed machine learning refers to the practice of running machine learning algorithms across multiple machines or distributed computing environments. Instead of relying on a single machine to process data, distributed ML leverages multiple processors or machines working in parallel. This allows for faster processing, better handling of large datasets, and the ability to scale ML models as your data grows.

While Apache Spark and Dask are both popular choices for distributed computing, they each have unique strengths and implementations. Let's dive into each of these tools and understand how they facilitate distributed machine learning workflows.

2. Overview of Apache Spark

Apache Spark is an open-source, distributed computing system that provides an easy-to-use interface for processing large-scale data. Spark can perform data processing tasks on distributed clusters, which allows it to process huge datasets in parallel.

Key Features of Apache Spark:

- **Distributed Data Processing**: Spark uses Resilient Distributed Datasets (RDDs) to store data in a distributed fashion across a cluster, allowing for parallel processing and fault tolerance.
- **In-Memory Computing**: Spark's in-memory computing engine speeds up processing by keeping data in RAM, instead of writing intermediate results to disk as with traditional MapReduce.
- **MLlib for Machine Learning**: Spark comes with a powerful library called MLlib, which contains many algorithms and tools for machine learning, such as regression, classification, clustering, and recommendation. MLlib can run on a distributed cluster, making it easier to scale ML workflows.
- **Scalability**: Spark can scale from a single machine to thousands of nodes, making it ideal for big data processing tasks.

How Apache Spark Scales ML:

Spark achieves its scalability by distributing tasks across a cluster of machines. The cluster can consist of a group of interconnected computers (nodes), each processing part of the data. Spark divides the input data into partitions and processes each partition independently on a different machine. This parallelization leads to faster processing times for ML models.

Spark's MLlib library supports a wide range of ML algorithms, including classification, regression, and clustering, which can all be distributed across nodes for parallel execution. In addition, Spark provides DataFrame-based APIs to streamline working with structured data, similar to how pandas operates on a single machine.

3. Overview of Dask

Dask is another open-source parallel computing library that is specifically designed to scale Python-based workflows. It is built with the goal of integrating seamlessly with the Python data ecosystem, providing a distributed version of tools like pandas, NumPy, and scikit-learn. Dask provides both dynamic task scheduling and parallel processing, making it a powerful option for scalable machine learning.

Key Features of Dask:

- **Flexible Parallelism**: Dask allows users to create a task graph for computation, which is then executed in parallel across multiple machines or cores. This flexibility means that you can scale your workloads from a single machine to a multi-node cluster with minimal changes.
- **Integration with Python Libraries**: Dask integrates with pandas, NumPy, scikit-learn, and other widely used libraries, making it easy for Python developers to scale existing workflows.
- **Dask-ML for Machine Learning**: Dask-ML is a scalable ML library built on top of Dask, providing tools to distribute training tasks and apply ML algorithms to large datasets efficiently.
- **Memory Efficiency**: Dask handles datasets that don't fit into memory by breaking them into smaller, manageable chunks and distributing the computation.

How Dask Scales ML:

Dask scales machine learning models by splitting data into smaller, chunks and performing operations on those chunks in parallel. Dask operates efficiently on larger-than-memory datasets by allowing users to manipulate out-of-core data in a distributed manner. Dask-ML, which is built on top of Dask, provides scalable versions of standard ML algorithms such as regression, classification, and clustering, as well as support for hyperparameter optimization and model evaluation.

Dask can also work well with scikit-learn and other familiar libraries by scaling their operations without the need for significant code modifications. This makes Dask a good choice for developers looking to scale up their existing ML workflows.

4. Comparison: Apache Spark vs. Dask

Both Apache Spark and Dask provide scalable machine learning frameworks, but they have different strengths depending on your use case.

Feature	Apache Spark	Dask
Ease of Use	Has its own API and syntax for ML (MLlib)	Seamless integration with Python's data ecosystem (pandas, NumPy, scikit-learn)
Parallelism	Distributed data processing via RDDs and DataFrames	Distributed parallel computing with dynamic task scheduling
Memory Efficiency	In-memory computing but can be expensive on large datasets	Handles out-of-core data processing effectively
Scaling	Scales from a single machine to a large cluster	Scales from single-node to multi-node clusters easily
ML Support	MLlib provides basic ML algorithms (regression, clustering)	Dask-ML offers scalable versions of popular ML algorithms, works well with scikit-learn
Compatibility	Works well with Hadoop ecosystem and big data tools	Works directly with Python-based libraries like pandas and NumPy

5. Implementing Distributed ML with Apache Spark

Here's a high-level overview of implementing a machine learning model using Apache Spark:

- **Setup Spark Environment**: Install and configure Apache Spark on a cluster or locally with the PySpark library.
- **Load Data into Spark**: Use Spark's DataFrame API to load and manipulate large datasets.
- **Train a Model**: Use MLlib to train a distributed ML model, such as linear regression or decision trees, across multiple machines.
- **Evaluate Model**: Evaluate the model's performance using MLlib's evaluation metrics such as accuracy, precision, and recall.
- **Save and Deploy**: Save the trained model and deploy it in production using a Spark-serving mechanism.

Example code for loading data and training a model in PySpark:

```
from pyspark.ml.regression import LinearRegression
from pyspark.ml.feature import VectorAssembler
from pyspark.sql import SparkSession
```

```
spark = SparkSession.builder.appName("MLExample").getOrCreate()
data = spark.read.csv("large_dataset.csv", header=True, inferSchema=True)

# Feature Engineering
assembler = VectorAssembler(inputCols=["feature1", "feature2"], outputCol="features")
data = assembler.transform(data)

# Train a Linear Regression Model
lr = LinearRegression(featuresCol="features", labelCol="target")
model = lr.fit(data)

# Evaluate the model
results = model.evaluate(data)
print("RMSE: ", results.rootMeanSquaredError)
```

6. Implementing Distributed ML with Dask

Here's how to implement distributed ML with Dask:

- **Setup Dask Environment**: Install Dask and Dask-ML.
- **Load Data**: Load large datasets using Dask DataFrame or Dask Array.
- **Train the Model**: Use Dask-ML to train machine learning models, leveraging parallelism across nodes.
- **Evaluate the Model**: Use Dask's parallelized evaluation functions to assess model performance.
- **Deploy**: Save the trained model and deploy it for production use.

Example code for training a model with Dask-ML:

```
import dask.dataframe as dd
from dask_ml.linear_model import LogisticRegression
from dask_ml.model_selection import train_test_split
from sklearn.datasets import make_classification

# Create a synthetic dataset for the example
X, y = make_classification(n_samples=1000000, n_features=20)
df = dd.from_array(X, columns=[f"feature{i}" for i in range(1, 21)])

# Split the data
```

```
X_train, X_test, y_train, y_test = train_test_split(df, y, test_size=0.2)

# Train a logistic regression model using Dask-ML
clf = LogisticRegression()
clf.fit(X_train, y_train)

# Evaluate the model
score = clf.score(X_test, y_test)
print(f"Model accuracy: {score}")
```

Both Apache Spark and Dask offer powerful solutions for scaling machine learning workflows across distributed systems, enabling you to handle big data and process large datasets with ease. Spark is well-suited for large-scale data processing in distributed clusters, especially in big data ecosystems, while Dask integrates more seamlessly with Python-based data tools and scales Python workflows more easily. By understanding the strengths of both frameworks, you can choose the best tool for your needs when working with big data for machine learning.

17.2 Handling large datasets efficiently

Working with large datasets is one of the most common challenges in machine learning (ML), especially as the data volume and complexity grow. Handling such datasets efficiently becomes crucial for ensuring that ML models can be trained in a timely manner without compromising performance or quality. As businesses and organizations collect vast amounts of data, making sure that your infrastructure can process, analyze, and derive insights from these datasets at scale is a necessity.

In this sub-chapter, we will explore different strategies and techniques for handling large datasets efficiently during the machine learning process. From data storage to distributed processing and optimization techniques, we'll cover the best practices to ensure that you can work with big data while minimizing computational overhead and maximizing resource utilization.

1. Challenges of Handling Large Datasets

Handling large datasets comes with several inherent challenges:

- **Memory Limitations**: When data doesn't fit into memory, traditional single-machine techniques struggle to process the dataset in a timely manner.

- **Storage Constraints**: Storing large datasets on disk can lead to slow read and write speeds, which impacts processing performance.
- **Processing Time**: Training machine learning models on large datasets requires significant computational power, often leading to longer runtimes.
- **Data Quality**: Large datasets can contain noisy, inconsistent, or missing data, which can affect model accuracy and efficiency.
- **Scalability**: Scaling ML workflows to process large datasets requires distributed systems or cloud-based infrastructure to handle parallel computation and data distribution.

2. Best Practices for Handling Large Datasets

To overcome these challenges, it's crucial to follow specific strategies and best practices to handle and process large datasets efficiently:

2.1 Data Preprocessing and Cleaning

Before diving into any machine learning task, it's important to preprocess and clean your data to improve both model performance and computational efficiency.

- **Handling Missing Data**: For large datasets, missing values can disrupt processing. Use imputation (filling missing values) or remove rows or columns with significant gaps. If the missing data is not important, dropping it can save on processing time.
- **Handling Outliers**: Large datasets often contain outliers or extreme values that can skew the performance of models. Identifying and handling outliers—either through transformation techniques (like normalization) or by removing extreme values—can help in making the model robust and improve performance.
- **Reducing Noise**: Noisy data can impact the quality of the insights extracted. Removing duplicate entries or applying noise reduction techniques such as smoothing can improve efficiency and the overall quality of the model.
- **Data Sampling**: For extremely large datasets, consider using sampling techniques to work with smaller subsets of data. Sampling can drastically reduce the amount of data to work with and enable faster experimentation while still retaining the original data distribution.

2.2 Efficient Data Storage

How data is stored and retrieved from disk plays a significant role in performance when dealing with large datasets.

- **Data Formats**: Use efficient file formats like Parquet and ORC, which are both columnar storage formats optimized for large datasets. These formats enable faster reading and writing compared to row-based formats (such as CSV).
- **Compression**: Data compression techniques, such as gzip or snappy compression, can help reduce the disk space required for large datasets and speed up file I/O operations.
- **Cloud Storage Solutions**: Consider using cloud-based storage solutions like Amazon S3, Google Cloud Storage, or Azure Blob Storage. These platforms provide scalable storage with fast access to large datasets and are optimized for handling big data.

2.3 Batch vs. Stream Processing

When working with large datasets, you have two main approaches to consider:

- **Batch Processing**: This approach involves processing large chunks of data at once. For example, you could load an entire dataset into memory, process it, and then discard the results. While batch processing works well for static datasets that do not require real-time updates, it can be slow and memory-intensive.
- **Stream Processing**: Stream processing involves processing data as it arrives. This is useful for real-time applications, such as fraud detection or recommendation systems, where you want to process data on the fly as new information is available. Tools like Apache Kafka, Apache Flink, and Spark Streaming are built for efficient stream processing.

2.4 Parallelism and Distributed Computing

To scale ML workflows and make processing large datasets efficient, parallelism and distributed computing are essential. Both Apache Spark and Dask, discussed in the previous sub-chapter, are designed to run distributed computations, which allow large datasets to be processed in parallel across multiple machines.

- **MapReduce Paradigm**: Spark and other distributed computing frameworks follow the MapReduce paradigm, which splits large datasets into smaller chunks and applies a function to each chunk in parallel. This allows for the parallelization of many tasks, such as data loading, cleaning, and feature extraction, making them significantly faster.
- **Sharding**: Sharding is the process of breaking down a large dataset into smaller shards or partitions. Each partition can then be processed on separate machines

in parallel. By doing so, you can distribute the workload and scale your ML tasks horizontally, increasing processing speed.

2.5 Memory Management

Memory management is key when handling large datasets. Here are some practices to optimize memory usage:

- **Out-of-Core Computation**: Out-of-core processing allows you to work with datasets larger than memory by streaming data from disk in chunks and processing one chunk at a time. Dask and Spark enable this type of memory-efficient processing by loading small portions of data into memory at once.
- **Lazy Evaluation**: Lazy evaluation refers to computing values only when they are needed, rather than computing everything upfront. Libraries like Dask and TensorFlow support lazy evaluation, allowing you to chain operations together and delay their execution until necessary. This can significantly reduce memory usage.
- **Efficient Data Structures**: Opt for memory-efficient data structures, such as Sparse Matrices, when dealing with high-dimensional datasets with lots of zeros. NumPy and Scipy offer sparse matrix representations, which help reduce memory overhead.

3. Distributed Frameworks for Big Data

Leveraging distributed computing frameworks like Apache Spark, Dask, and Hadoop can help in processing large datasets efficiently. Both Spark and Dask are designed to work with data that exceeds the memory capacity of a single machine, splitting the data into manageable chunks and processing them in parallel. These frameworks make it possible to scale ML models effectively across many nodes.

3.1 Using Apache Spark for Distributed Data Processing

With Spark, data can be distributed over a cluster using RDDs (Resilient Distributed Datasets) or DataFrames. This enables you to process data in parallel on multiple nodes, reducing the time it takes to complete tasks. Spark supports operations like grouping, filtering, and joins on distributed data, making it easier to scale out computations.

3.2 Using Dask for Scalable Computation

Dask works well with large datasets by breaking them into smaller chunks and applying parallel computations on those chunks. Unlike Spark, which uses RDDs and DataFrames,

Dask operates natively on pandas DataFrames and NumPy arrays, which means that if you're familiar with the Python data stack, working with Dask will be intuitive. Dask allows you to scale computations from a single machine to thousands of machines with little change in the code.

4. Optimizing ML Algorithms for Large Datasets

When training machine learning models on large datasets, there are several strategies that can make the process more efficient:

- **Stochastic Gradient Descent (SGD):** Traditional gradient descent may not scale well on large datasets due to its high memory and computational cost. SGD processes one sample at a time, making it more efficient for large datasets.
- **Mini-Batch Training**: For large-scale deep learning, using mini-batch training can help avoid memory overload by splitting the data into smaller batches. This allows for faster convergence and is less memory-intensive than full-batch gradient descent.
- **Approximate Algorithms**: For certain tasks, such as clustering or nearest neighbor search, approximate algorithms like Approximate Nearest Neighbors (ANN) can speed up computations without sacrificing too much accuracy.

Handling large datasets efficiently requires careful consideration of data storage, processing techniques, and model optimization strategies. By utilizing distributed computing frameworks like Apache Spark and Dask, leveraging parallelism, optimizing memory management, and applying efficient algorithms, it's possible to scale machine learning models to handle big data without sacrificing performance.

These strategies not only make it easier to handle vast amounts of data but also help speed up the ML workflow, enabling data scientists and engineers to focus on deriving insights and improving models rather than dealing with data bottlenecks. As the volume of data continues to grow, the ability to scale your ML pipelines becomes increasingly critical for staying ahead of the curve.

17.3 Parallel processing for ML models

Parallel processing is a critical technique for scaling machine learning (ML) workflows, especially when dealing with large datasets or complex models. As datasets grow larger and ML algorithms become more computationally demanding, parallel processing can significantly speed up model training, feature extraction, and other time-consuming tasks.

This sub-chapter will explore parallel processing techniques, tools, and best practices for scaling ML models efficiently.

1. What is Parallel Processing?

Parallel processing refers to the simultaneous execution of multiple tasks or operations. Instead of processing data sequentially, parallel processing divides a task into smaller sub-tasks that can be processed simultaneously by multiple processors (CPUs or GPUs). This approach dramatically reduces the time required for computation and makes it feasible to work with large-scale data, complex models, and computationally expensive algorithms.

For machine learning, parallel processing is used in several areas:

- **Data preprocessing**: Speeding up tasks like cleaning, feature engineering, and transformation.
- **Model training**: Distributing the task of training across multiple processors or machines.
- **Hyperparameter tuning**: Running multiple training jobs in parallel with different configurations.
- **Ensemble methods**: Training multiple models simultaneously and combining them for improved accuracy.

The essence of parallel processing is to break down tasks into smaller, independent pieces and distribute the load across multiple computing resources, whether that's CPUs, GPUs, or even distributed clusters of machines.

2. Types of Parallelism in Machine Learning

There are several types of parallelism in machine learning, and understanding how to use each type appropriately is essential for scaling models efficiently.

2.1 Data Parallelism

Data parallelism involves splitting a dataset into smaller batches and processing each batch independently. The idea is that the model architecture remains the same, but each batch of data is fed into separate processors for training. The key here is to ensure that the model parameters are updated simultaneously across all processors.

Example: When training a neural network, each mini-batch of data can be passed to different processors (such as GPUs). After processing the mini-batch, the gradient updates from each processor are combined to update the shared model parameters. This approach accelerates training by utilizing parallel computation without changing the model itself.

In frameworks like TensorFlow and PyTorch, data parallelism is often implemented through multi-threading or multi-processing. GPUs are especially effective for this type of parallelism because they are designed to handle thousands of computations in parallel, making them ideal for training deep learning models.

2.2 Model Parallelism

Model parallelism splits the model itself across multiple processors. Instead of dividing the data, the model is split into different parts, with each processor handling a subset of the model's layers or computations. This approach is useful when the model is too large to fit into the memory of a single machine or GPU.

Example: In a deep learning model with several large layers, some layers may be handled by one processor, while others are handled by different processors. The outputs from each processor are then combined to complete the forward pass and backpropagation.

Model parallelism is commonly used for very large neural networks, such as those found in natural language processing (NLP) or computer vision, where the model architecture itself is too large to fit in a single GPU's memory.

2.3 Task Parallelism

Task parallelism focuses on executing different types of tasks simultaneously. For instance, you can parallelize hyperparameter tuning, model evaluation, or even different stages of the ML pipeline, such as data preprocessing, training, and model evaluation.

Example: In a machine learning project, you could run multiple hyperparameter tuning experiments in parallel. Each experiment would train a different model configuration using different hyperparameters, and the best configuration could be selected afterward.

Task parallelism is often useful when different components of the ML workflow are independent of each other, and each task can be executed separately. This can be done efficiently with frameworks like Dask or Ray, which allow parallel execution of tasks across multiple machines.

3. Tools and Libraries for Parallel Processing in Machine Learning

To take full advantage of parallel processing, you need to utilize specific libraries and tools that enable parallel computation in machine learning. Here are some of the most popular frameworks and tools used for parallelism in ML:

3.1 TensorFlow

TensorFlow is one of the most widely used deep learning frameworks, and it offers robust support for parallel processing. TensorFlow can distribute model training across multiple GPUs, multiple machines, and even across different cloud platforms.

- **Data Parallelism**: TensorFlow's tf.distribute.Strategy API provides tools for parallel training on multiple GPUs or TPUs. It synchronizes gradient updates during distributed training, allowing for efficient scaling across large datasets.
- **Model Parallelism**: TensorFlow allows you to split your model across devices using techniques like multi-GPU model parallelism.

3.2 PyTorch

PyTorch, another popular deep learning framework, supports parallelism in a similar manner. PyTorch enables data parallelism through its DataParallel module, which automatically distributes batches across multiple GPUs.

DistributedDataParallel: PyTorch's torch.nn.DataParallel and torch.nn.parallel.DistributedDataParallel are used for data parallelism, while model parallelism can be achieved manually by splitting the model into sub-modules and distributing them across multiple GPUs.

3.3 Dask

Dask is a flexible parallel computing library that can be used to parallelize both machine learning tasks and data processing. Dask is especially useful for working with large datasets that don't fit into memory. It can scale from a single machine to a cluster of thousands of machines.

Dask-ML: Dask-ML provides scalable machine learning algorithms that are designed to work with Dask's parallel and distributed capabilities. It integrates well with other Python tools like scikit-learn, XGBoost, and TensorFlow.

3.4 Apache Spark

Apache Spark is a distributed data processing engine, and it is particularly well-suited for parallelizing ML workflows across a cluster of machines. Spark's MLlib provides a set of scalable machine learning algorithms that can be parallelized across multiple nodes in a cluster.

Spark's Resilient Distributed Datasets (RDDs) allow you to process large datasets in parallel by breaking them down into smaller chunks and distributing the workload across the cluster.

Hyperparameter Tuning: Spark provides built-in support for distributed hyperparameter tuning using techniques like grid search and random search.

3.5 Ray

Ray is an emerging framework for distributed computing that is gaining popularity for parallelizing machine learning tasks. It is highly flexible and can be used to parallelize tasks such as hyperparameter optimization, reinforcement learning, and even large-scale deep learning.

Ray Tune: Ray Tune is a scalable hyperparameter optimization library that allows you to efficiently search for the best hyperparameters in parallel across many trials.

4. Best Practices for Efficient Parallel Processing

While parallel processing can significantly speed up ML workflows, it's essential to follow certain best practices to ensure efficient use of resources and avoid common pitfalls.

4.1 Proper Hardware Setup

Ensure that you have the right hardware for parallel processing. Using multiple GPUs or TPUs is essential for scaling deep learning models. For distributed systems, ensure you have a high-speed network to minimize communication overhead between nodes.

4.2 Efficient Batch Sizing

When using data parallelism, finding the optimal batch size is crucial for performance. Too small a batch size might lead to high overhead, while too large a batch size might strain the memory. Fine-tuning the batch size for your hardware setup can lead to significant speed improvements.

4.3 Minimize Data Transfer

In distributed systems, excessive data transfer between nodes can significantly slow down the process. Aim to minimize data transfer by using data local to the node whenever possible, and reduce the number of inter-node communications.

4.4 Load Balancing

In parallel processing, tasks need to be evenly distributed across workers to avoid some workers being idle while others are overloaded. Implementing proper load balancing ensures that all resources are utilized optimally.

Parallel processing is a powerful technique for scaling machine learning tasks, enabling you to handle large datasets, train complex models faster, and make your ML workflows more efficient. By leveraging tools like TensorFlow, PyTorch, Dask, Spark, and Ray, you can harness the full potential of parallel computing to accelerate model development and experimentation.

As datasets continue to grow in size and complexity, parallel processing will become increasingly essential for keeping up with the demands of modern machine learning. Whether you're working with data preprocessing, training large models, or performing hyperparameter tuning, parallelism is key to improving both speed and efficiency in machine learning workflows.

17.4 Optimizing training with multi-GPU support

In machine learning, training models on large datasets or complex architectures can be computationally expensive and time-consuming. As a result, scaling up the training process is essential for achieving high-performance models in a reasonable amount of time. One of the most effective ways to scale machine learning training is through the use of multiple GPUs.

Multi-GPU training refers to the parallelization of the model training process across more than one Graphics Processing Unit (GPU), allowing the workload to be distributed across multiple devices. This can significantly accelerate training, reduce time-to-deployment, and enable training on larger datasets or more complex models that would otherwise be impossible to train on a single GPU due to memory limitations.

In this sub-chapter, we'll explore the concept of multi-GPU support in machine learning, how to optimize training with multiple GPUs, and how popular machine learning frameworks like TensorFlow and PyTorch handle multi-GPU training.

1. Why Use Multiple GPUs?

Training large machine learning models, particularly deep neural networks, often requires substantial computational resources. A single GPU can only handle a limited amount of data, and as model architectures become larger and more complex (e.g., transformers, deep convolutional networks), training on a single GPU may become impractical. The key benefits of using multiple GPUs for training are:

Speedup in Training: By splitting the training task across multiple GPUs, the overall training time can be reduced. Each GPU can process a different mini-batch or perform different parts of the computation simultaneously, allowing the model to be trained faster.

Larger Models: Some models and datasets are too large to fit into the memory of a single GPU. With multi-GPU setups, each GPU can hold a portion of the model or dataset, enabling the training of larger models or working with datasets that would otherwise be too large for the available hardware.

Improved Model Performance: Multi-GPU setups allow for better handling of larger datasets, potentially leading to better-trained models and improved generalization. By using more computing resources, you can experiment with more advanced model architectures and training strategies.

2. Types of Multi-GPU Training

There are different ways to use multiple GPUs for machine learning training, and the approach you choose depends on the hardware setup, model architecture, and machine learning framework. The two most common methods are data parallelism and model parallelism.

2.1 Data Parallelism

Data parallelism is the most widely used technique for multi-GPU training. In this approach, the entire dataset is split into smaller mini-batches, and each mini-batch is processed independently by a different GPU. The GPUs then compute gradients for their respective mini-batches, and these gradients are synchronized and averaged across all GPUs to update the model weights.

How It Works:

- The training data is split into smaller mini-batches.
- Each GPU processes its own mini-batch, computes gradients, and updates the model weights independently.
- The gradients from each GPU are averaged or summed together and then broadcasted to all GPUs to ensure that they all have the same updated model parameters.

This method is highly effective when you have large datasets because each GPU processes a fraction of the data in parallel, accelerating the overall training process.

Example: In TensorFlow, data parallelism is implemented through the tf.distribute.MirroredStrategy. This strategy creates copies of the model on each GPU, then synchronizes the gradients after each step, enabling faster training on multi-GPU systems.

2.2 Model Parallelism

In model parallelism, the model itself is divided into multiple parts, and each GPU is responsible for computing different sections of the model. This approach is used when the model is too large to fit into the memory of a single GPU.

How It Works:

- The model is split into segments (e.g., individual layers or blocks).
- Each GPU handles a different part of the model and computes its forward and backward pass for its assigned segment.
- Results from different GPUs are combined to update the model weights.

Model parallelism is typically used in very large models, such as transformer-based models, where the architecture requires substantial memory. It's more complex to implement than data parallelism, as it requires careful partitioning of the model across GPUs.

Example: PyTorch allows users to implement model parallelism by manually specifying which parts of the model should run on which device. Users can decide how to distribute the layers of the model across available GPUs.

3. Multi-GPU Training in TensorFlow

TensorFlow provides robust support for multi-GPU training, particularly through the use of tf.distribute.Strategy. The most commonly used strategy for multi-GPU training is the MirroredStrategy, which performs data parallelism across multiple GPUs.

3.1 MirroredStrategy

How It Works: MirroredStrategy mirrors the model on each GPU and synchronizes the gradients after each batch. Each GPU computes the gradients independently and then they are averaged across all GPUs, with the updates applied to each model replica. This ensures that each GPU maintains the same model parameters throughout training.

Code Example:

```
strategy = tf.distribute.MirroredStrategy()

with strategy.scope():
    model = build_model()  # Your model architecture
    model.compile(optimizer='adam', loss='mse', metrics=['accuracy'])

model.fit(train_dataset, epochs=10)
```

3.2 Performance Optimization

When using multi-GPU training, you need to ensure that the model is optimized to leverage the hardware efficiently. Some strategies include:

- **Variable sync**: Ensure that gradients are synchronized efficiently across GPUs to minimize communication overhead.
- **Gradient accumulation**: In scenarios with limited batch sizes, accumulating gradients over multiple iterations can reduce the communication cost.

- **Distributed batch size**: Increase the overall batch size when scaling to multiple GPUs, ensuring that each GPU processes an appropriately sized mini-batch.

4. Multi-GPU Training in PyTorch

PyTorch also offers multi-GPU support through two main techniques: DataParallel and DistributedDataParallel.

4.1 DataParallel

How It Works: In PyTorch's DataParallel, the model is replicated across all available GPUs, and each GPU computes the forward and backward passes for its portion of the input data. After each forward pass, the gradients are averaged and applied to the shared model.

Code Example:

```
model = MyModel()
model = nn.DataParallel(model)  # Wrap the model with DataParallel
model.to(device)  # Move the model to the device (GPU)

optimizer = optim.Adam(model.parameters())

# Training loop
for inputs, labels in dataloader:
    optimizer.zero_grad()
    outputs = model(inputs)
    loss = loss_fn(outputs, labels)
    loss.backward()
    optimizer.step()
```

4.2 DistributedDataParallel

How It Works: PyTorch's DistributedDataParallel (DDP) is more efficient than DataParallel as it minimizes the communication overhead between GPUs by utilizing a distributed training approach. It performs training across multiple nodes and devices, offering better scaling efficiency and speed.

5. Best Practices for Multi-GPU Training

To make the most out of your multi-GPU setup, consider the following best practices:

5.1 Batch Size and Learning Rate Adjustment

When moving from a single GPU to multiple GPUs, it's often necessary to adjust the batch size and learning rate to ensure optimal training. The batch size is typically increased proportionally to the number of GPUs. For instance, if you are using 4 GPUs, you can increase the batch size by a factor of 4. Additionally, the learning rate may need to be fine-tuned to maintain stable training.

5.2 Use Mixed Precision Training

Mixed precision training leverages both 16-bit and 32-bit floating-point operations, which can help speed up training and reduce memory usage without sacrificing model accuracy. Many modern deep learning frameworks, such as TensorFlow and PyTorch, provide native support for mixed precision, especially when using multiple GPUs.

5.3 Monitoring and Profiling

Monitoring the training process is critical to ensure that the GPUs are being utilized efficiently. Tools such as NVIDIA's nvidia-smi, TensorBoard for TensorFlow, and PyTorch Profiler can help identify bottlenecks in your model, whether it's the GPU utilization, memory usage, or communication overhead.

Using multi-GPU setups for training machine learning models allows you to scale your workloads efficiently, drastically reducing training time and enabling the use of larger datasets and more complex models. By leveraging parallelism, whether through data or model parallelism, machine learning practitioners can significantly improve the efficiency of their workflows. Tools like TensorFlow and PyTorch make it easy to implement multi-GPU training with just a few lines of code.

However, optimizing the training process with multiple GPUs requires careful management of resources, batch sizes, and synchronization of gradients. By following best practices and utilizing appropriate frameworks, you can achieve faster training and better scalability for large-scale machine learning projects.

17.5 Using cloud services for scalable ML

Cloud services have revolutionized how organizations deploy, scale, and manage machine learning (ML) models, especially when dealing with large datasets and computationally intensive tasks. Cloud platforms provide on-demand resources, high-performance computing capabilities, and robust infrastructure, allowing organizations to scale their machine learning projects efficiently without the need to invest in and maintain physical hardware.

In this sub-chapter, we will explore how cloud services are used to scale ML workloads, offering scalability, flexibility, and efficiency. We will focus on key cloud services for ML and how to leverage them effectively, including major providers like Amazon Web Services (AWS), Microsoft Azure, and Google Cloud Platform (GCP).

1. Cloud Platforms for Scalable ML

Several leading cloud platforms provide specialized services to facilitate scalable machine learning. These platforms offer a wide range of tools and infrastructure for training, deployment, and management of ML models, often with built-in support for distributed training, GPUs, and distributed data processing.

1.1 Amazon Web Services (AWS)

AWS is one of the most popular cloud service providers for ML, offering several tools to scale ML workflows effectively:

Amazon SageMaker: AWS's flagship ML platform, SageMaker, allows data scientists and developers to quickly build, train, and deploy machine learning models at scale. SageMaker offers several features, such as:

- **Built-in algorithms and frameworks**: SageMaker supports TensorFlow, PyTorch, Scikit-Learn, and other popular libraries.
- **Distributed training**: It provides the capability to distribute training across multiple GPUs or instances to scale up the training process.
- **Automatic Model Tuning**: SageMaker can automatically adjust hyperparameters to optimize model performance.
- **Managed Jupyter Notebooks**: SageMaker offers fully managed Jupyter notebooks for seamless experimentation.

Elastic Compute Cloud (EC2): AWS EC2 provides scalable compute capacity in the cloud. EC2 offers instances with GPU support, such as the p3 and p4 series, which are optimized for ML workloads, making it ideal for training large models or handling complex datasets.

Elastic MapReduce (EMR): EMR allows users to run big data frameworks, such as Apache Hadoop, Apache Spark, and Apache Hive. You can use EMR for distributed processing of large datasets, which can then be fed into ML models.

1.2 Microsoft Azure

Microsoft Azure is another powerful cloud platform with rich support for scalable ML. Key Azure services for ML include:

Azure Machine Learning Service: Azure ML provides an end-to-end platform for building, training, and deploying machine learning models at scale. Key features include:

- **Distributed training**: Supports distributed training using DataParallel and Horovod, allowing users to scale ML models across multiple compute nodes and GPUs.
- **Automated ML**: Azure ML offers an automated ML service, where users can define a problem, upload data, and let the platform automatically select the best algorithms and hyperparameters.
- **Managed compute clusters**: Azure provides compute clusters, which can be configured with virtual machines (VMs) optimized for ML workloads, such as GPU instances.

Azure Databricks: This is a collaborative Apache Spark-based environment designed for big data analytics and machine learning. It is particularly useful for training models on large datasets and supports integration with other Azure services.

1.3 Google Cloud Platform (GCP)

Google Cloud is another cloud platform that provides exceptional support for scaling machine learning workloads:

Google AI Platform: Google Cloud's AI Platform provides tools for building, training, and deploying machine learning models. Key offerings include:

- **Distributed training**: With the ability to run training jobs on multiple GPUs or TPUs (Tensor Processing Units), GCP can accelerate the training process and handle larger datasets.

- **Vertex AI**: A unified AI platform for building and deploying ML models that integrates tools for data preparation, model training, hyperparameter tuning, and monitoring.
- **Prebuilt models and APIs**: GCP offers pre-built models for tasks like image classification, natural language processing, and video analysis, which can be customized or fine-tuned for specific use cases.

BigQuery ML: Google's BigQuery ML allows users to build and deploy ML models directly on large-scale data stored in BigQuery. It leverages BigQuery's serverless architecture to scale effortlessly without worrying about infrastructure.

TensorFlow on Google Cloud: Google Cloud provides native integration with TensorFlow, which is optimized for training and deploying models on TPUs. Google's cloud also provides TensorFlow Enterprise, a fully managed environment for training deep learning models at scale.

2. Key Considerations for Using Cloud Services

While cloud services are an excellent option for scalable ML, there are several factors to consider when choosing a cloud platform and designing your workflow:

2.1 Cost Management

Cloud computing services are typically billed on a pay-as-you-go basis. While this provides flexibility, costs can quickly accumulate if you are not careful. Consider the following strategies to manage costs:

- **Cost estimation tools**: All major cloud platforms offer tools (e.g., AWS Cost Explorer, Azure Pricing Calculator) that help you estimate the cost of your ML workloads.
- **Reserved instances**: If your workloads are predictable, consider using reserved instances or committed use discounts, which can reduce costs in exchange for long-term commitments.
- **Spot instances**: Spot instances allow you to use excess capacity at a lower price, but they can be terminated with little notice, so they are best suited for non-critical tasks or batch processing jobs.

2.2 Resource Allocation and Scaling

Cloud platforms allow you to scale compute resources up or down depending on the needs of your ML workload. However, it's important to optimize resource allocation to avoid overprovisioning or underprovisioning:

- **Auto-scaling**: Many cloud platforms provide auto-scaling functionality, where resources can be automatically scaled based on the workload. For example, Azure and GCP offer auto-scaling for compute instances, and AWS can automatically scale EC2 instances based on demand.
- **Load balancing**: Ensure that workloads are evenly distributed across your available compute resources to prevent some instances from becoming overburdened while others remain idle.

2.3 Data Security and Privacy

Data security is a critical concern when working with cloud services, particularly when dealing with sensitive or proprietary data. Ensure that your cloud provider offers robust security measures, including:

- **Data encryption**: Ensure that data is encrypted both in transit and at rest.
- **Access control**: Implement role-based access control (RBAC) to limit access to resources and sensitive data.
- **Compliance**: If working with regulated industries (e.g., healthcare, finance), ensure that the cloud provider complies with relevant regulations (e.g., GDPR, HIPAA).

2.4 Integration with Existing Tools and Frameworks

Cloud platforms offer extensive support for popular ML frameworks, such as TensorFlow, PyTorch, and Scikit-learn. Be sure to check that your preferred frameworks and tools are supported by the cloud provider. Additionally, consider integrating cloud services with other tools, such as:

- **Data storage services**: Cloud storage services like AWS S3, Azure Blob Storage, and Google Cloud Storage are often used to store large datasets. Integration with these services is essential for efficient data handling.
- **Collaboration tools**: Tools like Jupyter Notebooks, GitHub, and Google Colab can be integrated with cloud services for better collaboration and version control in your ML projects.

3. Best Practices for Scaling ML with Cloud Services

To make the most of cloud services for scalable ML, consider these best practices:

3.1 Use Distributed Computing Resources

Leverage distributed computing frameworks, such as Apache Spark, Hadoop, or cloud-specific frameworks like Amazon EMR or Google Dataproc, to handle big data processing before training models. These distributed systems enable parallel processing of large datasets, which can be integrated into the ML pipeline for model training.

3.2 Take Advantage of Specialized Hardware

Cloud services provide access to specialized hardware, such as GPUs and TPUs, which are optimized for ML tasks. Be sure to use the most suitable hardware for your workload to maximize performance. For instance, use NVIDIA V100 GPUs or Google Cloud TPUs for deep learning models, which require substantial compute power.

3.3 Automate Pipelines

Use cloud-native tools like AWS Step Functions, Azure Pipelines, and Google Cloud Composer to automate your ML workflows. This can include everything from data collection and preprocessing to training, hyperparameter tuning, and deployment. Automation helps reduce human error and ensures consistency across your ML operations.

3.4 Monitor and Optimize Performance

Cloud platforms provide monitoring tools (e.g., AWS CloudWatch, Azure Monitor, Google Cloud Monitoring) that allow you to track the performance of your ML workloads. Regularly monitor GPU/CPU usage, memory utilization, and data throughput to identify bottlenecks in your workflow. Optimizing your workloads can help reduce costs and improve training efficiency.

Cloud services offer unparalleled scalability and flexibility for machine learning projects, enabling you to train large models, process big data, and deploy models at scale without the burden of managing on-premise infrastructure. By leveraging tools like Amazon SageMaker, Azure ML, and Google Cloud AI Platform, organizations can significantly accelerate their ML workflows, reduce time-to-market, and improve model performance. However, careful management of costs, resources, and data security is essential to ensure that cloud-based ML projects remain efficient, cost-effective, and secure. By following best practices and using cloud-native features, you can optimize your machine learning pipeline and achieve the best possible results from your cloud-based ML infrastructure.

18. LLMs & Generative AI in Real-World Applications

In this chapter, we explore the cutting-edge field of Large Language Models (LLMs) and Generative AI, focusing on how these advanced technologies are revolutionizing real-world applications. You'll learn how transformer-based models like GPT, BERT, and T5 are transforming industries through natural language understanding and generation tasks, such as content creation, chatbots, and text summarization. We'll cover the key concepts behind Generative AI techniques like text generation, image generation, and style transfer using models like DALL·E and Stable Diffusion. Through practical examples, you'll see how businesses are applying LLMs and generative models in sectors like marketing, healthcare, entertainment, and e-commerce to drive innovation and efficiency. By the end of this chapter, you'll have a strong understanding of how to leverage LLMs and Generative AI to solve complex problems and create innovative solutions that can transform industries. 💡✨

18.1 Understanding large language models (LLMs)

Large Language Models (LLMs) have become a cornerstone of recent advancements in artificial intelligence, enabling systems to generate human-like text, understand complex queries, and perform a variety of tasks involving natural language. LLMs are a subset of machine learning models, particularly designed to process and generate text by analyzing vast amounts of textual data. These models have emerged as a significant force in reshaping industries and opening new frontiers in AI applications, from chatbots and content creation to code generation and data analysis.

In this sub-chapter, we will explore what Large Language Models are, how they function, their capabilities, and their impact on various real-world applications. We will also look into some of the common architectures used to develop these models, such as GPT (Generative Pretrained Transformer) and BERT (Bidirectional Encoder Representations from Transformers), to give you a solid foundation for understanding their practical significance.

1. What Are Large Language Models (LLMs)?

At their core, Large Language Models (LLMs) are deep learning models that are trained on massive datasets consisting of text from books, articles, websites, and other written material. These models use this extensive training data to generate, comprehend, and manipulate language in a variety of ways.

1.1 The Role of Transformers in LLMs

The breakthrough in the development of LLMs came with the introduction of transformers, an architecture that revolutionized natural language processing (NLP). The transformer model, introduced by Vaswani et al. in the paper Attention is All You Need (2017), addressed several limitations of prior architectures like RNNs (Recurrent Neural Networks) and LSTMs (Long Short-Term Memory networks) by using self-attention mechanisms to process all parts of the input text simultaneously, rather than sequentially. This enables transformers to efficiently capture long-range dependencies in text and process much larger datasets.

Transformers work by processing an input sequence (e.g., a sentence or paragraph) and generating representations of the words in relation to each other. This structure is what enables LLMs to understand the context and nuances of language, making them highly effective for tasks such as machine translation, question-answering, and content generation.

2. Key Characteristics of Large Language Models

LLMs are distinct from traditional machine learning models due to their scale, architecture, and ability to generalize across multiple tasks. Some of the defining characteristics of LLMs include:

2.1 Scale and Pretraining

LLMs are characterized by their massive scale. Models such as GPT-3 (with 175 billion parameters) and GPT-4 (even larger) have billions, if not trillions, of parameters that allow them to perform complex language tasks. The scale of these models enables them to perform remarkably well across a wide range of NLP tasks without needing task-specific training.

Pretraining is a critical step in the development of LLMs. During pretraining, the model is exposed to a large corpus of text from the internet. It learns general patterns of language, grammar, context, and facts about the world. This unsupervised learning allows the model to acquire a wide-ranging understanding of language, which can later be fine-tuned for specific applications (e.g., customer service chatbots or medical question-answering).

2.2 Fine-Tuning for Specific Applications

While LLMs start with general knowledge from pretraining, they can also be fine-tuned on more specific datasets to specialize in particular tasks. Fine-tuning allows a model to focus on nuances that are relevant to a particular domain. For instance, a language model fine-tuned on medical literature can perform much better on tasks like diagnosing diseases or recommending treatments than a general model.

Fine-tuning is done by training the model on smaller, task-specific datasets. This makes LLMs versatile and applicable to a wide range of industries, from finance and healthcare to entertainment and marketing.

2.3 Natural Language Understanding and Generation

LLMs possess the ability to both understand and generate human-like text, which is crucial for a variety of real-world applications:

Understanding: LLMs can comprehend and process the meaning of text, allowing them to perform tasks such as text classification, sentiment analysis, and summarization. They can understand the context, identify entities, and infer meanings from ambiguous or incomplete sentences.

Generation: LLMs can also generate coherent and contextually relevant text, which is a powerful feature for applications like content creation, customer service chatbots, and even creative writing. The ability to generate meaningful and relevant text based on prompts makes LLMs highly flexible.

3. Notable Large Language Models

A variety of large language models have been developed by different research organizations and companies. The following models are among the most notable:

3.1 GPT (Generative Pretrained Transformer)

Developed by OpenAI, the GPT series of models, including GPT-3 and GPT-4, are some of the most powerful LLMs to date. GPT-3, with 175 billion parameters, is widely recognized for its ability to generate coherent and contextually relevant text across a variety of tasks.

- **Key Features**: GPT-3's strength lies in its ability to generate text from a given prompt, making it highly versatile for content creation, conversational AI, and coding tasks.
- **Real-World Applications**: GPT-3 has been used in applications such as AI-driven writing assistants (e.g., Jasper, Writesonic), code generation, automated customer support, and content recommendation.

3.2 BERT (Bidirectional Encoder Representations from Transformers)

Unlike GPT, BERT is primarily designed for understanding language and excels in tasks like question answering, sentiment analysis, and text classification. BERT uses a bidirectional approach, meaning it processes text from both directions, which helps the model better capture context.

- **Key Features**: BERT's ability to consider the entire context of a sentence—both left and right of a word—makes it highly effective for tasks that require deeper comprehension.
- **Real-World Applications**: BERT has been widely adopted for tasks such as search engine ranking, sentiment analysis, and document classification. Google Search, for instance, uses BERT to understand the meaning behind search queries more effectively.

3.3 T5 (Text-to-Text Transfer Transformer)

Google's T5 model treats every NLP task as a "text-to-text" problem, meaning that both the input and output are treated as strings of text. This unified approach simplifies the development process and allows T5 to handle tasks ranging from translation to summarization and classification.

- **Key Features**: T5's versatility in treating all tasks as text generation problems makes it highly flexible across diverse NLP tasks.
- **Real-World Applications**: T5 has been used for various applications, including document summarization, machine translation, and complex question-answering tasks.

4. Challenges and Limitations of LLMs

While LLMs are powerful, they are not without challenges and limitations:

4.1 Computational Resources

Training LLMs requires immense computational resources, including large clusters of GPUs or TPUs, which can be prohibitively expensive. Even inference—when the model is being used for real-time tasks—can demand significant computational power, especially for larger models.

4.2 Bias and Ethical Considerations

LLMs inherit biases present in the data they are trained on. If the training data contains biased or harmful information, the model may produce biased or unethical outputs. This is a critical concern for deploying LLMs in sensitive applications such as hiring, legal, or healthcare.

4.3 Generalization and Overfitting

Despite their impressive performance on a wide range of tasks, LLMs can still struggle with generalizing to new, unseen contexts or data. They may produce irrelevant or nonsensical outputs if the input is too far outside their training distribution.

5. Real-World Applications of LLMs

LLMs have made significant strides in real-world applications, transforming industries and changing how we interact with technology:

5.1 Content Creation and Copywriting

LLMs like GPT-3 are increasingly used in content generation tools, helping businesses and marketers create high-quality blog posts, articles, social media content, and product descriptions. This enables companies to scale their content production efforts while maintaining quality.

5.2 Chatbots and Virtual Assistants

Generative models like GPT-3 and BERT are widely used in building conversational AI, including chatbots and virtual assistants. These systems can answer questions, provide support, and engage in meaningful dialogues, making them ideal for customer service, tech support, and sales.

5.3 Code Generation and Programming

LLMs have also made an impact in software development, particularly through models like GitHub Copilot, which leverages GPT-3 to assist developers in writing code. These tools suggest code snippets, help debug errors, and automate repetitive tasks, significantly speeding up the development process.

5.4 Translation and Summarization

LLMs like T5 and BERT have shown significant improvements in machine translation, allowing for more accurate translations between languages. Additionally, they are widely used for summarizing long documents or articles into concise, digestible content.

Large Language Models (LLMs) have reshaped the landscape of natural language processing, offering unprecedented capabilities for understanding and generating human language. With applications across industries ranging from content creation to healthcare, LLMs are poised to play a pivotal role in future AI-driven solutions. However, as with all powerful technologies, they come with challenges, such as computational costs, biases in data, and ethical considerations. Nevertheless, as the technology matures, the potential of LLMs in real-world applications continues to expand, opening new doors to AI innovations and breakthroughs.

18.2 Fine-tuning pre-trained LLMs (GPT, BERT)

Large Language Models (LLMs) like GPT (Generative Pretrained Transformer) and BERT (Bidirectional Encoder Representations from Transformers) have set new standards in the field of natural language processing (NLP). These models, pre-trained on massive datasets, have a remarkable ability to understand and generate human-like text across a broad range of applications. However, their performance can be further enhanced for specific tasks through a process called fine-tuning.

Fine-tuning allows these models to adapt to particular datasets or domains, making them more effective and accurate in handling specialized tasks such as sentiment analysis, question-answering, text summarization, and more. In this sub-chapter, we will explore the process of fine-tuning pre-trained LLMs, focusing on GPT and BERT. We will dive into the steps required, the techniques used, and the real-world impact of fine-tuned models.

1. What Is Fine-Tuning in LLMs?

Fine-tuning is the process of taking a pre-trained LLM and training it further on a smaller, domain-specific dataset to adapt it to the requirements of a specific task. Pre-trained models, like GPT and BERT, are trained on large corpora of general text (such as books, websites, and articles), which allows them to acquire general language skills. However, for tasks requiring specialized knowledge, fine-tuning refines the model by exposing it to task-specific examples.

1.1 Why Fine-Tuning Is Essential

- **Adaptability**: While pre-trained LLMs can understand a broad range of languages, fine-tuning helps adapt the models to the particular nuances of a given domain (e.g., healthcare, finance, legal, etc.).
- **Improved Performance**: Fine-tuning typically leads to a significant boost in model performance, especially when working with specialized tasks. For instance, a general language model might struggle with medical texts, but fine-tuning it on a medical dataset improves its understanding of domain-specific terminology.
- **Cost and Efficiency**: Training an LLM from scratch requires enormous computational resources. Fine-tuning leverages the power of a pre-trained model, drastically reducing the time and cost of training while still achieving high accuracy.

2. Fine-Tuning GPT (Generative Pretrained Transformer)

GPT, developed by OpenAI, is a generative model designed for a wide range of NLP tasks. Fine-tuning GPT involves adapting the model for tasks that require generating human-like text, such as content creation, summarization, and even more complex tasks like code generation.

2.1 Fine-Tuning Process for GPT

Preparing the Data: Fine-tuning GPT requires a dataset tailored to the specific task. For instance, if you're fine-tuning for customer support, you would gather a dataset of previous conversations, frequently asked questions (FAQs), and support documentation. This data must be cleaned and preprocessed (e.g., tokenization, removing irrelevant data) to ensure optimal performance.

Setting Up the Model: Using frameworks like Hugging Face Transformers or OpenAI API, you can load the pre-trained GPT model. These frameworks provide the necessary tools to fine-tune large models efficiently on your hardware or in the cloud.

Training the Model: During fine-tuning, you use supervised learning with labeled data, where the model learns to predict or generate the correct output based on the input text. For example, fine-tuning GPT on a medical dataset would involve providing the model with medical questions and corresponding answers.

Adjusting Hyperparameters: Fine-tuning involves adjusting hyperparameters like learning rate, batch size, and number of epochs. These hyperparameters control how the model adjusts its weights and learns from the fine-tuning data.

Evaluation: After fine-tuning, the model must be evaluated to ensure it performs well on the specific task. Common evaluation metrics include perplexity (for text generation tasks) or accuracy/F1 score (for classification tasks).

2.2 Applications of Fine-Tuned GPT

Fine-tuned GPT can be applied across various industries:

- **Content Generation**: GPT fine-tuned on a specific writing style can assist in generating blog posts, social media content, or product descriptions.
- **Customer Support**: By fine-tuning GPT with historical chat logs, it can become an AI-powered chatbot capable of answering customer inquiries in real-time.
- **Code Generation**: GPT models fine-tuned with code-related datasets can assist in generating code snippets, debugging code, or providing programming suggestions.

3. Fine-Tuning BERT (Bidirectional Encoder Representations from Transformers)

BERT, unlike GPT, is primarily designed for understanding and analyzing text, making it ideal for tasks such as question answering, text classification, and sentiment analysis. Fine-tuning BERT involves using labeled datasets to adjust the model's weights for the specific task.

3.1 Fine-Tuning Process for BERT

Preparing the Data: As with GPT, fine-tuning BERT requires task-specific data. For a text classification task, you would need a labeled dataset where each text is associated with a specific category (e.g., positive or negative for sentiment analysis). This data must be tokenized and transformed into the format that BERT expects.

Setting Up the Model: Fine-tuning BERT also involves using pre-trained models available through libraries like Hugging Face or TensorFlow. BERT models are already available with different configurations (e.g., base or large), which can be chosen depending on computational resources and task complexity.

Training the Model: Fine-tuning BERT follows a supervised learning approach. The model is trained on the domain-specific dataset with an additional output layer designed for classification or other downstream tasks. For example, for sentiment analysis, the model learns to output probabilities for different sentiment classes.

Adjusting Hyperparameters: Fine-tuning BERT also involves adjusting hyperparameters such as learning rate, batch size, number of epochs, and optimization algorithm (often Adam). These settings influence the model's convergence and performance on the task.

Evaluation: Similar to GPT, fine-tuned BERT is evaluated using task-specific metrics. For classification tasks, accuracy, precision, recall, and F1 score are commonly used. For question-answering tasks, metrics like EM (Exact Match) and F1 score are used.

3.2 Applications of Fine-Tuned BERT

Fine-tuned BERT has a wide range of practical applications:

- **Sentiment Analysis**: Fine-tuning BERT with a dataset of product reviews enables it to classify new reviews as positive, negative, or neutral, allowing businesses to gauge customer sentiment.
- **Named Entity Recognition (NER):** BERT can be fine-tuned to recognize specific entities in a text (e.g., company names, dates, or locations), which is crucial for applications like resume parsing and legal document analysis.
- **Question Answering**: Fine-tuned BERT models are highly effective in question-answering systems, such as virtual assistants or customer support bots, where the model is trained on a dataset containing questions and answers.

4. Techniques and Considerations in Fine-Tuning

4.1 Transfer Learning

Fine-tuning essentially leverages transfer learning, which allows a model trained on a large dataset (like the general text corpus used for GPT and BERT) to apply its learned knowledge to a smaller, task-specific dataset. The idea is that general language understanding (like grammar, sentence structure, and semantic meaning) can be transferred from the pre-trained model to the fine-tuning task.

4.2 Regularization and Overfitting

While fine-tuning provides significant benefits, there is always the risk of overfitting—where the model becomes too specialized to the fine-tuning data and loses its ability to generalize to new data. Techniques like dropout, weight decay, and early stopping can be used to combat overfitting and ensure that the model remains robust.

4.3 Data Augmentation

In some cases, the fine-tuning dataset may be limited. Data augmentation techniques, such as back-translation (translating text to another language and then back to the original), paraphrasing, and adding noise to data, can be used to artificially expand the dataset and improve model performance.

Fine-tuning pre-trained LLMs like GPT and BERT enables the adaptation of these powerful models to specific tasks, enhancing their performance and utility across various real-world applications. Whether you're fine-tuning GPT for creative content generation or BERT for sentiment analysis, this process significantly improves a model's ability to perform specialized tasks. By leveraging techniques such as transfer learning, hyperparameter optimization, and data augmentation, fine-tuning allows businesses and developers to unlock the true potential of LLMs in practical, real-world scenarios.

As these models continue to evolve, fine-tuning will remain a cornerstone in the deployment of advanced NLP applications across industries, driving innovation and enabling smarter, more context-aware AI systems.

18.3 Generating text, images, and code with AI

Generative AI has made tremendous strides over the past decade, revolutionizing the way we create content. One of the most exciting advancements in the field is the ability of models like GPT, DALL·E, and Codex to generate text, images, and code—three highly impactful domains of content creation. These tools leverage large language models (LLMs) and specialized deep learning architectures, which enable machines to generate highly creative and coherent outputs.

In this sub-chapter, we will explore how AI models can generate these three types of content—text, images, and code—and the potential applications in various industries. We will focus on how generative models function, the underlying principles of their training, and practical examples of how they are being used in real-world scenarios.

1. Text Generation with AI

1.1 Overview of Text Generation

Text generation has long been a core application of LLMs, particularly models like GPT-3, GPT-4, and T5. These models are trained on large corpora of text data, which allow them to understand language structure, context, and style. The model is then capable of generating human-like text given a prompt or seed sentence, which it extends or refines based on the learned patterns.

1.2 Use Cases of Text Generation

Content Creation: AI models like GPT are widely used in content creation, including writing blog posts, news articles, marketing copy, social media content, and more. Given a topic or prompt, the model can generate readable, coherent, and relevant content in a fraction of the time it would take a human.

Chatbots & Virtual Assistants: Generative models enable the creation of intelligent chatbots and virtual assistants. By understanding and generating contextually relevant responses, they can simulate human-like conversations, answer questions, and provide recommendations.

Storytelling & Creative Writing: Authors and screenwriters are increasingly turning to AI for creative inspiration. Generative models can produce short stories, dialogue, and even entire novels, with some models capable of replicating specific writing styles or genres.

Translation & Paraphrasing: AI can also be used to generate translations or paraphrases of text, allowing for cross-lingual communication and the generation of varied expressions of the same idea.

1.3 Technical Insights into Text Generation

Text generation typically involves autoregressive models (such as GPT), which predict the next token (word, phrase, or character) in a sequence based on the preceding context. This step is repeated until a complete and coherent output is generated.

The most common techniques used in training these models include:

- **Tokenization**: Breaking text into smaller pieces (tokens), which are then processed by the model.
- **Transformers**: The underlying architecture for many of these models, based on self-attention mechanisms, which allow the model to weigh the importance of each word relative to the others in a sentence.
- **Fine-Tuning**: Adapting a pre-trained model on domain-specific data to improve its performance for particular use cases.

2. Image Generation with AI

2.1 Overview of Image Generation

Image generation is another exciting frontier in generative AI, with models like DALL·E (from OpenAI), Stable Diffusion, and GANs (Generative Adversarial Networks) paving the way. These models are capable of creating images from text descriptions, allowing users to generate highly detailed and creative visuals with minimal effort. The principle behind these models is similar to that of text generation—understanding patterns in visual data and using that understanding to generate new content.

2.2 Use Cases of Image Generation

Creative Arts & Design: Artists and designers are increasingly using generative AI tools to create artwork, concept designs, and illustrations. Given a textual description of a scene or character, models like DALL·E can generate stunning images that are then refined or used as the basis for further creative work.

Advertising & Marketing: Businesses are leveraging AI to produce advertisements, banners, social media posts, and marketing materials with minimal human intervention. Generative models can quickly create engaging images that are aligned with brand identities.

Fashion Design: Generative AI is also being employed in the fashion industry to design new clothing items and accessories. These models can generate novel patterns, clothing styles, and even predict trends based on visual input.

Video Game Development: Game developers use AI to create characters, environments, and textures. AI-generated images can be used in game design or to augment the creative process, enabling faster prototyping and the creation of expansive virtual worlds.

2.3 Technical Insights into Image Generation

Image generation relies heavily on architectures like GANs and Diffusion Models:

- **GANs (Generative Adversarial Networks):** GANs consist of two neural networks— a generator and a discriminator—working in opposition to create realistic images. The generator creates images, while the discriminator evaluates them for realism.
- **Diffusion Models**: These models work by gradually transforming random noise into coherent images, ensuring high-quality outputs through iterative processes.
- **Text-to-Image Models**: Recent advancements have integrated text-based input into image generation, enabling models like DALL·E to create images based on textual descriptions. The model learns the relationships between textual prompts and visual features to generate new, unseen images.

3. Code Generation with AI

3.1 Overview of Code Generation

Code generation is another powerful application of AI, where models like Codex (from OpenAI) and Copilot (powered by Codex) can generate source code from natural language prompts. These models have been trained on vast amounts of programming-related data, including open-source code, to learn programming syntax, functions, and logical structures.

3.2 Use Cases of Code Generation

Automating Code Writing: AI models can help developers by generating code snippets, completing functions, or even writing entire modules based on high-level descriptions. This dramatically reduces development time and increases productivity.

Bug Detection and Debugging: Generative AI models can also help in identifying potential bugs in code and suggesting fixes. This can be especially valuable for large-scale applications where manual debugging is time-consuming.

Code Refactoring: AI models can assist in improving the efficiency, readability, and performance of existing code by suggesting refactorings or restructuring code blocks.

Learning and Education: AI can also be used to help learners understand programming concepts by generating examples and exercises that demonstrate coding practices and solutions to common programming problems.

3.3 Technical Insights into Code Generation

Code generation models work similarly to text generation models, with the main difference being that they are trained on programming languages rather than natural language. These models:

- Learn the syntax, structure, and common patterns of various programming languages.
- Understand higher-level abstractions (like functions, classes, and APIs) and can translate human descriptions into executable code.
- Often use fine-tuning on domain-specific coding tasks to improve accuracy for particular use cases, such as web development, data science, or machine learning.

These models may generate code in languages like Python, JavaScript, Java, or others based on the prompt provided, and they can be used to automate repetitive tasks or generate code for specific functionalities, such as creating APIs or implementing algorithms.

4. Challenges in Generating Text, Images, and Code with AI

While generative AI models show tremendous potential, they also present challenges that must be addressed:

- **Creativity and Originality**: The balance between generating creative and realistic content without copying or mimicking existing works is a key challenge. In some cases, the model may inadvertently generate biased or irrelevant content.
- **Ethical Concerns**: The generation of deepfakes, misinformation, and harmful content poses ethical dilemmas, especially in the context of text and image generation.

- **Bias in Generated Content**: AI models may produce biased content depending on the data they were trained on, and this bias can be reflected in the generated output, whether text, images, or code.
- **Quality Control**: Ensuring that the generated content meets the desired quality standards is a significant challenge, especially when generating complex outputs like code or highly detailed images.

Generative AI models have revolutionized the way we create content across multiple domains. From generating coherent and contextually relevant text to creating stunning visuals and writing functional code, these models are transforming industries such as entertainment, marketing, software development, and more. By leveraging the power of advanced models like GPT, DALL·E, and Codex, businesses can automate tasks, enhance creativity, and streamline workflows.

However, as generative AI continues to evolve, it's crucial to address the ethical, technical, and social challenges associated with these technologies. By fostering responsible development and usage, we can ensure that AI-generated content serves to augment human creativity and productivity in meaningful and positive ways.

18.4 Building AI-powered assistants with LLM APIs

In recent years, the development of large language models (LLMs), such as GPT-3, GPT-4, and BERT, has dramatically transformed the capabilities of AI-powered assistants. These assistants, which leverage advanced natural language processing (NLP) techniques, can understand and generate human-like responses to a wide variety of inputs, making them essential tools in applications ranging from customer support to personal productivity.

Using LLMs through APIs, businesses and developers can build AI-powered assistants that help streamline processes, engage customers, and automate tasks across numerous industries. This section will walk you through the process of building such AI-powered assistants using LLM APIs, exploring the technical aspects, practical applications, and key considerations involved in the development process.

1. Understanding the Role of AI-Powered Assistants

1.1 What is an AI-powered Assistant?

An AI-powered assistant is a software application that uses artificial intelligence to perform tasks, answer questions, or simulate conversations with users. These assistants typically rely on natural language understanding (NLU) and natural language generation (NLG) to understand user input, interpret it, and generate meaningful responses.

There are various types of AI-powered assistants:

- **Virtual Assistants (e.g., Siri, Alexa, Google Assistant):** Personal assistants that help with daily tasks such as setting reminders, sending messages, playing music, and controlling smart devices.
- **Customer Support Assistants**: AI-powered chatbots designed to help customers with common inquiries, technical issues, or support requests.
- **Productivity Assistants**: Assistants that help with scheduling, note-taking, organizing workflows, and other productivity tasks.

By using advanced LLMs, these assistants can handle increasingly complex queries and provide more accurate, context-aware responses.

1.2 Applications of AI-Powered Assistants

AI assistants are being integrated into many real-world applications:

- **Customer Service**: Chatbots powered by LLMs can handle support tickets, provide 24/7 assistance, and resolve common issues without human intervention.
- **Personal Productivity**: Virtual assistants like Google Assistant and Apple's Siri help users stay organized by setting reminders, scheduling meetings, and managing tasks.
- **Healthcare**: AI assistants can triage patient symptoms, schedule appointments, or provide health-related information based on user queries.
- **E-commerce**: AI-powered shopping assistants can help users find products, recommend items, and assist in checkout processes.

With LLMs, these applications have become more intelligent, capable of understanding nuanced queries, adapting to different contexts, and handling a wide range of conversational scenarios.

2. Getting Started with LLM APIs

2.1 Overview of LLM APIs

Large language models like GPT-3 (developed by OpenAI) and GPT-4 provide developers with the ability to integrate AI capabilities into their applications via APIs. These APIs enable developers to send text input to the model, receive a text-based response, and implement conversational agents, content generators, or problem-solvers with minimal effort.

Some of the most popular LLM APIs include:

- **OpenAI API**: Provides access to models like GPT-3 and GPT-4, allowing developers to generate human-like text and build conversational agents.
- **Hugging Face**: Offers a wide range of pre-trained NLP models, including transformers for tasks such as text generation, question answering, and summarization.
- **Google Cloud AI**: Provides APIs for text generation, translation, and sentiment analysis using models like BERT and T5.
- **Azure Cognitive Services**: Offers language models and AI services for building chatbots, text analysis, and conversational AI applications.

The beauty of using these APIs is that developers do not need to worry about training models from scratch. Instead, they can focus on integrating the models into their applications and fine-tuning them to their specific needs.

2.2 Setting Up API Access

To use LLM APIs, the first step is to sign up for an API key from the service provider. Most of these platforms offer easy-to-follow documentation that explains how to set up API access. For instance:

- **OpenAI**: To use the GPT-3 or GPT-4 models, you need to create an account on OpenAI's platform, request an API key, and integrate it into your application.
- **Hugging Face**: Hugging Face provides pre-trained transformer models, and you can interact with them via their API (or via Python libraries like Transformers).
- **Google Cloud AI & Azure Cognitive Services**: Both offer API access for building AI assistants and integrating NLP capabilities, with detailed SDKs and code examples.

Once the API key is acquired, you can begin making HTTP requests to the API, passing in user inputs and receiving model-generated responses.

3. Building Your AI-Powered Assistant

3.1 Designing the User Interaction

Before diving into the technical aspects of integrating an LLM API, it's important to plan the flow of interaction with the AI assistant. Here are the steps for building a successful AI-powered assistant:

- **Understand the Use Case**: Determine the purpose of the assistant. Will it assist with customer service, act as a personal productivity tool, or handle specific tasks like product recommendations or scheduling?
- **User Input Format**: Consider how users will interact with the assistant. Is it through text, voice commands, or both? For text-based interactions, the system will need to handle input, preprocess it, and send it to the LLM API.
- **Response Handling**: Define how the assistant will respond. Should it provide short, concise answers or detailed explanations? Will it include links or images? This will determine how you structure the output from the LLM API.

3.2 Interacting with the API

The core of building an AI assistant using LLMs lies in how you interact with the API. For example, using the OpenAI API involves sending HTTP requests with input text and receiving generated responses. Here's a simple example in Python using the OpenAI API:

```
import openai

# Initialize OpenAI API with your key
openai.api_key = 'your-api-key'

# Send a prompt to GPT-3 and get a response
response = openai.Completion.create(
    engine="text-davinci-003",  # Choose a GPT-3 model
    prompt="What is the capital of France?",
    max_tokens=50
)

# Extract and print the response
print(response.choices[0].text.strip())
```

In this example:

- The prompt represents the question or command that you want the AI assistant to respond to.
- The max_tokens parameter specifies the length of the generated response.
- The response.choices[0].text.strip() part extracts the model's response, which is then printed.

The response can be further processed for specific applications, such as formatting it, adding additional logic, or structuring it into a conversation flow.

3.3 Fine-Tuning and Personalizing the Assistant

While LLM APIs provide powerful pre-trained models, fine-tuning can help tailor the assistant to specific needs. Fine-tuning involves training the model on additional, domain-specific data, such as customer queries for a support chatbot or industry-specific knowledge for a virtual assistant.

For example:

- **Custom Knowledge Base**: If building a customer service assistant, fine-tuning the model on a knowledge base specific to your business, including frequently asked questions, product catalogs, and support documentation, will enhance its performance.
- **Conversational Design**: Some platforms, like Dialogflow and Rasa, allow you to design conversation flows and integrate them with LLM APIs, ensuring smooth interactions and contextual awareness.

Fine-tuning may require access to specialized datasets or additional computational resources, but it can significantly improve the relevance and accuracy of the assistant's responses.

4. Key Considerations for Building AI-powered Assistants

4.1 Handling Ambiguity and Multiple Intents

One of the primary challenges when building AI-powered assistants is handling ambiguous queries or questions that may have multiple interpretations. AI models might struggle to choose the correct response unless properly trained or prompted.

Techniques to address this:

- **Clarifying Questions**: The assistant can ask follow-up questions to disambiguate user inputs.
- **Contextual Awareness**: Leveraging context from previous interactions (e.g., conversation history) helps the assistant generate more relevant responses.

4.2 User Feedback and Continuous Improvement

Once your assistant is deployed, gathering feedback from users is critical for continuous improvement. The assistant's responses can be monitored, feedback collected, and the model can be iteratively refined to enhance performance.

4.3 Ethical Considerations and Data Privacy

AI assistants need to operate responsibly by considering ethical concerns and protecting user data privacy. Key aspects include:

- **Data Encryption**: Ensure that any personal or sensitive information shared with the assistant is encrypted and stored securely.
- **Bias Mitigation**: Ensure that the assistant provides unbiased responses and is trained to recognize and avoid harmful language.

Building AI-powered assistants using LLM APIs is a powerful way to integrate advanced conversational capabilities into a wide range of applications. With easy access to state-of-the-art models like GPT-3 and GPT-4 through APIs, developers can quickly create intelligent systems that enhance user experiences, automate tasks, and streamline operations.

By carefully designing user interactions, fine-tuning models for specific use cases, and addressing technical and ethical challenges, businesses can leverage AI to improve customer engagement, productivity, and overall satisfaction. Whether you're building a virtual assistant, a customer service bot, or a productivity tool, AI-powered assistants can transform how we interact with technology.

18.5 Ethical concerns in generative AI

The rapid development and adoption of Generative AI technologies, particularly large language models (LLMs) such as GPT-3, GPT-4, and other deep learning-based models, have brought about profound shifts in the capabilities of AI systems. These models are capable of generating human-like text, images, and even code, which can have remarkable applications in content creation, customer service, education, and much more. However, with these advancements come a range of ethical concerns that need careful consideration to ensure that generative AI is used responsibly and for the greater good.

In this section, we will explore the key ethical concerns surrounding generative AI, with a focus on how they affect users, developers, and society as a whole. We will also discuss potential solutions to mitigate these risks and establish guidelines for the ethical use of generative AI in real-world applications.

1. Misinformation and Disinformation

1.1 The Risk of Fake News and Manipulation

Generative AI models like GPT-3 and GPT-4 can generate coherent, persuasive, and realistic text, which can be used to create news articles, social media posts, and blogs. While this has valuable applications, it also poses a significant risk in the form of misinformation and disinformation. These models can generate content that is entirely fabricated but appears authentic. This opens the door for malicious actors to create convincing fake news, manipulate public opinion, or spread harmful narratives.

Examples:

- **Fake Articles and News**: An AI model could be used to generate articles or social media posts that present false or misleading information, which could go viral and influence public perception.
- **Political Manipulation**: In elections or politically sensitive contexts, generative AI could be leveraged to create divisive content or propaganda that misleads voters.

1.2 Addressing Misinformation

To mitigate this ethical concern, several measures can be taken:

- **Fact-Checking**: Implementing automatic fact-checking systems for content generated by AI can help identify inaccuracies and prevent the spread of false information.
- **Content Verification**: By providing clear indicators that content is AI-generated, users can better distinguish between legitimate and synthetic content.

- **Regulations**: Governments and regulatory bodies can introduce laws to ensure responsible use of generative AI, especially in the context of political content and public discourse.

2. Bias and Discrimination

2.1 The Problem of Bias in AI Models

Bias in AI is a well-documented issue, and generative AI is no exception. Large language models are trained on vast datasets scraped from the internet, which means they inherit the biases present in those datasets. These biases can be based on factors such as race, gender, ethnicity, age, and socio-economic status, and can manifest in a variety of ways:

- **Stereotyping**: AI models may perpetuate harmful stereotypes by generating biased or discriminatory content. For instance, a generative AI model might output biased job recommendations based on gender or ethnicity.
- **Exclusion of Minority Groups**: The model might produce responses that underrepresent or marginalize minority perspectives and voices.

2.2 Reducing Bias in Generative AI

Efforts to mitigate bias in generative AI models should be made at both the training and application stages:

- **Diverse Datasets**: Ensuring that the datasets used to train these models are diverse and representative of various demographic groups can help reduce bias. It is crucial to evaluate datasets for potential biases related to gender, race, and other factors.
- **Bias Detection and Mitigation Algorithms**: Implementing tools that can detect and correct bias in the outputs generated by AI models can help ensure fairness. Techniques such as adversarial debiasing and fairness constraints can be used to reduce discriminatory behavior.
- **Human-in-the-loop**: In certain high-stakes applications, such as hiring or law enforcement, it may be necessary to have human oversight to ensure that AI-generated decisions are fair and free of bias.

3. Intellectual Property (IP) and Copyright

3.1 The Issue of Ownership

Generative AI can create a wide range of content—text, images, music, and code. However, the question of ownership becomes murky when it comes to content generated by AI. Who owns the rights to AI-generated content? Is it the creator of the AI system, the person who provided the input to the AI, or the entity that owns the AI model?

For example, an artist using a generative model to create digital artwork may not be sure if they hold the intellectual property rights to the final image. Similarly, AI-generated content such as articles, books, or advertisements could raise concerns about whether those works are subject to copyright protections or if they can be freely reproduced without crediting the creators of the models.

3.2 Resolving IP Issues in Generative AI

To address these concerns, clear legal frameworks need to be established:

- **Copyright Laws for AI-Created Content**: Legal systems may need to adapt and develop new guidelines for defining ownership of AI-generated works, ensuring that the creators or users of generative models have rights to the content they produce.
- **Transparency in Usage**: Developers and companies using generative AI should clearly communicate who holds the intellectual property rights of AI-generated works. This transparency will help avoid disputes in commercial applications and creative industries.
- **Fair Use and Licensing**: There should be proper licensing mechanisms that ensure AI-generated content does not infringe on the intellectual property of others, particularly when training models on publicly available data.

4. Privacy and Data Security

4.1 The Risk of Sensitive Data Leakage

Generative AI models can sometimes inadvertently generate content that includes sensitive or private information. This can occur if the model has been trained on private datasets or if it generates output based on user inputs that contain personal data. For instance, a chatbot powered by generative AI might leak private customer information during interactions, posing a serious privacy risk.

Examples:

- **Data Leaks**: Generative models trained on sensitive datasets could unintentionally reveal private information about individuals, such as names, addresses, or financial details.
- **Data Retention**: Some generative models retain user inputs, which could be accessed later by malicious actors or used to build user profiles without consent.

4.2 Addressing Privacy Concerns

To mitigate privacy concerns, the following strategies can be employed:

- **Data Encryption**: Ensuring that data is securely stored and transmitted to prevent unauthorized access.
- **User Consent**: Always obtaining user consent for data collection and clarifying how data will be used in training AI models.
- **Privacy-Preserving Techniques**: Techniques like differential privacy and secure multi-party computation can be used to ensure that private information is not exposed during model training or inference.

5. Accountability and Responsibility

5.1 Who is Responsible for AI Actions?

Generative AI systems operate autonomously, generating outputs based on their training data and inputs. However, if these outputs cause harm—such as generating offensive content, making biased decisions, or misleading users—who is held responsible? Is it the developers who created the model, the company that deployed the AI, or the user who interacted with it?

This raises important questions about accountability in AI development:

- **Liability**: In case of harm caused by AI, it's crucial to establish clear guidelines for determining liability. Is the company that deployed the model responsible, or does responsibility lie with the developer who trained the model?
- **Transparency**: Developers should be transparent about the limitations and potential risks of AI systems, so users can make informed decisions when interacting with them.

5.2 Establishing Ethical Guidelines

To navigate accountability issues, industry standards and ethical guidelines are necessary. These guidelines should cover:

- **Clear Communication**: AI developers and organizations must provide clear documentation about the capabilities, limitations, and potential risks of their models.
- **Governance Models**: Regulatory bodies could be established to oversee the use of generative AI technologies, ensuring that companies follow ethical standards and guidelines.

While generative AI has the potential to revolutionize industries and applications, its ethical implications must be carefully considered. The ability of large language models to generate content at scale presents risks related to misinformation, bias, intellectual property, privacy, and accountability. To ensure that generative AI benefits society as a whole, developers, businesses, and regulators must work together to establish ethical frameworks, safeguard against harm, and ensure transparency in the use of these powerful technologies.

By prioritizing ethical considerations, we can create a future where generative AI is used responsibly, fostering innovation while protecting the values and rights of individuals and communities.

19. AutoML & No-Code ML Tools

In this chapter, we explore the rise of AutoML and no-code machine learning tools, making it easier than ever for non-experts to build and deploy machine learning models. You'll learn how AutoML platforms automatically handle tasks like data preprocessing, model selection, and hyperparameter tuning, saving time and effort while achieving competitive results. We'll also dive into no-code ML tools that enable users to create models using simple drag-and-drop interfaces, empowering business professionals and data enthusiasts to solve complex problems without writing code. Through hands-on examples, we'll explore popular AutoML platforms like Google Cloud AutoML, H2O.ai, and Microsoft Azure ML, as well as no-code solutions like Teachable Machine and DataRobot. By the end of this chapter, you'll be able to leverage these tools to quickly create high-performance machine learning models and integrate them into real-world applications, democratizing the power of AI. □□□

19.1 Introduction to AutoML and its applications

Machine Learning (ML) has grown into one of the most transformative technologies of the modern era, offering the potential to unlock insights, automate complex processes, and solve problems across a wide range of industries. However, while the benefits of ML are undeniable, traditional ML development comes with its own set of challenges. These challenges stem from the complexities inherent in designing, training, and deploying models, which often require extensive expertise in mathematics, programming, and domain knowledge.

This is where AutoML (Automated Machine Learning) enters the scene. AutoML refers to the process of automating the design, selection, and training of machine learning models. The goal of AutoML is to make machine learning more accessible by allowing non-experts to build robust models without needing to deeply understand the underlying algorithms and complex workflows.

In this sub-chapter, we will explore what AutoML is, how it works, its applications, and the key tools that are revolutionizing how machine learning models are built and deployed. By the end of this section, you'll have a solid understanding of AutoML's potential, its use cases, and how it is democratizing access to machine learning.

1. What is AutoML?

At its core, AutoML seeks to simplify the machine learning pipeline by automating critical stages of the ML process, which include:

- **Data Preprocessing**: Automatically handling data cleaning, normalization, and feature engineering to prepare the data for model training.
- **Model Selection**: Automatically selecting the best model from a variety of algorithms based on the given dataset.
- **Hyperparameter Tuning**: Finding the optimal set of hyperparameters to improve the performance of the model.
- **Model Evaluation**: Assessing the model's accuracy, performance, and robustness using appropriate metrics.
- **Model Deployment**: Making the trained model available for real-world use by integrating it into a production environment.

This automation means that the machine learning process is simplified, and the need for in-depth technical expertise is reduced. Users, even without advanced knowledge of machine learning, can focus on the problem at hand while leveraging powerful ML tools to generate high-performing models.

2. How Does AutoML Work?

AutoML works through a series of automated steps that streamline the development of machine learning models. The key aspects of AutoML are:

2.1 Automated Data Preprocessing

One of the most time-consuming tasks in machine learning is preparing the data. AutoML platforms automate this process by taking raw, unstructured data and applying transformations that make it suitable for model training. This includes handling missing values, scaling numeric features, encoding categorical variables, and performing feature selection or dimensionality reduction.

For example, AutoML tools can automatically identify and handle missing data by imputing values or removing incomplete records. They can also automate feature engineering, where they identify relationships or transformations of raw data that might enhance model performance.

2.2 Model Selection

AutoML platforms come with a library of models (such as decision trees, support vector machines, neural networks, etc.), and they automatically test a wide range of these models to identify which one best fits the problem and dataset. For instance, if you are building a classification model, AutoML might test logistic regression, random forests, or gradient boosting models, then select the one that provides the best performance based on accuracy, precision, or recall.

This model selection process saves significant time compared to the traditional approach, where a data scientist manually chooses and tests different algorithms based on the dataset.

2.3 Hyperparameter Optimization

A critical part of machine learning is hyperparameter tuning, which involves adjusting the model's settings to improve performance. AutoML platforms automate hyperparameter optimization by systematically experimenting with different values of the hyperparameters (e.g., learning rate, batch size, regularization strength) and identifying the combination that results in the best model performance.

This process, often done through techniques such as grid search or random search, ensures that the model is fine-tuned for optimal results, without the need for manual intervention.

2.4 Model Evaluation and Validation

Once a model has been trained, AutoML tools automatically evaluate its performance using appropriate metrics. Depending on the type of problem, the evaluation might involve metrics like accuracy, precision, recall, F1 score, mean absolute error (MAE), or root mean squared error (RMSE).

AutoML platforms also apply cross-validation techniques, where the model is tested on multiple subsets of the data to ensure it generalizes well to new, unseen data. This reduces the risk of overfitting and ensures that the model is robust.

2.5 Model Deployment

Once the model is trained and evaluated, AutoML tools often include functionality for deploying the model into a production environment. The deployment phase typically involves creating an API, integrating the model into a business application, or embedding it into a device or system for real-time inference.

Some AutoML tools also enable model monitoring and retraining, which ensures that the model continues to perform well over time and adapts to any changes in the data distribution or external conditions.

3. Applications of AutoML

AutoML has a wide range of applications across different industries. By automating many aspects of the machine learning workflow, AutoML makes it possible for individuals and organizations to leverage AI technologies without requiring expert knowledge of machine learning. Below are some of the key areas where AutoML is being widely adopted:

3.1 Healthcare

In healthcare, AutoML can be used to develop predictive models for disease diagnosis, patient risk assessment, and medical image analysis. By automating the model-building process, AutoML tools allow healthcare professionals to focus on analyzing data and interpreting results rather than spending time on technical aspects of machine learning.

For instance, AutoML can help in diagnosing diseases like cancer by analyzing medical images (e.g., X-rays, MRIs) or genetic data. It can also be used for predictive analytics, such as forecasting patient admissions or predicting disease outbreaks.

3.2 Finance

In the finance sector, AutoML is used for credit scoring, fraud detection, algorithmic trading, and customer segmentation. Banks and financial institutions can leverage AutoML to analyze transaction data, identify patterns of fraudulent behavior, and develop strategies to mitigate financial risks.

AutoML tools can also be used to predict market trends, enabling hedge funds and traders to make data-driven investment decisions without deep technical expertise in data science.

3.3 Retail

In retail, AutoML can help businesses build recommendation systems that suggest products based on customers' previous purchases or browsing behaviors. These recommendation engines can drive higher sales and improve customer satisfaction.

AutoML can also be used for demand forecasting, inventory management, and customer segmentation, enabling retailers to optimize supply chains, predict trends, and personalize marketing campaigns.

3.4 Marketing

Marketers can use AutoML to automate customer segmentation, sentiment analysis, and personalized marketing campaigns. By using historical customer data, AutoML tools can help identify high-value customers, predict customer behavior, and tailor marketing efforts to maximize ROI.

AutoML can also be used to analyze social media data, enabling businesses to understand public sentiment and adjust their marketing strategies accordingly.

3.5 Manufacturing and Industrial Automation

In manufacturing, AutoML can help optimize production processes by predicting machine failures, quality control, and predictive maintenance. AutoML platforms can analyze sensor data from machinery to predict breakdowns before they happen, allowing companies to perform preventive maintenance and reduce downtime.

4. Popular AutoML Tools and Platforms

Several AutoML tools have emerged to meet the growing demand for machine learning automation. These tools are designed to simplify the process of building and deploying machine learning models for users with varying levels of expertise. Some of the most popular AutoML tools include:

- **Google Cloud AutoML**: Google's AutoML suite offers tools for image, text, and video processing, as well as natural language processing tasks. It is designed to be user-friendly and integrates with Google Cloud's ecosystem.
- **H2O.ai**: H2O.ai is an open-source platform that offers AutoML capabilities for tasks such as classification, regression, and time-series forecasting. It provides both a graphical interface and a programming API for flexible use.
- **DataRobot**: DataRobot is a comprehensive AutoML platform that automates model selection, feature engineering, and hyperparameter tuning. It supports a wide range of use cases, including business intelligence, predictive analytics, and deep learning.

- **Microsoft Azure AutoML**: Microsoft's Azure AutoML offers a cloud-based environment for automating the end-to-end ML process. It is highly customizable and suitable for a wide range of industries and applications.

AutoML has revolutionized the way machine learning models are developed, making it easier than ever for businesses and individuals to create powerful, data-driven applications without requiring deep technical expertise. By automating key aspects of the ML pipeline—such as data preprocessing, model selection, and hyperparameter optimization—AutoML platforms enable faster, more efficient model creation, with fewer technical barriers to entry.

From healthcare to finance, retail to marketing, the applications of AutoML are vast and growing. As AutoML tools continue to evolve, we can expect even greater accessibility and further democratization of machine learning, paving the way for innovative solutions across industries.

Ultimately, AutoML is not just about making machine learning easier—it's about unlocking the full potential of AI for everyone, regardless of technical skill, and empowering businesses and organizations to make smarter, data-driven decisions at scale.

19.2 Comparing popular AutoML platforms (Google AutoML, H2O.ai, Auto-Sklearn)

As the use of AutoML continues to grow, many platforms have emerged to cater to a wide variety of machine learning tasks, from image classification to natural language processing (NLP) and regression. Choosing the right AutoML platform depends on several factors such as the user's level of expertise, the complexity of the problem at hand, and the computational resources available. In this sub-chapter, we will compare three popular AutoML platforms: Google AutoML, H2O.ai, and Auto-Sklearn. Each of these platforms offers unique features, strengths, and use cases, so understanding their differences is crucial when deciding which one to use for a specific project.

1. Google AutoML

Overview: Google Cloud AutoML is a suite of machine learning products that enables users to build custom models without deep knowledge of ML. The platform is designed to simplify complex ML workflows by offering automated tools for model training, hyperparameter tuning, and model evaluation. Google AutoML supports a variety of machine learning tasks, including image classification, object detection, natural language processing, and translation. It is primarily a cloud-based service, integrated with Google Cloud, making it a good choice for users who are already embedded within the Google ecosystem.

Key Features:

- **Wide Range of Applications**: Google AutoML offers tools for text, image, and video processing. It includes services such as AutoML Vision, AutoML Natural Language, and AutoML Tables (for structured data).
- **Ease of Use**: Google AutoML is designed for users with little to no machine learning background. The user-friendly graphical interface allows users to upload their data and build models with minimal intervention.
- **Custom Model Building**: Users can train models based on their specific datasets. Google AutoML offers the flexibility to fine-tune the models by adjusting parameters or using pre-trained models.
- **Cloud Integration**: The platform is tightly integrated with Google Cloud, meaning that users can easily scale their models using Google's infrastructure and deploy them into production directly from the platform.
- **Model Deployment**: Google AutoML makes it easy to deploy models to the cloud, integrate them into applications, and monitor their performance.

Pros:

- **Highly Automated**: Google AutoML takes care of most aspects of the machine learning pipeline, from data preprocessing to model selection and training.
- **State-of-the-art Models**: Google AutoML uses cutting-edge machine learning models, including neural networks, and integrates with Google's pre-trained models for enhanced accuracy.
- **Scalability**: Because the platform is hosted in the cloud, users can easily scale their models to handle large datasets and complex tasks.
- **Integration with Google Cloud**: It integrates well with other Google Cloud services, which can be useful for businesses already using Google's ecosystem.

Cons:

- **Pricing**: While Google AutoML offers a pay-as-you-go pricing model, the costs can escalate for large-scale models or long-running tasks.

- **Limited Customization**: Although it's easy to use, some advanced users might feel restricted by the lack of deep customization options compared to open-source platforms.

2. H2O.ai

Overview: H2O.ai is an open-source machine learning platform designed for enterprise-level solutions. It provides a suite of tools that support AutoML, enabling users to build and deploy models for a wide range of use cases, including regression, classification, and time-series forecasting. H2O.ai's platform offers powerful ML algorithms, and its AutoML functionality is designed to handle complex business problems with ease.

Key Features:

- **Advanced Algorithms**: H2O.ai supports various state-of-the-art algorithms such as Gradient Boosting Machines (GBM), Deep Learning, and Random Forests. It also offers support for ensemble learning and automated feature engineering.
- **Scalability**: H2O.ai is designed to scale to handle big data workloads. The platform can work with large datasets across distributed computing environments and supports integration with Hadoop, Spark, and Kubernetes.
- **Open Source**: The platform is open-source, which makes it highly customizable for users who want to fine-tune their models or create specific solutions.
- **AutoML**: H2O.ai's AutoML capabilities are highly robust and include automatic preprocessing, feature engineering, model training, hyperparameter tuning, and model validation. It automatically selects the best model and parameters for a given task.
- **Interpretability**: H2O.ai includes tools for model interpretability, such as SHAP (Shapley additive explanations), making it easier for users to understand how their models make predictions.

Pros:

- **Enterprise-Grade**: H2O.ai is suitable for large organizations, offering enterprise-level scalability and integration capabilities.
- **Customizable**: Being open-source, H2O.ai allows advanced users to modify the platform's code to suit their needs.
- **Big Data Ready**: It is capable of processing large-scale datasets and is well-suited for industries where big data plays a central role.
- **Model Explainability**: The inclusion of interpretability features like SHAP helps users understand the decision-making process of their models.

Cons:

- **Complexity**: While it offers a powerful set of tools, the platform may be intimidating for beginners due to its complexity.
- **Limited Support for Non-technical Users**: H2O.ai requires a basic understanding of machine learning and may not be as beginner-friendly as Google AutoML.

3. Auto-Sklearn

Overview: Auto-Sklearn is an open-source AutoML library built on top of scikit-learn, one of the most popular machine learning libraries in Python. Auto-Sklearn automates the process of model selection, hyperparameter optimization, and ensemble learning. It is designed for users who are familiar with Python and want an easy-to-use yet powerful tool for building machine learning models.

Key Features:

- **Model Selection**: Auto-Sklearn automatically chooses the best algorithms for classification or regression tasks from a predefined pool of models available in scikit-learn.
- **Hyperparameter Optimization**: It uses Bayesian optimization to find the optimal hyperparameters for each model, improving the accuracy of the resulting machine learning models.
- **Ensemble Learning**: Auto-Sklearn automatically generates an ensemble of models by combining several models to create a more robust final model.
- **Scikit-learn Compatibility**: Since it is built on top of scikit-learn, Auto-Sklearn is highly compatible with scikit-learn's ecosystem, allowing users to seamlessly integrate AutoML into their existing machine learning workflows.

Pros:

- **Open Source and Free**: Auto-Sklearn is free to use and open-source, making it an excellent choice for developers on a budget or those who need to customize the tool for their specific use case.
- **Easy Integration**: Because it is built on scikit-learn, it integrates easily with other Python libraries, such as pandas, NumPy, and matplotlib.

- **Great for Classification and Regression**: Auto-Sklearn excels at classification and regression tasks, which are common in many real-world machine learning applications.

Cons:

- **Limited to Python**: Auto-Sklearn is built for the Python ecosystem, so it may not be suitable for users who prefer working in other languages.
- **Requires Some Technical Knowledge**: While Auto-Sklearn is more user-friendly than developing models from scratch, it still requires some familiarity with Python and scikit-learn.

4. Comparing the Platforms

Ease of Use:

- Google AutoML is the most user-friendly of the three, providing a drag-and-drop interface and minimal technical complexity. It's ideal for non-experts who need to build models quickly.
- H2O.ai is a bit more complex but offers a more powerful set of features, especially for big data use cases. It's suitable for enterprise users with more technical expertise.
- Auto-Sklearn is best suited for developers who are already comfortable with Python and scikit-learn. It provides a lot of automation but still requires some level of familiarity with coding.

Customization:

- Google AutoML offers limited customization but allows some fine-tuning of models through its interface.
- H2O.ai is highly customizable, especially because it is open-source. Developers can create custom algorithms and workflows.
- Auto-Sklearn allows users to modify models and integrate it easily with other Python libraries, though it may not offer as much customization as H2O.ai.

Scalability:

- Google AutoML is cloud-based and scales well with Google Cloud infrastructure.
- H2O.ai is designed for big data workloads and can scale across distributed systems.

- Auto-Sklearn does not scale as well as the other two, making it more suited for smaller to mid-sized datasets.

Pricing:

- Google AutoML operates on a pay-as-you-go model, which can become expensive depending on the model's complexity and the amount of compute power required.
- H2O.ai is open-source and free, but there are paid enterprise options with additional support.
- Auto-Sklearn is also open-source and free to use, making it the most budget-friendly option for individual developers or small teams.

The choice between Google AutoML, H2O.ai, and Auto-Sklearn depends on the specific needs of the user and the project at hand. Google AutoML is ideal for those who need a quick, scalable solution with minimal machine learning expertise. H2O.ai is best for organizations dealing with big data and requiring advanced features, scalability, and model interpretability. Auto-Sklearn offers a more technical, open-source solution for Python developers looking to automate machine learning workflows with minimal overhead.

By understanding the strengths and limitations of these platforms, you can choose the one that best aligns with your project's goals and your team's expertise.

19.3 No-code ML tools for non-technical users

In the past, machine learning (ML) was largely reserved for data scientists and engineers due to its complexity, steep learning curves, and the need for specialized coding skills. However, as the demand for AI solutions has exploded across industries, there has been a concerted effort to democratize ML by creating no-code ML tools. These platforms enable non-technical users to build, train, and deploy machine learning models without writing a single line of code.

No-code tools are empowering a wider audience, including business analysts, marketers, product managers, and other professionals, to integrate machine learning into their workflows and processes. In this sub-chapter, we will explore some of the most popular no-code ML tools available today, their key features, and how they make it easier for non-technical users to harness the power of machine learning.

1. What are No-Code ML Tools?

No-code machine learning tools provide intuitive, visual interfaces for building and deploying machine learning models. These platforms abstract away the technical complexity of ML, such as data preprocessing, feature selection, model selection, training, and evaluation. Instead, they enable users to interact with drag-and-drop components, sliders, and pre-configured templates to create their models.

No-code ML tools are designed to lower the barrier to entry for machine learning and artificial intelligence, allowing anyone with domain knowledge to use AI to solve real-world problems. Whether it's predicting customer behavior, classifying images, or automating tasks, these tools are democratizing machine learning for a broader audience.

2. Key Features of No-Code ML Tools

While each no-code ML tool offers unique features, there are several common functionalities that these platforms provide to help users get started:

1. Data Import and Preprocessing

- **Ease of Data Upload**: Users can easily upload their datasets from various sources such as spreadsheets, CSV files, cloud storage (e.g., Google Drive, AWS S3), or APIs.
- **Data Cleaning and Transformation**: These tools typically provide pre-built options for handling missing values, scaling and normalizing features, encoding categorical variables, and transforming data into formats suitable for training models.

2. Model Selection and Training

- **Prebuilt Algorithms**: Most no-code platforms offer a collection of ML algorithms like linear regression, decision trees, clustering, and neural networks that users can apply to their data.
- **AutoML Features**: Many no-code tools use automated machine learning (AutoML) processes to select the best model for the task at hand, based on the user's data and problem type.
- **Customization Options**: Users may be able to tweak certain hyperparameters and settings to better fit the needs of their particular use case.

3. Model Evaluation and Performance Metrics

- **Evaluation Metrics**: Users can assess the performance of their models using standard metrics like accuracy, precision, recall, F1 score, or mean squared error (MSE).
- **Model Comparison**: Many platforms offer a side-by-side comparison of different models, so users can choose the one that best suits their data and goals.

4. Deployment and Integration

- **One-click Deployment**: After a model is trained and validated, no-code tools allow for simple deployment, usually in the form of an API or web service. This makes it easy to integrate the model into production systems or applications.
- **Integration with Business Tools**: Some platforms allow users to integrate their models directly into business systems such as CRMs, marketing platforms, or customer support tools without the need for custom coding.

5. Monitoring and Maintenance

- **Real-Time Predictions**: Once deployed, the models can generate real-time predictions through APIs or dashboards, allowing non-technical users to interact with their AI models effortlessly.
- **Model Monitoring**: These platforms often include tools for tracking model performance over time, including metrics, predictions, and user interactions, to ensure models continue to operate effectively.

3. Popular No-Code ML Tools

Let's take a look at some of the top no-code ML tools available for non-technical users:

1. Google AutoML (Cloud AutoML)

Google AutoML is a robust cloud-based platform that offers a suite of machine learning products designed for users without coding expertise. It includes tools like AutoML Vision, AutoML Natural Language, and AutoML Tables, which allow users to build and deploy models for tasks such as image classification, text analysis, and structured data prediction.

- **Key Features**: Google AutoML offers a highly user-friendly interface where users can simply upload their data, choose the type of model they want to train (e.g., image, text, or tabular data), and let the platform automatically handle the heavy lifting of training and optimizing the model.

- **Best For**: Image and text analysis, as well as predictive modeling with tabular data (like sales forecasting or customer churn prediction).
- **Advantages**: One of the key advantages of Google AutoML is its seamless integration with Google Cloud, making it easy to scale models and deploy them within production applications.

2. H2O.ai Driverless AI

H2O.ai's Driverless AI is an enterprise-focused platform that offers advanced automated machine learning capabilities. It provides an easy-to-use interface where users can upload their data, select a target variable, and let the platform automatically perform tasks like feature engineering, model selection, and hyperparameter tuning.

- **Key Features**: The platform supports supervised and unsupervised learning, time-series forecasting, and deep learning tasks. It also includes AutoML and Explainable AI features to ensure that users can interpret model results.
- **Best For**: Users with slightly more technical background who need enterprise-grade features, such as predictive maintenance or financial forecasting.
- **Advantages**: Driverless AI's key advantage is its scalability and ability to handle large datasets. It also offers interpretable machine learning models, which are essential for regulated industries.

3. BigML

BigML is an intuitive, user-friendly platform that allows users to create machine learning models with minimal effort. The platform supports a range of ML tasks including classification, regression, clustering, anomaly detection, and time-series forecasting.

- **Key Features**: BigML includes a visual interface for data exploration, model creation, and performance evaluation. It allows users to train models with drag-and-drop functionality and offers features like automated feature engineering, model interpretability, and model validation.
- **Best For**: Small to medium businesses looking for an easy way to apply machine learning to their operations.
- **Advantages**: BigML's visual interface is simple, but the platform is also powerful enough to handle more advanced use cases. It also supports model deployment through REST APIs, making it easy to integrate models into web applications.

4. DataRobot

DataRobot is a powerful no-code platform that automates the process of building and deploying machine learning models. It supports a wide variety of use cases, from predictive analytics to time-series forecasting and classification tasks.

- **Key Features**: DataRobot offers an automatic model selection process where users simply upload their dataset, and the platform performs feature engineering, model selection, and hyperparameter tuning. The platform also provides model insights, validation tools, and scoring capabilities.
- **Best For**: Enterprises or teams with moderate to advanced machine learning needs.
- **Advantages**: DataRobot is known for its speed and accuracy in producing highly performant models. It also offers a variety of deployment options, from on-premise to cloud-based services.

5. Runway ML

Runway ML is an innovative no-code tool that simplifies the process of working with machine learning models for creative applications. It offers a wide range of pre-trained models for tasks such as image generation, text-to-image, object detection, and style transfer, making it a popular choice among artists and designers.

- **Key Features**: Runway ML provides users with access to pre-trained deep learning models and a user-friendly interface for manipulating these models to fit their creative projects.
- **Best For**: Artists, designers, and anyone involved in creative industries who want to leverage AI tools without the need for programming expertise.
- **Advantages**: The platform is highly intuitive and offers integration with creative tools like Adobe Photoshop and Unity, making it particularly useful for creative professionals.

4. Pros and Cons of No-Code ML Tools

Pros:

- **Ease of Use**: No-code tools eliminate the need for coding and technical expertise, empowering non-technical users to experiment with machine learning.
- **Rapid Prototyping**: These platforms allow users to quickly build prototypes without the usual overhead of data science projects, helping speed up decision-making.

- **Lower Barrier to Entry**: Non-technical users, such as business analysts, can apply machine learning techniques to their work without needing to understand algorithms or programming.
- **Cost-Effective for Small Projects**: Many no-code platforms offer flexible pricing models, including free plans or pay-as-you-go options, making them accessible to small teams or businesses.

Cons:

- **Limited Customization**: While no-code tools are user-friendly, they often have limited flexibility in terms of customization and advanced features, which may be a drawback for users with more specific needs.
- **Scalability Concerns**: Some no-code platforms may not scale well for large datasets or complex enterprise-level projects.
- **Dependence on Platform**: Users become dependent on the platform's capabilities and limitations, which may affect long-term flexibility, especially if the platform changes or gets discontinued.

No-code ML tools have opened up machine learning to a broader audience, making it easier for non-technical users to create predictive models and make data-driven decisions. Platforms like Google AutoML, H2O.ai, BigML, and Runway ML provide a wide variety of features, use cases, and levels of complexity to accommodate different types of users. By providing an intuitive interface and automating many of the complex steps involved in machine learning, no-code tools allow businesses and individuals to experiment with AI without requiring in-depth technical knowledge. While they may not replace the need for skilled data scientists in complex projects, no-code ML tools offer a powerful way for non-technical users to integrate machine learning into their daily workflows and create impactful solutions.

19.4 Automating feature engineering and hyperparameter tuning

Feature engineering and hyperparameter tuning are crucial steps in the machine learning pipeline that often require deep domain knowledge and technical expertise. These processes involve transforming raw data into meaningful features that improve the performance of machine learning models, and fine-tuning the model parameters to optimize its accuracy. However, for non-technical users or those looking to expedite their workflow, these tasks can be time-consuming and complex.

To address these challenges, the emergence of AutoML platforms and no-code ML tools has brought automation into the field of machine learning, including feature engineering and hyperparameter tuning. By automating these steps, these tools enable users to quickly and efficiently create machine learning models without needing advanced expertise in data processing or model optimization.

In this sub-chapter, we will explore the concept of automating feature engineering and hyperparameter tuning in the context of AutoML and no-code tools. We'll delve into the importance of both tasks, how they are automated, and the benefits they offer to users.

1. The Importance of Feature Engineering and Hyperparameter Tuning

Before discussing how these tasks are automated, it's essential to understand why feature engineering and hyperparameter tuning are critical for building effective machine learning models.

Feature Engineering

Feature engineering is the process of selecting, modifying, or creating new features from raw data that improve the model's ability to learn patterns and make predictions. In most machine learning projects, raw data (such as text, images, or sensor data) requires transformation into a more structured form (e.g., numerical features or categorical variables). Feature engineering can involve several steps, such as:

- **Handling Missing Data**: Filling or removing missing values.
- **Normalization and Scaling**: Adjusting numerical features to a common scale.
- **Encoding Categorical Data**: Converting non-numerical categories into numeric values.
- **Creating New Features**: Deriving additional features from the raw data (e.g., creating ratios or time-based features).

Effective feature engineering is vital for improving model accuracy. However, the process often requires domain expertise and experimentation, which can be labor-intensive for non-technical users.

Hyperparameter Tuning

Hyperparameter tuning involves adjusting the settings or hyperparameters of a machine learning algorithm to improve its performance. While algorithms have predefined parameters, there are often several settings (such as the learning rate, number of trees in a random forest, or layers in a neural network) that must be optimized. These settings can significantly influence model performance.

- **Manual Tuning**: Traditionally, hyperparameter tuning has been done manually through trial and error or grid search techniques, which can be computationally expensive and time-consuming.
- **Automated Tuning**: In contrast, automated hyperparameter tuning techniques allow algorithms to search through a range of hyperparameters and select the optimal ones in an efficient manner.

Without automated tools, hyperparameter tuning can be complex, especially when working with large datasets or intricate models. Automating this process significantly accelerates the model-building workflow.

2. How AutoML Tools Automate Feature Engineering and Hyperparameter Tuning

AutoML platforms and no-code ML tools simplify the process of feature engineering and hyperparameter tuning by automating them, enabling non-technical users to focus on other aspects of the project, such as understanding the business problem or evaluating the model's output. Let's explore how these tools automate each process:

Automating Feature Engineering

The process of automating feature engineering involves the creation and selection of relevant features from raw data through intelligent algorithms that recognize patterns and correlations.

Automatic Data Preprocessing:

AutoML platforms handle the preprocessing of data automatically. For example, missing values are imputed, and categorical features are encoded using techniques like one-hot encoding or label encoding. These platforms also perform feature scaling (e.g., standardization or normalization) to prepare the data for model training.

Feature Selection:

Auto-feature selection is an essential component of automating feature engineering. AutoML platforms analyze the relevance and importance of features using statistical methods or machine learning techniques. Recursive feature elimination (RFE) or tree-based methods are often used to identify and remove redundant or irrelevant features.

Feature Creation:

Many AutoML tools also have the capability to generate new features automatically. For example, they may generate interaction terms, polynomial features, or aggregate features from existing ones. This step can uncover hidden relationships within the data that could improve model accuracy.

Feature Transformation:

Transformations such as logarithmic scaling or discretization can be applied to features to enhance the model's ability to identify patterns. AutoML platforms often incorporate these transformations automatically based on the data type.

In summary, automated feature engineering removes the burden of having to manually preprocess and select features, ensuring that the data is prepared optimally for training without requiring expertise in this area.

Automating Hyperparameter Tuning

Automating hyperparameter tuning is a key feature of many AutoML platforms. Hyperparameters can greatly affect the performance of machine learning models, and finding the best combination of parameters can be time-consuming. AutoML platforms use advanced search strategies to automatically find the best hyperparameters for a given model.

Grid Search:

Grid search is one of the most common methods for hyperparameter tuning. AutoML platforms can perform grid search over a range of hyperparameters for various algorithms, systematically testing different combinations to find the best one. This approach can be computationally expensive but is efficient for small to medium-sized datasets.

Random Search:

In random search, the platform randomly selects combinations of hyperparameters within specified ranges and evaluates their performance. Random search is less exhaustive than grid search but often finds optimal results more quickly.

Bayesian Optimization:

Bayesian optimization is an advanced technique that builds a probabilistic model of the objective function. This method evaluates the hyperparameters in a way that uses past evaluations to predict where the best values are likely to be. It focuses on regions of the search space that are most promising, making it a more efficient method compared to grid or random search.

Genetic Algorithms:

Some AutoML platforms implement genetic algorithms for hyperparameter optimization. This technique uses principles of natural selection to evolve hyperparameters over generations, improving the model's performance with each iteration.

Automated Hyperparameter Optimization:

Once the algorithms are selected, AutoML tools perform hyperparameter tuning automatically, selecting the best-performing hyperparameters through techniques like cross-validation and early stopping to avoid overfitting.

By automating hyperparameter tuning, AutoML platforms reduce the need for manual intervention in the optimization process, ensuring that the best parameters are used without requiring technical expertise.

3. Benefits of Automating Feature Engineering and Hyperparameter Tuning

Automating feature engineering and hyperparameter tuning provides a number of benefits to users, including non-technical professionals:

1. Increased Efficiency:

Automation accelerates the model development process, reducing the time spent on tasks such as data preprocessing, feature selection, and tuning hyperparameters. This allows users to focus on higher-level tasks such as business analysis or decision-making.

2. Better Model Performance:

Automated techniques ensure that the features and hyperparameters are selected based on optimal statistical or machine learning methods, resulting in improved model accuracy and performance. The tools can perform complex operations that may be difficult or time-consuming for a non-technical user to execute manually.

3. Accessibility:

By automating these crucial steps, AutoML tools allow non-technical users—such as business analysts, marketers, and product managers—to engage with machine learning without the need for coding skills. This makes machine learning accessible to a wider range of professionals and accelerates innovation in business applications.

4. Reduced Risk of Human Error:

Manual feature engineering and hyperparameter tuning can introduce errors or biases, which can negatively impact model performance. Automation eliminates these risks, ensuring a more consistent and reliable process.

5. Scalability:

Automated processes can handle larger datasets and more complex models that might otherwise be difficult to manage manually. As businesses scale, these tools can continue to provide support, allowing users to work with big data without worrying about the intricacies of scaling.

Automating feature engineering and hyperparameter tuning through AutoML and no-code ML tools is transforming the machine learning landscape, making it more accessible to non-technical users. These automated processes not only save time but also enhance model performance, reduce the risk of human error, and increase the scalability of machine learning projects. As businesses and industries continue to adopt machine learning, the ability to leverage automated feature engineering and hyperparameter optimization will become increasingly valuable, enabling organizations to extract meaningful insights from their data with minimal effort.

19.5 The future of AutoML and its impact on ML careers

AutoML (Automated Machine Learning) and no-code ML tools have already made significant strides in democratizing machine learning (ML), enabling users without extensive technical backgrounds to leverage powerful algorithms and predictive models. As these tools evolve, they hold the potential to revolutionize industries and change the landscape of machine learning and data science careers. In this sub-chapter, we will explore the future of AutoML, its likely advancements, and how it will impact the careers of machine learning professionals.

1. The Growing Role of AutoML in ML

AutoML's primary goal is to make machine learning more accessible by automating the most time-consuming and complex tasks, such as data preprocessing, feature engineering, model selection, and hyperparameter tuning. In doing so, AutoML platforms enable data scientists, business analysts, and even non-technical users to develop machine learning models with minimal coding or expertise.

As machine learning continues to grow in popularity and becomes more embedded in various industries, the future of AutoML is looking incredibly promising. Here's why:

1.1 Expansion of AutoML Capabilities

The future of AutoML is centered on its increasing sophistication and its ability to automate more complex processes. Some areas of future growth include:

Advanced Model Architectures: AutoML platforms will become better at designing and selecting more sophisticated model architectures, such as deep learning models, reinforcement learning, and advanced neural network designs. Currently, AutoML tools excel with simpler models like decision trees, random forests, and linear regression. As their capabilities evolve, they will be able to handle more complex model types, opening up more use cases for industries like computer vision, natural language processing (NLP), and autonomous systems.

Automated Data Understanding: Future AutoML systems will likely improve their ability to automatically interpret and clean data, not only through standard preprocessing tasks but also by intelligently understanding the domain-specific features in raw data. This can include better handling of unstructured data, such as text, images, or audio, with minimal human intervention.

Multi-Modal Integration: As ML projects grow more complex and involve different types of data (such as structured, unstructured, and image data), future AutoML systems will be able to handle multi-modal data pipelines, effectively integrating information from various sources. This will allow organizations to run end-to-end machine learning workflows on diverse datasets in a seamless manner.

Self-Improving Systems: One exciting possibility for the future of AutoML is the creation of self-improving systems. These systems will analyze their past performance and optimize themselves continuously, learning from feedback loops and using it to make future predictions even more accurate.

2. Democratization of AI and Its Impact on Business

One of the biggest benefits of AutoML is the democratization of machine learning. As no-code and low-code tools become more powerful, they allow individuals and organizations from diverse sectors to take advantage of AI and machine learning without needing specialized skills.

2.1 Empowering Non-Technical Users

As AutoML platforms evolve, they will become even more user-friendly and accessible to non-technical professionals, empowering a wider range of individuals to build and deploy machine learning models. Business analysts, product managers, and marketers, for instance, will be able to integrate machine learning directly into their decision-making processes, reducing the reliance on data scientists for every task. This shift will accelerate the pace at which organizations can adopt AI-driven solutions and optimize their operations.

2.2 Reducing the Knowledge Gap

In many organizations today, there is a substantial knowledge gap between business leaders who understand the application of AI and data scientists who understand how to implement it. By making machine learning tools more accessible to non-technical users, AutoML platforms will bridge this gap, allowing organizations to achieve faster time-to-market and more responsive decision-making.

2.3 Increased Efficiency and Reduced Costs

AutoML platforms streamline the machine learning workflow, reducing the time required to go from concept to deployment. This increased efficiency allows organizations to save on resources and costs. They can develop AI-powered solutions more rapidly and scale them with less reliance on manual intervention, ultimately driving business innovation.

3. Impact on Machine Learning Careers

While AutoML opens up a world of possibilities for non-technical users, it also raises questions about the future of traditional ML roles. Will AutoML tools replace data scientists? How will the job landscape change for professionals in this field? Let's dive into these considerations.

3.1 Shift Toward Higher-Level Roles

AutoML tools are designed to handle repetitive, time-consuming tasks, such as model selection, hyperparameter tuning, and data preprocessing. As a result, data scientists and machine learning engineers will be freed up from many of these routine tasks, allowing them to focus on higher-level responsibilities like:

Problem Framing: Defining business problems and selecting the right machine learning models to solve them will remain a critical part of a data scientist's role. The need for domain expertise to understand complex business questions will not be replaced by AutoML.

Advanced Model Interpretation: While AutoML tools can create models and optimize them automatically, interpreting the results and making informed decisions based on model predictions requires a deeper understanding of the underlying principles. Data scientists will be responsible for validating model performance, addressing ethical considerations, and ensuring models meet business needs.

Ethical Oversight: Machine learning models are only as good as the data they are trained on. As AI tools become more prevalent, professionals will need to ensure that these models are ethically sound, free from bias, and aligned with organizational goals. Data scientists and ML engineers will continue to play a crucial role in this oversight, as AutoML platforms may lack the ability to independently account for all ethical issues.

3.2 Demand for Specialized Skills

While many routine tasks will be automated, the demand for highly specialized ML skills will continue to rise. Some areas where skilled professionals will remain essential include:

Deep Learning: While AutoML tools may simplify the process of building traditional models, deep learning models, such as neural networks, require a higher degree of expertise. Data scientists with deep learning skills will still be in demand for building and optimizing these complex models.

Reinforcement Learning: For cutting-edge applications like self-driving cars, robotics, and game AI, professionals who can design and implement reinforcement learning algorithms will continue to be sought after.

Research and Development: The development of new machine learning algorithms and techniques will always require research, which will remain an important part of data science. AutoML tools automate many tasks, but they do not replace the role of scientists who push the boundaries of AI technology.

3.3 Increased Focus on Collaboration

As AutoML becomes more widely adopted, collaboration between technical and non-technical teams will become more important. Data scientists will need to collaborate with business leaders, product managers, and subject matter experts to understand the problem at hand, provide context for automated results, and ensure the machine learning models align with organizational objectives.

Additionally, cross-disciplinary roles such as data engineers, MLOps specialists, and AI architects will play an increasingly important role in managing the deployment and scalability of automated models. These professionals will be responsible for optimizing AutoML tools and ensuring that the models they produce are reliable, scalable, and capable of handling large volumes of data.

4. Conclusion: A Paradigm Shift in ML Careers

The future of AutoML holds exciting potential. By automating repetitive tasks and making machine learning more accessible to non-technical users, AutoML is set to accelerate the adoption of AI across industries. It will not replace the need for skilled professionals but rather empower them to focus on more complex, creative, and strategic tasks.

The impact on careers in the ML field will be profound but also positive. Data scientists and machine learning engineers will see their roles evolve, with more focus on higher-level problem-solving, ethical oversight, and advanced model development. Professionals will need to adapt to this changing landscape by acquiring specialized skills and fostering collaboration across teams.

Ultimately, AutoML will be a tool that complements, rather than replaces, the expertise of skilled professionals, enabling them to deliver better, faster, and more impactful AI solutions. The future of AutoML offers endless opportunities to those willing to embrace the evolution of machine learning.

20. Final Thoughts & Next Steps

As we reach the conclusion of this book, we reflect on the journey you've taken from mastering foundational machine learning techniques to applying them in real-world projects. In this final chapter, we summarize the key concepts, strategies, and tools you've learned throughout the book and how they fit together to create practical, deployable machine learning solutions. We also discuss the future of machine learning, highlighting emerging trends such as quantum computing, AI ethics, and the integration of AI in various industries. We'll guide you on how to continue your learning journey with resources, communities, and ways to stay updated with the latest advancements. Finally, we encourage you to build your own projects, contribute to open-source initiatives, and keep pushing the boundaries of what machine learning can achieve. The path to becoming an industry-ready machine learning expert is just beginning—the real-world applications are waiting for you! 🚀💡

20.1 Building a portfolio with real-world ML projects

As you move through the exciting world of machine learning (ML) and artificial intelligence (AI), one of the most powerful ways to demonstrate your skills and knowledge is through a well-constructed portfolio. A portfolio acts as a concrete showcase of your work, helping potential employers or clients understand your capabilities and experience in the field. In this sub-chapter, we'll dive into how you can build an impressive portfolio with real-world ML projects, the importance of these projects, and strategies for showcasing them effectively.

1. The Importance of a Portfolio in Machine Learning

A portfolio is more than just a collection of projects; it's a narrative of your growth as an ML professional. It reflects your ability to handle real-world data, solve complex problems, and apply ML concepts practically. While resumes and certificates provide an overview of your qualifications, your portfolio proves that you can get your hands dirty with the actual tasks and challenges that come with real-world ML applications.

1.1 Proving Practical Experience

Employers and clients often look for practical experience that goes beyond theoretical knowledge. A portfolio demonstrates that you not only understand ML algorithms and concepts but can also apply them effectively to solve real-world problems. This makes it an essential asset for standing out in a competitive job market.

1.2 Showcasing Problem-Solving Skills

Machine learning isn't just about coding or training algorithms; it's about understanding the problem, defining it clearly, and then crafting a solution that addresses specific business needs. Through a portfolio, you can show that you can approach problems from a solution-oriented perspective, transforming raw data into valuable insights and actionable results.

1.3 Building Credibility

Having a portfolio that includes real-world projects, especially those that tackle industry-relevant problems, can significantly boost your credibility. Whether you are aiming for a career in a specific domain, such as healthcare, finance, or retail, or you want to demonstrate your general expertise in ML, your portfolio should reflect that.

2. Selecting Projects for Your Portfolio

Building a portfolio that resonates with potential employers and clients requires careful selection of projects. While the idea of including every single project you've worked on might be tempting, it's important to curate a collection of projects that truly highlight your strengths and skills. Here are a few pointers on how to choose the right projects for your ML portfolio:

2.1 Focus on Diversity

Showcasing a variety of projects will demonstrate your versatility and adaptability. Include different types of machine learning techniques, such as:

- **Supervised Learning**: For example, a project where you predicted house prices, customer churn, or loan default using regression and classification techniques.
- **Unsupervised Learning**: Projects like clustering or dimensionality reduction, where you explore patterns in unlabelled data.
- **Reinforcement Learning**: Projects that involve developing intelligent agents for environments like games, robotics, or simulations.
- **Deep Learning**: Projects focusing on neural networks, particularly for applications in computer vision, natural language processing, or audio processing.

- **Time Series Forecasting**: Projects predicting trends, such as stock prices, weather forecasts, or sales demand.

2.2 Focus on Real-World Applications

Select projects that are both technically challenging and relevant to current industry needs. Projects that solve tangible problems or demonstrate solutions to complex challenges are more attractive to employers. For example:

- **Predicting House Prices**: A classic regression problem that involves working with large datasets, understanding data relationships, and interpreting models.
- **Customer Churn Prediction**: A project that showcases your ability to work with business data and employ classification algorithms to predict churn risk.
- **Sentiment Analysis**: Leveraging NLP techniques to analyze customer sentiment from social media or product reviews.

Incorporating real-world business problems into your portfolio will also demonstrate your understanding of the domain you're working in, whether it's finance, healthcare, marketing, or e-commerce.

2.3 Highlighting Your Technical Skills

Include projects that allow you to show your technical expertise, such as working with machine learning frameworks (e.g., TensorFlow, PyTorch, Scikit-learn), cloud platforms (AWS, Google Cloud, Azure), data manipulation tools (Pandas, NumPy), and deployment tools (Docker, Kubernetes). Demonstrating your ability to work with these tools shows you can tackle end-to-end ML workflows, from data preprocessing to deployment.

2.4 Demonstrating the Entire ML Pipeline

A well-rounded project will cover all the stages of a machine learning pipeline, including:

- Problem definition and data exploration
- Data cleaning and preprocessing
- Feature engineering
- Model selection, tuning, and evaluation
- Deployment and maintenance

Ensure that the projects in your portfolio showcase your ability to handle each of these tasks. This demonstrates that you understand the full machine learning process, rather than focusing on just one aspect of it.

3. Structuring Your Portfolio

Now that you've selected a set of strong projects, the next step is to structure your portfolio effectively. A well-organized portfolio ensures that potential employers or clients can easily follow the work you've done and understand the impact of your projects. Here's a step-by-step guide to building a professional portfolio:

3.1 Choose a Platform for Hosting

While GitHub is the most common platform for hosting ML projects, there are other platforms you can use to showcase your work, such as:

- **Personal Portfolio Websites**: Create a website where you can detail each project, the approach you took, and the results. You can also link to the code repositories and demo applications.
- **Kaggle**: Kaggle offers a great platform for sharing projects, especially for those focused on datasets and competitions. You can showcase your solutions, explain your approach, and share notebooks with others.
- **GitHub**: GitHub remains the gold standard for hosting code. Ensure that your repositories are well-organized, with clear README files and relevant comments within the code. This makes it easy for others to understand your work.

3.2 Include a Detailed Readme

Each project in your portfolio should have a detailed README file that explains the following:

- **Project Overview**: A brief description of the problem you're solving and why it matters.
- **Approach**: Explain the machine learning techniques and algorithms used, as well as any challenges faced.
- **Results**: Showcase your results, such as evaluation metrics (accuracy, precision, recall, etc.), visualizations, or performance benchmarks.
- **Deployment**: If applicable, explain how you deployed the model (e.g., a Flask API, a web app, or a cloud-based solution).

- **Technologies Used**: List the libraries, frameworks, and tools employed in the project.

3.3 Include Visuals and Demos

Where possible, include visualizations, charts, and graphs that make it easier for viewers to understand your work. Visuals can help make your portfolio more engaging and provide a clearer understanding of your project's impact. Additionally, if feasible, provide a live demo of your work, either through a cloud platform or hosted application.

3.4 Add Explanations and Insights

Go beyond the technical details by explaining the insights you gained from your projects. Discuss what worked, what didn't, and how you iterated on your models. Reflecting on the challenges and lessons learned will give your portfolio more depth and show your capacity for critical thinking.

4. Updating and Expanding Your Portfolio

A portfolio should not be static. As you gain more experience and complete new projects, make sure to keep updating your portfolio to reflect your latest work and progress. Incorporate new techniques, challenges, and tools you learn over time, and showcase more complex projects that demonstrate your ability to handle advanced machine learning applications.

5. Conclusion: Building a Portfolio for Success

Building a portfolio with real-world ML projects is an essential step in showcasing your skills and proving your ability to apply machine learning in practical, meaningful ways. By carefully selecting diverse, relevant, and impactful projects, and presenting them with clarity and professionalism, you can significantly enhance your career prospects.

Your portfolio will serve as a living document of your growth as a machine learning practitioner. Whether you're aiming for a job, freelance opportunities, or career advancement, a strong portfolio will set you apart, making you a valuable asset in the rapidly growing AI industry. So, start building today—your future in machine learning depends on it!

20.2 Contributing to open-source ML projects

Contributing to open-source machine learning (ML) projects is one of the most rewarding ways to engage with the global community, grow as a practitioner, and build your personal brand. In this sub-chapter, we will explore how and why you should contribute to open-source ML projects, how it can accelerate your career, and provide a step-by-step guide to making meaningful contributions.

1. The Value of Open-Source Contributions

Open-source software has become the backbone of many machine learning applications, tools, and libraries. Some of the most widely-used libraries in ML, such as TensorFlow, PyTorch, Scikit-learn, and Keras, are open-source. These projects are not only essential to research and development but also provide an opportunity for anyone to contribute and make a lasting impact on the community.

Contributing to open-source ML projects offers multiple benefits that can accelerate your learning and career in profound ways:

1.1 Learning from Experienced Developers

Open-source projects often have experienced maintainers and contributors who can offer valuable feedback, best practices, and coding standards. By contributing to these projects, you will be exposed to high-quality code, sophisticated ML techniques, and cutting-edge research. This exposure can deepen your understanding of complex ML topics and help you improve your own coding skills.

1.2 Building Your Reputation and Credibility

Contributing to open-source is an effective way to establish your reputation within the global ML community. When you contribute to well-known projects, your GitHub profile will serve as a public record of your contributions. Over time, this will position you as an active and valuable member of the community. Your contributions may even lead to further opportunities, such as speaking engagements, job offers, or freelance projects.

1.3 Networking with Like-minded Professionals

Open-source projects are often collaborative in nature. Contributing to these projects allows you to network with other professionals who share your passion for ML. These interactions can lead to mentorship opportunities, collaborations, or even job referrals.

Building relationships with people in the industry can open doors to both personal and professional growth.

1.4 Enhancing Problem-Solving Skills

Working on open-source ML projects often involves solving problems that real users face. These can range from bug fixes and performance improvements to adding new features or algorithms. Contributing to such issues allows you to sharpen your problem-solving skills while also making meaningful changes that can have a widespread impact.

1.5 Gaining Experience with Version Control and Collaboration

Collaboration in open-source projects often involves using version control systems like Git and GitHub. Contributing to these projects will help you gain hands-on experience with these tools, which are crucial for modern software development. Understanding how to effectively work in a team using version control, managing pull requests, and reviewing others' code will enhance your skills as an ML practitioner.

2. Finding Open-Source ML Projects to Contribute To

Finding the right open-source ML projects to contribute to is a key step in making meaningful contributions. Here are some ways to find projects that align with your skills and interests:

2.1 Explore GitHub Repositories

GitHub is home to thousands of open-source ML projects, making it the primary place to look for contributions. Popular repositories include:

- **TensorFlow**: A powerful library for building machine learning models, especially deep learning.
- **Scikit-learn**: A well-established library for classical machine learning algorithms.
- **PyTorch**: A deep learning framework favored by many researchers and practitioners.
- **Keras**: A high-level neural networks API built on top of TensorFlow.

By searching for "good first issue" or "beginner-friendly" tags on GitHub, you can find issues that are suitable for newcomers. Look for projects that are well-documented and have a welcoming community to ensure that your experience is positive.

2.2 Participate in ML Competitions

Participating in Kaggle competitions is another way to contribute to the open-source community. While Kaggle competitions are often centered around model-building challenges, the solutions you develop can become open-source projects. You can share your kernels (Jupyter notebooks), collaborate with other participants, and offer valuable insights that the community can benefit from.

2.3 Join Specialized Communities and Forums

In addition to GitHub, there are specialized communities and forums where ML practitioners come together to work on open-source projects. Some popular platforms include:

- **OpenAI**: A non-profit AI research organization that often releases cutting-edge models and tools.
- **MLflow**: An open-source platform for managing the ML lifecycle, which has an active contributor community.
- **Hugging Face**: A company that focuses on NLP and provides access to large models and datasets. Hugging Face's transformer library is one of the most actively maintained ML repositories.

You can also explore resources such as Stack Overflow and Reddit's Machine Learning Subreddit, where discussions around open-source projects often take place. These communities will help you stay informed about ongoing projects and how you can contribute.

2.4 Contribute to ML Libraries You Use

If you are already using certain ML libraries or frameworks in your projects, contributing back to them is a great way to get involved. Many popular libraries, like FastAI, XGBoost, or LightGBM, actively accept contributions from users. These contributions can range from fixing bugs and improving documentation to implementing new algorithms or features.

3. How to Make Meaningful Contributions

Contributing to an open-source ML project can seem intimidating at first, but there are various ways you can start small and make valuable contributions over time. Here's a roadmap to guide your involvement:

3.1 Start with Documentation

One of the easiest ways to get started contributing to open-source projects is by improving the documentation. Clear, thorough documentation is critical to the success of any project. By fixing typos, adding explanations, or updating examples in the documentation, you can make a significant impact on the usability and accessibility of the project.

3.2 Tackle Open Issues

Most open-source projects maintain an issue tracker where contributors can identify problems or areas for improvement. Browse through the issues and look for "beginner-friendly" or "good first issue" tags, which are generally aimed at newcomers to the project. These issues could involve tasks like debugging, adding new features, or improving model performance. Once you identify an issue that aligns with your skills, fork the repository, work on a solution, and submit a pull request.

3.3 Improve or Implement ML Models

If you are comfortable with the underlying machine learning algorithms, consider enhancing the existing models in an open-source project. For example, you could improve the performance of an algorithm by experimenting with different hyperparameters or modifying the architecture. If you have a new model or algorithm that you think would be beneficial, you can propose adding it to the project.

3.4 Participate in Code Reviews

Once you gain experience, participating in code reviews is an effective way to contribute to the open-source community. Reviewing other contributors' code not only helps improve the quality of the project but also helps you learn from others. Code reviews allow you to understand different coding styles and better grasp various machine learning techniques.

4. Contributing to Open-Source ML Projects: A Step-by-Step Guide

Here's a step-by-step approach to get started with contributing to open-source ML projects:

Pick a Project: Start by identifying open-source ML projects that align with your skills and interests. GitHub, Kaggle, and specialized ML communities are good places to find projects.

Understand the Project: Before contributing, thoroughly explore the project. Read the documentation, understand the codebase, and check out the existing issues to see where you can help.

Start Small: Begin by tackling small issues, such as improving documentation or fixing minor bugs. Once you're comfortable, move on to bigger contributions, like improving algorithms or adding new features.

Fork and Clone the Repository: Create a fork of the project and clone it to your local machine. This allows you to make changes without affecting the original codebase.

Make Your Changes: Work on the changes you want to make in your forked repository. Ensure you follow the project's coding standards and best practices.

Submit a Pull Request: After making your changes, submit a pull request to the original repository. Clearly explain what you've done and why your changes will improve the project.

Engage with the Community: Respond to feedback from maintainers and other contributors, and be open to suggestions. Collaboration and communication are key to contributing successfully.

5. Conclusion: Contributing to Open-Source ML Projects

Contributing to open-source ML projects is a great way to gain hands-on experience, develop technical skills, build your professional network, and enhance your career. Whether you're improving existing models, fixing bugs, or writing documentation, every contribution makes a difference. By actively participating in open-source projects, you not only contribute to the ML community but also accelerate your personal growth as a machine learning professional. So, start exploring, start contributing, and watch your career in machine learning take flight.

20.3 Networking and advancing in the ML industry

In the rapidly evolving field of machine learning (ML), building a network and positioning yourself for career advancement is essential. While developing technical skills is crucial, networking and leveraging industry connections can significantly impact your growth and open doors to exciting opportunities. In this sub-chapter, we will explore strategies for effectively networking, establishing connections, and advancing in the ML industry, from attending conferences to online communities, mentorship, and personal branding.

1. The Power of Networking in ML

Networking isn't just about attending events and exchanging business cards—it's about building meaningful relationships that can accelerate your learning and career. In the context of machine learning, networking plays an essential role in the following ways:

1.1 Expanding Your Knowledge Base

Networking helps you learn from others in the field. Whether it's through casual conversations at a meetup or deep technical discussions during conferences, you'll be exposed to different perspectives and approaches. Conversations with other practitioners can introduce you to new tools, research papers, or real-world use cases that might inspire your own work.

1.2 Opening Career Opportunities

In the ML field, career growth is often driven by connections rather than just a résumé. Many job opportunities are found through word-of-mouth or referrals. Having a strong network gives you access to job openings, project collaborations, freelance work, and even research opportunities. These opportunities may not always be advertised publicly, so your network becomes a vital resource for uncovering hidden job markets.

1.3 Finding Mentors and Advisors

Mentorship is a cornerstone of professional growth in any industry, and machine learning is no different. Mentors offer guidance, share their experiences, and provide valuable advice on how to navigate your career. A mentor can help you refine your technical skills, introduce you to important research, and guide you through career decisions. Through networking, you can connect with potential mentors who can help you develop your expertise and avoid common pitfalls.

1.4 Building Collaboration Opportunities

The nature of ML projects—whether academic, open-source, or industry-based—often involves collaboration. Networking within ML communities helps you identify like-minded professionals to collaborate with on research papers, open-source projects, or product development. These collaborations not only improve your skills but can also lead to groundbreaking work that garners attention in the industry.

2. Ways to Network in the ML Industry

The ML community is vibrant and full of opportunities to connect. Networking can take many forms, both online and offline. Below are some effective strategies for building and maintaining a network in the machine learning industry.

2.1 Attending Conferences and Meetups

Conferences and meetups are fantastic venues to meet ML professionals from across the globe. These events bring together researchers, engineers, and industry leaders, making them excellent opportunities for learning and networking. Some popular ML and AI conferences include:

- **NeurIPS** (Conference on Neural Information Processing Systems)
- **ICML** (International Conference on Machine Learning)
- **CVPR** (Conference on Computer Vision and Pattern Recognition)
- **KDD** (Knowledge Discovery and Data Mining)

Conferences provide an opportunity to listen to cutting-edge research, engage in panel discussions, and meet with companies who may be hiring. Meetups are more localized events that allow you to connect with peers in your geographic area. Whether you're attending a large international conference or a smaller, more intimate meetup, these settings facilitate relationship-building and knowledge-sharing.

To make the most of these events, come prepared with questions, be open to discussing your work, and be proactive in reaching out to speakers, panelists, and attendees. Don't hesitate to introduce yourself and exchange contact information.

2.2 Participating in Online Communities and Forums

The rise of social media and online platforms has made it easier than ever to connect with ML professionals. Platforms such as Twitter, LinkedIn, and Reddit are excellent for staying informed, sharing ideas, and engaging with others in the community.

- **Twitter** is full of active ML researchers, developers, and organizations sharing papers, tutorials, and ideas. Follow people you admire, engage in conversations, and share your own work to increase your visibility.

- **LinkedIn** is a professional networking platform that allows you to connect with people in the ML industry, view job postings, and engage with content related to AI and ML. You can join ML groups, follow organizations, and expand your network by reaching out to like-minded professionals.
- **Reddit's** Machine Learning Subreddit is an excellent place to discuss new research, share your projects, and ask for advice. Participating in discussions on platforms like Reddit or Stack Overflow can lead to valuable connections and collaborations.

Additionally, consider joining specialized ML forums such as Cross Validated (a Stack Exchange site for statistics) or Kaggle forums where data scientists and ML practitioners collaborate, share solutions, and discuss new challenges.

2.3 Joining Online Courses and Bootcamps

Many machine learning enthusiasts and professionals continue their learning through online courses, bootcamps, or certification programs. These educational platforms often include forums and groups where you can interact with instructors and classmates.

Some top online platforms where you can meet fellow ML learners and practitioners include:

- **Coursera**: Offers courses from top universities such as Stanford, University of Washington, and others. Many ML courses include peer discussions, group projects, and opportunities for collaboration.
- **Udacity**: Features Nanodegree programs with a focus on hands-on projects and mentorship. The Udacity community often hosts networking events and forums for students and alumni.
- **fast.ai**: Known for its practical deep learning courses, fast.ai encourages an active community where learners share insights and discuss projects.

These courses often have associated forums, Slack groups, or Discord servers where you can connect with peers, share insights, and get help with challenges.

2.4 Writing and Sharing Knowledge

Another powerful way to establish connections and advance in the ML industry is by sharing your own knowledge. Writing blog posts, creating tutorials, or publishing research papers not only helps others but also raises your profile within the ML community. By creating content that addresses common issues, explains new concepts, or demonstrates how to use a machine learning library or tool, you position yourself as an expert in the field.

Platforms like Medium, Dev.to, and Towards Data Science are great places to publish technical articles. By sharing your learnings and experiences, you can engage with others who have similar interests and even attract potential collaborators or employers.

Moreover, hosting webinars or live coding sessions on platforms like YouTube, Twitch, or LinkedIn Live can help you engage with a global audience and further expand your network.

3. Personal Branding: Establishing Your Online Presence

In the ML industry, personal branding can be a powerful tool for advancing your career. By curating your online presence, you can showcase your skills, share your accomplishments, and establish yourself as a thought leader.

3.1 Create a Professional Portfolio

A well-maintained portfolio is essential for any machine learning professional. Your portfolio should include:

- A GitHub repository showcasing your projects, contributions to open-source, and research papers.
- A personal website or portfolio site that summarizes your work, technical expertise, and career achievements. You can also include case studies, blog posts, and links to your online profiles.
- An updated LinkedIn profile that highlights your skills, certifications, work experience, and accomplishments.

Your portfolio serves as an online résumé, demonstrating your work to potential employers, collaborators, and mentors. Having a visible, organized, and easily accessible portfolio is a key factor in getting noticed.

3.2 Engage with Thought Leaders

Engage with established professionals in the ML industry by commenting on their blog posts, sharing their work, and participating in discussions. Thought leaders often provide valuable insights that can help you grow as a professional, and connecting with them can lead to collaboration or mentorship opportunities.

4. Leveraging Mentorship for Career Advancement

Mentorship plays a pivotal role in career advancement, especially in a complex field like machine learning. Having a mentor can help you:

- **Avoid common mistakes**: Mentors can offer advice on navigating challenges in both technical and non-technical aspects of your career.
- **Provide personalized feedback**: Mentors can evaluate your work and provide actionable suggestions for improvement.
- **Expand your network**: Mentors often have extensive networks and can introduce you to others who can help you grow professionally.

To find a mentor, consider reaching out to professionals you admire through platforms like LinkedIn, or ask for mentorship opportunities at conferences, meetups, or online communities.

5. Conclusion: Networking as a Key to Career Growth

Networking is a powerful tool for advancing in the ML industry. By actively engaging with the community, attending events, collaborating on projects, and building your personal brand, you create opportunities for learning, career advancement, and growth. Networking goes hand-in-hand with continuous learning and practice, and when done right, it can open the door to exciting projects, collaborations, and career breakthroughs. Embrace networking as an ongoing process, and the rewards will follow throughout your journey in the machine learning field.

20.4 Emerging trends in ML and AI research

As we continue to explore the exciting landscape of machine learning (ML) and artificial intelligence (AI), it's crucial to stay informed about the emerging trends shaping the future of these fields. The pace of innovation in ML and AI is accelerating, and with each passing year, new breakthroughs and methodologies emerge, making it an exciting time for both beginners and experienced practitioners. In this sub-chapter, we will explore some of the most promising and transformative trends in ML and AI research, providing you with a glimpse into the future and how these advancements could impact industries and careers.

1. The Rise of Large Language Models (LLMs) and Generative AI

One of the most exciting advancements in recent years is the rapid development of Large Language Models (LLMs), such as GPT-3 and BERT. These models have demonstrated remarkable capabilities in understanding and generating human-like text, making them invaluable in tasks such as natural language processing (NLP), sentiment analysis, machine translation, and content generation.

LLMs are now not only excelling in text generation but are also being adapted for multimodal tasks—including text, images, and video generation. Generative AI, which includes models capable of creating new content such as text, images, and even code, is poised to revolutionize industries like creative writing, marketing, gaming, and software development.

The future of LLMs holds the potential for even larger, more sophisticated models that can seamlessly generate text, understand nuances in complex queries, and integrate multiple modalities for more accurate and human-like interactions. These models are not only pushing the boundaries of AI but also reshaping how we think about creativity, problem-solving, and human-computer interaction.

2. Reinforcement Learning (RL) for Real-World Applications

Reinforcement Learning (RL), a subfield of machine learning inspired by behavioral psychology, continues to gain momentum in research and practical applications. RL has already shown immense success in training autonomous agents to perform complex tasks, such as in self-driving cars and robotics.

RL enables models to learn by interacting with an environment, receiving feedback (rewards or penalties), and continuously adjusting their strategies to optimize performance. The Deep Q-Networks (DQN) and AlphaGo successes demonstrated RL's power in high-stakes, dynamic environments, but the potential for RL extends far beyond games.

In the coming years, RL is expected to play a pivotal role in areas like:

- **Healthcare**: RL models could assist in personalized treatment planning, drug discovery, and optimizing healthcare delivery systems.
- **Energy management**: RL algorithms can be used to optimize energy consumption in smart grids and reduce operational costs.
- **Finance**: Reinforcement learning could optimize portfolio management, trading strategies, and risk assessment.

Research into RL will likely focus on improving scalability, efficiency, and the ability to work in real-world, noisy environments. We can also expect more hybrid models that combine reinforcement learning with supervised or unsupervised learning techniques to handle complex tasks.

3. Federated Learning and Privacy-Preserving AI

As concerns about data privacy and security continue to grow, Federated Learning has emerged as a powerful solution that allows AI models to be trained across decentralized devices while ensuring that sensitive data never leaves the device. This approach has the potential to address concerns around data privacy and security by enabling privacy-preserving AI models that do not require centralized data storage.

In federated learning, a model is trained locally on devices (such as smartphones, IoT devices, and edge devices), and only the model updates (gradients) are shared with a central server, which aggregates them to improve the model. This eliminates the need to move personal or sensitive data to the cloud, making it particularly relevant for industries such as:

- **Healthcare**: With federated learning, sensitive medical data from patient records can be kept local to ensure privacy while still enabling valuable insights and model improvements.
- **Finance**: In financial institutions, federated learning can be used to train models for fraud detection, credit scoring, and risk assessment without compromising customer privacy.
- **Smart devices**: AI-powered devices such as smartphones, wearables, and home assistants can benefit from federated learning by continuously improving on-device AI models without uploading sensitive personal data.

The future of federated learning holds great promise, particularly with the increasing importance of data governance and privacy laws like GDPR. As the world becomes more connected through IoT, federated learning can pave the way for creating intelligent systems without compromising user privacy.

4. Explainable AI (XAI) and Model Interpretability

As AI systems become more complex and embedded in critical decision-making processes, the need for explainable AI (XAI) is growing. Model interpretability is a crucial aspect of ensuring that AI-driven decisions are transparent, accountable, and understandable to human users.

XAI aims to provide insights into how AI models arrive at their conclusions, making them more transparent, interpretable, and trustworthy. In high-stakes domains such as healthcare, finance, and law enforcement, understanding the reasoning behind AI decisions is vital for building trust and enabling ethical decision-making.

Incorporating explainability into machine learning models often requires techniques like:

- **Feature importance**: Identifying which features contribute most to model predictions.
- **Surrogate models**: Using simpler, more interpretable models (e.g., decision trees) to approximate the behavior of more complex models like deep neural networks.
- **Shapley values**: A game-theoretic approach to determine the contribution of each feature to the model's prediction.

In the coming years, XAI will be central to advancing AI adoption, particularly in industries where safety, fairness, and transparency are non-negotiable. We can expect continued research into developing more interpretable models and tools that can be used to demystify even the most sophisticated AI systems.

5. Quantum Computing and ML

Although still in the early stages, quantum computing holds the potential to revolutionize machine learning by dramatically speeding up computation and solving problems that are currently intractable for classical computers. Quantum algorithms can potentially provide exponential speedups for optimization tasks, large-scale simulations, and high-dimensional data analysis, which are central to many machine learning applications.

In the realm of machine learning, quantum computing could impact various areas, including:

- **Optimization**: Quantum algorithms could improve optimization processes in ML, leading to faster and more accurate solutions for tasks like hyperparameter tuning, clustering, and feature selection.
- **Quantum-enhanced ML models**: Quantum machine learning (QML) algorithms may be developed to handle large datasets and complex tasks, unlocking new capabilities that are currently not feasible with classical ML models.
- **Simulating complex systems**: Quantum computers are particularly suited for simulating quantum systems, which could benefit fields like materials science, drug

discovery, and chemistry, where simulating molecular interactions is computationally expensive.

While we're still in the early stages of quantum computing, the next few years will likely see significant advancements in quantum algorithms and hardware, which could make quantum-enhanced machine learning a reality.

6. AI for Sustainability and Climate Change

With the growing urgency of climate change, AI is playing an increasingly important role in developing solutions to tackle environmental issues. Researchers are exploring how machine learning and AI can be used to:

- **Optimize energy consumption**: AI can help optimize energy use in buildings, factories, and homes, contributing to significant reductions in carbon emissions.
- **Predict and model climate change**: Machine learning models can be used to simulate climate scenarios, predict environmental changes, and improve disaster preparedness and response.
- **Sustainable agriculture**: AI can enhance precision farming, helping farmers use fewer resources, reduce waste, and optimize crop yields.

As global sustainability efforts continue to gain momentum, machine learning will become an integral part of addressing climate change challenges, driving innovations in renewable energy, resource management, and environmental monitoring.

7. Conclusion: The Future of ML and AI

Machine learning and AI are continuously evolving fields, with new breakthroughs on the horizon that promise to transform industries and society as a whole. From large language models and reinforcement learning to quantum computing and AI for sustainability, the future of ML is filled with exciting possibilities. As practitioners and researchers, staying informed and adaptable to these emerging trends will be crucial for continuing to push the boundaries of what's possible with AI.

By understanding these emerging trends, you can better position yourself to contribute to the exciting developments in ML, engage in meaningful research, and apply cutting-edge techniques to real-world challenges. The future of ML and AI is bright, and it's up to you to be a part of shaping it.

20.5 Final words and roadmap for the next AI breakthroughs

As we conclude this journey through the world of real-world machine learning projects, it's important to pause and reflect on the exciting path ahead. You've gained an in-depth understanding of how to apply machine learning concepts to solve tangible, real-world problems, but the world of AI and ML is rapidly evolving, and the future holds even more thrilling possibilities.

In this final section, we'll look ahead to the next big breakthroughs in AI, offering a roadmap of where the field is headed and how you can continue your journey as a machine learning practitioner. Whether you're interested in continuing your work with ML models, diving deeper into research, or exploring new interdisciplinary areas, this roadmap will provide you with the tools and vision to thrive in the ever-changing world of AI.

1. Staying Current: The Accelerating Pace of AI Research

One of the most exciting aspects of machine learning and AI is the speed at which the field is progressing. Every year, new algorithms, techniques, and tools emerge, pushing the boundaries of what's possible. To stay at the forefront of AI, it's crucial to continuously update your knowledge and adapt to the latest trends.

There are several ways you can keep your skills fresh:

- **Follow key conferences**: Major ML and AI conferences such as NeurIPS, ICML, and CVPR are where many groundbreaking ideas and papers are presented. These conferences provide a platform to learn about the latest research, network with experts, and discover innovative tools.
- **Join AI communities and forums**: Platforms like Kaggle, Reddit's Machine Learning community, Medium, and Twitter host discussions around the latest breakthroughs and trends. Engaging with these communities can help you keep a pulse on the newest developments.
- **Experiment with cutting-edge technologies**: The best way to stay current is by experimenting with the latest tools and frameworks. Explore emerging AI paradigms such as transformer models, neuro-symbolic AI, federated learning, and quantum machine learning. Trying these out in real-world applications will help you refine your skills and keep your projects on the cutting edge.

2. Key AI Research Areas to Watch in the Coming Years

As you look forward to future AI advancements, it's worth paying attention to several key research areas that are poised to reshape the landscape in the years ahead. These include:

a. Explainable AI (XAI)

With the increasing reliance on AI in critical decision-making, understanding how models arrive at their conclusions is vital. XAI is an active area of research that focuses on creating models that are not only accurate but also interpretable. Future breakthroughs will likely focus on making complex deep learning models more transparent, providing humans with the ability to understand and trust the AI systems they work with.

b. Neuromorphic Computing and Brain-Inspired AI

Neuromorphic computing takes inspiration from the structure and functioning of the human brain. This field aims to create more energy-efficient models capable of learning in a more biological way. Future breakthroughs in this area could lead to significant improvements in brain-computer interfaces, cognitive AI, and autonomous agents that can learn and adapt in real-time environments with much more natural intelligence.

c. Generative AI (GANs and Beyond)

Generative models like Generative Adversarial Networks (GANs) have already shown their potential to generate high-quality images, music, and even text. In the near future, we can expect even more sophisticated models that create original works of art, help in drug discovery, design innovative products, and improve simulations for various industries.

d. Reinforcement Learning (RL) in Real-World Applications

While RL has already been applied to problems like game playing and robotics, there is still much to explore when it comes to deploying RL in real-world settings. As industries like autonomous vehicles, robotics, and finance continue to adopt RL, researchers will focus on making it more stable, efficient, and applicable to complex, real-world environments.

e. AI for Social Good

AI's role in solving social, environmental, and humanitarian challenges is rapidly expanding. AI for social good includes efforts to fight climate change, improve public health, and enhance socioeconomic opportunities. Expect to see AI applications that are designed not just for profitability but also for creating a more equitable and sustainable future.

3. The Role of Interdisciplinary Knowledge

As AI becomes increasingly intertwined with many fields, future breakthroughs will likely occur at the intersection of machine learning and other disciplines. Some promising areas include:

- **AI + Ethics**: With growing concerns about AI's societal impact, ethical considerations will be at the forefront. Bridging AI with ethics and law will be essential to address issues related to bias, fairness, privacy, and transparency.
- **AI + Neuroscience**: The fusion of AI and neuroscience is opening up new pathways for creating more intelligent systems and understanding the human brain. Breakthroughs in this area may lead to the development of more human-like AI agents and enhanced brain-machine interfaces.
- **AI + Creativity**: AI-powered tools are already being used in creative fields like writing, art, and music. Future advances in generative models will enable even more personalized and sophisticated creative applications, changing the way we think about artistry and human creativity.

By exploring these interdisciplinary areas, you can contribute to cutting-edge research and leverage your ML expertise in new and exciting domains.

4. Building a Career in AI: Preparing for the Future

The future of AI and ML offers exciting opportunities for both new entrants and seasoned professionals. As the demand for AI skills continues to grow across industries, there are several steps you can take to position yourself for success:

- **Build a strong portfolio**: Showcase your skills by working on diverse, real-world ML projects. The more varied your portfolio, the more attractive you will be to potential employers and collaborators.
- **Contribute to open-source**: Engage with open-source projects to enhance your skills, gain visibility, and contribute to the broader AI community. Platforms like GitHub offer opportunities to work on collaborative projects and solve real-world problems.
- **Continue learning**: ML and AI are vast and rapidly evolving fields. Stay ahead by regularly taking online courses, attending workshops, and reading the latest

papers. Platforms like Coursera, edX, and Fast.ai provide excellent learning resources.

The future of AI is limitless, and by continuing to learn and innovate, you can play an essential role in the breakthroughs that lie ahead.

5. The Road Ahead: From Research to Real-World Applications

Ultimately, the future of AI hinges on translating research breakthroughs into practical applications. The journey from conceptualizing an AI model to deploying it in a real-world environment is a continuous cycle of innovation and iteration. By following these trends and staying connected to the research community, you'll be well-equipped to contribute to the next generation of AI breakthroughs.

The next few years are likely to see AI integrated into almost every aspect of society—business, healthcare, education, entertainment, and beyond. By engaging in lifelong learning, embracing interdisciplinary approaches, and contributing to cutting-edge research, you can ensure that you remain at the forefront of this incredible field.

As you move forward, remember that AI's potential is boundless, and the possibilities for innovation are only limited by our imagination. Keep pushing the boundaries, continue learning, and most importantly, stay curious. The world of AI is waiting for you to make your mark.

Final Thoughts: Your Role in Shaping the Future of AI

In closing, the future of machine learning and AI is filled with excitement, challenges, and incredible opportunities. By following the roadmap laid out in this chapter and continuing to advance your knowledge, you will be well-equipped to contribute to the next wave of AI innovations that will define the future. Whether you're working on cutting-edge technologies, applying AI to real-world challenges, or researching new frontiers, you are part of an ever-evolving and transformative journey that will impact generations to come.

Stay focused, stay passionate, and always be open to the new frontiers of AI. The next breakthrough is just around the corner—be ready to embrace it!

Machine Learning is shaping the future, but mastering it requires more than just understanding algorithms—it demands real-world experience. **Real-World ML Projects: Hands-on Learning** is a practical guide designed to help you bridge the gap between theory and industry applications through hands-on, end-to-end projects.

This book takes you on a journey through 10 real-world machine learning projects, covering key domains like finance, healthcare, retail, NLP, and computer vision. You'll learn how to collect and clean real-world data, train models, evaluate performance, and deploy ML solutions at scale. From predicting house prices and detecting fraud to building chatbots and deploying Edge AI, each project follows an industry-standard workflow—ensuring you gain skills that are highly relevant to today's job market.

Beyond building models, this book dives into MLOps, model deployment, and scalability—critical aspects often overlooked in traditional ML education. You'll explore CI/CD pipelines, monitoring strategies, and cloud-based deployment, preparing you to take your ML solutions from development to production.

By the end of this book, you won't just be familiar with machine learning—you'll have a portfolio of real-world projects, hands-on experience with industry tools, and the confidence to apply ML in practical scenarios. Whether you're an aspiring data scientist, an engineer looking to integrate AI, or a business professional exploring data-driven solutions, this book provides everything you need to succeed in the real world of machine learning.

🚀 *Turn your knowledge into action and start building impactful ML projects today!*

To my dear readers,

Thank you for joining me on this journey through **<u>Real-World ML Projects: Hands-on Learning</u>**. Writing this book has been an incredible experience, but what truly brings it to life is your curiosity, passion, and dedication to learning machine learning in a hands-on way.

I deeply appreciate the time and effort you've invested in reading, practicing, and applying the concepts in this book. Whether you're a beginner taking your first steps or an experienced professional expanding your skills, I hope these projects have empowered you to build, deploy, and scale real-world ML solutions with confidence.

A heartfelt thank you to everyone who has supported this book—my family, friends, mentors, and the amazing AI community. Your encouragement and feedback continue to inspire me to share knowledge and push the boundaries of what's possible with machine learning.

Finally, I would love to hear about your journey! If this book has helped you, please feel free to share your projects, thoughts, and feedback. Your success is the greatest reward, and I look forward to seeing how you apply these lessons to make an impact in the world of AI.

Keep learning, keep building, and keep innovating!

With gratitude,

Gilbert Gutiérrez